I0816025

ECKIE

ECKIE

Walter Eckersall and the Rise of Chicago Sports

CHRIS SERB

UNIVERSITY OF NEBRASKA PRESS
Lincoln

Manufactured in the United States of America

The University of Nebraska Press is part of a land-grant institution with campuses and programs on the past, present, and future homelands of the Pawnee, Ponca, Otoe-Missouria, Omaha, Dakota, Lakota, Kaw, Cheyenne, and Arapaho Peoples, as well as those of the relocated Ho-Chunk, Sac and Fox, and Iowa Peoples.

For customers in the EU with safety/GPSR concerns, contact:
gpsr@mare-nostrum.co.uk
Mare Nostrum Group BV
Mauritskade 21D
1091 GC Amsterdam
The Netherlands

Library of Congress Control Number: 2025000612

Designed and set in Adobe Jenson Pro by Katrina Noble.

For my parents, Tom and Ann

CONTENTS

ILLUSTRATIONS

PREFACE

As a young adult, I once volunteered at a Special Olympics competition at Eckersall Stadium, on Chicago's far South Side. That day brings back warm memories of sportsmanship and fellowship. But the name on the stadium, "Eckersall," was random to me, with no real meaning attached.

I first encountered the man behind that name, Walter Eckersall, in the anthology *The Best American Sports Writing of the Century*. One of editor David Halberstam's selections was "Eckie," written by Ring Lardner in 1932. Lardner begins by talking about Eckersall as a fellow sportswriter and close friend, then recounts his days as a University of Chicago football legend between 1903 and 1906.

I had never heard of Eckersall beyond a name on a stadium, so I sought to learn more . . . and came up almost empty-handed. Only one book had ever been written about him. *Eckersall of Chicago*, self-published by an amateur historian in 1957, is a slim volume that discusses Eckersall solely as an athlete, not as a person.

I found more information in Robin Lester's 1995 book *Stagg's University*, a scathing look at the University of Chicago's often hypocritical early football history. While the book's focus is coach Amos Alonzo Stagg, Lester also explores Eckersall's football heroics, academic failings, and questionable life choices.

Several years later, while researching my book *War Football*, I encountered Eckersall again, in the sports pages of the *Chicago Tribune*. From Lardner and Lester, I knew that the football hero later transitioned into sports journalism. But until I read his original *Tribune* stories, I had no idea how prolific, insightful, and influential Eckersall was as a writer. In addition, in a clear conflict of interest today, Eckie often officiated the same games he covered, placing him in the middle of the action at many of the greatest moments of 1920s football.

I originally conceived *Eckie* as a straight biography. But as I dug deeper, I realized that his career was interwoven with the growth of Chicago from a sporting backwater to a major player on the national and international stage, in three significant and interrelated ways.

As a league, state, and national champion in three different sports at Hyde Park High School, Walter Eckersall became the first prep superstar in Chicago history, forging the path that many significant athletes would follow.

As quarterback at the University of Chicago, Walter Eckersall was the city's and the region's first true college football hero, and the means through which Coach Stagg won a national championship with an undefeated season in 1905.

As a prominent and influential sportswriter for the *Chicago Tribune*, Walter Eckersall was the lens through which Chicago readers came to understand sports: not only in his expert area of football but also in boxing, track and field, swimming, speedskating, and a host of obscure sports.

This book also explores other areas: A young superstar's troubles, as Eckersall was arrested for theft, struggled with alcohol, and had a shotgun wedding and messy divorce. Racism in sports, where Eckie stood apart from his peers as a strong advocate for Black athletes. The re-establishment of professional boxing in the city, with Eckersall vigorously publicizing the newly sanctioned sport. The rise of pro football, which Eckie turned his back on at an unfortunate time. And the "seedy side" of sports with its gamblers and mobsters and fixers, whose paths Eckersall frequently crossed.

—

Today, Eckersall has been largely forgotten. The few historians who still study him give mixed evaluations. His football greatness remains unchallenged, but other portions of his life have come under heavy scrutiny. In *Stagg's University*, Lester exposes Eckersall's academic and moral flaws. In *Stagg vs. Yost*, John Kryk highlights the unethical arms race between Michigan and Chicago to sign Eckersall out of high school, with Eckie all too willingly reaping the benefits. In *Shake Down the Thunder*, Murray Sperber hints that Notre Dame coach Knute Rockne manipulated Eckersall, seeking to sway Eckie's news coverage, All-American selections, and officiating decisions.

Social media hasn't done Eckersall any favors. On Twitter, self-appointed experts mock Eckersall's small stature:

"Reminder: The 1904 first-team all-american fullback named Walter Eckersall was 5/7 and 141 pounds. (Second reminder: I would've won the 1904 Heisman)."[1]

"I would've dusted that 140 pound fullback."[2]

"That was my first thought too. That fullback is a high school freshman, who the f— is he blocking? Nobody, that's who."[3]

"I was 6'3 219 with a 4.7 40 yard dash and probably the 7,739,725 best football player in the world at the time. I would've sent Walter Eckersall back to the 1800s."[4]

These pictures are incomplete, and understandably so. Eckersall is a secondary character in those books, and those tweets are just a bunch of noise. But all these factors led me to look deeper into Eckersall's life and career. I devoured every contemporary account about him as a high school, college, and semiprofessional athlete, while becoming probably the only person (other than Eckersall himself) to read all 5,500 bylined *Chicago Tribune* stories that he churned out over twenty-three years.

—

From the beginning, Chicago fans have practically worshipped their sports heroes. Some, such as Isiah Thomas, Kirby Puckett, and Donovan McNabb, were homegrown but became stars in other towns. Others, including Ernie Banks, Stan Mikita, Walter Payton, and Michael Jordan, moved to the city from elsewhere, then found themselves embraced and adopted by locals. A handful were born and raised in Chicago, then remained during their sporting lives: "Papa Bear" George Halas, Chicago Cubs stalwart Phil Cavarretta, longtime DePaul basketball coach Ray Meyer, and Chicago Bears linebackers George Connor and Dick Butkus.

That last group includes Walter Eckersall, who came before any of the others. For thirty years, Walter Eckersall was synonymous with Chicago sports. And for those same thirty years, Chicago sports grew tremendously, largely driven by Walter Eckersall. This book attempts to bring Eckie back into the spotlight that once shone so brightly on him, in the context of larger social themes and within the framework of the rise of Chicago sports.

ACKNOWLEDGMENTS

I wish to thank the following for their assistance:

My dad, Tom Serb, who inspired my love of sports and Chicago history and who closely read an early draft of this book, and my mom, Ann Toland Serb, who taught me how to write.

John Binder, professor emeritus of history at the University of Illinois at Chicago, who took a strong interest in this project and closely read an early draft.

Mark Schipper, author and college football historian, who wrote about Eckersall for his "5th Down College Football" website and who first connected me with Professor Binder.

Bill Savage—professor of English at Northwestern University, Chicago historian, lifelong friend, and cousin-by-marriage—who helped me develop my narrative framework.

Historians, journalists, authors, and friends Clayton Trutor, Jim Leeke, Joe Ziemba, Chris Willis, Timothy Brown, Dave Revsine, Christine Brennan, Rob Peterson, Aimee Crawford, Liam Ford, and Robert Loerzel, for their help and encouragement along the way.

The team at University of Nebraska Press, especially editor Rob Taylor, who believed in this project from the start.

The staffs of the University of Chicago Library, Northwestern University Library, and Chicago History Museum; Marianne Mather, senior visual editor of the *Chicago Tribune*, and Tony Dudek of Tribune Content Agency; Gregory Bond, curator of the Joyce Sports Research Collection at University of Notre Dame's Hesburgh Libraries; Brad Green, curator of University of Alabama's Bryant Museum; and Rosalynn Anderson, librarian at Hyde

Park Career Academy. Thanks also to the staff of Oak Woods Cemetery, for helping me find the Eckersall family grave.

As always, I owe my deepest thanks to my wife, Emily, and our daughters, Helen and Maggie, for their love, inspiration, support, and patience.

ECKIE

PART 1

1886–1903

1

Woodlawn

Located about halfway between downtown Chicago and the city's border with Indiana, the Woodlawn neighborhood is best known today as the site of the Obama Presidential Center, honoring the legacy of the former U.S. president and longtime Chicagoan. In its not-too-distant past, Woodlawn was a center for community activism and the advancement of civil rights. Before that, Woodlawn was at the center of massive, rapid demographic change, as the neighborhood shifted from 83 percent white to 89 percent Black between 1940 and 1960.[1]

Today's Woodlawn bears little resemblance to the neighborhood where Walter Eckersall grew up, and even less to the one where his parents settled. Like many Chicagoans of the late nineteenth century, Walter Eckersall Sr. and Minnie Killerlain moved to the area from far away. Walter was born in 1848 in Stalybridge, a textile-manufacturing town in northwest England, and arrived in the United States in the late 1860s. Shortly after his arrival, Walter met Minnie, who was born to Irish immigrants in Vermont in 1850 and moved to Wisconsin as a child. The couple married in Chicago on September 22, 1871, two weeks before the Great Chicago Fire that threw the city into chaos but also spurred tremendous growth.[2]

Woodlawn, where the newlyweds settled, was spared much of this chaos, along with much of the growth. The neighborhood was then part of Hyde Park Township, which was independent from Chicago. Originally settled by Dutch farmers, Woodlawn had between five hundred and a thousand residents scattered through two square miles. That same area has about twenty-five thousand residents today and had more than eighty thousand at its peak.[3]

One of the area's early attractions was Oak Woods Cemetery, a beautifully landscaped 180-acre burial ground south of Sixty-Seventh Street and east of Cottage Grove Avenue. The now-historic cemetery has become the final resting place for politicians, mob bosses, sports heroes, musicians, and civil rights activists. In 1872 Walter worked as a caretaker at Oak Woods, moving with Minnie into a small cottage on its grounds. During this time, the name "Walter Eckersall" first appeared in the *Chicago Tribune,* when he took out a classified ad seeking help tending his horses and garden.[4]

The Eckersalls soon moved out of the cemetery and into a small house on Sixty-Fifth Street between Drexel and Maryland Avenues. The house was conveniently down the street from Holy Cross Catholic Church, which opened in 1891. Walter Sr. does not appear to have been formally religious, but Minnie was a lifelong Catholic who raised their children in the faith.[5]

Walter spent his adulthood in working-class occupations. At different times, he worked as a gardener, a laborer, and a construction foreman for a rapid-transit railroad line. Along the way, Walter also pursued a few improbable dreams. In October 1879 he participated in a six-day race-walking tournament in New York City with a grand prize of $5,000, worth more than $150,000 today, along with a host of lesser prizes. (Walter didn't win anything.) In January 1886 Eckersall was awarded U.S. patent #334,761 for a spring-loaded burglar alarm, though it's doubtful he made much money from this invention.[6]

Over time, the Eckersalls welcomed three sons and two daughters. Arthur was born in 1876; Elmer in 1877; Etta in 1879; Walter Jr. *sometime* in the mid-1880s; and Jessie in 1889. Walter Jr.'s birth date is consistently given as June 17, but the year remains unclear. The College Football Hall of Fame lists his birth year as 1886. On his World War I draft registration card, Walter recorded it as 1885. In the 1900 census and on his gravestone, his birth year is given as 1883. And on his marriage and death certificates, Walter's birth year is listed as 1884. Any year within this narrow range would mesh with the dates of Walter's major milestones. Most likely, he was born in 1884 or 1885.[7]

Over the course of four short years during Walter Jr.'s childhood, three major events radically transformed his neighborhood. In 1889 Chicago quadrupled in area when it annexed Hyde Park and three other large townships, bringing much-needed services to those areas. In 1892 the University of Chicago, funded by oil baron John D. Rockefeller, opened in the Hyde Park neighborhood, just north of Woodlawn. And in 1893 Jackson Park, on the eastern edge of Woodlawn, hosted the World's Columbian Exposition, also known as the Chicago World's Fair, drawing more than twenty-seven million visitors to architect Daniel Burnham's stunning, though temporary, "White City."[8]

This period saw a tremendous building boom in Woodlawn, shaping it into a solidly residential neighborhood, without the industrial corridors that developed to the southeast and west. Caught up in this bubble, Walter Sr. made an ambitious financial gamble.

In January 1893 he built a three-story hotel at Sixtieth Street and St. Lawrence Avenue. Eckersall's project cost $100,000, the equivalent of nearly $3 million today. This type of speculation ran rampant just before the fair, though it's not clear how a common laborer came up with the down payment for such an investment. During the fair, Eckersall rented out rooms for a dollar a day, charging an additional thirty cents apiece for meals. He advertised his hotel as the "Finest Location in the World's Fair District."[9]

Walter Sr. was one of many speculators in the area at the time of the fair, and their buildings serviced the massive influx of visitors. When the fair closed, demand dried up just as quickly, leading to a housing glut right when the country plunged into a general depression. The fate of Eckersall's project is unknown, but since he was again a common laborer by 1900, it's likely that the hotel failed.

When he reached school age, Walter Jr. attended Woodlawn School at Sixty-Fourth Street and Lexington Avenue (today's University Avenue). From an early age, Walter—never "Walt" or "Wally" but whose youthful nickname "Eckie" stuck for the rest of his life—displayed tremendous speed. According to one legend, young Eckie would hang around the Washington Park Race Track at Sixty-First Street and Cottage Grove, charging trainers a small fee to watch their horses while they took their meal breaks. If the horses somehow got away, Walter promised, he was fast enough to catch them.[10]

Sometime during his grammar school days, Eckie discovered football. Decades later, he recalled learning the game in the lot where Holy Cross Church would later be built. This memory was probably faulty; when Holy Cross was completed in 1891, Walter was only five or six, not quite football-playing age. But there was plenty of other open space to explore in Woodlawn throughout his youth. A neighbor later remembered Eckie and his friends playing adventure games in vacant lots along Sixty-Third Street. Young Walter undoubtedly gained his first football experience on this kind of open land.[11]

At home, Walter was further exposed to sports by his siblings. Oldest brother Arthur, then age nineteen, played halfback for an independent or "prairie" football team, the Calumets, in 1895. Either Arthur or Elmer, or possibly both, played for two different prairie teams in 1896. Elmer was an all-around athlete who ran track for an Amateur Athletic Union team, played baseball for a team from the steel company where he worked, and competed in long-distance bicycle races. It's unclear whether Etta played sports, but youngest sister Jessie was an ice-skater, tennis player, and dancer who would later teach high school physical education.[12]

Walter's first appearance on a college gridiron came in November 1897, when the University of Illinois hosted the Carlisle Indian School at the old Chicago Coliseum, about a half mile east of the Eckersall house. Since the "home" team was 120 miles from its campus, organizers needed to recruit some local help.

"As I was one of the neighborhood boys, it was my good fortune to carry water from the side lines to the Illinois players," Eckersall recalled. "I doubt if there was a man on either team who was prouder or happier than I, on the occasions on which I was called upon to trot out before the crowd."[13]

Carlisle beat Illinois 23–6 that day, in the third of four college games held indoors at the Coliseum. Attendance at each averaged ten thousand, and the Woodlawn venue seemed poised for a bright future. But that Christmas Eve, the supposedly fireproof building burned to the ground. A new Chicago Coliseum would open three years later, but far north of Woodlawn, in the neighborhood now known as the South Loop.

Even with the Coliseum gone, Walter could still watch football nearby. Marshall Field, home of the University of Chicago, stood at Fifty-Seventh Street and Ellis Avenue, just over a mile from the Eckersall home. The Maroons, coached by the soon-to-be-legendary Amos Alonzo Stagg, first fielded a team in 1892, became a charter member of what would become the Big Ten conference in 1896, and quickly emerged as a regional powerhouse.

While still in grammar school, Eckie did whatever he could to catch a glimpse of Stagg's teams. The Woodlawn boys couldn't afford tickets, so they would peek through knotholes or scale rooftops to watch the Maroons in action.

"My impressions of these games . . . are fresher in my memory than most of those in which I officiated in later years," Eckersall recalled in 1926. He remembered especially one "struggle of Titans," when Chicago hosted the University of Pennsylvania in 1899. "I witnessed the game from a telephone pole. It ended in a 5 to 5 tie."[14]

Young Eckersall appreciated the mental side of football. Late in that game, with the score tied, Chicago drove into Penn territory. There, Penn's All-American guard Truxtun Hare taunted his opponents.

"His attitude proclaimed defiance as he glared at the Chicago quarterback and seemed to dare him to send plays in his direction," Eckersall remembered. "[Chicago quarterback Walter] Kennedy accepted the challenge. Three times in succession [Frank] Slaker, the Chicago fullback, was hurled against Hare, and three times he was thrown back. . . . It appeared to me that psychology saved Pennsylvania that day."[15]

Eckie came to feel a special awe in the Maroons' presence.

"We little fellows couldn't buy footballs, but we caught the spirit of the game from watching Stagg's players racing around in practice and in real games," Eckersall said. "We had bully times in those days. I guess we all dreamed of being football heroes."[16]

Soon, he would have the chance to turn those dreams into reality.

2

Pre-1900 High School Sports

When Walter Eckersall was a baby in Woodlawn, high school sports in Chicago were similarly in their infancy. By the time Eckie reached adolescence, the scene was growing rapidly, chaotically, and controversially.

High school sports had been born in the prep schools of the Northeast in the 1850s. These all-male institutions borrowed their traditions, including athletics, from English boarding schools. Embracing the philosophy of "muscular Christianity," prep schools increasingly strived for the ideal of a sound mind in a sound body. Early schoolboy athletics included soccer, rowing, track, and baseball. These were limited to intramural or interclass contests at first, but schools eventually began competing against one another.[1]

Chicago lagged behind the East Coast in part because the region was settled later, and in part for structural reasons. Early Chicago was a blue-collar city, with few high schools. Until 1875 the city had only one public secondary school, along with a handful of private schools. About two-thirds of public high school students were female, aiming toward teaching careers. Boys who did enroll often dropped out after a year or two, to do manual labor in a society where an eighth-grade education was deemed more than sufficient.

In the late nineteenth century, that framework shifted radically. Parents increasingly sent their children to high school, to give them better opportunities than they had enjoyed. Between 1890 and 1918, public high school enrollment in the United States grew more than sevenfold, even though the overall population had less than doubled. Within a generation, high school education became the norm rather than the exception.

In 1875 Chicago High School split into three schools: North Division, South Division, and West Division. Soon afterward, two all-male vocational schools opened. Annexations and organic population growth brought additional high schools into the system. By 1900 the city had thirteen public high schools, up from that lone Chicago High School twenty-five years earlier.

Interscholastic sports in the city were born in 1884 with a round-robin baseball tournament between North Division, Lake View, and Hyde Park. Baseball interest waxed and waned over the next few years, but by 1890 a Cook County High School League was formed with teams from the city and its close-in suburbs. In that first season, Evanston High School won the baseball title with a perfect record.[2]

Chicago-area high schools began competing in track and field after baseball, but they established a formal track championship before baseball. In July 1889 five teams held a league championship at Wanderers' Cricket Grounds, located at Thirty-Seventh Street and Indiana Avenue. The Cook County League meet soon became a season-ending fixture for the area's schools.[3]

In 1893 the University of Illinois began hosting an Interscholastic Track Meet of the best teams from around the state—or more accurately, the best public school teams (the meet wouldn't unconditionally welcome private high schools until the 1970s). The Illinois meet served as the official high school state championships. In the state meet's first ten years, Chicago schools placed at least two teams in the top ten each year and won four team titles, while Chicago athletes won forty-four individual state titles.[4]

High school football in the Chicago area was first played by Evanston High School in 1879. In 1884 South Division created the first high school team within city limits. The following year, a league was formed with five teams, at a time when only seventy-five high schools played the sport nationwide. But by 1887, interscholastic football in Chicago was suspended because of growing concerns over injuries.[5]

The sport quickly recovered. In 1889 the Cook County High School Football League was organized. Hyde Park shut out all four of its opponents to win the inaugural league championship.[6]

In 1890 three new teams joined the league, and South Division beat Hyde Park in the season finale to win the title. A few days later, it was revealed that South Division used three "ringers" who weren't actually students. The student managers who ran the league expelled South Division but only for football. South Division continued to compete in baseball and track, and was readmitted for football in 1897.[7]

The dispute highlighted a major organizational flaw. High school sports were coordinated not by faculty members or responsible adults but by teenage students. And the Cook County League was managed by a "Board of Control" made up of students, with no adults in sight.[8]

Decades later, Walter Eckersall, still in grammar school when these abuses were happening, noted the "Wild West" atmosphere of high school sports in the 1890s:

> [The] teams had not been composed entirely of high-school students. The managers of the school teams, themselves high-school boys, made the rules that governed the high-school league and they changed the code at will. . . . The programs of some of the players included one hour of gymnasium work, one hour of singing, two hours of drawing, and eleven other hours devoted to the easiest subjects they could select. Not that it made much difference what these subjects were; there was no requirement that they keep above any certain mark in their studies. They could get zero for all their courses and still play—and some of them did.
>
> Under these conditions the high-school managers played anyone they could induce to go to school. Several of the players were voters; one, I remember, was twenty-eight years old. Several of the high-school players served in the Spanish-American War as soldiers and as sailors on board the fleet that won the naval battle off Santiago, then returned to school and played on their old high-school teams.[9]

Eckersall may have exaggerated but not by much. In November 1896 the *Chicago Tribune* ran an editorial headlined: "High School Football League Competition Becoming a Farce." The writer noted, "The team which protests the longest and hardest gets the games. Yesterday at its meeting, the game between Evanston and Englewood, which Englewood won by a decisive score, was protested because there was offside play and slugging in the game. . . . The usual oratory was indulged in, and a vote of six to three awarded the protest to Evanston . . . although the grounds of protest were flimsy."[10]

Childish antics spilled over to the league's meeting rooms. In 1896 students trashed the downtown hotel conference room that the league had rented for Board of Control meetings, and they promptly got expelled from the hotel. The board scrambled to find new quarters at a different hotel a few blocks away.[11]

Throughout the 1890s in all three major sports, the Cook County League clung to student management rather than faculty control. Although the newspapers referred to team managers and league officers as "Mr.," these were very clearly kids making adult decisions. Yet, the newspapers hardly batted an eye at the situation.

After ten years of student-run competition, faculty members finally got involved. In February 1898 representatives from eighteen high schools met to reform the Cook County League. Significantly, this meeting took place at the Chicago Board of Education, not in a student-rented hotel suite.

The revamped Board of Control would now consist of one faculty member from each school, although in a concession to students, the faculty representatives would be selected by student-run athletic associations rather than by school principals. While the Board of Control would rule on eligibility and protests, a separate Board of Managers, comprising one student from each team, would determine rules of competition and hire game officials.[12]

—

By the turn of the twentieth century, high school sports in Chicago had reached their adolescence, although with a significant number of growing pains. Over the next couple of decades, faculty and students would continue to struggle for control as the number of schools expanded, new sports were introduced, and girls fought for their own right to compete.

But the high school scene had not yet featured a true superstar. A rotating cast of fairly anonymous characters filled team lineups, to be replaced by a new cast the following season. Game and meet coverage at the time rarely listed athletes' last names. The names of the schools, not of the athletes, garnered the attention—in part due to the conventions of sports reporting then, and in part because no individual had yet stood out.

In the fall of 1899, Walter Eckersall—short and skinny and somewhere between thirteen and sixteen years old—arrived at Hyde Park High School. While he would achieve nothing remarkable in the classroom, on the playing fields Eckie would seize the public's imagination over the next four years and emerge as Chicago's first prep sports hero.

3

Hyde Park High School

Founded in 1863, Hyde Park High School is one of the oldest high schools in Illinois. In 1894 a new school building opened on Kimbark Avenue between Fifty-Sixth and Fifty-Seventh Streets, one and a half miles from the Eckersall family home. The new building was decked out with modern amenities such as a large assembly hall, a seven-thousand-volume library, science laboratories, and an art studio.[1]

Perhaps most significantly for young Walter Eckersall, Hyde Park had a modern gymnasium with an indoor track. Over the next four years, Eckersall would participate on Hyde Park teams that dominated sports in the city, the state, and even the country. Three athletes from that era stood out: Eckersall; Sam Ransom, an African American student who excelled in four sports; and Tom Hammond, who came straight from central casting with his tall stature, broad shoulders, and good looks. Of the trio, Eckie looked the least like an athlete: 5 feet 6 inches tall and skinny, with slumped shoulders and a fragile appearance that masked his toughness, leadership ability, and world-class speed.

Arriving at Hyde Park's football tryouts in Washington Park in 1899, Eckersall declared his intention to play quarterback. The coach took one look at the scrawny freshman and moved him to end. Years later, Eckie remembered "hurling myself under the heavy formations that made for my wing, and burying my 118 pounds under a ton or two of players."[2]

1. Hyde Park High School's three best athletes of the early 1900s line up at football practice. From left: Tom Hammond, Sam Ransom, Walter Eckersall. SDN-001000, *Chicago Daily News* collection, Chicago History Museum.

Eckersall left out one key detail: He didn't make Hyde Park's varsity. All the pounding he took came anonymously on Hyde Park's scrub team.

In the spring of 1900, Eckersall and Ransom began to emerge in both track and baseball for the "Blue and White" (Hyde Park's school colors, which served as its athletic nickname until the 1940s). Eckersall competed in sprints, relays, and even the pole vault as he tried to figure out his proper place on the track. Ransom competed mainly in the long jump and high jump.[3]

In baseball, Ransom started as varsity catcher, earning praise for his excellent arm and glove. One of the pitchers Ransom regularly caught was Fred Beebe, who would go on to a seven-year career in the Major Leagues. Eckersall also made the varsity, starting at shortstop.

Against West Division High School on June 8, Eckersall had two runs on two hits, but he also made two errors in a 12–4 victory. A week later, in the Cook County League championship game against Austin, Eckersall scored a run and helped turn a double play but had two more errors as Hyde Park lost, 9–8. Ransom was selected first-team catcher on the all–Cook County League team, a sign of the respect the freshman was earning in a mostly white sports environment.[4]

—

As the 1900 football season began, Eckersall, Ransom, and Hammond all won starting spots on the Hyde Park varsity team. Hyde Park's coach for that season, former University of Chicago All-American Walter Kennedy, tinkered with lineups, playing Eckersall at end and Hammond at guard for a couple of games. By midseason, Eckersall claimed the starting job at quarterback, Hammond at fullback, and Ransom at halfback, positions they would retain for two and a half years. The young trio showed flashes of brilliance all season but also struggled at times.

The football they played looked very different from the game we know today. The ball was fatter and rounder, easier to kick but harder to throw or catch—although the ability to throw didn't matter much, since forward passing wouldn't be legal until 1906. The field was 110 yards long, 10 yards longer than a modern field. Each game was split into two halves, rather than four quarters; the length of halves was negotiated by the competing teams and ranged from twenty to thirty-five minutes. There were no "end zones," only a "goal line" that a ball-carrier had to cross in order to score. On offense, teams had three downs to gain 5 yards, instead of four downs to gain 10. The player who received the snap (usually, though not always, the quarterback) couldn't carry the ball past scrimmage until at least one other player had touched it. Even with this restriction, teams still employed the quarterback as a running threat through reverses, laterals, and other misdirection plays.

Touchdowns and field goals were each worth 5 points, goals-after-touchdown 1, and safeties 2. Teams that scored received the ensuing kickoff, and defenses stayed on defense until they could stop their opponents' attack. Sideline coaching was illegal, though teams figured ways around this ban. Players who subbed out of a game had to stay out, so unless there was an injury or the game was a blowout, the starters stayed on the field for the entire game, playing offense, defense, and special teams.[5]

Hyde Park opened 1900 with a 5–0 loss to the University of Chicago. (Most major colleges back then played a couple early-season games against high schools.) In its next game, Hyde Park fought to a scoreless tie with Chicago's junior varsity. In the team's third game, Ransom scored Hyde Park's first touchdown of the season and Hyde Park earned its first win, 5–0, over a team of warehousemen from the Marshall Field department store.[6]

In mid-October Hyde Park finally started playing other high schools. The team was competitive but didn't stand out. Between October 10 and November 17, the Blue and White won four games, lost once, and tied twice. Although Eckersall started all these games, his name was singled out in the newspapers only once, for a 35-yard run in a win over Evanston.[7]

On November 24, in a nonconference game against East Aurora High School, Eckersall scored his first career touchdown on a 60-yard punt return. This play accounted for Hyde Park's only points, as East Aurora won 16–5.[8]

Hyde Park finished the regular season undefeated, though twice tied, in the Cook County League. On November 30 Hyde Park squared off with undefeated North Division for the league title. In a clear conflict of interest, Northwestern University player Al Johnson, who was coaching North Division and whose brother was starting fullback, served as timekeeper. A suspicious Coach Kennedy kept time informally on his own.

A Hyde Park halfback bobbled the opening kickoff, panicked, then flipped the ball back to Eckersall at the 5-yard line. Eckie looked downfield, sized up the kick coverage, then dashed up the sideline "like a frightened rabbit" for a 105-yard touchdown, though Hyde Park missed the extra point. After a couple exchanges of punts, a missed field goal by North Division, and a Hyde Park fumble, Harry Johnson (the timekeeper's brother) rushed for a short touchdown and kicked the extra point, giving North Division a 6–5 halftime lead.

Hyde Park drove deep into North Division Territory three times in the second half, only to lose the ball twice on downs and once on a fumble. In one ugly, probably racially motivated incident, a North Division halfback punched Ransom and was thrown out of the game.

Late in the game, Hyde Park blocked a punt and recovered on North Division's 5-yard line. By Kennedy's clock, there should have been forty-five seconds left in the game. But as Eckersall barked out his signals, official timekeeper Johnson blew his whistle. No play; game over.

As North Division left the field, Coach Kennedy told his boys they'd been cheated, ordering Hyde Park to line up and rush in for an unopposed touchdown. Kennedy now appealed the official score, claiming an 11–6 victory for Hyde Park.

Al Johnson denied any shenanigans and said that in the interest of fairness, he gave Hyde Park thirty extra seconds before ending the game. Without any solid proof, the Board of Control abided by the official ruling. North Division won the game, and championship, by a single point.[9]

Eckersall learned two important lessons from this lost championship: first, as a player, to keep the game moving along quickly, and second, as an official, to be as fair as possible.

The controversial loss brought a disappointing end to Walter Eckersall's first season of varsity football, but he had shown tremendous promise. And the trio of Eckie, Ransom, and Hammond would be together for two more seasons. Hyde Park's football future looked bright.

—

At 5 feet 6 inches tall, Eckersall wasn't built to play basketball, but the 5-foot-9 Ransom and 6-foot Hammond were. In the winter of 1900–1901, the pair started every game for Hyde Park, which beat North Division 23–22 for the Cook County League title.[10]

In the Illinois state track championships, Eckersall placed fifth in the 100-yard dash, while Hyde Park tied for eighth as a team. In the Cook County League championships, Eckersall took third in the 220-yard dash, then nosed out Bill Hogenson of English High School to win the 100, closing his sophomore season with his first major track title.[11]

In baseball, Eckersall again started at shortstop, with Ransom catching. Ransom stood out in wins over the Armour Institute and South Division, Eckersall hit a double and scored three runs in a win over Englewood, and Eckersall and Ransom each scored two runs in a win over Austin High School.[12]

To wrap up the season, Ransom hit a double and a home run against North Division, while Beebe threw ten strikeouts. Hyde Park's 9–3 win sealed the Cook County League championship, Eckersall's second league title in two different sports in just eight days.[13]

—

With Eckersall leading his team in the triple roles of quarterback, captain, and coach, local newspapers expected Hyde Park to have a winning team in 1901. But they didn't expect the shocking result of the first game, in which Hyde Park beat University of Chicago, 6–0. Eckersall made the play of the game: From Chicago's 40-yard line, he handed off, circled backward, then took a pitch and scampered outside, racing to the 5-yard line. Hammond then punched the ball in for a touchdown, the only score of the game.

Eckie clearly learned his lesson from the North Division loss the previous November. "The men lined up rapidly after each scrimmage, the signals were given without an instant's hesitation, and the ball was going down the field before the maroons began to realize what was happening," the *Chicago Tribune* noted. This up-tempo style of offense would be a hallmark of Eckersall's play for the next six years.[14]

Hyde Park faced East Aurora in its second game. In each half, East Aurora drove inside Hyde Park's 5-yard line. Both times, Hyde Park took over on downs and immediately punted out of danger. With only seconds left to play, Eckersall fielded an East Aurora punt and weaved through the field for an apparent 55-yard touchdown, but the referee ruled he had stepped out of bounds at the 25. Game over, a 0–0 tie.[15]

Hyde Park's third game was a forgettable 63–0 loss to the University of Wisconsin in Madison. The following Wednesday, against University of Chicago's JV, Ransom ran for a touchdown and Eckersall kicked a field goal in a 17–5 win.[16]

As Hyde Park reached the heart of its schedule, the Blue and White looked unbeatable. Eckersall would later cite opponents' racism as a key factor: "The slogan of all Hyde Park's opponents was 'Get the Negro!' The harder opposing players tried to disable Ransom, the harder he played, and I have heard players on opposing teams say they would have been victorious if they had played the game instead of trying to put Ransom out."[17]

On October 12 Hammond scored the game's only touchdown, and Eckie kicked the extra point as Hyde Park beat North Division 6–0. The next Wednesday, Ransom scored a touchdown in a shutout win over South Side Academy. The following Saturday, Hyde Park beat South Division in another shutout.[18]

In late October, Hyde Park lost a rematch against Chicago and lost another game to the Chicago Dental School. Hyde Park returned to its winning ways against Evanston High School. Eckersall and Ransom each scored a touchdown in the first half, and Hyde Park seemed headed toward a blowout victory. At halftime, Evanston offered to forfeit if it could play the rest of the game as an "exhibition" using two academically ineligible players. Hyde Park agreed. Late in the game, one of the ineligibles got away for a long run to the Hyde Park 20. From there a teammate kicked a field goal. Hyde Park still won comfortably, 29–5.[19]

Against Englewood, Hammond scored three touchdowns in a 33–0 win. Hammond scored another touchdown as Hyde Park beat Elgin High School 10–0 in a nonconference game. In the last regular-season game, Hyde Park dominated West Division 57–0. Hammond scored five touchdowns and Ransom scored one, but "Eckersall was the star of the game," the *Chicago Tribune* noted. He returned a kickoff 85 yards for a touchdown, returned another kickoff 80 yards, had a 55-yard rush, kicked a field goal, and regularly pinned West Division deep with his booming punts.[20]

This set up a rematch with North Division for the Cook County League championship at Marshall Field. Both teams enlisted college coaches as volunteer mentors: Chicago coach Amos Alonzo Stagg helped out at Hyde Park, while Dartmouth coach and Chicago native Walter McCornack prepped the North Division boys.

Leading up to the game, Eckersall gave his first-ever newspaper interview, telling the *Chicago Tribune*: "Every Hyde Park player is going into the game to play until he can't stand. Then a substitute will be sent in, and we have an abundance of good utility men. We expect to win, but no one is overconfident, for we expect a close contest."[21]

Early in the first half, Eckersall connected on a 40-yard field goal. In the game's closing minutes, he fielded a punt, broke a tackle, and sprinted

2. Hyde Park High School football team, Cook County League champions of 1901. Walter Eckersall, center, is holding the ball; Sam Ransom stands just to Eckersall's left; and Tom Hammond stands just to Ransom's left. SDN-000369, *Chicago Daily News* collection, Chicago History Museum.

down the right sideline for a 60-yard touchdown, for an 11–0 Hyde Park victory and the Cook County League championship. Fans hoisted Eckersall on their shoulders and carried him half a mile back to school, where the celebration on Kimbark Avenue lasted into the night.[22]

Hyde Park finished the season with a 10-3-1 record, 8-0-1 against high schools. The Blue and White had outscored high school opponents by a total of 180–5, and those 5 points didn't really count, since Evanston scored them after forfeiting. Eckersall, Ransom, and Hammond emerged as stars, and all three were named first-team All-Cook County League.[23]

Late in the season, the *Chicago Inter Ocean* wrote the first newspaper feature to focus exclusively on Eckersall, complete with a full-length picture of the star, hands on his hips and a scowl on his face:

> The great success and reputation attained by the football team of the Hyde Park High school this fall has been largely due to its captain and leader, Walter Eckersall. Captain Eckersall himself has not only gained an enviable reputation as a football player, but he is also captain of this year's track team and short stop on the baseball team. This is his second year on the football team, and he is already acknowledged the best quarter back and kicker in the High School league and will doubtless make the all-star team for the second time in his short career.
>
> On the track Eckersall is one of the fastest men in the high schools of Chicago. . . . In baseball he makes intricate plays with the polish of a veteran and in football his speed, generalship, kicking, and tackling make him a dangerous man for even university teams. Eckersall has yet two years at Hyde Park, at the end of which time he is expected to become a valuable addition to the athletic teams of some near-by university.[24]

—

The following spring, Eckersall appeared invincible on the track. He lost only one individual sprint race (to a college runner) while also contributing to several winning relay teams.[25]

With Sam Ransom as captain, the baseball team lost to Chicago and Wisconsin, but beat Chicago's JV team twice. Hyde Park also lost to the all-Black Chicago Union Giants, though Eckersall, Ransom, and Hammond each scored a run against the professionals.[26]

In late April Hyde Park ran into a problem. Distance runner Fred Hall, third in state in the mile the previous year, had a failing math grade at midterms. The Cook County League ordered Hyde Park to bench Hall until he got his grades up.[27]

Hyde Park defied the league, entering a meet at Northwestern University. Hall won the mile, Eckersall won the 100- and 220-yard dashes, Ransom took third in the discus, and Hyde Park captured the team title.[28]

Days before the state meet, the Board of Control came down firmly, suspending Hyde Park for the rest of the season—not only in track but also in baseball, since Eckersall, Ransom, and Hammond played both sports.[29]

Hyde Park considered running in the state meet anyway, since the Cook County League wasn't in charge of that event. Hyde Park's principal vetoed the boys' plan. South Division, which Hyde Park had already beaten in a dual meet, won both the state and county team titles. Grumbling over their suspension, the Hyde Park athletes plotted to form a rival league, free from any pesky eligibility requirements.[30]

Hyde Park's plan came to nothing. With its track season lost, Hyde Park appealed the baseball team's suspension. The Board of Control ruled that Hyde Park could play baseball but only if it benched the track athletes. The school dropped its appeal.

Before disbanding, Hyde Park played an exhibition game against North Division. Eckersall, Ransom, and Hammond each had two hits, and Eckersall and Hammond each stole two bases as Hyde Park crushed North Division 12–1, a pyrrhic victory in a shortened season.[31]

4

High School Superstar

Before the 1902 football season, several area schoolboys transferred into Hyde Park, hoping to team with Walter Eckersall, Sam Ransom, and Tom Hammond. Two became starters, but the other newcomers, even those who had been stars at their old schools, wound up buried on the bench.[1]

Eckie had been captain-coach in 1901, but this year he solicited help from an adult: his AAU track coach, Lee Grennan. Chicago coach Amos Alonzo Stagg, who let Hyde Park host games at Marshall Field and witnessed practice often, probably gave the boys as much feedback as Grennan ever did.[2]

Unlike the previous year, Hyde Park couldn't pull off a season-opening upset against Chicago, though the Blue and White came close. Chicago scored the first touchdown and made the extra point for a 6–0 lead. That score would hold for most of the game.

"The Hyde Park boys, however, outplayed the maroons at nearly every point," the *Chicago Tribune* noted. "Hyde Park . . . played an open running game, with double passes and trick plays that kept the opposing team guessing. Eckersall's punting was superior to anything the maroons could show."

Late in the game, Hyde Park halfback Marion Wolfe forced a fumble, scooped up the ball, and ran 105 yards for a touchdown. Tackle Ted Knorr, who doubled as Hyde Park's place-kicker, appeared to tie the game with the extra point, but the umpire whistled that play dead: Hyde Park hadn't given Chicago time to line up. Knorr missed his second attempt, and the Blue and White lost 6–5.[3]

Hyde Park fell behind early in its second game, to the University of Chicago's JV. Eckersall tried to get something going in the second half, faking a punt before taking off and running with the ball. The defense wasn't fooled, and Eckersall was tackled near the sideline.

A Chicago halfback came over to clean up the play, piling on Eckersall out of bounds. Eckersall came up swinging, the tiny quarterback trying to take on a college player who outweighed him by forty pounds. Eckie's feisty reaction was the high point of the game for Hyde Park in a 5–0 loss.[4]

Next, Hyde Park traveled to Madison to play University of Wisconsin. Early in the game, Eckersall faked a punt from his own 10-yard line, then scampered around left end for a 50-yard run, "which came so near being a touchdown that it took the breath away from the rooters," reported the *Chicago Tribune*. Hyde Park couldn't get any closer, and Wisconsin scored a touchdown on its next drive.

Later in the first half, Eckie tried a field goal from the Wisconsin 10. The Badgers blocked the attempt right into the hands of Hammond. At the time, blocked kicks were considered "live" and could be advanced by either team, so Hammond grabbed the ball and ran for a touchdown. Hyde Park missed the extra point and trailed by just 1 point at halftime.

Wisconsin wore the high school boys down in the second half, adding three more touchdowns in a 24–5 win. Hyde Park had started the season 0-3, but its competitive play against colleges set the stage for a memorable season.[5]

In Cook County League competition, Hyde Park scored nearly at will in 1902. With Eckersall directing the attack, the Blue and White compiled:

A 72–0 victory over South Division. Eckersall had a 110-yard kickoff return touchdown and added an extra point, Sam Ransom ran for three touchdowns, and Tom Hammond ran for two touchdowns.[6]

A 28–0 win over North Division. Eckersall, Hammond, and Ransom each scored a touchdown and Eckersall added a 20-yard field goal.[7]

A 74–0 shellacking of West Division. Eckie scored 37 points on a field goal, two extra points, and six touchdowns, which included a 50-yard punt return and two kickoff returns of 80 yards each. Tom Hammond added 17 points on two touchdowns and seven extra points.[8]

A 57–0 win over archrival Englewood. Eckersall and Ransom each scored touchdowns, and Tom Hammond ran for three.[9]

The Cook County League turned down North Division's request for a rematch in a championship game and declared the Blue and White undisputed champions for 1902. Yet, the season felt hollow. After playing twelve games in 1900 and fourteen games in 1901, Hyde Park had only played seven in 1902. And despite their dominance against high schools, the three losses to colleges dragged down Hyde Park's overall record. The team hoped for one more game against good competition and started to look out of state for a matchup.[10]

Initially, Hyde Park agreed to a game at Louisville Manual High School, Kentucky's state champions, on November 29. After Hyde Park's manager signed a contract, Louisville Manual came back with a demand: Ransom couldn't play in the land where slavery had been legal less than forty years earlier and where Jim Crow still reigned. The *Chicago Tribune*, while sympathetic toward Ransom, declared that a "contract is a contract" and that the team should play without its African American halfback.[11]

Eckersall had other ideas, promising to boycott if Ransom had to sit. The school's administration and alumni overwhelmingly backed his decision.

"They all said it would be a shame for the team, for which Ransom has fought so hard, to agree to a game in which he should be barred," said an alumni spokesman. "Nobody at Hyde Park has ever thought of discriminating against Ransom because of his color. He takes his place at the banquet table or other places where the boys of the team are without any one ever thinking about the color of his skin."[12]

(With the Hyde Park game canceled, Louisville Manual arranged a substitute game against Louisville Male High School. In a classic case of karma, Male beat Manual 10–5.)[13]

Hyde Park continued to seek an opponent, finally sending a challenge to Brooklyn Polytechnic Prep. The befuddled Eastern team wondered if the telegram was a joke. Assured that it was real, Poly Prep agreed to an expenses-paid trip to Chicago.[14]

Later authors hailed Poly Prep as champions of New York City, or even as the best team in the East. Eckersall would recall that Brooklyn Poly "had won the Long Island interscholastic championship . . . [and was] heralded as the equal of most minor college elevens of its section."[15]

In reality, the Brooklyn school was a poor choice. Poly had not only lost the Long Island title but placed third in that four-team league.[16]

Stagg signed on again as volunteer coach. "Those [Hyde Park] boys play well for a high school team," he said. "Brooklyn will have to play good football to beat that Hyde Park team."[17]

Sensing a rout, Poly Prep hoped to temper expectations. "This team is simply going as a representative Eastern eleven, and not as a champion eleven," said a faculty spokesman. "We wish that [was] understood distinctly, and the Western people understand it in that light."[18]

Midwest colleges had played Eastern colleges before. But because it was the first East versus Midwest high school game on record, the newspapers hyped up this angle.

"The game is expected to bring out the comparative quality of play of representative scholastic teams of the east and west," the *Chicago Tribune* asserted. The *Tribune* also stated, without evidence, that "the 'Poly' prep team that plays Hyde Park high school on Saturday is one of the strongest teams in the east. . . . Poly can be relied upon to put up a fast, scientific, and spectacular game."[19]

Poly Prep was anything but fast, scientific, or spectacular on game day, on a snowy Marshall Field. The slippery turf should have at least slowed down Hyde Park's speedsters, but Poly Prep was simply "Outclassed and Bewildered," as one sub-headline in the *Brooklyn Daily Eagle* sadly read.[20]

Hyde Park scored two minutes into the game and never looked back. Eckersall ran his team at a furious clip. Under the rules of the day, the team scored on had to kick off. Poly Prep kicked off often and spent most of the game on defense as Hyde Park scored nearly at will.

Although Poly Prep had nothing to do with the Louisville Manual controversy, Eckie seemed intent on proving a point. He kept calling Ransom's

3. A capacity crowd watches Hyde Park humiliate Brooklyn Poly Prep, 105–0, on a snowy Marshall Field in 1902. Hyde Park is lined up for a snap on the right side of the picture. SDN-001074, *Chicago Daily News* collection, Chicago History Museum.

number, and Ransom kept scoring: seven touchdowns, for 35 points. Eckersall had three touchdowns himself, all on plays of at least 60 yards, while Hammond scored a touchdown and kicked fifteen extra points. In the end, Hyde Park absolutely crushed Brooklyn Poly, 105–0.[21]

The game ended with one item of concern: Eckie broke his collarbone in the second half, missing the final eleven minutes. This would be the only significant playing time Eckersall would ever miss due to injury.

Captain Eckersall was satisfied with his final high school game. "We expected to win by a good sized score, but never thought of running up such a big total," he told the *Chicago Tribune*. "The eastern team was not as strong as we expected, although our team never feared the outcome. We won by fast, open football, which was too much for Brooklyn."[22]

Eckersall ended his high school football career with back-to-back Cook County League titles; only the controversial ending against North

Division in 1900 prevented a three-peat. During Eckersall's three varsity seasons, Hyde Park went 17-3-3 against high schools, including a 13-0-1 record in his junior and senior years. Since the 29–5 win over Evanston in 1901 was technically a forfeit, no high school team had even scored on Hyde Park in those last two seasons. In a further show of dominance, the Blue and White placed ten starters on the eleven-player All-Chicago High School team for 1902.[23]

—

In track, Eckersall won all his indoor races, at distances ranging from 35 to 300 yards. That March, Eckersall won the Central AAU championship in the 75-yard dash, beating a future Olympic medalist.[24]

As outdoor season began, Hyde Park's mile relay team emerged victorious in a runoff to compete in the Penn Relays. Coach Stagg contributed $100 to Hyde Park's travel expenses, a generous gesture that is a clear recruiting violation by today's standards.[25]

At Philadelphia, Hyde Park's Norman Barker started off poorly, finishing his leg in fourth place out of the five teams. Running second, Hammond passed two opponents to move Hyde Park into second position. Phil Comstock lost some ground on the third leg, and Eckersall received the baton in third place. Then Eckersall found another gear, surging past runners from Brooklyn and Washington to finish first, capturing the de facto national high school title for Hyde Park.[26]

Eckersall appeared invincible on the track. But one week later, he met his match: Bill Hogenson, whom Eckersall narrowly beat for the Cook County League 100-yard title two years earlier. In a meet at Northwestern, Hogenson beat Eckersall in both the 100 and the 220, although Hyde Park managed to win the team title.[27]

Eckersall rebounded for the Illinois state championships. (Hogenson did not compete; he had transferred to a private school, and only public schools were invited.) Eckie tied the meet record in the 50-yard dash, and he set new records in the 100- and 220-yard dashes. He also anchored Hyde Park's winning ⅔-mile relay team.

4. Hyde Park mile relay team, high school national champions at the 1903 Penn Relays. From left: Walter Eckersall, Phil Comstock, Tom Hammond, Norman Barker. AAS Papers, Box 316, Scrapbook 18, Hanna Holborn Gray Special Collections Research Center, University of Chicago Library.

Eckersall's four state titles helped Hyde Park capture the team title. His state record in the 220 would stand for twenty years, and his 100-yard record lasted for twenty-five years. His shared record in the 50, discontinued as a state event after 1929, still stands.[28]

The Cook County League meet was canceled for 1903 because of a date conflict with an "Anti-Cigarette League" meet (pre-PC slogan: "To show that its members are not merely 'girl-boys'"). Instead, Hyde Park's track season ended at a high school meet at the University of Chicago. Hogenson beat Eckersall again, winning the 100 and the 220, with Eckie finishing a close second in both events. In the anchor leg of the sprint relay, Eckersall again

5. Hyde Park baseball team, Cook County League champions of 1903. Captain Sam Ransom is seated in the middle row, center; Walter Eckersall sits to Ransom's right. SDN-001546, *Chicago Daily News* collection, Chicago History Museum.

faced Hogenson and led Hyde Park to victory, closing his high school track career with a win.[29]

—

The 1903 high school baseball season proved anticlimactic; Hyde Park was simply too good for its competition.[30]

Hyde Park swept all its high school opponents, beating West Division, North Division, and English High and taking down an out-of-state opponent in Goshen (Indiana) High School. Eckersall's personal highlight came against English High, when he hit a grand slam in the fourth inning of an 11–9 victory.[31]

On June 19 Hyde Park faced Oak Park for the league title. "The boys on both sides were confident of winning and considerable money was bet on the result," the *Chicago Inter Ocean* noted, without a hint of judgment against gambling on a high school game.[32]

Eckersall had a quiet game: one hit and six fielding assists, along with two errors. Ransom had a hit, stole two bases, and scored three runs in a 5–2 win that sealed the Cook County League championship. The following day, Hyde Park played Delavan (Wisconsin) High School and won 13–2, Eckie's final appearance in a Blue and White uniform.[33]

During Eckersall's career, Hyde Park won two Cook County League titles in football and two more in baseball, while the 1902 football team was regarded as best in the country. In track, Hyde Park won a state team title, and Eckersall four state titles, a Central AAU title, a national relay title, and a Cook County League championship.

While colleges were interested in Eckie's track and baseball potential, they were most eager to see him line up for their teams on the football field. His leadership skills, self-confidence, and football IQ would prove just as valuable as his tremendous athletic ability. And a pending rule change would make Eckersall even more valuable. Starting in 1903, the quarterback could now run past the line of scrimmage directly, as long as he crossed at least 5 yards outside the point of the snap.

College coaches drooled over Eckersall's potential, making him the most sought-after recruit of his era.

5

High School Sports after Eckersall

After Walter Eckersall left Hyde Park, high school sports in Chicago continued along the trajectory he helped start. One immediate result was intersectional football games, inspired by Hyde Park's 1902 battle with Brooklyn Poly Prep.

In 1903 North Division High School traveled east and crushed Brooklyn Boys High School, 75–0. North Division turned west a couple years later and lost a close game to Seattle High School on New Year's Day 1907, leading Seattle to declare itself "Champions of the United States."[1]

Englewood High School went on its own western trip two seasons later, splitting games in Montana and Denver in December 1908. After Englewood's train left Chicago, the school board demanded to know who had granted permission. Englewood's principal punted, saying that any authority lay with the boys' parents and not the school.[2]

Englewood arranged another trip out West the following year. This time the school board said an emphatic no to football "junkets."

"I am informed that the boys have received a guaranty of $1,500 from Butte and a like guaranty from Seattle," said the school board president. "This looks too much like turning the boys' sport into professionalism."[3]

City high schools were now banned from intersectional games, but this ban didn't apply to suburban Oak Park High School. In 1910 first-year coach Bob Zuppke took his Cook County League champions to Seattle and Portland over Christmas break. In 1911 Oak Park hosted St. John's Prep of Danvers, Massachusetts; in 1912 Zuppke's team played Everett (Massachusetts) High School at Boston's Fenway Park. Oak Park won all four intersectional games, and his success at Oak Park led Zuppke to a Hall of Fame coaching career at University of Illinois.[4]

The Chicago schools' intersectional ban was either forgiven or forgotten by 1912, when Wendell Phillips High School (the new name of South Division) traveled to the Pacific Northwest for three games over Christmas break. Altogether, Chicago-area high schools recorded thirteen wins, seven losses, and one tie in intersectional games between 1902 and 1917.

By the 1920s, out-of-state foes had caught up in talent and tactics, and Chicago limped to a losing record in intersectional games. In the 1930s, the Great Depression halted most of these exhibitions. Two series that survived involved African American teams. Between 1925 and 1948, Wendell Phillips (which had shifted to majority Black in less than ten years) and DuSable High School played seventeen games against segregated schools from Kentucky, Missouri, and Oklahoma.[5]

Otherwise, intersectional high school football died out. It resumed in the 1990s, driven not by the schools but by television. Each year, ESPN airs about a dozen high school football games, of which only a handful are truly intersectional, as ESPN tries to create a somewhat artificial conversation about a national champion at the high school level.

That type of championship-caliber game traces its lineage to 1902. Intersectional high school football was a Chicago creation, with Walter Eckersall, Sam Ransom, and Tom Hammond as its pioneers.

—

One question was never fully answered during Eckie's playing days: Who was in charge of high school sports, the kids or the grown-ups?

After 1898 the revitalized Cook County League Board of Control, now run by faculty members, reined in the worst abuses. Academic standards were now enforced, and the board expelled teams for full seasons when members had been caught breaking rules.[6]

But the high schoolers chafed at adult supervision. In 1900 several members threatened to withdraw from the Cook County League and start a rival conference under student control.

"Just consider the situation at present, of the league being run by a lot of men who know nothing about football," said one anonymous student. "Protests are decided not according to rules of football, but in favor of the member who is the best orator."[7]

This rival league never materialized. Two years later, another coup attempt fizzled.[8]

Behind the facade of faculty supervision, high school kids still largely ran the athletic show. The few adult coaches were usually alumni or former college players, not teachers. Team managers were selected more for popularity than competence, yet they wielded tremendous power regarding scheduling, rule-making, and the disbursement of net proceeds.

Perhaps most bizarre, most high school athletes were also members of fraternities. These secret societies imitated their collegiate counterparts with chapter houses, initiation rites, and hazing, while seeking popular, high-status classmates as pledges. This exclusivity ran counter to emerging democratic currents in education that sought to make all aspects of schooling, including extracurriculars, widely accessible.[9]

(Walter Eckersall belonged to one of these frats. Historian Robert Pruter included a picture labeled "Hyde Park fraternity, 1903," in a scholarly article that touches on the fraternity issue; Eckersall is clearly visible in the group of twenty-eight boys. In May 1903 the *Chicago Tribune* noted the star had suffered a minor injury "while Eckersall was scuffling in a fraternity house at school." But the fraternity issue didn't gain much outside scrutiny until Eckersall was a freshman in college, where he naturally pledged Alpha Delta Phi.)[10]

A 1905 *Chicago Tribune* editorial asked:

> Are high school fraternities inconsistent with democracy? The high schools themselves . . . are a product of the idea that the poor boy and the rich boy should have equal opportunities. Is it right that in such schools small cliques should be formed on the basis of social prestige?

> Is it right that a distinction should be erected between the boy who has money or ingratiating attractiveness and the boy who is not so favored? . . . High school fraternities by the almost unanimous opinion of the teachers and principals of Chicago have a bad moral effect upon their members and create a feeling of caste resentment among non-members. From the evidence in hand it seems probable that the fraternity system is not suited to pupils of high school age. They are not yet old enough for it.[11]

In March 1904 school superintendent Edwin Cooley pressured the Cook County League to grant him greater oversight over athletics. He tightened academic standards and banned freshmen from varsity football. Cooley also capped the age of high school athletes at twenty-one years. Schoolboys bristled, but they could do little. Cooley then turned toward the fraternities.[12]

"The high school fraternity tends to the formation of cliques and detracts from the efficiency and discipline of schools," Cooley said at a school board meeting in May 1904. "They divert the attention of students from their studies and should be abolished."[13]

The Board of Education agreed, banning fraternity and sorority members from high school extracurriculars. Most students shrugged their shoulders.

"It will simply make the secret societies more secret," stated one student. "Our 'frats' have been organized for years and we do not propose to see them driven to the wall. We shall meet away from the schools and surround our meetings with such secrecy that the board members will not know that they exist."[14]

At Hyde Park, the principal told players that they had to choose between their teams and their frats. The players responded with lawsuits. Four games into the 1904 football season, a Cook County judge granted an injunction allowing the frat boys to play. Their return didn't make much difference as Hyde Park, just two years removed from Walter Eckersall's stellar senior season, limped to a 1-8 record.[15]

In 1906 the school board passed a new antifrat rule. Later that year, principals at Hyde Park and Wendell Phillips discovered that several athletes still belonged to fraternities, and again ordered them to quit. The players returned to the courts. After more than a year, the Illinois Supreme Court ruled in favor of the school board.[16]

"I am in favor of a more stringent rule than the one we have," Cooley commented. "I would smite these organizations hip and thigh if I had my way. I believe they are enemies of the school system. . . . [You] will find the fraternities in everything bad there is in the schools, from crooked athletics down—or up."[17]

Cooley was finally granted his four-year-old wish. In March 1908 the Board of Education banned fraternities altogether, effective the following September. Several students defied the order and were immediately suspended.[18]

After one attempt at mediation, the school board president was aghast at the frat boys' attitudes. "The conduct of the boys who attended that conference showed exactly why we are stamping out the fraternities," he said. "They were impudent and ill mannered. . . . I have become pretty clear as to what they need, the boys, I mean. If they could be taken out behind the school building and given a good old fashioned spanking it would do more real good than all the rules the board can pass."[19]

The suspended students again appealed to the courts. This time, their case was swiftly dismissed. High school fraternities, a strange sideshow in the life of schoolboy athletics, had now faded into the background.[20]

—

After roughly twenty-five years of student-run competition and a ten-year period in which students and faculty struggled for power, the adults had finally taken control of high school sports in Chicago. Governance would soon change in other ways.

The Cook County League continued to expand and included twenty members by 1904. The number of sports grew as well, and they now included basketball, tennis, soccer, and indoor baseball. The league also began offering girls' basketball, tennis, and track.[21]

As new public high schools opened in the city, several joined the Cook County League. The league also welcomed a couple more suburban schools.

In 1911 the league admitted a Catholic school, St. Philip, which won the baseball championship in its first season.[22]

St. Philip wanted to compete again the following year, and two other Catholic schools also applied. The Board of Control refused to vote, instead referring the decision to a committee. The resulting delay guaranteed that the Catholic schools couldn't play league football that fall. The three snubbed schools joined with several others to form the Chicago Catholic League.[23]

The Catholic League's first season coincided with the Cook County League's last. With a growing roster of schools, "the Cook County league became so cumbersome it was necessary to bring about a dissolution," the *Chicago Tribune* reported. The new Chicago Public League consisted solely of public high schools within the city limits. Castoffs formed the Suburban High School League, which stuck around, with five original members still participating, until 1970.[24]

At first, the Chicago Public League struggled to find its footing. But the Suburban League thrived, capturing ten team titles in the state track meet during the league's first twelve seasons. Evanston won the inaugural Suburban League title in basketball, then defeated Public League champion Bowen en route to a Midwest regional title. In swimming, Suburban League champion Oak Park soundly beat Public League champ Hyde Park in a postseason meet. In football, Oak Park swept through the Suburban League's inaugural season of 1913, winning all ten games by an average of 45 points.[25]

Also in 1913, the Catholic League football champions from DePaul Academy sought a game with Public League champ Hyde Park for a true "city championship," but they were spurned. That championship finally took place in 1927, when the Catholic League's Mount Carmel beat Schurz of the Public League in front of fifty thousand fans at Soldier Field. The game has been played in all but four seasons since then.[26]

The Prep Bowl was the premier high school athletic event in Chicago for decades, drawing huge crowds and generating large sums for charity. The 1937 game between Austin and Leo stands out, not for the quality of the game (the Public League's Austin, led by halfback Bill DeCorrevont, beat Leo of the Catholic League 26–0) but for the size of the crowd, estimated at 125,000.[27]

The Public League went 12-6-2 over the first twenty Prep Bowls, and the series was tied as late as 1963. But early parity between the conferences would drastically shift over time. Through the 2024 season, the Catholic League holds a 64-28-2 overall advantage versus the Public League.[28]

—

Another shift in athletic governance started when the Illinois High School Association was born in December 1900. In 1908 IHSA started sponsoring a basketball tournament, which instantly proved popular. An IHSA official coined the term "March Madness" in 1939, decades before the NCAA co-opted the slogan. Chicago-area schools had little to do with the tournament's early years, as the "state basketball championship" was essentially a small-town and rural affair.[29]

In 1926 IHSA joined the University of Illinois as cosponsor of the state track and field meet; eventually, the university ceded full control to the association. As that spring's championships approached, six Public League schools applied to join. Soon the entire league was admitted. Meanwhile, the Catholic League remained outside IHSA's governance and was ineligible for state competition.[30]

Joining IHSA came at a cost. The Cook County League and, later, the Public League had been early proponents of girls' sports, which the association discouraged. "The high school girls of this state who are under supervision of this association should not appear before the public promiscuously in interscholastic basketball games," IHSA declared in 1907. "The game is altogether too masculine. . . . [The] exercise in public is immodest and not altogether ladylike."[31]

In casting its lot with IHSA, the Public League crippled girls' sports for decades. From the 1920s through the 1950s, the Chicago area produced Olympic-caliber female athletes such as swimmers Sybil Bauer of Schurz and Ethel Lackie of University High, and track athletes Annette Rogers and Helen Filkey of Senn, Betty Robinson of Thornton, and Mabel Landry and Barbara Jones of St. Elizabeth. But these athletes were developed by their Amateur Athletic Union teams, the Chicago Park District, or the Catholic Youth Organization; none could compete through their high schools.

In 1973 the Catholic League finally joined IHSA, coinciding with the association's decision to start sponsoring football playoffs. Membership paid off quickly for the league. St. Laurence won IHSA's 5A (then the largest class) football title in 1976, the first of forty-four state football titles for Catholic League teams through 2024. Meanwhile, the Public League has struggled in state competition, winning just two titles over the same span.[32]

One casualty of the IHSA football championships has been the Prep Bowl. Both the Catholic League's and the Public League's best teams would compete in the state playoffs, so the Prep Bowl became a consolation prize. This meant fewer fans and less media coverage. The Prep Bowl continues, but as it nears its hundredth edition, the bowl's relevance and future are in question.[33]

As the Catholic League dominated in football, the Public League's strength came in boys' basketball. In 1958 Marshall High School won the Public League's first state basketball title. Through 2025, Chicago Public League boys' teams have won thirty-five state titles, compared to just nine for Catholic League schools.[34]

In the 1970s, IHSA began offering girls' sports, not out of goodwill but by legal coercion, forced by Title IX of the Civil Rights Act of 1964. By this time suburban high schools had grown in size, strength, and funding compared to their urban counterparts, but Chicago's girls managed to hold their own. Through 2025, Public League teams have won sixteen girls' state basketball titles, led by Marshall High School and legendary coach Dorothy Gaters. Mother McAuley of the Girls Catholic Athletic Conference (parallel to the Catholic League and formed when most Catholic high schools were still single-sex) has won seventeen state championships in girls' volleyball, while the Public League's Morgan Park High School has captured seven girls' team track titles.[35]

—

In Walter Eckersall's own time, sportswriters covered him closely and highlighted his exploits for Hyde Park, making Eckie Chicago's first prep superstar.

What was it about Eckersall that drew such attention? Chicago-area high schools had a few great athletes before him: three-sport champion Wal-

6. Publicity photo of Walter Eckersall on the practice field during his Hyde Park High School days. SDN-000362, *Chicago Daily News* collection, Chicago History Museum.

ter McCornack of Englewood, West Division pole vaulter Charles Dvorak, Oak Park distance runner Sidney Hatch, Englewood football player and shot-putter Robert Maxwell. But Chicago newspapers hardly covered any of these athletes until they achieved prominence in college or at the Olympics.

Maybe the sportswriters admired Eckie's all-around brilliance. Maybe they were cheering for the "little guy," since Eckersall was usually the smallest player on the field. Maybe it was his attitude, the way he appeared indifferent and stoic on the sidelines or between races, then launched furiously into action when it was time to perform. Maybe it was simply his winning record, as a league, state, and national champion in multiple sports and multiple years.

Whatever the reason, Chicago newspapers treated Eckie differently than any prep athlete before him, with big pictures, large headlines, and highest praise: "Eckersall is without doubt the best all around athlete turned out by local schools in many years"; "Eckersall was again the star of the Hyde Park team, and when he got the ball on a kick-off or punt he sifted through the West Division players like chaff through a sieve"; "Eckersall proved himself again a strong man in the dashes. . . . [He] is regarded fast even for a college athlete"; "Captain Eckersall lived up to his reputation and made a spectacular run of over 100 yards down the field"; "Eckersall proved that he is still the leading sprinter among the high school boys"; "Eckersall [is] probably the best known high school athlete in the country."[36]

While Eckie may have been the first schoolboy to receive the superstar treatment, he was far from the last. A new superstar received larger-than-life press coverage every few years. These included Eckersall's future Chicago teammate Wally Steffen, a multiple-sport star at North Division; Ralph Metcalfe of Tilden, who won nine state track titles and went on to win four Olympic medals in the 1930s; Austin halfback DeCorrevont, who scored thirty-four touchdowns in 1937 and would sign autographs at celebrity appearances while still in high school; and Fenwick's three-sport star Johnny Lattner, who later became the first (and, to date, only) Chicago native to win a Heisman Trophy, for Notre Dame in 1953.[37]

Starting in the 1960s, a long line of Public League basketball players earned superstar status and became household names. These included Cazzie Russell of Carver, who became the first no. 1 overall NBA draft pick from Chicago; Westinghouse's Mark Aguirre, who stayed home to lead DePaul to an NCAA Final Four, then also became a no. 1 overall pick; Ben Wilson of Simeon, the top high school player in the country before his tragic murder in 1984; Farragut's high-flying duo of Kevin Garnett and Ronnie Fields, who won back-to-back "Mr. Basketball" state MVP honors in the mid-1990s; and Simeon's Derrick Rose, another "Mr. Basketball" and no. 1 pick who would win the NBA's Rookie of the Year and MVP honors for his hometown Chicago Bulls.[38]

As Title IX slowly brought girls' sports up to par with boys', female superstars emerged to rival their male counterparts. The two greatest female athletes in Illinois high school history—East St. Louis track and basketball star Jackie Joyner and Naperville Central basketball star Candace Parker—were *not* from Chicago or Cook County. Still, at least two local girls can rightly claim places in the Illinois high school sports pantheon. Cappie Pondexter of Marshall won a state title and two "Ms. Basketball" awards, then won Olympic gold and WNBA titles as a player before returning home to coach the Chicago Sky. And Alexandria Anderson of Morgan Park became the most decorated track athlete in Illinois history with fourteen state titles; she later won an NCAA title and a World Championship gold medal.[39]

All these superstars received the same types of headlines, feature articles, and splashy photos that Walter Eckersall earned at the turn of the twentieth century. In driving the hype around Eckersall, Chicago's sports journalists created the framework for the superstar culture that would endure over many decades.

For most of these high school superstars, the biggest question that emerged during their senior years became: Where will this athlete go to college? As the 1903 football season approached, this was the overriding question surrounding Walter Eckersall, one that wouldn't be answered until the last minute.

PART 2

1903–6

6

The Recruit

At the turn of the twentieth century, college football recruiting was just as dirty as it is today. Maybe even dirtier, because with no NCAA (that organization would be founded in 1906), there was minimal oversight. Yet, the general public remained unaware of most recruiting abuses. Coaches desired to keep positive public images; jilted schools were afraid to throw stones, to protect their own glass houses; and recruits didn't want the gravy train of benefits to end. Most recruiting secrets remained buried for decades, but in real time, a few bold reformers tried to expose corruption.

In 1905 muckraking journalist Henry Beach Needham wrote an exposé on abuses in the East for *McClure's Magazine*, while Edward Jordan wrote a similar series on dirty recruiting in the Midwest for *Collier's*. Those articles highlighted colleges that ignored woeful academic records; offered gifts of theater tickets or fancy dinners; awarded full-tuition athletic scholarships, technically illegal but easy to hide as need-based aid; provided lucrative on-campus jobs that required little actual work; and made promises of future employment. All these were features of Eckersall's case.[1]

The recruiting of Walter Eckersall began in earnest during his junior year at Hyde Park and featured three major competitors: Chicago, Michigan, and Wisconsin.

Chicago coach Amos Alonzo Stagg did much of his recruiting by mail. His archives are packed with hundreds of letters between the coach and his targets. Among Eckersall's contemporaries, Stagg sent five letters and a foot-

7. Amos Alonzo Stagg supervises University of Chicago football practice in 1901. University of Chicago Photographic Archive, apf1-07894, Hanna Holborn Gray Special Collections Research Center, University of Chicago Library.

ball to 1902 recruit Mark Catlin, and six letters to 1905 recruit Wally Steffen, who replied at least four times.[2]

There is no surviving recruiting correspondence between Stagg and Eckersall. Then again, Stagg didn't need to waste stamps when Eckersall lived only a mile from campus. The Midway had already turned into something of a second home for Hyde Park athletics. Stagg let Eckie's teams use Chicago's indoor track for dual meets, practice on campus often, and host twenty football games at Marshall Field, almost three times as often as the team played at its nominal "home field" of Washington Park.

With the doors to Chicago's gym open, Stagg quickly saw Eckersall's talent and paid special attention to the budding star. In Eckersall's junior and senior years, Stagg worked closely with Hyde Park late into the football season, serving as a volunteer coach for games with North Division in 1901 and Brooklyn Poly Prep in 1902.

8. Michigan coach Fielding Yost at the beginning of the "Point-a-Minute" era. BL012505, Bentley Historical Library Image Bank, University of Michigan Library Digital Collections.

Wisconsin got into the recruiting game by bringing Hyde Park up north to play. In both 1901 and 1902, Wisconsin coach Phil King paid for Hyde Park to travel to Madison for early-season football games. In 1902 Wisconsin also brought Hyde Park's spring sports teams up to campus, for several baseball games and a dual track meet.[3]

Michigan coach Fielding Yost also coveted Eckersall, keeping tabs on Eckie through alumni emissaries and coming to Chicago for the Hyde Park–Brooklyn Poly Prep game. "That Hyde Park team is a good one," Yost told the papers. "I like its fast style, which resembles Michigan's." After the game, Yost commented approvingly on the play of Eckersall, Sam Ransom, and Tom Hammond, then added: "No, I have not signed any of them yet."[4]

Stagg's recruiting advantage came from proximity and familiarity. King's came from the beauty of the Madison campus, shown off in those three Hyde Park visits. And Yost's came from the championship program he had built in Ann Arbor.

In 1901 Michigan hired Yost, who had been successful in four previous, but brief, coaching stops. During Yost's first two seasons, Michigan went 22-0 while averaging 54 points per game. The Wolverines tied Wisconsin for the Big Nine title in 1901 and won the championship outright in 1902. Michigan also won the inaugural Rose Bowl in 1902 with a 49–0 throttling of Stanford.

Halfback Willie Heston was Yost's star on those "Point-a-Minute" teams. Heston scored seventy-two touchdowns at Michigan, still a school record. By the loose standards of the time, the twenty-four-year-old Heston, a law student who had already earned a bachelor's from San Jose State, had played his fifth season of college football in 1902 but still had two years of eligibility remaining. Yost salivated at the thought of pairing Heston with Eckersall and tried to steer the phenom toward Ann Arbor.

By October 1902 the *Chicago Tribune* asserted that Eckersall would play for Stagg at Chicago and that Michigan hadn't shown much interest. That changed, quickly. In one bold maneuver, Michigan men invited the high school senior to an alumni "smoker," a cigar-and-liquor banquet the night before the Chicago-Michigan game at Marshall Field in November 1902. After one toast to Eckie, the enthusiastic crowd of two hundred roared with approval for the young star. At this point, Michigan alums thought they had the inside track on securing Eckersall.[5]

"If he does not go to Ann Arbor it will be funny," said one banquet guest, apparently oblivious to the irony that Michigan itself was using "funny" means to flip Eckie away from Stagg.[6]

In an ethically questionable move, Stagg donated $100—worth about $3,500 today—to send Eckersall and his Hyde Park mile relay team to Philadelphia for the Penn Relays. Still, by the summer, the *Chicago Tribune* reported that Eckie was a likely Michigan commit. Eckersall remained silent.[7]

By July a new rumor emerged: Eckie was heading back to high school. He was still three credits short of graduating from Hyde Park, and since he only played JV football as a freshman, he might still have one season of varsity eligibility.[8]

That rumor quickly dissipated, and the recruiting battle between Michigan and Chicago continued. According to paranoid intelligence gathered by the opposing camps, Michigan alumni promised to pay Eckersall's tuition. Chicago pledged a no-show job at a university office. Michigan offered under-the-table payments. Chicago guaranteed Eckie a coaching job after college. The stakes kept getting higher, at least according to the rumors that flew between Ann Arbor and Chicago and the secret reports kept by both Yost and Stagg.[9]

Both teams held informal preseason practices in early September. Stagg held his on campus at Marshall Field, while Yost took his team to Ludington, a resort town on the Lake Michigan coast. Eckie was a no-show at either camp.

Finally, Eckersall made up his mind: On September 14 he appeared on Marshall Field for the first official day of practice. More than twenty years later, Eckersall summed up his final decision:

> Summer of 1903 passed without my having decided which college to attend, although, like all the members of the Hyde Park High School champions, I had been "rushed" by the students and alumni of practically all of the colleges in the Western Conference. . . .
>
> Practice had started at the University of Chicago, which was near my home, and one day I drifted over to Marshall Field to look at the candidates at work. I crawled into one of the stands unnoticed and watched the men at work. The thud of the pigskin stirred my love of the game. I left the stand and made my way to where the candidates for the team were to practice.
>
> "Give me a suit," I said, and I spent the rest of the afternoon with the University of Chicago candidates.
>
> Many stories have since been told as to how and why I entered the University of Chicago instead of some other institution, but the one I have related is the truth.[10]

Eckie's account certainly didn't include the *whole* truth. Regardless, Chicago had beaten Michigan for the prized recruit.

Still, Michigan refused to concede. That evening, boosters showed up at the Eckersall home, dragging Walter out of bed and badgering him for hours, promising free tuition and a no-show job and assorted other benefits to abandon Chicago in favor of Michigan. Eckersall caved and accepted a train ticket to Ann Arbor for the following morning. Chicago fans got wind of this move and tipped off Stagg, who then showed up at the station and snatched Eckersall from the platform just before his train arrived.[11]

Now Eckersall would definitely be a Chicago Maroon. But the drama surrounding his recruiting was far from over.

—

While Eckie was the gem of his recruiting class, several Hyde Park teammates were also courted by Big Nine schools. Michigan wound up with six starters from 1902, most notably Hammond. But Hammond was a rising senior and far short of graduation, so Yost hired a tutor to help him pass his entrance exams. He was an immediate starter, and Michigan went 33-1-1 during his three varsity seasons. One other Hyde Park player became a part-time starter for Yost; the rest didn't pan out.

One Hyde Park player Yost did *not* recruit was Ransom. During three decades of college coaching, Yost, whose father fought for the Confederacy during the Civil War, never had a Black player. Chicago and Wisconsin did recruit Ransom, who initially chose Chicago.

Ransom looked sharp in preseason camp. "Any one who knows Ransom's history can tell by the way Ransom has started out at Chicago that he is out to make this fall's team," the *Chicago Tribune* reported. "In his freshman year at Hyde Park Ransom started in to work hard and was always one of the most faithful trainers . . . and he has started in the same manner to make the Chicago team."[12]

But on September 14, the same day Eckersall first showed up for practice, Ransom left the team. He had started high school in January 1900 and was still one semester short of graduation. Even though Chicago had admitted him as a "sub-freshman" like Eckersall, Ransom thought he would be better off finishing high school.[13]

The following year, Ransom went to Beloit College in southern Wisconsin. He became a multisport star at the small school, while Stagg missed out on a man who would have been *his* only Black player at Chicago—a loss that Eckersall always regretted.

So Eckersall, now a committed Maroon, started his college career a few blocks from his childhood home, under the tutelage of one of history's great college coaches.

7

Coach Stagg, President Harper, and Their University

Recent Yale University graduate Amos Alonzo Stagg—"Lonnie" to his friends—claimed he wanted to enter the ministry when he signed up for graduate-level divinity classes in 1888. More likely, the twenty-six-year-old, a star baseball pitcher and football backup, was trying to extend his days as a college athlete.

His timing was perfect. Stagg emerged as a starter at end and helped guide Yale to its greatest football season ever: thirteen shutout wins and no losses. More important for Stagg's future, he took a class on biblical literature with Professor William Rainey Harper, then in his third year as Yale's Semitic languages chair.[1]

Stagg remained at Yale for one more year. On the football field, he made Walter Camp's first-ever All-America team in 1889. After baseball season, he left school without finishing his divinity degree. Stagg later claimed that ministry wasn't a good fit due to his aversion to public speaking, although neither future players nor banquet audiences ever found him lacking in this area.[2]

Stagg moved on to the International YMCA College at Springfield, Massachusetts, where he trained to become a YMCA physical director. One of his fellow students there was James Naismith, best known today as the inventor of basketball. Stagg took charge of the Springfield football team, for his first coaching experience.

9. Amos Alonzo Stagg as a Yale football player in the late 1880s, around the time he first met Professor William Rainey Harper. University of Chicago Photographic Archive, apf1-07896, Hanna Holborn Gray Special Collections Research Center, University of Chicago Library.

"There were forty-two students all told, and I still am a little proud of the fact that from such a handful I produced teams that defeated a number of New England colleges and made the best of them exert themselves," Stagg later said.[3]

This claim is a bit of a stretch. The Springfield "Christian Workers"— with Stagg and Naismith in the lineup even though both were graduate students, with Stagg playing his seventh season of intercollegiate sports— didn't play the "best" opponents, going 5-3 against prep schools, small colleges, and major college JV teams.

That fall, Harper, impressed with both Stagg's athletic prowess and religious fervor, requested a meeting. Oil magnate and devout Baptist John D. Rockefeller had recently tabbed the equally devout Baptist Harper to lead his new university in Chicago. Over breakfast in Manhattan in September

1890, Harper made an offer to the similarly devout, but Presbyterian, Stagg: Together, we can build something great.[4]

—

Rockefeller's university took a circuitous route to Chicago. The tycoon founded Standard Oil in Cleveland in 1870; organized his company into a far-reaching "trust," which made him and his partners absurdly wealthy; and moved the company's headquarters to New York in 1885. Though Rockefeller never attended college, he had made large donations to Denison University, Barnard College, and Cornell University, along with Indian University (today's Bacone College) in Oklahoma and Spelman College, a historically Black women's college in Atlanta.

After settling in New York, Rockefeller was frequently visited by Rev. Augustus Strong, his former pastor in Cleveland whose son would later marry Rockefeller's daughter. Strong had become president of Rochester Theological Seminary, to which Rockefeller had also donated generously. In conversations with Rockefeller, Strong argued that Baptists needed an elite graduate university of their own, since their children were far outnumbered by mainstream Protestants at schools such as Harvard, Yale, and Princeton. Strong offered to head this university, with Manhattan as its location. The cost would be $20 million—a bargain, in terms of both Rockefeller's enormous wealth and his desire to save souls.

Rockefeller balked at the price tag as well as Strong's insistence on Rockefeller as sole benefactor. Strong continued to push but overplayed his hand. Ultimately, Rockefeller denied his old pastor's dream. Yet, Strong had planted an idea, of endowing a first-rate Baptist university *somewhere*.[5]

A couple members of Rockefeller's inner circle suggested Chicago and courted the philanthropist more gently than Strong had. They noted that the Baptist church was growing faster in the Midwest than in the East, and that construction costs were cheaper in Chicago than New York. And they proposed a more modest undergraduate school, with the potential to later add graduate schools.

The idea gained significant traction in 1887 when Rockefeller met Harper, who at that point was only loosely associated with the Chicago project. The previous year, Yale University had courted the thirty-year-old scholar, then teaching at Baptist Union Theological Seminary in then-suburban Morgan Park, fifteen miles southwest of downtown Chicago. Rockefeller, a trustee and major donor to Baptist Union, urged the administration to try its hardest to retain Harper.[6]

Harper spurned Morgan Park for Yale, which helped the Chicago project due to his newfound proximity to Rockefeller. Harper and Rockefeller first met neither in Manhattan nor at Yale, but at Vassar College in Poughkeepsie, New York, where Rockefeller's daughter Bessie was a student.

"[Harper] used to come, as the guest of Dr. James M. Taylor, the president, to lecture on Sundays; and as I frequently spent week-ends there, I saw and talked much with the young professor, then of Yale, and caught in some degree the contagion of his enthusiasm," Rockefeller wrote some twenty years later. "Dr. Harper was a man of exquisite personal charm. . . . As a friend and companion, in daily intercourse, no one could be more delightful than he."[7]

In October 1887, not long after their first meeting, the pair spent the day together in Manhattan, where Rockefeller truly fell under Harper's spell. Rockefeller soon gave Harper rare "open door" access. They met frequently in Manhattan and at Vassar, dined often, even rode bicycles together. Along the way, Harper outlined his vision for an innovative Baptist university in Chicago.

By May 1889 Rockefeller agreed to make a lead gift of $600,000 to this new university, if another $400,000 could be raised within the year. With days to spare, fundraisers met this goal, and the university was founded with $1 million in capital and ten acres of land donated by department store magnate Marshall Field. Located just north of the mile-long, block-wide Midway Plaisance Park, "the Midway" soon became shorthand for the university itself.[8]

Harper had big dreams for Chicago. (Expensive dreams, too. By the time of Rockefeller's last donation in 1910, he had contributed $35 million—more than $1.1 billion today and nearly double what Reverend Strong had asked for his proposed Manhattan university.) While Rockefeller urged him to begin modestly with an undergraduate college, Harper insisted that Chicago would start as a full university, with both undergraduate and graduate schools. Harper also embraced several experimental ideas. His innovations

10. University of Chicago benefactor John D. Rockefeller and founding president William Rainey Harper at a celebration marking the university's tenth anniversary. University of Chicago Photographic Archive, apf3-01968, Hanna Holborn Gray Special Collections Research Center, University of Chicago Library.

included a university press; a nighttime extension school for working adults; and the country's first Latin American studies curriculum.[9]

President Harper also envisioned another new type of university department, which led to his breakfast meeting with Stagg in 1890.

—

Harper offered Stagg $1,500 per year to head Chicago's Department of Physical Culture and Athletics. When Stagg failed to immediately answer, Harper upped his offer to $2,000. As Stagg mulled things over, Harper bid against himself to raise the ante again, pledging $2,500 and a tenured associate professorship.

Stagg considered Harper's offer for two months, then graciously accepted, in religious terms: "After much thought and prayer I feel decided that my life can best be used toward my Master's service in the position which you have offered." But Stagg also hedged his bets, entertaining feelers from Harvard, Yale, Penn, and Johns Hopkins, even as he pledged loyalty to this still-unrealized dream of a university.[10]

Ultimately, Stagg kept his promise, arriving at Harper's new "campus"—one mostly completed building, a handful of buildings under construction, and no athletic facilities—in September 1892. What Chicago lacked in amenities it made up for in energy, as both the campus and the nearby World's Columbian Exposition rapidly rose from the ground.

Harper envisioned the Department of Physical Culture and Athletics as a means for the physical development of regular students. Freshmen and sophomores would take three quarters of athletics each academic year, while juniors and seniors needed to take two quarters. At the same time, Harper encouraged Stagg to develop teams that would publicize the new university, carrying Chicago's standard far and wide.

"I am most heartily in favor of [intercollegiate athletics]," Harper wrote to Stagg. "I want you to develop teams which we can send around the country and knock out all the colleges."[11]

With this appointment, Stagg became the first permanent coach in college football history. Before Stagg, college coaches, often the previous season's captain, usually filled the role on a temporary basis, a year or two at most. Many teams still didn't have coaches at all, relying on captains to organize practices and on managers to schedule games.

At the same time, Chicago became the first school where the university and its faculty, rather than students and alumni, retained control of athletics. President Harper insisted, at least on paper, on strict amateurism, good sportsmanship, and a high standard of scholarship. Stagg, who had turned down offers to play pro baseball because he thought "the whole tone of the game was smelly," publicly embraced all three ideals, though he frequently stretched the definitions of both "amateurism" and "scholarship."[12]

Before he ever taught a class or coached a game, Stagg was already big news in the big city. "A. Alonzo Stagg is not among the least of President Harper's notable acquisitions," the *Chicago Inter Ocean* remarked when the university formally opened in 1892. "Indeed, as the sound mind predicates the sound body it might be claimed that Mr. Stagg is the most important man in the faculty, for he is to have charge of university athletics."[13]

—

For that 1892 season, Stagg posted notices on campus bulletin boards and cobbled together a ragtag football team. A couple students had played in high school, but most were novices, some of whom, Stagg noted, were "well up in years." Stagg, now thirty years old himself, pulled double duty by playing halfback in his ninth and final season as a "college" athlete.

"The squad was so weak that I had no choice but to play on the team," Stagg later wrote. "There was no secrecy about my presence in the line-up, and no objection by our opponents. The game was too young and weak for such a situation to be thought particularly unusual."[14]

Even with Stagg in the lineup, Chicago went just 2-4-1 against colleges in its first season. In 1893, with Stagg finally retired as a player, Chicago improved to 6-4-2. In 1894 Chicago adopted maroon as both its team color and nickname. After the regular season, Stagg proposed a Christmas break trip to play games in San Francisco, Los Angeles, and Salt Lake City.[15]

"President Harper was entirely agreeable, as he was toward anything legitimate that put the university's name in print," Stagg recalled. "But he left it to me to find the money." The team went 2-2 over the four games and took in almost $3,000 in revenue, but lost a net of $100 after expenses. "The deficit was charged to advertising, and was worth it," Stagg said, as he spread the University of Chicago brand westward.[16]

While Stagg and his Maroons returned from their groundbreaking trip, President Harper and five of his peers were involved in a groundbreaking event of their own. On January 11, 1895, Harper met with the presidents of Northwestern, Wisconsin, Minnesota, Illinois, and Purdue at the Auditorium Hotel in Chicago. These "six wise men" discussed the future of intercollegiate sports and recommended reforms.[17]

At a February 1896 meeting that built on the previous year's conference, Stagg met with representatives of six other schools (this time, Michigan joined the group) at Chicago's Palmer House to further discuss those reforms. This second meeting is widely considered the birth of what was then known as the Western Conference, today the Big Ten. It also led to the start of regular conference football competition in the fall of 1896.[18]

Chicago went 15-2-1 that season, although losses to Northwestern and Wisconsin left the Maroons in fourth place in the seven-team league. Chicago finished second to Wisconsin in 1897, and second to Michigan in 1898. Stagg won his first title in the conference's fourth season, going 4-0 in league play in 1899.

From there, Chicago slumped, dropping to sixth place in the "Big Nine" (Iowa and Indiana joined that season) in 1900 and finishing in a three-way tie for last place in 1901. The Maroons rebounded in 1902 by finishing second.[19]

Stagg earned a reputation as an innovator, credited with introducing or contributing to countless inventions, formations, and communication systems during a career that ultimately spanned sixty-nine seasons, fifty-seven of which were as head coach. Since the profession was brand-new and the rules were frequently evolving, Stagg had plenty of opportunities for creativity. His contributions include the huddle, the tackling dummy, the blocking sled, the reverse, indoor football games, intersectional football games, the man-in-motion, the pre-snap backfield shift, and numbered jerseys.[20]

With all these innovations, Stagg was called a "genius," even a "wizard." Or, increasingly, the "Old Man," even though he was only thirty-seven when receiving that nickname. But even the best coach needs good players to execute his schemes, and Stagg was no exception.[21]

After that first ragtag team of 1892, Stagg quickly raised his level of talent. His best player of that first decade, Clarence Herschberger, made first-team All-American at fullback in 1898, Camp's first such selection from outside the East. The captain of the 1899 championship team, Walter Kennedy, made second-team All-American twice. Herschberger was from downstate Peoria and Kennedy from Iowa, but Stagg increasingly targeted the fertile recruiting grounds of Cook County League schools, to which he generously (and self-interestedly) donated Marshall Field for major games.

As a relatively small private school, Chicago faced recruiting disadvantages compared to the big land-grant schools in its conference. Some of these disadvantages were offset by the opportunity to play in a big city—and by the chance to play for a brilliant coach like Stagg.

After beating out Fielding Yost for the top recruit of the 1903 class, Stagg hoped that Walter Eckersall could finally help him achieve his football vision.

8

Freshman Phenom

The college career of Walter Eckersall began under a cloud of controversy. Before he ever took a snap, Eckie was suspended by the Amateur Athletic Union, the self-appointed, often-sanctimonious guardian of "pure" athletics in the United States.

Throughout high school, Eckersall participated in AAU track. He ran with his brother Elmer for the First Regiment Athletic Association, which competed locally with the likes of the Chicago Athletic Association and nationally with peers in other cities. While still in high school, Eckie won AAU races in Cincinnati, Indianapolis, Milwaukee, and St. Louis, and won the Central AAU championship in the 75-yard dash.[1]

In August 1903 the National AAU suspended Eckersall for professionalism but not for taking money to play sports. Instead, the union discovered he had played a few baseball games in 1902 for the Chicago Spaldings of the low-level Inter-State League. It's not clear whether the Spaldings had any paid players, but some of Spaldings' opponents were, without doubt, semiprofessional.[2]

The Spaldings were a mediocre team, and Eckie didn't receive any money, but such technicalities didn't matter to the AAU. Those few games would hang over Eckersall's head for more than two years.[3]

Coach Amos Alonzo Stagg and AAU president Walter Liginger engaged in a game of chicken over Eckie's eligibility. On September 15 Liginger announced that anyone who played football against Eckersall that fall would also be suspended from the AAU. Stagg replied that the AAU should butt out, since it had no jurisdiction over college athletics.[4]

"I do not want to take a position that appears 'sassy,' but there is no question as to our rights," he said. "I am unwilling to believe that any college team in the country would refuse to play the Maroons just because Eckersall was a member of the team."[5]

Stagg was playing a dangerous game. College track teams competed regularly at AAU meets, and Stagg needed to stay in the union's good graces if he wanted his Chicago athletes to be eligible for the Olympics the following summer.

Liginger backed off in late September, saying his threats were misinterpreted. Meanwhile, Eckersall prepared for his freshman football season.[6]

—

In 1903 the Chicago Maroons were coming off a second-place finish in the Big Nine. The best of Chicago's seven returning starters was guard Robert Maxwell, then known by the literal "Big" but later by the ironic "Tiny." Ends Fred Speik and Mark Catlin and fullback Hugo Bezdek also returned.

Chicago's starting quarterback from 1902, Lee Maxwell, hoped to reclaim his old position. But from the first practice, Eckersall was obviously the best choice to run the Maroons.

Eckersall benefited from one rule change in 1903: The player receiving the snap could now run directly with the ball, as long as he was 5 yards outside the point of the snap. This style of outside running meshed well with Eckersall's speed.

But would speed suffice? "Eckersall . . . is good enough to make any college team, but I hardly think he will last the season," the coach of Beloit College remarked. "He is too light."[7]

It's easy to understand those comments. Whether he was seventeen or twenty, Eckersall simply looked . . . little, more like a waterboy than a football player, especially in the single-platoon days, when the 135-pounder would be expected to tackle fullbacks or ends in the open field.

Stagg opened the season as he usually did, with a few warmup games against high schools and small colleges. He tinkered with lineups, substituted frequently, and treated these games as extended tryouts.

Against Englewood High School, Stagg rotated Eckersall, Lee Maxwell, and law student Charles McMillan at quarterback. Eckersall only played ten minutes, but his talent was instantly clear in the 40–0 victory. "When Eckersall took control a marked difference was noticed in the play, which became faster and was better directed," the *Chicago Tribune* noted.[8]

Eckersall later insisted that the three quarterbacks were evenly matched: "Lee Maxwell, McMillan, and I were used alternately at quarter, and none of us could consider himself the regular."[9]

Stagg knew otherwise. Lee Maxwell would be Eckersall's primary backup at quarterback and started a few games at end, while McMillan would quit football by October. These Maroons were clearly Eckersall's team.

Still, Stagg broke his freshman in slowly. Eckie had a 45-yard kickoff return against Lombard College of Galesburg, Illinois, and a 70-yard kickoff return and a 50-yard rush against Lawrence University of Appleton, Wisconsin. But Eckersall didn't score over those first five games. His primary role was simply to call plays.[10]

His other job was to train. After coming to the bench in a 108–0 blowout win over Monmouth College, Eckie spoke extensively to the *Chicago Inter Ocean*:

> The training itself is a hard thing. It is both hard in what we have to do and what we have not to do. Do you know what a football player has to give up? If he is a smoker he must quit. If he likes a glass of beer he must swear off. If he is a society light and ballroom figure he must reform. If he likes the theater he must forget it until after Thanksgiving day. . . . Smoking wrecks a man's "wind." Drinking destroys his reserve strength. Late hours at a theater or a dance or a fraternity gathering takes the ginger out of him. There must be discipline everywhere and all the time. . . . Victory is worth more than all that a player gives up, and there is only one time to play football while there is much time

> coming for dances and the theater, for smoking and staying up late, and for thinking of something other than end runs and line bucks.[11]

The benefits of that training showed on October 3, when Eckersall played his first Big Nine game and scored his first collegiate points against Indiana. He returned a punt 75 yards for a touchdown, returned a kickoff 75 yards for another touchdown, and drop-kicked a 45-yard field goal. Bezdek added two touchdowns, but Eckersall was singled out as "the Bright Star" in Chicago's 34–0 win.[12]

Eckersall played only the first half in a 23–0 win over Cornell College of Mount Vernon, Iowa. He recovered a fumble and played strong defense in his second Big Nine game against Purdue, but he didn't score in a 22–0 victory. Eckie and most of the first-stringers sat out the Maroons' 40–0 win over their last minor opponent, Rush Medical College.[13]

Back in the lineup on October 17, Eckersall faltered against Northwestern. He struggled to run the ball, fumbled a punt, and fumbled a snap. Northwestern's cheermaster taunted the freshman, calling out: "Eckersall, Rah-Rah-Rah, Rotten" to the small group of Purple fans at Marshall Field. A *Chicago Tribune* subhead stated: "Eckersall Not So Brilliant."

But Northwestern also struggled. At one point, the Purple drove to Chicago's 4-yard line, but Catlin forced a fumble on the following play. The game ended in a 0–0 tie and a moral victory for Northwestern, which went on to win a share of the school's first-ever conference title that fall.[14]

A few days after the Northwestern game, the AAU hastily scheduled an eligibility hearing for Eckersall. Sensing an ambush, Stagg advised Eckersall to stay home.[15]

At the hearing, the union board voted to permanently ban Eckersall from amateur athletics, based on new evidence. The AAU's star witness was Nathan MacChesney, a Michigan alumnus who had previously offered to pay Walter's tuition at Michigan. According to MacChesney, Eckie turned him down not owing to any grand moral principle; Chicago simply offered a better deal.[16]

At the hearing, MacChesney relayed Eckersall's own (alleged) words:

Chicago was allowing Eckersall into school without conditions or exams.

Eckersall would receive a full scholarship, worth $120 a year, to play football.

Eckersall would earn $40 to $45 a month for a no-show job in a university office.

Eckersall would receive free room and board.

Stagg would line a coaching job up for Eckersall after his playing days were over.[17]

Eckie denied the allegations. "I am not receiving, and never have received, salary or any offers of salary or any other illegitimate inducement from the University of Chicago," he said. "If Mr. MacChesney says so, I can only say that he lies."[18]

Stagg issued a two-thousand-word statement, refuting MacChesney's charges point by point and asserting that Eckersall's only aid was a work-study program that benefited low-income students, only a handful of whom were athletes.

To Stagg, MacChesney wasn't credible, since he had illegally offered to pay Eckersall's Michigan tuition, then attempted to poach him from Chicago: "He ought to be the last person in the world to attempt to cast suspicion on the athletic authorities of another institution."

Stagg took a further swipe at Michigan for admitting Tom Hammond: "It is reasonable to believe it would be as easy for Mr. Eckersall to enter the university after four years of preparation at Hyde Park as for another member of the Hyde Park team to enter the University of Michigan this year after three years of preparation at the same school." (Stagg was strategically silent on the fact that Eckersall, like Hammond, hadn't graduated from Hyde Park.)[19]

Eckersall turned back to football with renewed focus against Illinois. The Illini went up 6–0 early in the game, but the team was forced to punt on its next series. Eckersall caught the ball at his own 50, then started up the right sideline. Within a few yards, an Illini player tried to trap Eckersall and force him out of bounds.

Eckie suddenly stopped, let his opponent's momentum carry him across the sideline, then cut back to the middle of the field, darting past two more Illini for a 60-yard touchdown. "It was the most beautiful and sensational run seen on the South Side grounds since the days of [Clarence] Herschberger," declared the *Chicago Inter Ocean*, comparing Eckie to Chicago's first-ever All-American.

Chicago added another touchdown late in the first half, and in the second half, Catlin returned an Illini fumble 40 yards for a touchdown, in an 18–6 Chicago win.[20]

Chicago's twelfth game, against Wisconsin, was the first road game of Eckie's college career. Marshall Field could seat twenty-five thousand fans, while Chicago was both centrally located and the conference's biggest city by far. Stagg used these advantages to dictate terms to his opponents, on both location of games and division of gate receipts. Because of Stagg's bullying tactics, the Maroons hosted thirty-eight games over Eckersall's four seasons and went on the road only five times.[21]

In Madison, Eckersall drop-kicked three field goals, worth 5 points each at the time, while his punting regularly pinned Wisconsin deep in its own territory. Chicago left Camp Randall Field with a 15–6 victory, all 15 Chicago points scored via Eckersall's toe.[22]

The Maroons were sloppy in their next game against the Haskell Indian School, with Chicago fumbling, on average, every six plays. Still, Chicago opened up a 12–0 first-half lead off touchdowns by Bezdek and Catlin. Haskell's offense came alive in the second half under sixteen-year-old end Pete Hauser, who would later star at the Carlisle Indian School. Hauser scored all 11 of Haskell's points on a 45-yard field goal, a 36-yard touchdown run, and an extra point. The Maroons scored another touchdown late and stopped Haskell's final drive at the 15-yard line to escape with a 17–11 win.[23]

Chicago then traveled to West Point, New York, to face Army. The Cadets scored on their first possession but missed the extra point. The Maroons scored a touchdown early in the second half and converted the extra point for a 1-point lead. Late in the game, Chicago had to punt from its own end zone. Eckersall boomed a high one to Army quarterback Horatio Hackett, who called for a fair catch at Chicago's 40-yard line. As Hackett tried to secure the ball, it popped loose; Chicago end Speik scooped it up and rumbled toward the goal line.

But the referee whistled the play dead: Catlin interfered with Hackett's opportunity to make the catch. The penalty gave Army 15 yards and the opportunity for a free kick. Army made the 25-yard field goal for a 10–6 win, and Eckersall suffered the first loss of his college career.[24]

The loss stung but didn't matter in the Big Nine race, which would come down to Chicago's Thanksgiving Day game against Michigan. Northwestern had already finished conference play undefeated, guaranteeing the Purple at least a share of the title. Minnesota secured its own share with a Thanksgiving Day win over Wisconsin. So, the Michigan-Chicago winner would share a three-way conference championship.

Sensing an epic contest, Stagg's mentor Walter Camp, the "Father of American Football," came to Chicago to watch the game. The matchup didn't live up to the hype. On a snowy day at Marshall Field, Eckersall played the worst game of his college career. All Eckie did well was tackle, bringing down star halfback Willie Heston several times when he was the only player standing between Heston and the end zone. Otherwise, observers said, Michigan could have scored 50 on the overmatched Maroons.

Eckersall had one embarrassing miss against Heston, lunging at the All-American's knees on an end run. Heston simply hurdled over the freshman and raced 30 more yards, until Speik tackled Heston short of a touchdown.

(That Heston hurdle has long been celebrated for something that didn't happen: According to legend, Eckersall rose from the ground, got back to full speed, and tackled Heston from behind. The story was first told by Carlisle All-American end Al Exendine, who was at the game, in a 1917 interview. Exendine's story was repeated often, most notably by syndicated columnist Grantland Rice in 1924; the attribution was dropped; and the legend took on a life of its own. While Eckersall was faster than Heston, he wasn't *that* fast. Exendine probably confused Heston's hurdle with an entirely different play. *Chicago Tribune* reporter Harvey Woodruff tried to correct the legend in a 1932 column, even interviewing Heston to get his version. But the myth endured, adding an unnecessary embellishment to Eckie's impressive record.)[25]

11. Michigan halfback Willie Heston, who dominated Walter Eckersall in their first meeting in 1903. BL010982, Bentley Historical Library Image Bank, University of Michigan Library Digital Collections.

For the Wolverines, Heston scored two touchdowns, and Hammond kicked three extra points and two field goals. Eckersall struggled to run the ball and punted poorly. Michigan dominated the Maroons 28–0, the only shutout loss of Eckersall's college career.[26]

"I guess that we were rotten," a humbled Eckersall told the *Chicago Tribune*. "I know that every one of the fellows would have given anything to have won. But we were beaten, and beaten badly."[27]

Chicago finished 1903 with a 12-2-1 record. In Big Nine play, Chicago went 4-1-1, fourth in the conference. While Eckersall didn't put up gaudy numbers himself, his three touchdowns each came on returns of at least 60 yards, and he added four field goals. His defense was excellent, and his punting routinely gave Chicago the advantage in field position.

Several selectors, including the *Chicago Tribune* and the *Chicago Inter Ocean*, named Eckersall first-team All-Western quarterback. Camp saw things differently.[28]

"The race for quarter-back is certainly a close one between [Sig] Harris, of Minnesota, and Eckersall, of Chicago," Camp noted, before naming Harris first-team All-Western and third-team All-American. For 1903, Eckersall was left without any Walter Camp honors for the only time in his career.[29]

—

That career could have proven quite short: After the Michigan game, Eckersall stopped going to class. Rumors spread that the star had dropped out of school, or had signed with a Major League Baseball team, or was transferring to Wisconsin or Michigan.

Eckie spoke up a week later: "I am coming back to the university tomorrow. I have just been resting after football work. I have no intention of dropping out of college either this quarter or next." But he was a no-show at classes the next day.[30]

On December 11 Coach Stagg talked to his star for the first time since Thanksgiving.

"The boy was disappointed and sore at the criticism he received after the Michigan game, and feeling so, he did not go back to college," Stagg told the *Chicago Tribune*. "Then, when his action was severely commented on, he realized his error and was ashamed to go back. I told him we all make foolish mistakes sometimes and he said he would go back to the university and live this one down."[31]

But Eckie told a different story to Hammond. "I made the mistake of my life in going to Chicago," he wrote, asking Hammond to put in the good word regarding a possible transfer. Michigan's athletic department answered no, in part because he was unlikely to receive a letter of good standing from Chicago, and in part due to an "objectionable personality" rule.[32]

With that door closed, Eckersall returned to school on December 15. His three-week absence, coupled with his already subpar academic work, guaranteed that he would be ineligible for varsity sports during winter quarter.[33]

Eckersall was still allowed to compete in junior varsity events. In February 1904 he won the 35-yard dash in one JV track meet and the 50-yard dash in another. In March he won the 50 and anchored the winning sprint relay team in an intramural meet between Chicago's freshman and sophomore classes.[34]

Stagg hoped Eckersall would regain eligibility for the spring, and penciled Eckie into his varsity baseball and track lineups. Yet, the bad news continued, based on poor academic advice. Eckersall passed all his winter classes, but he needed to take and pass one additional class to offset his previous failures.

"The dean did not inform Eckersall on this particular rule, and hence Eckersall feels he has not been given a square deal," the *Chicago Inter Ocean* reported. The young athlete again thought about leaving Chicago, this time to join a Minor League Baseball team.[35]

Ultimately, Eckie decided to stay and bear down on his studies. At the end of spring, Eckersall and Stagg received the good news: the quarterback would be eligible for football in 1904.[36]

9

All-American

In June 1904 the University of Chicago track team had a once-in-a-lifetime opportunity: to compete at the Olympic Games in St. Louis or, more precisely, at the "Olympic Intercollegiate Championships," a college track meet loosely tied to the real Olympics. Organizers declared that "college rules" instead of AAU rules would apply for the intercollegiate meet. Since Eckie was academically eligible, and an amateur in the Big Nine's eyes, he could run.[1]

Princeton protested Eckersall's presence. James E. Sullivan, whose name remains synonymous with amateur athletics, presided at a hearing and ruled in Eckersall's favor. The rusty sprinter finished fourth in the 220-yard dash. Eckersall's lone point didn't matter; Chicago won the meet by 10 points and received a handsome trophy.[2]

While several Chicago track athletes continued to train for the actual Olympics, Eckersall headed to Paw Paw Lake in southwest Michigan, where his parents had bought a summer cottage the previous year, for a few weeks of vacation. While there, Eckersall ran into another setback: a case of malaria. As he remained in Michigan to recover, Eckie transformed from a football hero into a real-life one.[3]

On August 24 two young men were sailing on the lake when their boat capsized. One of the men submerged quickly and drowned while the other clung to the swamped hull. Hearing cries for help, Eckersall swam out and towed the distressed boater to safety. News of the rescue was picked up on the press wires, and in a preview of Chicago's 1904 football team, the *Chi-*

cago Inter Ocean referred to "Eckersall, life saver, general all round hero, and, incidentally, when not otherwise engaged, quarter back."[4]

—

For 1904, Chicago returned the core of the previous year's team. The biggest loss was starting lineman Robert Maxwell, who was academically ineligible; Maxwell then transferred to Swarthmore. Promising freshmen included two of Eckie's former Cook County League rivals, lineman Art Badenoch of Englewood and halfback Leo DeTray of North Division. End Fred Speik was elected team captain.

Coach Amos Alonzo Stagg again lined up early games against high schools and small colleges, and again used Eckersall sparingly. When Eckie did play, Stagg had him focus on his place-kicking. As with most things football-related, Eckie was a natural. He kicked four extra points in a 40–5 win over Lombard College; added four more and also place-kicked a 42-yard field goal (reduced in value to 4 points this season) in a 72–0 win over Englewood High School; kicked two extra points in a 29–0 win over Lawrence University; and kicked one in an 18–0 win over North Division High School.[5]

When Chicago opened Big Nine play against Indiana, sportswriters noticed significant improvement in Eckie's poise, confidence, and play selection. Eckersall made the defensive play of the game early. An Indiana halfback broke through the line for a 30-yard gain; Eckersall, playing deep, sprinted across the field and caught him at the 25-yard line. Indiana fumbled on the next play, squandering its best chance at scoring.

On offense Eckersall distributed the ball generously, as five Chicago backs rushed for touchdowns. Eckersall scored his lone touchdown defensively on a 25-yard fumble recovery and added one of Chicago's six extra points in a 56–0 win.[6]

Against Purdue, Eckersall drop-kicked a 33-yard field goal to give Chicago a 4–0 lead late in the first half. Hugo Bezdek later rushed for a touchdown, and DeTray added two more touchdowns. The Maroon offense was otherwise sloppy, coughing up several fumbles. But Purdue lacked the size or speed to take advantage, and Chicago won 20–0.[7]

12. Walter Eckersall eludes a tackler at Marshall Field and breaks into the clear. SDN-004921, *Chicago Daily News* collection, Chicago History Museum.

Hoping to give his stars some rest, Stagg held his starting backfield out of the team's next game against Iowa. Backup quarterback Lee Maxwell struggled to move the offense, and Chicago led just 4–0 at halftime.

Stagg inserted his starters in the second half, and the difference was noticeable. "The Chicago team in the second half was as much like the Chicago team in the first half as an automobile is like a dray wagon," the *Chicago Inter Ocean* reported. "Iowa managed to overturn the dray wagon several times and was always able to block it at critical times. But the automobile raged back and forth across the field a thing invincible."

On one kickoff, Mark Catlin caught the ball, then pitched it to Eckersall, who sprinted 90 yards for a touchdown. Eckie stepped up the pace of the game and read the Iowa defense well, sending other backs toward weaknesses in the Hawkeye line. DeTray scored four touchdowns, and the Maroons thrashed Iowa 39–0.[8]

Against undefeated Northwestern on October 22, fifteen thousand spectators showed up at Marshall Field, including a who's who of Chicago business and society people and, as the *Chicago Tribune* noted, "girls galore—college girls, city girls, old girls, young girls, girls in autos, traps, and tandems, girls in sweaters, with a swagger stride, and girls muffled in feather boas."

Early in the first half, Northwestern's quarterback fumbled near midfield, and lineman Ed Parry recovered for Chicago. Northwestern would get no closer to Chicago's goal all afternoon.

In the second half, the Maroon offense roared to life. Eckersall had more than 200 all-purpose yards, rushed for a 5-yard touchdown, drop-kicked two field goals, and place-kicked an extra point. Bezdek and DeTray each added two touchdowns in a 32–0 win, and the Maroons improved to 4–0 in conference play.[9]

Against Illinois on October 29, the first half featured tough defense, long punts, and a battle for field position. Illinois nearly won that battle late in the half, when Eckersall lined up to punt from his own 30-yard line. The snap was bad, and Illinois recovered deep in Chicago territory. Illinois pushed ahead for 10 more yards, but Chicago's defense stopped Illinois on third-and-one, and the first half ended in a 0–0 tie.

Early in the second half, Eckie appeared to give Chicago the lead on a 60-yard punt return, dodging multiple tacklers down the right sideline for a touchdown. But the linesman ruled that Eckersall stepped out of bounds at the Illinois 40-yard line. The *Chicago Tribune* thought the official made a bad call: "There were scores of nonpartisan witnesses in good position to sight along the side line who will take their oaths that Eckersall did not come within eighteen inches of the side line at any time."

From there, Eckersall punted, and Illinois fumbled. Parry scooped up the ball and ran in for a touchdown, and the extra point put Chicago ahead 6–0.

Then, Eckersall made a costly mistake. From midfield, Illinois end Claude Rothgeb took the ball on an end-around play. From his safety position, Eckersall ran over, crouched, and wrapped his arms around Rothgeb's waist. But Rothgeb wriggled free, one of the few times in his career that Eckersall missed an open-field tackle. Rothgeb gained 30 yards before DeTray brought him down. From there, Illinois methodically drove for a touchdown, and the extra point was good. Neither team moved the ball consistently after that, and Illinois escaped with a 6–6 tie.[10]

Stagg's team regrouped for the next game, an intersectional matchup against Texas. Michigan coach Fielding Yost and halfback Willie Heston attended, skipping their own game against Drake to scout the Maroons. From the press box, reporters pranked Yost by issuing fake announcements that Drake had scored twice on mighty Michigan. Chicago fans heckled the pair throughout the game, but Yost and Heston took the taunts in stride.[11]

Texas received the opening kickoff and marched downfield. A Texas halfback broke through the line for a 40-yard gain, but Eckersall made a touchdown-saving tackle at his own 20. A few plays later, Texas fumbled. Eckersall scooped up the ball and scampered more than 100 yards for Chicago's first touchdown.

Eckie's brilliant play turned all momentum toward the Maroons. The defense shut Texas down, while seven different Chicago players scored touchdowns. Early in the second half, Eckersall drop-kicked a 40-yard field goal. Stagg then emptied his bench, but Texas could do nothing against Chicago's backups. The 68–0 beating remains the worst loss in the storied history of Texas football.[12]

Next came the biggest game of the season: against Michigan, in a battle for western supremacy. Michigan entered with a 9-0 record and had outscored opponents by a total of 545–10. The game in Ann Arbor, Chicago's only road game of the season, would be the last of the great Heston's career.

Yost gave Stagg some classic bulletin-board material when he declared, "We have never had a great deal of trouble beating Chicago." Arrogant but true: In three previous games under Yost, Michigan had outscored Chicago 71–0.[13]

More than twenty thousand fans saw "one of the bitterest and most desperate battles ever fought over the greensward of Ferry field" and "an exhibition never equaled before on a western gridiron," the *Chicago Tri-*

bune declared. The *Chicago Inter Ocean* compared the game to the battle of Thermopylae, with Chicago captain Speik playing the role of Spartan King Leonidas.

A Chicago-based apparel company promised a new suit to whoever scored the game's first touchdown. After receiving the kickoff, Chicago quickly advanced the ball to midfield, and it looked like a Maroon would win that suit. But the opening drive stalled on a penalty, and Eckie had to punt.

On Michigan's first series, Heston and Tom Hammond both made big gains as the Wolverines methodically drove inside Chicago's 5-yard line. From there, quarterback Fred Norcross called on halfback Shorty Longman, a tough inside runner.

"Longman had a chance with only half a yard to go, but the Maroon line held," Hammond recalled almost thirty years later. "Finally I had a chance at about the same distance and the fellows shoved me over. . . . Incidentally a dress suit was quite a possession for a college sophomore then."[14]

On Michigan's next series, Heston skirted around right end for 45 yards, but Eckersall made a touchdown-saving tackle at the 10. On the next play, Hammond broke through the Chicago line. Although Eckie tried to wrap him up, Hammond dragged his old friend into the end zone for another touchdown. At this point, the game was shaping up like the 1903 blowout.

Then Eckersall flipped the field with a 90-yard punt. Eckie caught Michigan's return punt at midfield and ran it back 20 yards. Chicago continued to chip away at the Michigan defense, until a 10-yard touchdown run by Bezdek cut Michigan's lead to 10–6.

On Chicago's next series, Eckersall took a huge risk on third-and-two from his own 25. He lined up to punt but instead slipped the ball into Bezdek's arms. The trick nearly worked, but Bezdek was tackled inches short of the first down. Michigan then pounded the ball inside, until Heston scored Michigan's third touchdown, for a 16–6 lead.

Early in the second half, Heston made a run around his left end, but the ball was stripped and bounced around on the turf. Down 10 points, Eckersall knew he needed to take a chance. Instead of jumping on the ball for a safe recovery, he sprinted ahead at full speed, reached down, bobbled the ball, reached again, then finally secured it, racing 40 yards for a touchdown. The extra point narrowed Michigan's lead to 4 points.

But Eckersall could only do so much by himself. Late in the game, with four Maroon starters sidelined with injuries, Michigan used its size and strength to full advantage. "Giants they were," the *Chicago Tribune* noted. "Beside them Stagg's 6 footers looked like schoolboys." Hammond ran for another touchdown, and Michigan won the game 22–12.

In four years together, Yost and Heston had compiled a 43-0-1 record, including four wins over Chicago. If there was any moral victory here, it was that the Maroons had put up one of the best fights against any Michigan team of the "Point-a-Minute" era.[15]

Chicago closed its season by hosting Wisconsin on Thanksgiving Day. Early in the first half, Eckie was forced to punt from his own 20. For the first time in his career, he shanked one, booting the ball sideways and out of bounds. Wisconsin seized the opportunity, driving 20 yards for the game's first touchdown, though the extra point failed. Late in the first half, Bezdek rushed for a touchdown to give the Maroons a 6–5 lead.

In the second half, DeTray returned a Wisconsin fumble 15 yards for Chicago's second touchdown. Under a recent rule change, at this point Wisconsin had the option of either kicking off or receiving. In close games where field position mattered, teams often chose to kick off, to try to pin their opponents deep. That's what Wisconsin decided here.

A stiff wind held the ball aloft long enough for Eckersall to field it at the 5-yard line. He sprinted up the right sideline, veered left at the 30, then stutter-stepped to avoid a tackle near midfield. The field was clear ahead, and Eckersall raced for a 105-yard touchdown, which the *Chicago Inter Ocean* called "the prettiest run ever seen on a Western field." Wisconsin added a late touchdown, but the game ended with the score 18–11 in Chicago's favor.[16]

The Maroons finished the season 10-1-1, and third in the Big Nine with a 5-1-1 conference record. Eckie had scored 63 of his team's 410 points on six touchdowns, five field goals, and thirteen extra points.

Sig Harris's hometown *Minneapolis Journal* named Harris first-team all-conference for 1904. All other major selectors, including Walter Camp, chose Eckersall as first-team all-conference quarterback.[17]

13. Walter Eckersall in his University of Chicago baseball uniform. University of Chicago Photographic Archive, apf1-05923, Hanna Holborn Gray Special Collections Research Center, University of Chicago Library.

Though Camp thought Eckersall was the best quarterback in the West, he thought Penn's Vince Stevenson was the best in the country. But Camp had to find room for Eckersall on his All-America team: "This man Eckersall can punt 60 yards, drop-kick with disconcerting accuracy. . . . He is a remarkable tackler, and as for running in a broken-up field, he is a wonder."

So, Camp changed Eckie's position, naming him first-team All-American at end. Caspar Whitney, considered a close second to Camp among national football authorities, also toyed with positions, naming Eckersall first-team All-American at fullback. With these selections, Eckersall became only the third non-Easterner to make first-team All-American, after Clarence Herschberger and Heston.[18]

—

In December Eckersall joined the track team and looked sharp in practice, winning the 40-yard dash in one time trial and the 50-yard dash in another. In his first varsity track meet for Chicago, against Illinois in February, Eckersall injured his leg in a preliminary heat and couldn't run in the final. He returned a few weeks later for a meet against Wisconsin. Eckie advanced from the preliminaries of the 35-yard dash, but he didn't place in the final.[19]

Frustrated by his nagging injury, Eckie quit the track team and shifted focus to baseball. Eckie's season started with promise: Playing third base, he scored two runs on two hits in a win over the Armour Institute. From then on, his play was subpar. He went hitless while stranding a runner on third in a one-run loss to Michigan; went hitless and had three errors, one of which allowed the game-winning run, in a one-run loss to Northwestern; and scored a run but had two costly errors in a loss to Illinois.[20]

Eckersall batted just .167, ranking eighth out of twelve Maroon regulars. He committed ten errors for a .697 fielding average, worst on the team. Chicago went 15-12 overall but just 4-11 in Big Nine play. While Eckie did just enough on the diamond to earn a varsity letter, 1905 was a forgettable baseball season for the football star.[21]

In the meantime, his AAU case dragged on. In January Eckersall applied for reinstatement. As he awaited an answer, the Illinois Athletic Club, located in downtown Chicago, invited the Maroons to a track meet. Inside sources predicted that AAU president Walter Liginger would reinstate Eckersall, allowing him a triumphant return at the IAC meet.[22]

A few days before the meet, the Central AAU held another Eckersall hearing. This time the professional baseball charges were dismissed. The only issue on the docket was a new allegation that Eckersall had accepted $1.50 for winning a foot race in Woodstock, Illinois, in 1902. The race's organizer remembered giving *someone* the prize money, but at the hearing, he said that he didn't recognize Eckie. The Central AAU board then voted unanimously for reinstatement.[23]

Liginger refused to budge, however. He stated, cryptically, that he had received damaging new evidence against Eckersall. He also insisted that even if Eckersall were innocent, the National AAU couldn't act until its annual meeting, still eight months away.

Eckersall dropped out of the IAC meet. His nagging leg injury may have influenced him as much as the controversy. But in what can only be interpreted as a giant "Screw You" to Liginger, Eckersall volunteered as a scorer for the meet, for which Liginger had already signed on as head referee.[24]

So Eckersall's AAU suspension continued, without resolution, into a third straight football season.

10

Champions of the West

Unlike his busy summer of 1904, Walter Eckersall made few headlines in the summer of 1905. A subpar spring quarter forced him to go to summer school. Eckie passed those classes and was cleared to play that fall.[1]

With Willie Heston now graduated from Michigan, 1905 looked like Chicago's best shot at a championship in years. End Mark Catlin had taken Fred Speik's role as captain, but Speik was back as an assistant coach. Besides Eckersall and Catlin, the Maroons returned starting fullback Hugo Bezdek, halfback Leo DeTray, and tackle Ed Parry. Sophomore Merrill Meigs, in only his second year of organized football, claimed an open spot at guard. Linemen Art Badenoch and halfback Fred Walker, both substitutes in 1904, earned starting roles, while Jesse Harper became Eckie's primary backup at quarterback.

Coach Amos Alonzo Stagg also brought in a tremendous freshman, quarterback Wally Steffen of North Division High School. But Steffen couldn't play right away. The Big Nine had recently voted to make freshmen ineligible for varsity football, a ban that would remain for most of the next seventy years.[2]

The Maroons had all put on muscle in the offseason. "The average of the team will be well up in the 180s, which will approximate closely the weight of Michigan this fall," the *Chicago Tribune* reported. Since his freshman year, Eckie had also gained some weight but still only weighed 142 pounds. Early in training camp, Stagg introduced new strength and flexibility exercises he dubbed "football jiu jitsu," which seems closer to modern-day plyometrics.[3]

14. Walter Eckersall cracks a smile after pitching the ball during practice at Marshall Field. *Chicago Tribune*/TCA.

Preseason hype for Chicago football was the greatest in the program's fourteen-year history. "The Midway coach has the best material in his career at the University of Chicago," the *Tribune* noted. "Stagg's one great task, it seems, will be the rounding into a machine of his eleven men of experience, weight, and speed that will go through the season to the championship with an untarnished record."[4]

In one preseason practice, Eckersall, sporting a custom pair of square-toed shoes, converted thirty out of thirty-six field goal attempts at distances ranging from 35 to 45 yards. After practice, the quarterback said that he hoped to beat his current school record of three field goals in a game.[5]

Stagg again used Eckie sparingly in early-season games against minor opponents. He only played in the first half and never attempted a rush in shutout wins over North Division High School and Lawrence University of Appleton, Wisconsin. Chicago's third game, against Wabash College, proved much tougher. The small Indiana school frequently took on big-time opponents in the early twentieth century, beating several and earning the nickname "Little Giants." Chicago struggled to secure the ball, and Bezdek fumbled several times.[6]

Though he didn't score any touchdowns that day, "Eckersall brought thrills to the spectators in returning punts and kickoffs," the *Chicago Tribune* reported. "Time after time, when he seemed completely surrounded by Wabash tacklers, he broke away and dodged or side stepped for little dashes of twenty-five yards." Bezdek and Harper both ran for touchdowns, and Eckie added a 23-yard field goal as Chicago escaped with a 15–0 win.[7]

A hard tackle against Wabash left Eckersall with a sore knee. He would have played through the injury for a conference game, but since the next game was against another "minor" opponent, Eckie sat out. Unfortunately, that game was against Beloit College, featuring Eckie's old friend Sam Ransom.

Ransom made several tackles for loss in the first half, and the Maroons led just 11–0 at halftime. But Ransom was injured early in the second half, and Chicago exploited his absence, rolling up four second-half touchdowns in a 38–0 win. The lackluster first half disappointed Stagg, who conducted a hard practice immediately after the game.[8]

—

Conference play opened on October 7 against Iowa. Early in the game, Parry blocked an Iowa punt and recovered it in the end zone for a touchdown. Harper scored three touchdowns on short rushes, and Bezdek added a 70-yard touchdown run. Eckersall got into the action when he returned a punt

70 yards for a touchdown of his own. The Maroons won convincingly, 42–0. But Stagg seemed dissatisfied.

"I am not at all pleased with the showing made by the men, and I think the large score was due more to the weakness of the Iowans than to the strength of the Maroon offense," he said. "I used only the simplest sort of plays in today's game, not because I was afraid that the Michigan and Wisconsin spies might see my best plays, but I am afraid that the present team is not capable of executing any intricate plays."[9]

Despite his apparent disappointment, Stagg didn't think Indiana posed much of a threat the following week. Stagg skipped that game to scout Wisconsin, leaving assistant Speik in charge. Stagg told Speik to sit Eckersall and Bezdek, to give the pair some more rest.[10]

It's unclear why Stagg didn't take Indiana seriously. Under new coach Jimmy Sheldon, who had played on Stagg's 1899 conference championship team, the Hoosiers had won their first three games of 1905, all by shutout.

Without Eckersall or Bezdek on the field, or Stagg on the sidelines, "Capt. Catlin and his men put up a listless, spiritless exhibition of the sport for their first period," the *Chicago Tribune* reported. Late in the first half, an Indiana halfback rushed for a 45-yard touchdown, and Indiana's 5–0 lead held up through halftime.

For the second half, Speik defied Stagg's orders, inserting Eckie and Bezdek into the game. "[Eckersall] looked at us scornfully," recalled Meigs more than forty years later. "'What in hell is the matter with you fellows?' he barked. He really gave each member of the team a solid kick in the pants. 'Now let's go!' he ordered, and we really went."[11]

Behind Eckersall, the Maroon offense sprang to life. Bezdek scored on a 15-yard run early in the second half, the extra point giving Chicago its first lead. On the team's next series, Eckie kicked a 20-yard field goal. Walker added a 33-yard touchdown late in the game, and Chicago escaped with a 16–5 victory.[12]

—

Before the Wisconsin game, Stagg was optimistic even though the undefeated, unscored-on Badgers would be Chicago's toughest opponent yet.

"We are now at our best," Stagg told the *Chicago Tribune*. "I have all the confidence in our battering ram, Hugo Bezdek. If the team stands by Eckersall, Chicago is sure to walk down the field over the Badgers. . . . I believe we will land the victory."[13]

Chicago was fired up for off-the-field reasons. Two weeks earlier, Wisconsin captain E. J. Vanderboom had secretly taken Steffen to Madison, trying to convince the freshman to leave Chicago and transfer up north.

"The pressure became so strong that I could not resist," Steffen admitted. "I was ashamed to make the trip and hoped to get up there and get back before any one would know about it. . . . An hour after my arrival I told them that I would not remain."

Vanderboom disputed Steffen's account. "He explained to me that the situation at Chicago was unsatisfactory and distasteful to him," the Wisconsin captain said. "Whatever was done was done on Mr. Steffens' [*sic*] own initiative."[14]

The Wisconsin game was played on a suspiciously muddy Camp Randall Field. It hadn't rained in Madison for two days, and Stagg thought the Wisconsin grounds crew intentionally flooded the field to slow Eckersall down. "The field was in surprisingly poor condition," an angry Stagg said after the game. "If the field was actually flooded it is the most contemptible trick I have ever run across in my association with the game."[15]

A throng of Wisconsin rooters taunted Chicago's star quarterback with the chant: "Eckie, Eckie, Break Your Necky, Eckersall!" Two minutes into the game, Chicago faced third-and-four from its own 30-yard line, with the ball near the left sideline. Eckie lined up to punt, which seemed like his only option in the three-downs-to-make-five-yards era. Instead, Eckersall made one of the most brilliant play calls ever witnessed by future Hall of Fame coach Gil Dobie, who was scouting this game for Minnesota. Dobie remembered:

> Standing like a little, listless old man as he waited for the snapback, Eckersall seemed the personification of defeated hopelessness, robbed of all desire for offensive action and contented merely to fend off immediate danger. . . . But Eckersall did not kick. Instead, shedding his seeming dejection, he sprang into rapid, vivid action. Timing his move-

> ments beautifully, he ran in behind center and, crouching low, turned to his left. Then—doing that which had been regarded as impossible—he circled thru the narrow opening between the left end and the side-line. Wisconsin's right end was left standing flat-footed, so surprised he did not even touch the maroon quarter with his finger tips. The Badger backfield, with the exception of its safety man, had been drawn toward Chicago's right side by the feigned punt. That astounding run, started on Chicago's 30-yard line, did not end until Eckersall was downed . . . on Wisconsin's 30-yard line.[16]

The run set the tone for the game and kept Wisconsin off balance. The Badgers now knew that Eckersall *could* spring a 50-yard run seemingly at will and that he *would* call plays that defied logic. Dobie thrilled at the psychological games that Eckie played with the Badgers: running when he should have punted, handing off when he should have kept the ball, and running outside when his blockers massed in the middle and vice versa.

But Wisconsin's defense stiffened whenever Chicago approached the goal. So, Eckersall tried to beat the Badgers with his leg. His first field-goal attempt came from 47 yards out but fell short of the goal posts. He later tried a drop-kick from the 15-yard line, but at a sharp angle, and missed again. On yet another attempt, Eckersall missed a 25-yard kick.

"My shoes were covered with several inches of mud all the time and it was almost impossible for me to kick with any degree of accuracy," Eckie complained after the game.

Late in the first half, Eckersall fumbled at his own 15-yard line, and Wisconsin recovered. The Chicago defense held, so Wisconsin tried a field goal. Three Chicago players stormed through the line, blocking the Badgers' 20-yard attempt.

Wisconsin started the second half with a long drive. From the Chicago 35, Wisconsin tried another field goal, and again the Maroons blocked it. A few plays later, Eckie faced another third down, similar to the situation that had led to his fake punt in the first half.

"Obviously he would not try that trick again," Dobie recalled. "But in Eckersall's case the thought persisted that his opponents would reach such a conclusion. . . . So he did that which it was apparent he could not do—and for the second time, got away with it; this time for a run of forty yards."

Neither of Eckersall's fake punts led directly to points, but they kept Wisconsin off balance. After more back and forth, Eckie made another long run, to the Wisconsin 20. On first down, and already zero for three on field goals, he defied logic again by deciding to kick. Or maybe his logic was perfect: With the Badger defense set to defend the run, Eckersall faced no pressure. The ball sailed through the uprights perfectly for a field goal.

The rest of the game was a battle for field position, one that Eckersall won. Eckie boomed five punts of at least 50 yards to pin the Badgers deep. When time was finally called, the Maroons had prevailed with a narrow 4–0 win.[17]

"Properly speaking, the great strategy which brought the Maroon its victory over Wisconsin did not rest in a single play, but in the repetition of that play at carefully foreseen psychological intervals," Dobie later said. "Thus carried out, the football world was afforded the spectacle of a tactical demonstration which, in my opinion, has never been surpassed and perhaps never equaled. It thrills me to the marrow even tho nearly twenty years have passed."[18]

—

At practice the next Monday, Stagg surprised his starters with a day off, and a carriage tour of the South Side's parks and boulevards. The team stayed loose and relaxed in practice that week, with Stagg taking extra care to not risk injury after two tough games in a row.[19]

Michigan coach Fielding Yost was in the stands for Chicago's next game, at Northwestern. Stagg ordered his players to use "straight" football so as not to tip off Yost to any trick plays or creative formations. Instead, the Maroons rammed the ball right down Northwestern's throat. Bezdek, described as "a Human Catapult," scored three touchdowns in the first half. Eckersall never attempted a rush. He missed a 25-yard field goal in the first half but made one from 15 yards in the second as Chicago won easily, 32–0.[20]

Chicago had an open date on November 4, so Stagg took the team to Champaign to scout the Michigan-Illinois game. Mindful of the Maroons' presence, Yost copied Stagg's strategy of the previous week and played only "straight" football, as Michigan pounded the Illini, 33–0.[21]

The following week, a bombshell hit national newsstands. *Collier's*, a popular general-interest magazine, began publishing "Buying Football Victories," a four-part series exposing academic fraud and unethical behavior in the Big Nine. To muckraking journalist Edward Jordan, Eckersall was exhibit A of all that was wrong with college athletics:

> Walter Eckersall, the Chicago quarter and All-American end, is simply an "athletic ward" of the University of Chicago, retained under her system of official "maintenance" as a factor in building her athletic prestige. . . . Although short three of the minimum number of required credits for the admission of the most poorly prepared freshman, Eckersall entered Chicago, and received free tuition during his entire course, with no return except in kicking and tackling ability. . . . Eckersall has twice been disqualified by the Chicago faculty for poor academic work, but never during the football season. His studies are always "made up" at that time. It is immaterial and extraneous from the present real athletic issue that Eckersall is charged with professionalism. But it is something that the university is bartering her gold-fed academic prestige for a muscular leg, and using funds endowed for needy students to offset the bids of rivals of equal culpability. That is the meat of the athletic issue.[22]

DeTray and Steffen were similarly cited as bad examples. Jordan quoted Steffen's alleged reply to one booster during his recruiting battle: "You fellows can't get me at Northwestern, and they can't get me at Wisconsin. You haven't got the money."[23]

Chicago vigorously disputed Jordan's article. "The charges are absurd," said University registrar Thomas Goodspeed, who noted that he had cooperated with Jordan's investigation. "[Jordan] expressed great surprise when he saw that out of 150 students working for the university there were but fifteen athletes on the list. Just why Mr. Jordan should go to the trouble of twisting his statements in order to make them read as though every athlete in the university was receiving money from the school is more than I can say."

Eckersall displayed similar outrage, remarking, "I can show the receipts for my tuition and room, and the receipts for my board at the training table. The charges made against me in that article are lies."[24]

—

In the next game against Purdue, the Maroons struggled to move the ball early and limped into halftime leading just 4–0 on an Eckersall field goal. In the second half, Eckersall kicked another field goal, Bezdek and DeTray added touchdown runs, and Purdue never crossed midfield. The Maroons won 19–0, but according to the *Chicago Tribune*, "at the finish few of the 10,000 spectators knew any more about whether the maroon could defeat Michigan than before."[25]

With the increased scrutiny brought by the *Collier's* article, one might have expected Eckie to bear down on both his studies and his football. Instead, Eckie and Walker went out to blow off some steam, heading downtown to a play and returning to campus after their 10 p.m. curfew.

The next day, captain Catlin told Eckie and Walker that they had to apologize to Stagg or they would be kicked off the team. Eckersall called Stagg's bluff and refused. Stagg started practice with Harper at quarterback, while Eckersall and Walker stubbornly stood on the sidelines. After half an hour, Eckie and Walker realized that Stagg was willing to lose a game, or even a championship, to prove a point. The pair apologized and went back to work.[26]

The following Saturday, the Maroons faced Illinois at Marshall Field. From two minutes in, when he kicked his first field goal, this game belonged to Eckersall. He drop-kicked five field goals, tying a major-college record for drop-kicks that still stands. Eckie also rushed for a 30-yard touchdown, scoring 25 points by himself. Whenever Chicago's offense stalled, Eckie pinned his opponents deep with punts of 50, 65, and 70 yards. Led by Eckersall, Chicago put together another dominant performance in a 44–0 win.[27]

"That Eckersall is a great player," Illinois coach Fred Lowenthal said after the game. "He could make any team play behind him." But Lowenthal also warned: "As regards Chicago and Michigan, I think that the Wolverines

15. Panorama view of the twenty-seven-thousand-person crowd at the Chicago-Michigan game at Marshall Field, November 30, 1905. LC-USZ62-128940, Library of Congress Prints and Photographs Division.

have a shade the better of it. . . . I do not think that Eckersall will gain much against Michigan, as they will be laying for him."[28]

—

Chicago's win set up the original Game of the Century: Chicago versus Michigan at Marshall Field on Thanksgiving Day, November 30, for the conference title.

Three weeks before the game, Michigan boosters placed postcards for sale, in both Chicago and Ann Arbor, with a picture of their team labeled as "Champions of the West, 1905." To many, this result seemed inevitable. Even without Heston, Michigan had outscored its twelve opponents 495–0. Most bookies quoted Michigan as a 2-to-1 favorite, but some promised as much as a 10-to-1 payout for a Chicago win.[29]

Stagg, always a meticulous game-planner, focused on this contest with near-obsession. In his archives, 117 pages of scouting notes survive, far more than the 30 pages or so that he accumulated for most big games.[30]

On Thanksgiving Day, twenty-seven thousand fans—including East Coast football experts Walter Camp and Caspar Whitney—packed the stands of a cold, snowy Marshall Field for the showdown. One missing fan was Chicago's founding president, William Rainey Harper, terminally ill with cancer. Harper originally planned to watch from a room across the street, but because he was too weak to sit up, one of his sons kept him updated via telephone instead. Coach Stagg used his former professor's illness as a motivational tool, imploring the Maroons to win for their dying president.[31]

The two teams prepared to unveil innovative offensive plays that their genius coaches had devised for this game. But both offenses would stall, and the Chicago and Michigan defenses instead showed why they had combined for twenty-one shutouts that season. The creative formations and trick plays that Stagg and Yost had prepared would prove worthless. This would be a classic game of old-school, smash-mouth football.

On their first series, the Maroons gained 3 yards on two downs, and Eckersall dropped back to punt. Then, a critical error: Eckersall fumbled the snap at his own 25, and Michigan took over on downs. Michigan quarterback Fred Norcross gave the ball right back to Chicago, fumbling on *his* first down. Chicago recovered, and Michigan had squandered a great chance at scoring.

Much of the first half was a punting duel between Eckersall and Michigan end Johnny Garrels; each punted at least ten times. One early special-teams blunder by Michigan would prove costly. After Eckersall punted from his own 30-yard line, Michigan's 230-pound tackle Joe Curtis rammed into the diminutive quarterback, "striking him with knee and shoulder, and hurling him a dozen feet away to the ground." As Eckersall lay motionless, the umpire threw Curtis out of the game for roughing.

The stands fell silent, concerned for both the hero and his team. Under the rules of the time, any substitution would keep Eckie out for the remainder of the game. "For several minutes it seemed as if he might not regain consciousness," the *Chicago Tribune* reported. "But after hard work by his teammates and trainer, finally he was able to totter, dazed, to his place."

This account was part hyperbole by the *Tribune*, part acting by Eckersall. According to one (certainly biased) report from the Michigan camp, Tom Hammond walked over to Eckersall as he lay on the ground.

"Walter, are you going to stand for this dirty business? Get up and be a man!" When Eckersall said nothing, Hammond supposedly continued, "Well, you and I have been friends a long time, Walter, but we're through now."[32]

Whether Eckersall was acting, officials nationwide were placing renewed emphasis on roughing penalties during a very deadly season on the gridiron.

"The fouling of Eckersall by Curtis was too palpable to go unnoticed by the officials, and there was nothing else to do but rule him out of the game," the umpire explained. "His offense was made worse through the fact that he had been warned once for rough tactics, but in spite of this he deliberately fouled Eckersall."[33]

Early in the second half, Michigan blocked an Eckersall field-goal attempt, and Norcross recovered at his own 15. The spirited group of Michigan fans responded with a rehearsed cheer, inspired by Wisconsin's from a few weeks earlier:

> Gee hee, Gee ha, Gee ha-ha-ha, Eckersall!
> Eckersall, Eckersall!
> When you're running with the ball,
> You will get an awful fall,
> Eckersall, Eckersall!
> Eckie, Eckie, break your neckie,
> Eckersall!

Eckersall and Garrels continued to exchange punts. One deep Garrels punt, followed by a Chicago offside penalty, pinned the Maroons at their own 7-yard line. From there, on third down, Eckie faced a dilemma, as Camp described:

> If he attempted a run, and Michigan stopped him, she was perfectly sure to score. If he punted against the wind, the chances were very

> strong indeed that if the ball went out into the field it would be heeled and Michigan would kick a place-kick goal. If he endeavored to kick it out of bounds on either side, the angle would be such that it would still leave Michigan within scoring distance. It was a hard proposition, but he faced it and did the bold thing. . . . [He] undoubtedly saved Chicago by his nerve.[34]

Out of the corner of his eye, Eckie saw Michigan's defense shifting right in an effort to block the punt, leaving a gap up the left side. Eckersall called the signals for a punt; the ball was snapped; and instead of punting, he sprinted around his left end. It was the kind of risky, do-or-die play that looks brilliant if it works and awful if it doesn't. That day, Eckersall's gamble was brilliant. He carried the ball past the 25-yard line, gaining first down and giving Chicago new life. Eckie followed with a deep punt, pushing Michigan past midfield. In just two plays, Eckersall had placed Michigan back on its heels.

After another exchange of punts, Garrels copied Eckersall's trick. He lined up to punt from his 20, then tucked the ball and ran into the open field. Eckie, who had dropped back to return the punt, "was all that stood between Chicago and defeat," the *Chicago Tribune* reported.

"Twenty-eight yards Garrels had covered when the maroon quarter gathered for his spring. Diving low, he grabbed the runner firmly, but the shock nearly tore him loose, and only by clinging to one of Garrels' feet could Eckersall stop his foe."

But Eckie did stop Garrels, one of the textbook open-field tackles he had mastered during his career. Michigan fumbled on the next play, and the Maroons recovered. Eckie punted to the Michigan 5; Garrels punted back to the Michigan 45. Chicago gained 3 yards on two plays and faced third-and-two from the Michigan 42.

Then Eckersall, Badenoch, and Catlin combined to make the Play of the Game in the Game of the Century.

Eckersall dropped back to midfield to punt. Michigan's Denny Clark, a substitute halfback pressed into service due to an injury, lined up deep to receive. Eckie kicked a beauty that soared high into the air. Instead of letting the ball go, Clark fielded it behind the goal line. Then, instead of downing the ball for a touchback, Clark tried to run. Badenoch hit him, hard, at the 2-yard line. Clark slipped out of Badenoch's grasp, but Catlin threw Clark backward, then fell on him behind the goal line.

There was no "forward progress" rule then; a player was down where he was down. In this case, Clark was down for a safety and 2 points for Chicago.

Yost pulled Clark out of the game, a despondent Clark sobbing on the sidelines. But a few minutes were still left. Michigan got the ball back three times but struggled to gain any ground.

More than a decade later, Eckersall recalled:

> Tom [Hammond]'s blood began to boil. He pleaded with Capt. Norcross to be allowed to carry the ball. When it was given him he tore into the line like a bull, but he did not have the assistance to make the required distance. He urged his fast tiring teammates to get together and himself mixed in every play. . . . Tom shouted, "Try trick plays, damn it; we might just as well be licked by forty points!" At this stage Tom tore off his head guard and attempted to get away on all sorts of plays. Fake punts, criss-crosses, delayed passes, shoestring plays, and even the hidden ball trick were tried to no avail.[35]

At one point, the Wolverines just missed blocking an Eckersall punt. On the next series, Hammond broke around the left side of the line, but Eckie ran over from midfield and stripped the ball. Finally, Michigan tried one of Yost's special plays: a complicated triple lateral, which Chicago stopped for no gain. Garrels and Eckersall traded punts once more, and the game ended with the ball in Michigan's possession at midfield.[36]

Chicago had beaten Michigan, a 2–0 masterpiece far more exciting than its low score would indicate. Fans hoisted Stagg and Catlin up on their shoulders. Stagg danced joyfully with his players and embraced senior fullback Bezdek, who had no highlights that day but had done much of the grunt work.

"Beautiful, Bezdek—beautiful!" the coach rejoiced. With fans lighting a bonfire in the middle of campus, the celebration continued well into Thanksgiving night.[37]

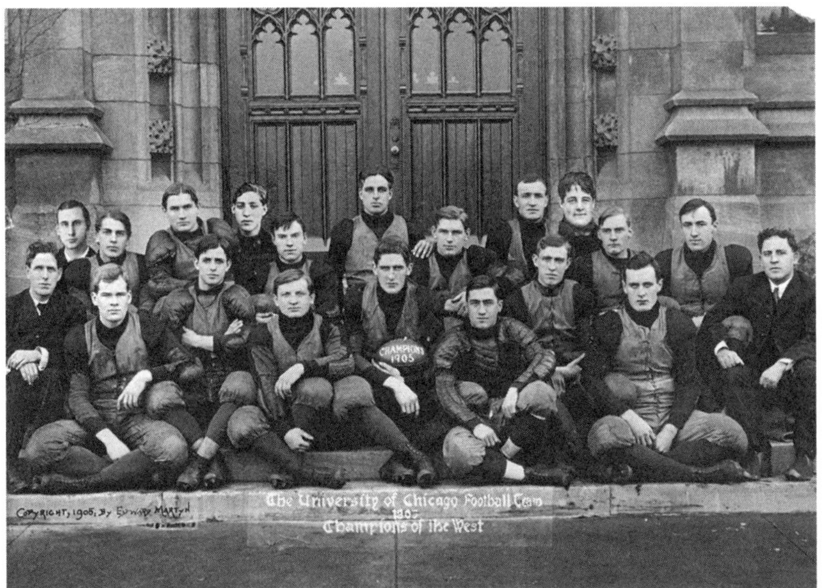

16. University of Chicago's Big Nine and national championship team of 1905. Walter Eckersall sits on the bottom-most step, just to the right of captain Mark Catlin, who is holding the football. University of Chicago Photographic Archive, apf5-03228, Hanna Holborn Gray Special Collections Research Center, University of Chicago Library.

"I believe we are just about two points better than Michigan this year," Eckersall said after the game. "There is not a great deal of difference between the two teams, but Chicago is better and deserved to win." Thinking also about Chicago's 4–0 win over Wisconsin a few weeks earlier, Eckersall added, "One might say Chicago won the championship without a touchdown. It shows just how closely matched the three leading teams were."[38]

Yost praised Chicago on "one of the best and hardest fought games I ever witnessed." But he lamented Curtis's ejection. "As it is, we have no sour grapes to offer except that the action hardly seemed warranted. . . . But we are beaten and we congratulate Chicago on the great victory."[39]

With this win, the Maroons not only won the Big Nine title but also ended Michigan's then-record 56-game unbeaten streak. Chicago students celebrated again with a pep rally a few days later. Catlin, Bezdek, and Eckie all gave speeches, the 1905 letterwinners were announced, and the evening ended with another bonfire. At a team meeting the following night, Chicago's returning players unanimously elected Eckersall captain for 1906.[40]

Among the fans in the stands on Thanksgiving was a twenty-year-old from Niles in southwest Michigan, who had just started his career as a sportswriter.

"In common with everybody else from Michigan, I felt murderously inclined toward Eckie that day, and not until I got to know him would I admit to myself or anyone else that all he had done was play a great and victorious game of football against a school that had held a monopoly on football glory in the hinterlands since 1900," Ring Lardner wrote more than twenty-five years later. "And it was the first time my girl friend has ever seen me cry."[41]

—

Eckersall was the consensus All–Big Nine quarterback and repeated as a Walter Camp All-American, this time at his actual position of quarterback.[42]

Camp praised every aspect of Eckie's game: "His runs from fake kicks were strong. . . . He won the Wisconsin game himself by a drop kick. . . . He is a first-class punter, getting from fifty to sixty yards, and his punt against the wind across Michigan's goal line was the kick that eventually resulted in a safety, defeating Michigan."[43]

Like Camp, Whitney named Eckersall a first-team All-American for the second time, although once again at fullback; Whitney reserved the quarterback slot for a Yale player. Whitney also attempted a very flawed national ranking of teams, placing Chicago fourth, behind undefeated Yale and Penn and two-loss Harvard. Neither Michigan nor Wisconsin appears on Whitney's fourteen-team list; yet, his rankings included 4-4-1 Army at no. 7, 7-4-0 Brown at no. 9, and 4-3-2 Columbia at no. 12.[44]

History has looked more favorably on Chicago's 1905 team. After the Associated Press began formally ranking football teams in 1936, various organizations started choosing retroactive champions. Four major selectors named Chicago national champion for 1905, while only one picked Yale. A more recent look at the season, conducted by football researcher James Vautravers, declared Chicago and Yale co-champions.[45]

—

A few days before the Michigan game, the National AAU reinstated Eckersall, unconditionally. After two and a half long years, he was free to compete in AAU track, although now with three seasons of football-related wear and tear on his legs.[46]

As in previous offseasons, rumors swirled about Eckersall's plans. He was dropping out of school to go into business. Eckie and Bezdek were signing with a pro baseball team. Eckersall would compete in soccer instead of track. Hammond, still angry about Eckie's alleged "flop" in the Chicago-Michigan game, was going to provide definitive evidence that Eckersall was a professional.[47]

In fact, Eckie had a quiet winter. He dabbled with soccer, but only as a conditioning tool. He signed up for a Bible study class with a few other athletes. He went to Detroit, briefly, on what he mysteriously described as "business affairs." And in a harbinger of other things to come, he wrote his first-ever bylined article for the *Chicago Tribune*.[48]

Eckie joined the track team when indoor practice started on January 16, although the bigger news was conveyed by that day's *Chicago Inter Ocean* headline: "Football May Be Abolished at the Midway." After a deadly year on the gridiron, the Football Rules Committee was trying to make the game safer. If football couldn't clean up its act, the game might disappear.[49]

Those conversations were taking place at a high level, with no player input. All athletes could do was keep practicing and competing.

In early February Eckersall won the 50-yard dash at an intramural time trial. On February 10 he competed, but did not place, in a meet at Boston's Mechanics Hall, his first AAU competition since 1903. He ran a dead heat with an Illinois sprinter in the 35-yard dash at a meet in mid-February, and he won the 50-yard dash in another meet with Illinois in early March.[50]

Eckie was running well and declared he would skip baseball to focus on track. Then in early April, without explanation, he quit track and rejoined the baseball squad.[51]

Chicago was much improved in 1906, and so was Eckersall. The team went 19-7 overall and 9-6 in conference, good enough for third place. Eckie

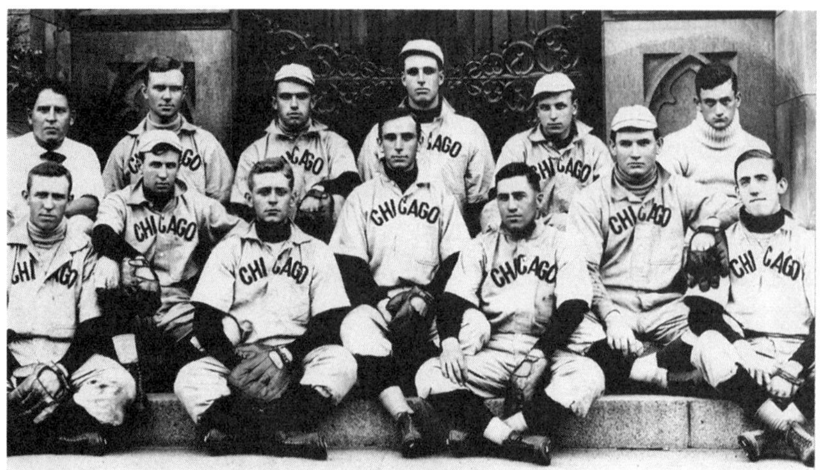

17. University of Chicago baseball team, 1906. Walter Eckersall sits on the bottom-most step, third from left. University of Chicago Photographic Archive, apf5-02815, Hanna Holborn Gray Special Collections Research Center, University of Chicago Library.

batted .250, fourth-best among regulars. He moved from third base to the outfield and had an .893 fielding percentage, significantly better than his team-worst .697 the previous season.

Eckie had a couple personal highlights that spring. He walked, stole two bases, and scored the winning run against Northwestern. In a home game against Michigan (whose fans had taunted Eckie at Ann Arbor days earlier), he hit a triple and stole home in a 9–3 rout. In another game at Michigan, Eckie drove in the go-ahead run in the tenth inning for a 5–4 victory.[52]

Eckersall was steady, but far from a star. Perhaps the best thing one can say about his 1906 baseball season is that, unlike the previous season, he didn't single-handedly cost his team any games.

With baseball and school over, Eckie put aside his worries for a few weeks, spending most of the summer of 1906 at Paw Paw Lake before his final season of college football.[53]

11

Year of Reform

Chicago's win over Michigan in 1905 was one of the great football games of all time. It was also very nearly one of the last football games of all time.

In October 1905 President Theodore Roosevelt summoned several top Eastern football authorities to the White House and demanded that they do something about the sport's excessive roughness. The football men, including Walter Camp, released a public statement promising to do their best to clean up the game.[1]

But on-field behavior grew worse. In the Harvard-Yale game, a Yale player roughed Harvard's All-American guard Francis Burr on a fair catch, breaking his nose and knocking him semiconscious. Shockingly, referee Paul Dashiell didn't call a penalty. Less shockingly, a clearly concussed Burr stayed in the game.

Dashiell apologized to Roosevelt, but the damage had been done. And the damage was mounting. Mass-formation football was causing large numbers of serious injuries and a growing number of deaths. In a telegram to President Roosevelt, reprinted under the provocative headline "Football Year's Death Harvest," the *Chicago Tribune* reported nineteen gridiron deaths and 137 serious injuries that season. (The *Tribune* wanted it both ways, condemning the sport on Sunday yet devoting four full pages to the Chicago-Michigan game the following Friday.)[2]

After the 1905 season ended, several colleges suspended their football programs, including Columbia, California, Stanford, and Northwestern.

Rumors of a nationwide ban began circulating. Those who wanted to save football needed to do something, fast.

The forward pass, which the Football Rules Committee had debated for years, promised to open up the game by moving away from mass formations. Camp resisted, but the newly created Intercollegiate Athletic Association of the United States (which rebranded itself as the NCAA in 1910) outvoted Camp and legalized the forward pass, although with heavy restrictions. The rule-makers also agreed to Camp's suggestion of increasing the distance needed for a first down, from 5 yards to 10.[3]

Camp hated the forward pass. So, initially, did Michigan's Fielding Yost. But Amos Alonzo Stagg embraced the change.

"I do not agree with Mr. Yost on the new rules," Stagg said. "There will be less of the old plugging game, there will be more open field running, more thrilling passing. . . . Spectators will be able to follow the ball. The game will be opened up . . . and will be less rough and less dangerous than before."[4]

The Big Nine also added strict new policies to reduce the emphasis placed on football. Training tables were abolished. Athletes could play no more than three seasons, although Eckersall's class was "grandfathered" in (for football only) for a fourth. Teams were now limited to five games per season. Practice couldn't start until school started, which meant October 1 for the University of Chicago. The end of the season was similarly trimmed, with the last game played on the Saturday before Thanksgiving. This policy would remain, with only occasional exceptions, for more than a hundred years, making the Chicago-Michigan Thanksgiving Day spectacle of 1905 especially memorable.

The University of Chicago faculty, swept up in the spirit of reform, went even further than the conference. The faculty voted to require athletes to take and pass at least three classes per quarter, up from the previous two.

"This new move is unfair to the athletes," complained Walter Eckersall, who had already been academically ineligible twice under the less-stringent rules. "It is putting a burden on our shoulders."[5]

To pare down the schedule, Chicago's athletic board canceled the two biggest games, against Michigan and Wisconsin. Big games were too commercial and drew too close to the line of professionalism, the faculty argued.

On paper, the last tough game on Chicago's schedule was against Minnesota, which had lost only one game over the previous three seasons. The Maroons' other conference opponents had combined for just one league win in 1905.

The matter was never put up for debate or comment. The faculty senate and athletic board met in secret and announced the cancellations several days later. Captain Eckersall expressed his team's disappointment: "It comes a little hard for one playing his fourth year to face a milk and water schedule."[6]

—

With all this change as a backdrop, Eckersall returned in mid-September to hold "captain's practice" and experiment with the new rules. He originally held practice at Marshall Field, but when Stagg arrived a few days later, he stopped this: The letter of the law prohibited any football activities on campus before October 1. So, Eckersall took his team to Jackson Park to tinker with the forward pass.[7]

18. Collectible photo of Walter Eckersall wearing a University of Chicago letterman's sweater. University of Chicago Photographic Archive, apf1-05929, Hanna Holborn Gray Special Collections Research Center, University of Chicago Library.

For the 1906 season, Wally Steffen would be joining the varsity. Steffen was nearly as fast as Eckersall, giving the Maroons a tremendous one-two punch in the backfield at the dawn of open play.

After less than three weeks of formal practice, Chicago opened its season on October 20 against Purdue at Marshall Field.

"University of Chicago athletes take to the sterilized game of football like ducks to water," the *Chicago Tribune* declared. "Capt. Eckersall kept his fast maroon back field on the jump, reeling off play after play with a speed and comparative certainty which fairly baffled his opponents. . . . The way in which the maroons ran off their intricate plays was little short of marvelous, considering the short time they have had to develop them. There was an unexpected smoothness."

Eckie called end runs, reverses, double-reverses, and delayed handoffs, but he didn't throw any passes. Stagg knew that Indiana coach Jimmy Sheldon and Minnesota coach Henry Williams were in the stands to scout the Maroons, and he didn't want to tip his hand to those future opponents.

Early in the game, Eckie rushed for a 25-yard touchdown. He added a 65-yard punt return touchdown at the start of the second half and boomed several deep punts. Steffen also ran for the first two touchdowns of his career. Chicago's only apparent flaw was its kicking, as Purdue blocked both of Eckersall's field-goal attempts.

While Chicago stuck with the running game, Purdue experimented with the pass. The Boilermakers completed two but also lost the ball twice, once on an incompletion (under the original rules, a pass that hit the ground without touching a player was a turnover) and once on an interception. Chicago returned that interception 65 yards for a touchdown, the exclamation point on a 39–0 victory.

"It was a good game to watch and a good game to play," Stagg said. "I certainly was satisfied with the new rules, and I think before the close of the season the game will be bully sport. . . . I do not think there could be any adverse criticism about this style of contest."[8]

In Chicago's second game, against Indiana, play was fairly even through the first forty minutes. Eckersall drove his team into field-goal range several times. His 20-yard attempt was blocked; he then missed three more attempts. Midway through the first half, Eckersall finally connected on a 45-yard drop-kick, for a 4–0 Chicago lead.

A few plays later, an Indiana halfback zipped through ten Chicago players on a punt return, with only an open-field tackle by Eckersall preventing a touchdown. From there, Indiana quarterback Bunny Hare drop-kicked a field goal of his own to tie the game at 4–4.

19. Walter Eckersall breaks a tackle against Purdue at Marshall Field on October 20, 1906, en route to a 25-yard touchdown run. SDN-004920, *Chicago Daily News* collection, Chicago History Museum.

Late in the first half, Hare was forced to punt from deep in his own territory. Eckie caught the ball on a bounce at his own 35-yard line and cut straight up the middle of the field, dodging six Indiana defenders on the way. Hare attempted an open-field tackle near midfield, but Eckersall wriggled out of his grasp and kept churning his legs, until he was finally brought down at the 2-yard line. On the next play, Eckie handed off for a touchdown and a 10–4 halftime lead.

Early in the second half, Eckie tried his first-ever forward pass, but the ball narrowly eluded Fred Walker, resulting in a turnover. A few plays later, Indiana kicked another field goal, cutting Chicago's lead to just 2 points.

The Maroons now found a sense of urgency that was lacking earlier. Hare fumbled an Eckersall punt, and Chicago recovered deep in Indiana territory. Two plays later, Steffen feigned an end run, then cut back to the middle, going untouched for a 15-yard score. A couple of series later, Steffen dodged through the worn-out Indiana defense for a 35-yard touchdown. Chicago added two more late touchdowns for a 33–8 victory that was much closer than the score would indicate.

"The game was a hard one for the players," Eckersall said. "All this punting adds a great deal to the strenuousness of the play." The *Chicago Tribune*'s scorekeeper credited him with twenty-five punts, while the *Chicago Inter Ocean* counted twenty-one. Eckersall scored just 4 points, but he had more than 200 all-purpose yards, controlled field position with his punting, and made that touchdown-saving tackle. As usual, Eckie impacted the game in all kinds of ways.[9]

The next Tuesday, Eckersall, Walker, and Ed Parry all skipped practice. Stagg wondered if they might have gotten into an accident; one rumor spread that the group had been kidnapped by fans of their next opponent, Minnesota. The absence did give Stagg a chance to give Steffen, Eckersall's heir apparent, some practice reps at quarterback. Unlike the forced apology for Eckie's and Walker's missed curfew from the previous season, there were no public consequences for this missed practice.[10]

Eckersall skipped practice again that Saturday, but this absence was excused. Coach Stagg took him to Minneapolis on Chicago's open date to watch two future opponents, Minnesota and Nebraska. Bobby Marshall, one of the few Black players in major-college football and a second-team All-American in 1905, kicked two field goals for the Gophers in a 13–0 win.

"Minnesota is, of course, a strong team . . . but it is not as fast as it is reported to be, and I am becoming confident of a Chicago victory," Eckersall said after the game. "Marshall's work in scoring the two place kicks was nothing phenomenal. Both were from inside the twenty-five yard line."[11]

"I am sorry the Minnesota people have the opinion that we believe them to be weaklings," Stagg said the following day, attempting to walk back Eckersall's comments. "Eckersall is sorry he has been quoted to this effect. He does not believe it at all."[12]

—

The weather in Chicago was awful when Minnesota came to town on November 10. Some fifteen thousand spectators braved heavy rain to watch the biggest game at Marshall Field this season, between the two best players in the Big Nine: "Without disparagement to the other twenty men in the game, it was Marshall against Eckersall," the *Chicago Tribune* said.

The muddy field prevented the forward passes and other open plays that Stagg and Williams had developed. Instead, this would look like a game under the old-time rules, which would favor Minnesota and its heavy, experienced line.

Chicago threatened first. On third-and-two, Eckie tried a field goal from the Minnesota 43, but the attempt went wide. Minnesota punted on its next series, and Eckersall fumbled the slippery ball at his own 40. Chicago's defense held strong, and Marshall tried a field goal. His attempt also missed, and the two teams locked into a stalemate.

Just over twenty minutes into the game, Marshall swept past the Chicago end for a 20-yard run. Only a perfect open-field tackle by Eckersall prevented a touchdown. Minnesota stalled again, and Marshall kicked from the Maroons' 38. This time the ball went low but straight, barely clearing the goal post for a 4–0 Minnesota lead.

With time running out in the first half, Chicago had its best opportunity of the game. From midfield, Minnesota quarterback Art Larkin punted to Eckersall, waiting at the 20-yard line. He sprinted down the right sideline and dodged through the Gopher defense until only Larkin remained between him and the goal line. Eckie slowed down just a bit, to let a Maroon teammate catch up to block Larkin.

As it turned out, Eckie didn't need that blocker; Larkin slipped, and Eckersall found an open field ahead of him. But by slowing down, Eckie allowed Marshall to catch up to the play. As Eckersall tried to re-accelerate, Marshall lunged from behind, tripping the Chicago quarterback by the ankles.

It was a beautiful 45-yard return by Eckersall—and an even more beautiful touchdown-saving tackle by Marshall. Chicago gained 10 more yards in two plays, but the half ended before Eckie had a chance for another field-goal attempt.

The second half was much like the first: "It was punt, punt, punt again, with an occasional effort to gain ground by rushing, in which neither team was successful to any degree," the *Chicago Tribune* noted.

In one critical sequence, Marshall was short on a 38-yard field-goal attempt; Eckie scooped up the miss and returned it 25 yards. He followed up with a 55-yard punt. Larkin punted right back but only managed 20 yards. Chicago was now clearly winning the battle for field position, and another good punt might put the Maroons in position to at least tie the game. From midfield, Eckersall booted one, high and deep. Larkin caught the ball at his own 5-yard line, took a couple steps backward, then knelt for a safety.

Larkin was skewered in the press for what looked like a boneheaded play, similar to Denny Clark's mistake in the Michigan-Chicago game of 1905. "Larkin lost his head," the *Chicago Tribune* commented. It was "a headless play," the *Chicago Inter Ocean* opined. The *Minneapolis Journal* defended Larkin by saying the goal line had been washed away by rain, so Larkin thought he was taking a touchback instead of a safety.

In reality, Larkin's play was brilliant, the kind of play Eckersall himself, as a football writer many years later, would praise.[13]

Larkin explained his thinking a couple days later. "The rain had totally obliterated the lines and when I made the play I thought it was a touchback," he told the *Minneapolis Journal*. "If the lines had been visible I would have done the same thing, since there were a hundred and one chances for Chicago to score a field goal or even a touchdown, if I had carried the ball forward. It was not a play like the one by which Chicago beat Michigan last year."[14]

Minnesota's kick after the safety went past midfield. Two Maroon rushes gained nothing, and Eckersall punted again, another beauty to Minnesota's 10. But Marshall returned the ball 25 yards, giving the Gophers some breathing room.

Chicago never threatened again. Five more punts followed, and time expired with the ball in the Maroons' possession at their own 20-yard line. Stagg's men had fallen 4–2, their hopes of a second straight championship washed away by the November rain.[15]

20. Cartoon mocking Walter Eckersall and Amos Alonzo Stagg after Chicago's narrow loss to Minnesota on a rainy afternoon. *Minneapolis Journal*, November 11, 1906.

Eckersall was gracious in defeat. "Minnesota deserves full credit for its victory," he told the *Chicago Tribune*. "We all willingly grant the game to our opponents for their superiority today."

At the same time, Eckie blamed the rain. "If the game had been played on Friday I think we would have won, but the weather is a factor in football," he said. "With our light team it was well nigh impossible to make any decent advances, which we might have done with firm footing."

Stagg praised his senior quarterback: "Eckersall played one of the best games in his career. His punting was even better than usual, with the odds so much against him. It was unfortunate for him he could not have had a dry field today. I believe he alone could have won the game. His generalship was ideal."[16]

(Privately, Stagg thought otherwise, writing twenty-five years later: "Eckersall did not try a single forward pass because the ball was slippery. I always felt that he made a mistake, that he should have at least tried some passes.")[17]

—

The following Saturday, Chicago played the last Big Nine game of Eckersall's career against Illinois, finally unveiling some of the innovative plays that Stagg had wanted to showcase against Minnesota.

"Forward passes, double, triple, and criss cross passes, onside kicks and fakes of various kinds were reeled off," the *Chicago Tribune* reported, "with a speed which indicated Chicago's purpose to vindicate itself as far as possible for its defeat of a week previous."

On Chicago's second play from scrimmage, Eckersall faked a run, then lobbed a short pass to Steffen, who had slipped out of the backfield unnoticed. Steffen outraced the entire Illinois backfield for an 85-yard touchdown, the first completed pass in Chicago history.

Eckie threw for 170 yards and two touchdowns, while adding 120 yards and a touchdown rushing and a 20-yard field goal. He also made the defensive play of the game. After a Steffen fumble, Illinois drove inside the Chicago 2, then stalled twice. Already down 22–0, Illinois decided to go for a touchdown instead of a field goal. On third-and-goal from less than a yard out, an Illinois halfback plunged into the gap between Chicago's right guard and right tackle.

Just then, Eckie, though the smallest player on the field, filled the hole and knocked the runner backward, and Illinois turned the ball over on downs. Eckersall punted; Illinois called a fair catch at the Chicago 42, which allowed them to try a field goal from a free kick, without any defensive rush. The kick fell short, and it was now clear that Illinois wouldn't score.

But Chicago continued to score at will. Steffen ran for four touchdowns, to go along with his touchdown catch. Besides Steffen and Eckersall, three other Maroons scored touchdowns. Chicago won 63–0, the largest conference win in program history.[18]

On the same day that Chicago throttled Illinois, Minnesota and Michigan lost nonconference games. But those didn't count in the Big Nine standings. Minnesota, Michigan, and Wisconsin would all share the title with undefeated conference records. Despite losing by only 2 points to a top opponent on a muddy field, Chicago finished fourth in the Big Nine.

—

On November 24 at Marshall Field, Eckersall suited up for the Maroons for the last time, against Nebraska. The Nebraska defense focused on containing the quarterback and didn't let him get away with any of his signature runs. So Eckie relied on two other aspects of his game, one new and the other old: forward passes and drop-kicks, respectively. He completed nine of his eleven passes on the day and drop-kicked five field goals, tying the school and major-college record that he had set against Illinois the previous year.

One of Eckie's incompletions hit the ground before any player touched the ball, which was a turnover under 1906 rules. Nebraska pushed the ball over the goal line three plays later, the first touchdown surrendered by Chicago all season.

At halftime, University of Chicago registrar Thomas Goodspeed called Eckersall up to a makeshift stage and gave a ten-minute speech extolling Eckie's virtues. Goodspeed then presented the captain with a diamond-studded gold watch, a gift from the university community. Instead of numbers, the watch had pictures—Stagg's where the "12" would be, Eckie's where the "6" would be, and Chicago's other starters around the dial.

"So he will have to learn a new set of signals for this new machine," the *Chicago Inter Ocean* noted. "He will tell the time of day something after this fashion: 'It is now Parry after Walker,' or 'It's just Russell to Steffen.'"

In the second half, Nebraska continued to bottle up Eckersall, so he continued to pass. Late in the half, Nebraska lost a fumble deep in Chicago territory. Eckersall faked a punt, then threw to a wide-open Steffen, who broke into the clear for a 98-yard touchdown. A few minutes later, the game, and Eckie's college career, ended with a 38–5 Maroon victory.[19]

Afterward, Eckersall gave a lengthy interview to the *Chicago Tribune*:

> It was a pleasure for me to end my career with my fellow players fighting with such good spirit. The boys even outdid themselves. . . . This is probably my last appearance on an athletic field. . . . When I get through college I will go into business. I will not coach for money, neither will I play football or baseball for money. If I have spare time I may assist Mr. Stagg in coaching the team next fall, but this is quite doubtful. I wish it to be understood clearly that I will not become a profes-

21. University of Chicago registrar Thomas Goodspeed presents a watch to Walter Eckersall at halftime of his last college game on November 24, 1906. SDN-005066, *Chicago Daily News* collection, Chicago History Museum.

> sional coach. I am glad to a certain extent that this is my last game, but I have to think that these four years of college never can be duplicated in my life. I have had my fill. I think it is enough.[20]

—

Eckie made first-team All–Big Nine at quarterback for the fourth straight year, while Steffen was first-team halfback. The *Chicago Tribune* acknowledged several other good conference quarterbacks, including Indiana's Hare and Minnesota's Larkin. "But Eckersall is so far superior in . . . generalship, passing, running with the ball, catching punts, and kicking, that Hare and Larkin would not be mentioned except that they are excellent quarterbacks. Eckersall is, in fact, the most valuable man to any team in the country."[21]

Eckersall also made Camp's All-America team for the third straight year. This placed him in rare company. Of nearly three hundred players to make

Camp's All-America first team through the years, only seventeen made it three times, and Eckersall was the only one of those not to play at one of the "Big Four" of Yale, Harvard, Princeton, and Penn.

Caspar Whitney also named Eckie to his All-America team, though again as fullback. Whitney ranked Chicago as the no. 12 team in the country. In Whitney's eyes, 4-1 Chicago rated behind 9-3 Carlisle, 7-2-3 Penn, and, inexplicably, even 3-5-1 Army. Minnesota, at no. 11, was the only other Western team that Whitney ranked.[22]

In forty-one college games, Eckersall had scored 201 points on fourteen touchdowns, twenty-eight field goals, and fifteen extra points, while accounting for 15 more points with three touchdown passes. In those days of iron-man all-around players, he added to his offensive and return prowess with tremendous punting, drop-kicking, and tackling. He was the best all-purpose player of his era, perhaps the best of all time.

Eckie was also a winner. In four seasons, the Maroons went 37-4-2 while outscoring opponents by an average of 26 points. Twenty-seven of those wins had been by shutout. Among contemporary Western teams, only Michigan and Minnesota were in the same orbit.

Now it was over. And like any top athlete whose competition days had ended, Walter Eckersall had to figure out what to do with his life now that the cheering had stopped.

12

Maroon Football after Eckersall

With Walter Eckersall calling plays and leading the team, University of Chicago football had achieved the greatness that Amos Alonzo Stagg envisioned when he accepted President William Rainey Harper's 1890 offer. Now that the Maroons had reached the top, they stayed there for a while.

In 1907 Wally Steffen succeeded Eckersall at quarterback. In the season opener, he put up Eckie-like numbers with nearly 400 all-purpose yards, a touchdown run, and a field goal, while completing five of eight passes for 90 more yards. Steffen continued to put up similar performances throughout that fall. Chicago won the Big Eight title (Michigan had dropped out of the league that season), and Steffen made third-team All-American.[1]

Steffen was even better in 1908, and so was Chicago. In Big Eight play, Steffen rushed for seven touchdowns, passed for two more, and had four return touchdowns. Chicago went 5-0 in the conference, although the Maroons tied their lone out-of-conference foe. Later evaluators would rank Chicago the no. 4 team in the country for 1908.[2]

This time, Walter Camp named Steffen first-team All-American at quarterback. During his Chicago career, Steffen accounted for 171 total points in just sixteen career games. Eckersall had accounted for 45 more points, but he had also played twenty-five more games.

The Eckersall years kicked off a sustained period of excellence for Coach Stagg. Between 1905 and 1914, Chicago won four conference titles. The Maroons' 0.803 winning percentage was best among major teams in the

22. Wally Steffen, Eckersall's partner in Chicago's 1906 backfield and successor at quarterback, would be a two-time All-American. University of Chicago Photographic Archive, apf4-03825-001, Hanna Holborn Gray Special Collections Research Center, University of Chicago Library.

Midwest, just as football in the region was achieving parity with (and, to many experts, surpassing) the Eastern version of the game.

Chicago's undefeated, untied championship in 1905 marked one apex to Stagg's coaching career; its undefeated, untied championship in 1913 was the other. Unlike the days when quarterbacks were the Maroons' stars, the 1913 team was led by Paul Des Jardien, a six-foot-five center out of Chicago's Wendell Phillips High School who bore the ironic nickname "Shorty." A tremendous blocker on offense, Des Jardien frequently dropped off the line to play "free center" or "roving center" on defense, an early example of what would later be recognized as the linebacker position.[3]

Chicago won all seven of its games and easily took first place in the conference (now the "Big Nine" again, with newcomer Ohio State aboard).

Des Jardien earned first-team All-American honors, and Chicago would retroactively be recognized as the national champion.[4]

Stagg achieved another honor in 1913, one he never sought for himself. Over the previous year, Marshall Field had been rebuilt and expanded, with concrete stands replacing the old wooden ones. The university dropped the Marshall Field name and started using the bulky "Athletic Field of the University of Chicago." Within weeks, *Chicago Tribune* sports editor Harvey Woodruff called for a renaming:

23. Like Eckersall before him, Paul Des Jardien led University of Chicago to an undefeated season and a national championship in 1913. University of Chicago Photographic Archive, apf5-00556, Hanna Holborn Gray Special Collections Research Center, University of Chicago Library.

> The new handle is cumbersome. It is too long for colloquial or newspaper use. University field, College field, or Chicago field might be popular and possible—but WHY NOT CALL IT STAGG FIELD? Stagg's name has been synonymous with University of Chicago athletics since the university was founded in 1892. . . . Chicago alumni generally feel that no more fitting tribute could be paid to the "Old Man" than to name for him the field on which he has achieved many notable victories against odds. An official request from the alumni for that name is not improbable, but why wait? WHY NOT CALL IT STAGG FIELD?[5]

The *Tribune* didn't wait for a formal decision. The day after Woodruff's editorial, the newspaper began using the name. Other newspapers used it occasionally, but the *Tribune* did so aggressively, repeating "Stagg Field" in print more than eighty times between Woodruff's suggestion and the end of the season.[6]

By then, the *Tribune*'s repetition made the renaming a foregone conclusion. In mid-November, Chicago's alumni association submitted a formal petition to adopt "Stagg Field." The board of trustees approved this name change the following fall.[7]

Shortly after the renaming, Chicago football slumped. The 1916 team went 3-4. The 1917 Maroons were slightly better, finishing 3-2-1. But 1918 was a disaster.

Stagg chalked up his struggles to World War I. "I had begun to whip up a fairly good team together when most of them were called to the colors," Stagg wrote. "To fill the dates already scheduled, we had to conjure up a new team composed principally of freshmen."[8]

Those freshmen went winless in the Big Ten (Michigan had rejoined the conference in 1917). The war hurt the Maroons in another way. Four letterwinners died in action, including starting linemen Spike Shull and Harold Goettler from the 1913 national championship team. A second-team All-Conference pick, Goettler gained a measure of immortality beyond the gridiron. As an army pilot, he earned the Medal of Honor for dropping food and supplies to the so-called Lost Battalion in October 1918, a mission during which he was shot down and killed.

"But the college athlete did more than die," Stagg wrote. "He lived magnificently, volunteered almost to a man, was accepted to a man because of his physical condition, and usually became an officer by virtue of the qualities that won him a place on the team."[9]

After the war, Stagg and his team rebounded. Between 1919 and 1924, the Maroons won 75 percent of their games and two Big Ten titles. The 1924 team had one of the strangest records of any champion: three conference wins, no losses, and three ties. That season, Stagg pulled off perhaps his greatest coaching feat against Illinois. The undefeated Illini were a 3-to-1 favorite, and experts wondered how Stagg could contain mighty halfback Red Grange.

Stagg's answer: don't even try. "For strategy I fell back on that good old military aphorism . . . the best defense is an attack," Stagg later wrote. "Not for us the negative 'Stop Grange!' The command was 'Forward! Get the jump! Attack! Attack! Then attack some more!'"[10]

Chicago scored a touchdown on its first series, then added another on the first play of the second quarter. Illinois scraped and fought back, but never took the lead. Despite Grange's three touchdowns and 300 yards of offense, Chicago and Illinois tied 21–21. The *Chicago Tribune* hailed the tie as the biggest upset of the season. Illinois lost to Minnesota the following week, sealing the Big Ten title for the Maroons.[11]

Stagg hoped that the 1924 season might serve as the foundation for another period of excellence. Instead, it was the beginning of the end.

After Harper's successor as president, football-friendly Harry Pratt Judson, retired in 1923, new administrators became alarmed at the academic performance of Chicago's athletes. The dean noted, "This exceedingly discreditable record indicates either that the football men are of mentally low grade, or that the conditions under which they live during the football quarter are such as to prevent them from doing their work properly." Chicago responded by enforcing academic standards that had long been ignored.[12]

The timing was unfortunate. Football soared in popularity throughout the country in the 1920s, and Chicago's Big Ten counterparts had no moral qualms about recruiting academically questionable players.

At the same time, most Big Ten schools built new stadiums during the 1920s, giant concrete-and-steel football cathedrals that seated fifty thousand to seventy thousand fans. Marshall Field—later, Stagg Field—had long been the premier venue in the Midwest but had fallen behind its peers in the 1920s. Stagg hoped to build a shiny new stadium south of campus in Woodlawn, which may have happened if Harper or Judson were still president. Instead, he had to settle for marginal improvements to his namesake.

Through the 1910s, the Maroons were the only football team on any level with a broad following among Chicagoans. Pro football didn't yet exist

24. The play of inaugural Heisman Trophy winner Jay Berwanger was a rare bright spot for University of Chicago football in the 1930s. University of Chicago Photographic Archive, apf1-00641, Hanna Holborn Gray Special Collections Research Center, University of Chicago Library.

on a widespread scale. Chicago's only significant local rival, Northwestern, had struggled for most of its existence. Notre Dame was still considered a "minor" team. For nearly three decades, Stagg enjoyed a virtual monopoly on Chicago football fandom.

In the 1920s, that landscape changed. Northwestern dramatically improved, winning three Big Ten titles in a six-year span. Notre Dame emerged as a major power under coach Knute Rockne and gained a large following among Chicagoans, especially Catholics. Notre Dame even temporarily moved into the city, playing at Soldier Field in 1929 during the construction of Notre Dame Stadium. Meanwhile, big-time professional football finally arrived in the city with the birth of the National Football League in 1920 and the signing of Grange by the Chicago Bears in 1925.

These combined factors—higher academic standards, an outdated stadium, and increased competition from Northwestern, Notre Dame, and pro football—spelled trouble for the Maroons. In 1925 Chicago slumped to a

3-4-1 record, and things only got worse from there. In Stagg's last eight seasons, the Maroons went just 9-31-1 in conference.

The university's new "boy president," Robert Maynard Hutchins, who took over at age thirty in 1929, viewed athletics as a distraction from the true purpose of a university. That, coupled with Maroon football's declining quality, made its final course inevitable.

University policy forced Stagg to retire at age seventy after the 1932 season. He went on to spend fourteen seasons as head coach at the University of the Pacific, then continued to work as an assistant coach, finally retiring for good at age ninety-six. Stagg's successor, Clark Shaughnessy, was a brilliant football mind and Hall of Fame coach who developed the modern T-formation. But Shaughnessy never had the athletes at Chicago to carry out his vision. Shaughnessy's Maroons went 5-25-2 in the Big Ten during his seven-year tenure. His lone bright spot was the 1935 performance of halfback Jay Berwanger, a first-team All-American, recipient of the *Chicago Tribune* Silver Football as Big Ten MVP, and winner of the first Heisman Trophy. But even the Berwanger-Shaughnessy combination could only garner a 4-4 overall record in their best season together.[13]

In 1939 Chicago staggered to a 2-6 record. The losses included an 85–0 beatdown by Michigan and an equally embarrassing 6–0 loss to tiny Beloit College. Within a month of the season finale, President Hutchins called for the abolition of football at the university; the board of trustees unanimously approved.[14]

The Maroons had enjoyed a forty-eight-season run that included the tremendous heights achieved by Eckersall, Steffen, Des Jardien, and Stagg but also the dismal lows of the final fifteen years.

Chicago would resume playing at the NCAA's College Division level in 1969 and in the newly formed Division III in 1973. But in 1939, somewhat mercifully, big-time football at the University of Chicago had faded into the past.

PART 3

1907–30

13

The Myth of Frank Merriwell

Like many young boys in the 1890s, Walter Eckersall would have been familiar with the popular "nickel weekly" stories about Frank Merriwell. The fictional Yale halfback—who also played baseball, ran track, and rowed crew—had a knack for snatching victory from the jaws of defeat with his last-second heroics. Frank's character was just as exemplary as his play on the field. He succeeded in school, was unfailingly honest, treated women with respect, steered clear of alcohol and cigarettes, and was a natural leader, in sports and in life. In these stories, Merriwell won the respect and admiration of his peers, while giving bullies and scoundrels their comeuppances, solving mysteries, and of course beating Harvard.[1]

With annual sales in the millions, the Frank Merriwell stories in *Tip Top Weekly* were the creation of Gilbert Patten, writing under the pseudonym Burt Standish. The author bore little resemblance to his own hero. Patten never went to college, was twice divorced, smoked, and experienced little success until he created Frank Merriwell in 1896, when he was nearly thirty.

The moral of these stories was clear. Sports, especially football, developed All-American values. And All-American boys gravitated toward football, which forged them into not only better athletes but also better men.

This myth resonated with football's biggest backers, reinforcing the popular philosophy of muscular Christianity. Walter Camp believed that athletics were necessary to develop character in a world that was rapidly growing softer. He chided those who urged youths to focus solely on academics, writing in 1885: "How many parents urge their sons on coming to college to study hard and stand high! How few exhort them to play hard and be athletic!"[2]

Whereas some reformers and muckrakers considered football a brutal, negative influence, Camp thought football created character-building traits such as discipline, teamwork, and communication skills. Camp's mentee, Amos Alonzo Stagg, saw things similarly, although the former divinity student also believed that football created not only a strong man but also a *good* man.[3]

In the early twentieth century, football had perhaps no greater booster than President Theodore Roosevelt. To Roosevelt, football was an integral part of "the Strenuous Life" that Americans needed to embrace.

"The great growth in the love of athletic sports, for instance, while fraught with danger if it becomes one-sided and unhealthy, has beyond all question had an excellent effect in increased manliness," Roosevelt wrote in 1900, when he was governor of New York. "A boy needs both physical and moral courage. Neither can take the place of the other. . . . In life, as in a football game, the principle to follow is: Hit the line hard; don't foul and don't shirk, but hit the line hard!"[4]

To Camp, Stagg, and Roosevelt, athletics made one a better student, a better person, a better Christian, a better leader, a better soldier in times of war, and an ideal gear in the corporate machine in times of peace.

Numerous football alumni had succeeded on the field, in school, and in life. After starring at Yale, Camp became chair of one of the world's largest clock manufacturers. Dudley Dean, Harvard's All-American quarterback of 1890, helped lead the charge up San Juan Hill during the Spanish-American War, then became a mining executive. Harlan Stone, starting guard at Amherst in the early 1890s, became chief justice of the U.S. Supreme Court. Georgia Tech quarterback Leonard Wood and Lafayette fullback Peyton March both served as U.S. Army chief of staff. A couple generations later, West Point halfback Dwight Eisenhower and Michigan center Gerald Ford both became president.

"But, whatever and wherever they may be," wrote football historian Parke Davis, "they are pursuing their serious lives aided by the traits of character, intelligence, initiative, judgment, aggressiveness, courage, and honor in which they were specially trained on the foot ball gridirons of America."[5]

Somewhere along the way, Eckersall failed to get the memo.

At Chicago, Eckie was originally admitted as a "sub-freshman" because he hadn't even graduated high school yet. Throughout college, Eckersall took only the minimum number of courses required for athletic eligibility, while also skipping class frequently. Eckersall should have been more than 80 percent through his bachelor's degree by the end of his senior football season. Instead, he had barely one-third of the required credits.[6]

Still, Eckersall approached winter quarter 1907 as if nothing were wrong. He showed up for preseason track practice in January, hopeful that the Big Nine would "grandfather" his class for spring sports eligibility. Barely a week later, conference officials dashed Eckersall's hopes, insisting on a firm application of the new rules. No track or baseball for the senior class. Eckersall's career as a college athlete abruptly ended not on the field but in a conference room.[7]

Rumors spread that Eckersall would drop out of school. Eckie denied this, insisting that he planned to graduate on schedule that June. (Graduating was impossible, however, since he would have, at best, half the required credits by then.)[8]

University administrators kept their eyes on the former star, especially since he had no more public relations value. Eckersall quickly gave them reason to act. On January 24 a downtown Chicago tailor pressed charges, alleging that Eckersall had defrauded him of clothing worth $40 (about $1,300 today). Wire services picked up the story, and Eckie was once again national news.[9]

Eckersall came up with the $40, plus $8.50 in court costs. More accurately, his *friends* came up with the $48.50. Eckersall didn't have any money at his court appearance, so he phoned his fraternity for help.[10]

Eckie's latest misadventure, combined with his academic woes, forced the university's hand. Official correspondence referred to Eckersall's "deplorable and unfortunate actions," "loose morals," "bad debts," and "traitorous personal friendships." The day after the charges were filed, acting university president Harry Pratt Judson ordered: "Mr. Eckersall is not to be permitted to register in the Univ. again—for cause."[11]

Just two months after receiving that beautiful watch from the school, Eckersall was finished at Chicago, as both an athlete and a student. Yet, the expulsion took place quietly and was never reported in the press. Eckersall kept up the ruse, telling the *Chicago Tribune* that he was taking winter quarter off but would re-enroll in April. Adding to the deception, Eckie's picture appears with the rest of the class of 1907 in Chicago's yearbook. Eckersall's expulsion wouldn't be widely known to the public until Amos Alonzo Stagg biographer Robin Lester uncovered it almost ninety years later.[12]

Unfazed, Eckersall continued to participate in fraternity activities. A few days after his expulsion, he was high scorer in a campus bowling tournament. After the results appeared in the student newspaper, university officials barred Eckersall from on-campus activities "because of non-residence," leaving his fraternity brothers confused and knocking Alpha Delta Phi out of first place.[13]

—

In June 1907 Stagg announced his assistant coaches for the upcoming football season. Usually, he hired the previous year's captain as an assistant, but Stagg chose Hugo Bezdek instead. Despite his status as the greatest athlete in school history, Eckie was snubbed.

"Mr. Stagg's selection caused a little surprise at the Midway as it was thought Walter Eckersall would be his first assistant this fall," the *Chicago Tribune* reported. "Eckersall, however, was left out of consideration."[14]

Stagg probably wanted to hire Eckersall, but based on his expulsion, the university wouldn't allow it. Eckie tried to deflect the perceived slight by announcing that he would become a game official, claiming he could earn more money that way than as an assistant coach.

At the same time, Eckersall inquired about open coaching jobs at Purdue and Nebraska. Stagg's reference could have been a huge help here. Colleges frequently asked Stagg for coaching candidates, and Stagg eagerly touted his former Maroons: twenty-one of Eckersall's Chicago teammates would become head coaches, including two, Bezdek and Jesse Harper, who would become Hall of Famers.[15]

Yet, Stagg's folders full of recommendations include only one for Eckersall, for the Utah State job in 1907. And Stagg threw Eckie's name in at the end; the bulk of his letter was an endorsement of Fred Walker. Stagg's words seem to damn Eckie with faint praise: "You might be able to get W.H. Eckersall, 675 East 65th Street. Eckersall, as you know, is a wonderful athlete, and strong in all lines; but I hardly think he would make as good a coach as Walker, although he has some very good points."[16]

Stagg and Eckersall remained close, and Stagg knew what a great football mind Eckersall possessed, so it's puzzling to note Stagg's lack of enthusiasm toward a potential Coach Eckersall. A closer look at his correspondence reveals why Stagg may have hedged.

Athletic directors usually inquired about personal character, and even state-run colleges often asked for a good Christian. For most of his former athletes, Stagg replied with enthusiasm: Jimmy Sheldon was "a clean, wholesome-minded fellow." Fred Speik was "absolutely reliable and trustworthy and a man of fine personal character." William Boone and Harper "are fine fellows, men of excellent habits and strong personalities." Mark Catlin "is thoroughly clean and upright." Wally Steffen was not only "a man of very strong personality and genial"; Stagg also noted, "I doubt very much if you will find anywhere a stronger man to fill the position."[17]

Compared to such high praise, Stagg's lone, halfhearted recommendation of Eckersall as a backup choice for an obscure job stands out, negatively. Perhaps the public charges of theft, the private whispers of "loose morals," and the secret expulsion caused Stagg not to place his own reputation on the line for a risky endorsement.

—

The University of Chicago's files on Eckersall refer to "loose morals" but never cite specifics. Was he a drinker? A gambler? A womanizer? Officials never recorded, and newspapers never reported, the details. Eckie himself remained secretive about his personal life until, almost two years after his expulsion, he was very publicly tied to a woman.

In December 1908 Eckersall was seeing a young actress named Elizabeth Jahn, a German-born, Chicago-raised twenty-one-year-old who lived at Twenty-Sixth Street and Indiana Avenue, about five miles north of the

Eckersall home. The two spent a Friday evening together and were back at Elizabeth's place shortly after midnight.

Eckie headed home to Woodlawn, and Elizabeth stayed up talking with her roommate, an actress named Marguerite Wiswell. Around two o'clock in the morning, Marguerite shot herself in the abdomen, in what she claimed was an accident. She was rushed across the street to Mercy Hospital with a serious wound that was originally thought to be fatal.[18]

Elizabeth called Eckie at his parents' home. He returned quickly and tried to shield Elizabeth from reporters. Rumors spread that the shooting was a suicide attempt, or that Elizabeth shot her roommate, or that Eckie was somehow involved.[19]

The story spread on the press wires and appeared in newspapers from Los Angeles to Nebraska to New York. The details were murky, but one fact was clear: The very private athlete was now very publicly revealed to be dating.

Eckie's private life soon turned private again, and for a time the world heard nothing more about the couple. But they clearly continued seeing each other. In August 1909 Walter and Elizabeth, who went by "Lizzie" with her family but whom Eckie nicknamed "Jappy," quietly eloped in Indiana. With the modern-day assistance of vital records databases, the reason is now clear: In December, just four months after the wedding, Jappy gave birth to a daughter, also named Elizabeth, or "Betty."[20]

Eckersall would face a very public scandal if the shotgun nature of his wedding was discovered. So, the Eckersalls covered their tracks. When Betty was a baby, they would lie about their wedding date, stating they had been married in 1908. Later, they would lie about Betty's age, pushing her birth year back to 1910. Generally, though, Walter hid his marriage altogether. Although a brief item on the wedding appeared in the *South Bend (IN) Tribune*, the press wires didn't pick up that story. When the marriage was publicly revealed later, some of Eckie's friends expressed surprise. (Eckersall did trust Stagg, who wrote in an October 1909 letter: "I have preserved your secret.") Some later researchers incorrectly concluded that Eckersall was a lifelong bachelor.[21]

Initially, Eckersall tried to make his marriage work. Unlike the widespread rambling of his later career, Eckie stayed close to home in the fall of

1909, mostly covering University of Chicago home games. Once Betty was born on December 20, Eckie took nearly a month off work.

But Eckersall couldn't stay out of the game for long. By March 1910 he was covering multiple local sporting events a week: indoor track meets, amateur wrestling matches, basketball tournaments, swim meets. He also hit the road for a few days, joining Coach Stagg to help Arkansas coach Bezdek install a modern passing offense during spring football practice.[22]

By census time in April, the Eckersalls were already living apart. Walter lived with his parents and sisters in Woodlawn, while Jappy and four-month-old Betty stayed in a boarding house a mile and a half northeast. Tellingly, Jappy listed herself as married, while Walter Sr. listed Eckie as single.[23]

What should have been glaringly obvious, and would become increasingly more obvious as his career went on, is that Walter Eckersall was never cut out for marriage or family life. He lived in a sporting world and very much a man's world, which included: football fields, boxing gyms, locker rooms, "dopesters" with their gambling tips, promoters hyping their latest stars, constant train travel, meals taken in hotel cafes, and late nights in companionship with similar sporting men, either in the newsroom or at a saloon.

Eckie's life simply didn't have room for a wife or a child.

In hindsight, Jappy may have been a victim of what we now recognize as codependent behavior. She had suffered a significant childhood tragedy at age ten, when her father was murdered outside a brothel in Chicago's infamous Levee district. Years later, she may have been trying to overcome her own trauma by choosing a somewhat broken bad boy as a partner, then trying to "fix" him.[24]

The attempt didn't work. In December 1911 Jappy filed for divorce in a scathing petition, charging Walter with cruelty, lack of support, and habitual intoxication. Jappy also sought a restraining order to keep Eckie from harassing her. The story was picked up by the press wires and ran in newspapers across the country.

Most papers—including the *Chicago Tribune*, in the awkward position of both employing Eckersall and reporting on him as a public figure—ran brief items on the divorce, leaving out the details. But a few publications included salacious tidbits. Jappy claimed Eckie had thrown beer in her face, squandered his income on wild living, and maintained "association with other women." Perhaps Jappy's saddest piece of testimony was reported by the *Chicago Daily News*: "I have seldom seen him sober."[25]

The divorce was finalized in February 1912, and Walter was ordered to pay Jappy $12 a week in alimony. Yet, he struggled to make these payments. By January 1915 Jappy took Walter to court again, complaining that he was behind on his alimony by almost $350, the equivalent of more than $10,000 today. At the same time, Walter appears to have had little relationship with his now-five-year-old daughter.[26]

The brief, doomed marriage was the latest evidence of poor character in Walter Eckersall's young adulthood. He was an academic failure and attempted thief. He had been kicked out of college for loose morals. His mentor refused to recommend him for a job. He had impregnated a woman out of wedlock, covered up his shotgun wedding, and abandoned his wife and child. He was irresponsible and had a drinking problem.

Eckie was nothing like the fictional Frank Merriwell, except on the athletic field. And his window for athletic success was rapidly closing.

14

Semipro

As Walter Eckersall's college football career ended, a big game was planned for Chicago, the first major professional football contest ever held in the city. The game was to take place on Thanksgiving Day 1906 at South Side Park, home of the Chicago White Sox, between Chicago and Michigan alumni.

Eckersall and Willie Heston would captain the rival teams. To make the game palatable to the public, some proceeds would be earmarked for homeless youth.[1]

Michigan president James Angell and acting Chicago president Harry Pratt Judson objected to the game and exchanged telegrams. (Angell to Judson: "We strongly disapprove, what is your attitude?" Judson to Angell: "No such game will be permitted.") There was little either president could do formally, but both worked behind the scenes to ensure that the game was canceled.[2]

A substitute game was then organized between the Massillon Tigers, champions of the semiprofessional Ohio League, and a hastily assembled Western All-Star Team. Heston, who had played in one pro game for the Canton Bulldogs the previous year, would play for the All-Stars. But Eckersall, still hoping to participate in spring sports for Chicago, steered clear of playing.

Eckie refereed instead. For his health, this decision might have been for the best. The *Chicago Inter Ocean* called the game "a bone breaking contest." Heston broke his leg while making a tackle midway through the second half, ending his pro football career after only two games.[3]

25. Manager, owner, and part-time player Cap Anson, center, on the field at Anson's Park in Woodlawn. SDN-054107, *Chicago Daily News* collection, Chicago History Museum.

In January 1907 Eckersall announced that he would remain an amateur. He wouldn't play, or even coach, for money.

"The greatest football player the west has ever produced, the greatest player in the country today, is to be a godfather to clean sport in the west," read the dispatch on the wire services. "He will lend his influence to all that is best in the college arena, but he never will attempt to reap any financial returns."[4]

Days later, unbeknownst to the public, Eckersall was expelled from Chicago. Barely a month after that, Cap Anson, baseball royalty as nineteenth-century player-manager of the team that became the Chicago Cubs, started a new semipro baseball club, and he declared his desire to sign Eckie. Eckersall wasn't a legitimate Major League or even Minor League Baseball prospect, but he could get regular playing time in Chicago's bustling semipro scene.[5]

"Anson's Colts," adopting the name the Cubs had used from 1890 to 1897, started play in late April at the newly built Anson's Park at Sixty-First Street and St. Lawrence Avenue, less than a mile from the Eckersall home. But Eckie didn't report right away; he was still hoping to join Amos Alonzo Stagg's football staff as an assistant coach, and pay-for-play status would disqualify him. After the University of Chicago snubbed him, Eckersall joined the Colts in mid-June as starting right fielder.[6]

Eckersall was now irrevocably a professional athlete. When news of the signing leaked, a Wisconsin newspaper chided Eckie as a hypocrite: "When Eckersall left school he . . . extolled the merits of amateurism and announced his virtuous intention to keep away from professionalism. Manifestly the microbe has begun to get in its work on the young man, and he has succumbed to its conquering power. Perhaps its [*sic*] destiny!"[7]

Eckie's new boss, Anson, is considered by historians to be largely responsible for Major League Baseball's "color line" that lasted from the 1880s until 1947. But in baseball's lower levels, Anson needed to put fans in the seats, so his Colts regularly played all-Black teams.

That's how Eckersall's semipro debut, on June 16, 1907, came against the Chicago Leland Giants, led by player-manager Rube Foster. With the Colts down 2–0, Eckie walked, stole a base, and scored a run to cut the deficit to 2–1. Later, Eckersall doubled and scored as part of a five-run rally in a 6–2 Colts win.[8]

Competing in the Chicago Baseball League of semipro teams, the Colts finished the season around .500. In the documented games that Eckersall played in 1907, the Colts won sixteen, lost twelve, and tied once. Eckersall played better baseball for Anson than he ever had for the Maroons. He had twenty-nine hits and scored twenty-eight runs in those twenty-nine games.

The Colts usually played two to three games a week, so Eckie's time at Paw Paw Lake was limited, but he still got up to Michigan a couple of times that summer. While there, he improbably became a real-life hero for the second time.

On July 10 a young couple was paddling a rowboat when the man had a medical episode, likely a seizure. He fell out of the boat and sank, as his girlfriend screamed. Eckie swam out and rescued the victim, towing him back to shore, where doctors revived him. This dramatic rescue showed that even if Eckersall were no Frank Merriwell in terms of morality, he was still capable of public, and very literal, heroics.[9]

—

Anson's Colts wrapped up their season in September, and Eckersall's mind turned toward football. The problem, as Eckersall later said: "Professional football was virtually unknown in Chicago." By 1907 a few high-level pro teams like the Massillon Tigers competed in Ohio. But the "Sunday game" wouldn't really emerge for another eight to ten years, wouldn't become truly organized until the founding of the NFL in 1920, and wouldn't capture the public's imagination for decades.[10]

But Eckersall still had the urge to play. His duties at the *Chicago Tribune* would prevent him from playing in the Ohio League, so he organized, coached, and quarterbacked a semipro team that would play in the middleweight division of the Chicago Football League. This "prairie football" league included a mix of semipro and strictly amateur teams. While lesser teams played in public parks, good teams played at stadiums with grandstands; Eckie's team would use Anson's Park.

Other prairie teams went by the names of their neighborhoods or sponsoring athletic clubs: the Armour Squares, the Pullmans, the Hurons, the Calumets. Eckie's team was unique in adopting the name of its star. They were known simply as the Eckersalls.

Eckie was the only big name in the Chicago Football League, so as a point of pride, his competitors aimed to neutralize the league's only star. For the most part, this strategy worked—Eckie settled for the role of field general, reading defenses, calling plays, and distributing the ball.

The Eckersalls started 1907 with three straight shutout wins. Eckersall didn't score any touchdowns but kicked three extra points and seven field goals over these first three games.[11]

Eckie missed the team's next three games when his *Tribune* commitments took him out of town. The Eckersall-less Eckersalls kept rolling, shutting out those three opponents. After returning to the lineup, Eckie led the team to two more shutout wins.[12]

On Thanksgiving Day, the Eckersalls played the All-Suburbans. In the first half, an All-Suburban halfback recovered an Eckersalls' fumble at his own 10-yard line and dashed into the open field. Showing flashes of his old-time speed, Eckie was able to stop him, but not before the latter had returned the ball 95 yards. Another All-Suburban player punched the ball in on the next play, the first points surrendered by the Eckersalls all season.

Toward the end of the first half, an Eckersalls end ran 40 yards for a touchdown, but the left tackle missed the extra point. No explanation was given on why Eckersall, who had previously done most of the team's place-kicking, didn't kick this one. The All-Suburbans clung to their 6–5 lead for most of the game, and Eckie seemed headed for his first loss as a pro. But late in the second half, an Eckersalls halfback broke through the line for a 70-yard touchdown. Eckie added the extra point for a narrow 11–6 victory.[13]

The Eckersalls advanced to the league's semifinals, against the Thistles. Eckersall made a touchdown-saving tackle at the 5-yard line and drop-kicked a 40-yard field goal in a 6–0 win. This gave the Eckersalls a berth in the championship game against the Mohawks at West Side Park, home of the Chicago Cubs.[14]

Eckersall predicted a blowout victory but didn't factor in the possibility of bad weather. The *Chicago Tribune*'s post-game recap started with a one-word paragraph: "Mud." That summed up the whole contest, played under horrible conditions. Eckie tried to drop-kick field goals three times, but each attempt was blocked. The four thousand fans—a great crowd for a prairie football game, lured by the chance to see Eckie one more time—went home disappointed at the 0–0 tie.[15]

The Chicago Football League scheduled a rematch for December 15. But previous opponents of both teams filed protests, claiming that the other had used players over the middleweight limit of 155 pounds. When neither team responded to the allegations, the league declared both teams ineligible for the championship.[16]

The Mohawks disbanded for the season, but Eckersall decided to step up in weight class and challenge the First Regiment Athletic Association, undefeated in the heavyweight division. A few days before the game, Eckersall announced that this appearance would be his last as a player.[17]

The game, back home at Anson's Park, was an even fight most of the way. The First Regiment outweighed the Eckersalls by fifteen pounds per man and used that weight in the first half by pounding the ball up the middle. But the Eckersalls' defense stiffened whenever their opponents approached the 20-yard line. Early in the second half, the First Regiment worked the ball into Eckersalls' territory again but turned the ball over on downs.

Then Eckie, who hadn't gotten free for a run all afternoon, changed his strategy to a pass-heavy attack. He completed three straight to his ends for 35, 20, and 35 yards. The last pass was good for a touchdown.

A First Regiment guard was offsides on the touchdown play, and his captain incorrectly believed the penalty made the play "dead." Penalty yardage should be awarded, the captain argued, and then the teams should line up for another play.

Eckie, already working part-time as a game official, insisted that the ball remained "live," and that he could decline the penalty and accept the touchdown. The officials ruled in Eckie's favor. In protest, the First Regiment walked off the field. The Eckersalls won the game, and the heavyweight championship, 6–0.[18]

The Eckersalls went 11-0-1 in 1907 while outscoring opponents 203–6. Eckersall didn't score any touchdowns, although he did pass for one against the First Regiment. Between his field goals and extra points, Eckie had also kicked for 44 points.

—

In the spring of 1908, Eckersall rejoined Anson's Colts. Before the season started, Anson announced that he would play part-time. At first, this possibility seemed unlikely. Anson turned fifty-six at the start of the season and hadn't played regularly since 1897. True to his word, though, Anson came off the bench in the ninth inning of the team's first game and hit a single, then was replaced by a pinch runner in a 14–3 win.[19]

From surviving accounts, it appears that Anson didn't play again for six weeks. When he returned to the field, he hit another single. Then Eckersall, as Anson's pinch runner, came around to score in the Colts' 13–5 victory.[20]

26. Walter Eckersall puts the ball in play for Anson's Colts in 1908. SDN-054075, *Chicago Daily News* collection, Chicago History Museum.

The Colts started the year with seven straight wins, and Eckersall scored nine runs on eight hits during that streak. By the end of May, the Colts had a 9-2 record and looked like a real contender in the Chicago Baseball League.

Then labor strife arrived, when five of Anson's best players demanded salary guarantees. This violated semipro norms; splitting gate receipts was the commonly accepted practice and marked the biggest difference between semipro baseball and the Minors. Anson promptly cut all five and had to rebuild his team. Anson himself played a larger role, starting nineteen of the team's final twenty-four games.[21]

The Colts finished the season with a documented record of 24-17-1. Eckersall improved a bit from 1907. In thirty-eight games with surviving box scores, Eckie had forty-one hits and scored twenty-nine runs.

—

Although professional track and field didn't exist in the early twentieth century, Eckersall tested his speed a couple times. At a special competition for semipro baseball players in July 1907, Eckie raced a 100-yard dash, a 30-yard sprint to first base, and a dash around all four bases. Competitors would run in baseball spikes instead of track shoes.

Though he hadn't sprinted regularly for more than four years, Eckersall was a heavy favorite at the meet, at Logan Square Park on Chicago's near Northwest Side. In the 100, Eckie was passed in the final 10 yards by another speedster, Johnny Malloy of the Logan Squares. Malloy also won the dash around the bases. Eckie fared better in the sprint to first base, tying Malloy, then winning a runoff by one-fifth of a second. This wasn't quite the performance expected of a track legend like Eckersall, but at least he had won one of his three events.[22]

The following year, Eckie couldn't even manage that. "Walter Eckersall of the Ansons, former University of Chicago football hero and a premier sprinter at Hyde Park high school some years ago, was the disappointment of the meet," the *Chicago Inter Ocean* remarked. "It was apparent his stamina was gone."[23]

Eckersall didn't make the finals in any of his events. Though only in his midtwenties, he looked old and slow.

Eckie never raced competitively again. He had peaked at the Illinois high school state championships of 1903 and had fallen far behind over the next five years.

—

For the 1908 football season, the core of the semipro "Eckersalls" stayed together, without its namesake. Playing at Anson's Park and adopting the "Anson's Colts" name, Eckie's former team won another Chicago Football League title.[24]

Eckie had been stretched thin in 1907, playing semipro football while sportswriting and officiating. By 1908 he had quit playing football but started coaching at St. Viator College, a Catholic school in Bourbonnais, Illinois, about fifty miles south of Woodlawn.[25]

Landing a "name" coach like Eckersall was big news at the all-male school, which only had about 250 students. The school's monthly magazine captured some of the hype:

> The increased speed which the football squad daily acquires, the intricate plays which they are constantly mastering, the "never say die spirit" which is always in evidence, all these things and others which we need not mention indicate that the men at the helm know their business and know it well. Walter H. Eckersall . . . is a man whose personality will appeal to every gentleman, whose conduct on the football and other athletic fields interested lovers of fair play, whose knowledge of the game ably fits him for the position of coach of any squad. . . . Eckersall has aroused the spirit of his men and instilled in them a confidence of the same species that landed him the position of All American quarter back.[26]

St. Viator went 5-4 with Eckersall at the helm in 1908, a record boosted by wins over two high schools and two athletic clubs. Against big-time competition, Eckie's team got crushed: 63–0 against Marquette, and 46–0 against Notre Dame. St. Viator even lost a game to a high school.[27]

As a player, Eckersall had been passionate and intense, extremely involved in all aspects of the game. But as a coach, he was unusually hands-off. Unlike Stagg or Fielding Yost, so indelibly linked to their teams, Eckie's name rarely appeared in print in association with St. Viator.[28]

Eckersall seemed more invested in his alma mater than in the team he was getting paid to coach. One afternoon in October, Eckie and a handful of former teammates showed up at Marshall Field and challenged Chicago's current varsity to a scrimmage. Eckie rushed for three touchdowns against a Chicago team that would go undefeated and win the conference title, but he had failed to appear that day where he belonged, on St. Viator's practice field.[29]

Eckersall not only missed many St. Viator practices but also skipped several games due to his sportswriting commitments. Big-time coaches would do this once or twice during a season: skip a minor game to go scout a major opponent. But there's no such thing as a minor opponent when high schools are beating your team.

Eckie simply didn't seem to care very much about St. Viator football. Coaching clearly took a back seat to sportswriting and officiating. Perhaps Stagg had been right all along in not recommending the football genius for a coaching job.

—

St. Viator closed its season on Thanksgiving Day with a 28–5 win over Chicago's St. Ignatius College (today's Loyola University of Chicago). Eckie again skipped the game, not to write about football but to play it. He had accepted an expenses-paid trip to play in Minneapolis against the Deans, a semipro team featuring Bobby Marshall.[30]

Eckie borrowed a handful of players from Anson's Colts, along with some former college players. But the Deans had one clear advantage: teamwork. The Deans had practiced together all season and had played three games, all wins.

The game quickly became a battle between the two stars. In the first half, Marshall kicked a 35-yard field goal to put the Deans ahead, 4–0. Throughout the game, Eckersall passed the ball well but failed to gain much ground running on a slippery field. Marshall's punting consistently pinned the Chicagoans deep, and the Eckersalls' one serious threat at a touchdown was thwarted when a Deans halfback batted down an Eckersall pass.

Late in the second half, the Eckersalls caught a break by recovering a fumble in Deans' territory. From there, Eckie tried a field goal. The kick was blocked, but Eckersall fell on the ball, resulting in an Eckersalls first down instead of a turnover under the rules of the day. Eckie tried another field goal, was blocked again, and recovered again. Undaunted, Eckersall kicked a third time. This time the drop-kick was perfect, and the game ended in a 4–4 tie.[31]

The Minneapolis game was supposed to be a one-time deal, but Eckersall received another challenge from Eddie Cochems, coach of St. Louis University. The New Year's Day game between the Eckersalls and a team of All-Stars would be played indoors at the brand-new St. Louis Coliseum. A crowd of five thousand showed up, and Eckersall netted $300, his biggest payday as a professional.

Cochems's All-Stars included Rube Waddell, the eccentric Hall of Fame pitcher for the American League's St. Louis Browns who had played some sandlot football. Eckersall later recalled:

> Apparently Waddell had been instructed to tackle and rough me whenever he had the chance. Whether I ran with the ball, kicked, or passed, Waddell would make it his business to tackle and throw me. His tactics got on my nerves and I decided that the football field was no place for Waddell. I called my players together and told them what Waddell was doing. We abandoned for a few minutes any effort to gain ground, and made him the target of our rushes. He finally was compelled to leave the game because of the battering he received.[32]

Eckersall drop-kicked a field goal on his team's opening drive, then followed up with two more drop-kicks. In the second half, the All-Stars kicked a 30-yard field goal. St. Louis never threatened again, and the Eckersalls won 12–4.[33]

This game marked two milestones. First, it was the only time Eckersall ever wrote a news story about a game he played. (He modestly buried his own role, stating in the fourth paragraph of a five-paragraph story: "Chicago's points were scored by Eckersall's three drop kicks in the first half.") Second, this was the last time Eckie ever suited up as a football player.

"The rewards of the professional game were small," Eckersall recalled in the 1920s. "My total return for about half a dozen games was less than $1,000. There is considerable difference between this figure and the ones given as the profits of the professional players of today, but it must be remembered that at the time football was still in its infancy as far as the general public was concerned."[34]

In eleven games with Eckie in the lineup, the Eckersalls had won nine times, lost none, and tied twice. Eckie scored 60 points on twelve field goals and twelve extra points, and he also passed for a touchdown. Perhaps all that was missing from Eckersall's semipro resume was, unusually considering his college record, a touchdown of his own. Still, his undefeated run as a professional served as a nice coda to Eckie's stellar football career.

—

As the spring of 1909 neared, Eckersall got ready for a third season with Anson's Colts. He was on the preseason roster and was suggested as likely team captain. Yet, sometime in February, Eckersall switched allegiances, leaving the Colts for a semipro team in the west suburban town of River Forest, twenty miles from the Eckersalls' Woodlawn home.[35]

The River Forests were billed as an "All Collegian" team, but none had been college baseball stars. Besides Eckersall, the biggest name was pitcher Doc Hillebrand who, like Eckersall, was better known for football than baseball, as a two-time All-American tackle at Princeton. Some players had Minor League Baseball experience, and one would briefly make the Majors. Mostly, though, the team was a bunch of guys like Walter Eckersall, fringe players hoping to impress some scout enough to earn a contract offer.[36]

Early in the season, Eckie appeared ready to make that leap. He started the year with an eleven-game hitting streak, scoring seven runs during that stretch. But the River Forests struggled as a team, going 3-7-1 in those games.

As summer progressed the River Forests continued to slump, and so did Eckersall's bat. Eckie went hitless in ten of his final twenty-two games. For the season, his batting average hovered just above .200. Such statistics simply didn't garner Minor League Baseball offers.

The River Forests finished 1909 with a documented record of 16-20-1. The true class of the Chicago Baseball League was Foster's Leland Giants, who went 31-9 in the league, seven games ahead of second place. Of course, the Leland Giants were a Major League–caliber team, prevented from competing with baseball's best through no fault of their own. The blame for Major League Baseball's color line rests, squarely and ironically, with managers such as Anson, whose team finished 1909 far down the standings to a superior all-Black team.[37]

In the spring of 1910, Eckersall joined the Red Sox, which played at the former Anson's Park after financial troubles cost Cap his team and his stadium. In the season opener, Eckie hit a double in a one-run loss. A few days later, he went hitless in another one-run loss. Then, Eckersall hung up his bat and glove for good. Ten years after he burst onto the Chicago sports scene as a Hyde Park freshman, Walter Eckersall had transitioned from "athlete" to "retired athlete."[38]

Not coincidentally, 1910 marked another transition for Eckie. He went from part-time football expert for the *Chicago Tribune* to full-time sportswriter, paving the path for a productive and influential sports journalism career.

15

Sports and the World's Greatest Newspaper

In 1907 the *Chicago Tribune*, just ten years younger than the city itself, celebrated its diamond anniversary.

"THE TRIBUNE is 60 years old today," said one editorial. "From a small sheet in an obscure western town it has grown to be the chief newspaper in a great metropolis and to deserve the title 'the world's greatest newspaper.'"[1]

Whether or not the *Tribune* had earned that moniker, the paper grew and prospered along with its city. In the early years, circulation hovered between one thousand and two thousand as editors tried to navigate a neutral political ground between Democrats and Whigs, and between the antislavery and "states' rights" factions.

Two key events launched the *Tribune* toward sustained success: the birth of the Republican party and the arrival of Joseph Medill. When the party was formed in 1854 by opponents of slavery, the thirty-one-year-old Medill became a major organizer in Cleveland. In 1855 Medill moved to Chicago and purchased part-interest in the *Tribune*. He swayed his partners over to his political views, and by the end of the year, the paper declared: "Believing that the spread of Liberty and not of Bondage, is the saving principle of the Republic, the Tribune has enlisted into the ranks of the National Republicans, not for a campaign, but during the war. . . . [The *Tribune* believes that] slavery or involuntary servitude is inconsistent with all principles, civil or religious."[2]

Under Medill, the *Tribune* supported both the Republicans and their Illinois standard-bearer, Abraham Lincoln. The paper played a large role in securing Lincoln's bid for U.S. Senate in 1858; in supporting Lincoln's successful presidential campaigns of 1860 and 1864; and in garnering support for the Union cause during the Civil War. The *Tribune* helped Lincoln succeed, and the paper's connections to Lincoln and the Republicans, in turn, helped the *Tribune* succeed.

Medill served long stints as managing editor and editor in chief and eventually became majority owner. (He also served as Chicago mayor for two years, right after the Great Chicago Fire of 1871.) Under Medill's stewardship, *Tribune* circulation grew dramatically: from 1,400 in 1855, to 4,000 in 1857, to 24,000 in 1860. Weekday circulation exceeded 40,000 for the entire Civil War, then continued to climb, nearing 100,000 by the end of the century.[3]

The *Tribune* produced a steady diet of what its editors thought readers needed to know: Business news. Political news. War news. News on health emergencies and fire hazards. News on engineering innovations that raised the city out of the mud and provided safe drinking water. News on the constant building and rebuilding that defined the energetic young city.

Sports coverage was an afterthought. Shortly after its founding, the *Tribune* covered a half-mile novelty race between a white man on a horse, a Black man, and a Native American. (The Black man, a barber named Louis Ishbell, won because the horse had trouble making a U-turn.) By 1855 the *Tribune* began covering harness racing. In 1858 the paper's first baseball story noted that a team from suburban Downers Grove had beaten Chicago's Union Base Ball Club, but it failed to list a score or any player names. By 1863 the paper published wire stories on out-of-town boxing matches, even as editorial writers spoke out strongly against the sport.[4]

One 1867 *Tribune* editorial highlighted the rough crowd that traveled from Chicago to Indiana to witness a big fight, beginning with a staggering subject of more than three hundred words:

One hundred and five gamblers, faro-dealers and keepers of gambling hells, one Justice of the Peace, all the pimps who could raise five dollars for their fare thither, two Chicago Aldermen, two hundred and nineteen brutal bullies who hang about the saloons and live by what they can pick up in a robbery here, a garroting there, and a plug muss yonder, one Dept. Superintendent of Chicago Police, one man known to be a murderer, two Captains of Police, any quantity of confidence men, three Sergeants of Police, sixteen professional garroters, four detectives of the police force, forty men recently out of jail, ten or a dozen Board of Trade men of questionable antecedents, forty-one of the worst of the Chicago hackmen, eleven Chicago lawyers, two hundred and twenty keepers of low doggeries, nine Chicago physicians, eighty bawdy-house keepers, twenty members of the Chicago press who went to report, twelve suspected forgers, one Master in Chancery, one ex-clergyman who is up to any crime, twelve hotel keepers, fifty-two burglars, six peddlers of nuts, apples, flash papers and obscene books, forty men about town—these, with about five hundred citizens of all occupations, men of supposed but doubtful decency, mixed in with a thousand more or less of the most degraded specimens of humanity of which the worst places in a large city can boast—the professional thieves, loafers, rummies, cut-throats—the riff-raff and scum of moral cess-pools in which populous places abound—the beetle-browed, sullen-visaged ruffians, the flashily-dressed pickpockets, the nasty and revolting young men with wicked and disgusting visages, who have prematurely given themselves up to a life of vice and infamy—all armed, all inflamed and maddened by liquor—all seeking the gratification of their greed in the expected winning of bets, and all lashed up to a pitch of fury little short of demonical by the spectacle of barbarism and blood—these made up the disreputable crowd that went out of Chicago on Wednesday to witness the long-talked-of prize-fight.[5]

Preachiness aside, sporting items were rare for practical reasons: There simply weren't many competitions in town. In a brief end-of-year sports roundup in 1865, the paper admitted, "As yet Chicago is rather too much in the development stage to have much time for sport."[6]

With so little sporting news to cover, the *Tribune* didn't bother.

Even in the East, where the sports scene was more mature, there was no such thing as a "sports page" yet. Event coverage was sporadic and seemingly random. Sports stories were written as spot news items by city desk reporters, pulled off police or political beats to cover competitions that the reporters themselves didn't really understand.[7]

For the *Tribune*, that changed once pro baseball came to town in 1870.

—

Professional baseball spread rapidly after the end of the Civil War, as community-based amateur teams began adding paid ringers. An uneven playing field followed; so did gambling and fraud. The *Tribune* noted this trend when the Washington Nationals blew out the amateur Chicago Excelsiors, 49–4, in 1867. Days before this game, the Nationals lost to an amateur team from Rockford, Illinois, in what the paper thought was a set-up job.

"It was a regular confidence game, familiar to every attendant upon races," railed one *Tribune* editorial. "It was an operation intended to induce the sporting men of Chicago to venture their money. They did so and the Nationals have pocketed it. It is estimated that $20,000 changed hands. . . . It is painful, however, to see this noble exercise, thus abused and prostituted, a healthful game perverted into a gambling operation, as demoralizing as racing or cockfighting or tiger fighting. That which was intended for the benefit of the body, is turned into something which is to corrupt the soul."[8]

In the *Tribune's* view, professional sports, and the gambling that went hand in hand, destroyed wholesome fair play. But all was forgiven, or at least forgotten, three years later when Chicago got its own pro baseball team, the White Stockings. The team's first game, a 47–1 win over the St. Louis Unions in April 1870, dominated sports news, which was allotted three-quarters of a column (out of ten columns per page) on the *Tribune*'s fourth, and last, page.[9]

Pro baseball quickly became a regular part of the *Tribune*'s sports coverage. Later in 1870, recaps of White Stockings games took up more than two full columns, and the *Tribune* also shared dispatches about other cities' pro teams. But sporting news still competed for space on the paper's back page with cultural news, weather reports, and classified ads.[10]

The *Tribune*'s coverage of the White Stockings, a team that survives today as the Chicago Cubs, grew each year. The paper reported on the organization of the National League in 1876, with the White Stockings as a charter member, and followed as the team won six league championships behind player-managers Albert Spalding and Cap Anson. When the White Stockings drew forty thousand fans for a four-game series with the New York Giants in 1888, the *Tribune* declared that "Chicago is a city of baseball maniacs."[11]

As the size of the paper expanded—to twelve or sixteen pages for the daily edition, and double that on Sundays—sports coverage also grew. By 1888 sports would take up most of one page in the daily edition, and just more than a page on Sundays. Sports also moved off the back page and into the heart of the paper.

By this point, more than half of the *Tribune*'s sports coverage was dedicated to horse racing, which grew in popularity after 1884 when the Washington Park Race Track opened in Woodlawn. That year, Washington Park started hosting the one-and-a-half-mile American Derby thoroughbred race, which garnered three and a half columns of *Tribune* coverage. This expanded to almost a full page by 1886, and to two pages by 1889. In 1890 Derby coverage moved onto the paper's front page.[12]

The *Tribune* faced a moral dilemma. The public wanted more sports news, and the editors were willing to oblige. A growing number of readers were no longer simply sports fans, however; they were gamblers and bookies seeking information. The *Tribune* benefited from newspaper sales to these "sporting men," but moralistic editors wanted to rein in vice.

"[Bookmakers] are worse even than thieves or highwaymen. They give their victim no chance," stated one 1894 *Tribune* editorial. "[T]he Washington Park club throws around itself a cloak of respectability and even of fashion, while in reality it is a kindergarten where many a young man takes his first lesson in gambling. They get their education from the bookmakers and when they have completed their curriculum in pools at the race tracks they are graduated into the gambling-house."[13]

Ultimately, the sporting men won out. By 1897 the *Tribune* billed itself as *the* source for information on the sports world, as seen in one *Tribune* advertisement that ran for several years: "For Reliable Sporting News Read THE TRIBUNE."[14]

—

Increasingly, that sporting news included football.

When intercollegiate football emerged on the East Coast in the 1870s, the *Tribune* ignored it. But when a group of youths on the Near South Side formed the "Chicago Football Club" in 1875, the *Tribune* latched on with interest.

The *Tribune*'s stories carry little description of actual play, focusing instead on roughness: "Several heels were unceremoniously tramped upon and blisters raised; portions of the cuticle were removed from the hands and faces of more than one contestant; shirts, shoes, and clothing bore incontestable evidences of many a run and scuffle for the ball; but it was rare sport, so they all said, and they seemed to know, for they came away with glowing countenances and remarkably good appetites."[15]

In May 1879 Chicago hosted the first major-college football game in the Midwest between University of Michigan and Racine College. The *Tribune*'s game story was light on the details but noted what voyeuristic readers wanted to hear: "No bones were broken, but Torbert was stretched on the turf once. A bucket of water, however, revived him."[16]

By 1885 the *Tribune* picked up a four-hundred-word item off the press wires on Princeton's upset win over Yale for the college championship. In 1886 the *Tribune* ran brief items on Yale victories over Penn, Harvard, and Princeton. By 1889 the *Tribune* started covering local high school football.[17]

Yet, after the Chicago Football Club disbanded in 1879, the city lacked a true home team for news coverage. Northwestern didn't consistently field teams until 1888; even then, most games were against high schools or YMCAs, and were ignored by the press. Any newspaper coverage focused on high school games or East Coast college games, at least until the pivotal year of 1892.

That's when the University of Chicago started playing football under coach Amos Alonzo Stagg. That's also when the Chicago Athletic Association started its own team of former college players. The CAA's star was Pudge Heffelfinger, a former teammate of Stagg at Yale. The *Tribune* followed along as CAA beat Northwestern, got crushed by Harvard, and lost close games to Penn and Princeton.[18]

The CAA closed its season with a Thanksgiving Day home game against the Boston Athletic Association. Appealing to civic pride, the *Tribune* crowed, "The game will unquestionably be the best football game ever played west of New York City." Boston beat the CAA (without Heffelfinger, who had defected to a Pittsburgh team for $500, becoming the first known professional football player) in front of nearly five thousand fans, by a score of 18–12. The *Tribune* gave this game front-page coverage, with eight stories and twenty illustrations. Football had finally arrived in Chicago, and at the *Chicago Tribune*.[19]

The CAA played for a few more seasons. Gradually, though, Stagg's Maroons and the other teams in the newborn Western Conference took over the sports pages.

By 1900 the *Tribune*'s Sunday sports section had grown to four full pages during football season. Games involving Chicago or Northwestern received prime position on the first page of sports or, for a really big game, the front page of the paper itself. Other Big Nine games might take up three-quarters of a column's worth of space. Wire stories on East Coast games were usually brief, only a couple of paragraphs.[20]

Reflecting nationwide trends, the *Tribune*'s sports coverage had improved in both depth and breadth since the 1870s. But in many ways, the sports pages were still archaic. Bylines were rare. Text was arranged "tombstone" style, in seven blocky columns. Large headlines were followed by four or five descriptive "subheads" or "decks." Any pictures were posed portraits of well-known players. Cartoons and diagrams occasionally broke up the visual monotony.

Design improved in the early 1900s, most notably in the form of action photos. Content-wise, the football also improved, as the *Tribune* covered some great college teams: Fielding Yost's "Point-a-Minute" Michigan teams, Walter Eckersall's championship team at Chicago, and undefeated teams at Wisconsin in 1901 and Minnesota in 1903.

Just as Eckersall was being expelled from the University of Chicago, the paper's managing editor and general manager, James Keeley, sought to make further improvements to *Tribune* sports. So, Eckersall found himself in the right place at the right time.

—

Keeley's editorship straddled those of Joseph Medill, who died in 1899, and Medill's grandson Robert R. McCormick, who became editor and publisher in 1914. Largely forgotten amid these towering figures, Keeley was also a pioneer, an ace reporter and editor who ushered the paper into the twentieth century. Keeley presided over perhaps the greatest scoop in *Tribune* history when he published an "Extra" on the U.S. victory at the Battle of Manila Bay during the Spanish-American War. Once the presses were rolling, Keeley called the White House to tell President William McKinley, who hadn't received the news yet.[21]

Though Keeley focused on the *Tribune*'s news-gathering apparatus, he also had a strong belief in the "personal service" aspect of a metropolitan newspaper. Keeley launched a "How to Keep Well" column, with advice from physicians; a "Friend of the People" column, where readers could lodge civic complaints about broken streetlights or uncollected garbage; and "The Good Fellow," a seasonal effort to provide Christmas baskets to the needy, which led to the creation of Chicago Tribune Charities. In 1903 Keeley hired political cartoonist John T. McCutcheon. Later, he hired Burton Rascoe as drama critic.

In Keeley's philosophy, it was no longer enough for a paper to tell readers what they needed to know. Now, a paper had to tell readers what they wanted to know—even if they didn't know exactly what they wanted yet.

After improving other sections of the paper, Keeley turned to sports. In 1904 he hired Hugh Keough, whose "In the Wake of the News" became the first regular sports column in the United States. In 1907 he hired cartoonist Clare Briggs, whose "Days of Real Sport" depicted regular city children at play. He increasingly gave bylines to sportswriters and brought in new talent, notably hiring Ring Lardner in 1909; Lardner would take over "In the Wake of the News" in 1912.[22]

With the growing popularity of football, Keeley thought the newspaper could use a football expert. Conveniently, Eckersall was just wrapping up his first season of semipro baseball and hadn't landed one of the college coaching jobs he coveted. Keeley reached out, and his offer steered Eckersall to a lifelong career.

16

The Scribe

Before 1907, Walter Eckersall showed no inclinations toward a writing career. In his first quarter of college, he was the lowest-ranked student in his English composition class. He never contributed to the University of Chicago's campus newspaper, the *Daily Maroon*. In December 1905 he wrote one article for the *Chicago Tribune*, a look back at the previous year in college athletics. And that was all, the full extent of Eckersall's undergraduate portfolio.[1]

After his Chicago expulsion, Eckersall handwrote a pleading letter to Walter Camp, asking for help in finding football-related work: "I am very desirous of still taking some sort of an active part in the game of football. I would consider it a personal favor if you would give me your consideration."[2]

If Camp answered, that reply has been lost. But shortly after Eckie's letter, Camp farmed out a piece of freelance work to his recent All-American: a chapter about quarterback play for Camp's upcoming book, *How to Play Foot Ball*.[3]

Eckie threw himself into the job, churning out a three-thousand-word essay. The chapter wasn't well written. Eckersall alternated between vague platitudes, like "A team should have the utmost confidence in its quarterback," and hyper-specific instructions, like "If the full-back is to make a straight buck on the right of center, the quarter should pivot on his left foot, quarter of the way round, and with his left hand *place* the ball in the pit of the stomach of the full-back, and vice versa if he bucks on the left side." Still, he now had a professional writing credit.[4]

Soon after Eckie turned in that assignment, *Chicago Tribune* editor James Keeley hired him as the paper's football expert. Eckersall's limited experience didn't matter. Journalism was a teachable skill, so a vibrant newsroom offered opportunities for on-the-job training. Best of all, from Keeley's perspective, Eckersall was a "name," and names helped sell newspapers.[5]

Eckie's first regular *Tribune* article, "Gridiron Gossip by Eckersall," appeared on September 15, 1907. Eckersall begins his professional writing career this way: "The day for football practice is at last on hand, and all the coaches will begin their arduous tasks of rounding out winning elevens. The athletes are arriving at their respective colleges from all points, preparatory to practice call. On Friday, the 20th, the big nine teams take their initial practice, while the small colleges already have had their preliminary work."[6]

Eckersall's 1,500-word story violated many emerging norms of newspaper journalism. The article lacks focus and organization. Perhaps worst of all, almost a quarter of Eckie's story consists of a rambling quote from a Theodore Roosevelt speech, dripping with machismo and praising the greatness of football.

The writer quickly improved, learning the "inverted pyramid" style in which a story begins with an information-packed introduction, or "lede." His status as a football legend allowed Eckie easy access to players and coaches for interviews. His knowledge of strategy and rules gave him valuable insights; by passing these on, he made his readers feel like "insiders," too. And his accounts of game action—initially covering only football but later expanding to any sport that could be played—are descriptive and insightful.

An early example of Eckie's improving writing style appears in his lede on October 27, 1907, after Carlisle upset the University of Pennsylvania: "Penn was beaten by a better team. That is the tale of the humiliating defeat of the Quakers at the hands of the Carlisle Indians before 25,000 spectators at Franklin field, Philadelphia, on Saturday."[7]

Eckersall had clearly been coached by seasoned writers and editors. And with a large percentage of his stories reported from the road, a "rewrite man" could sort the details into a coherent whole. Eckie's friend Ring Lardner once described a 1908 experience on the *Chicago Examiner*'s rewrite desk:

Shroudy was going to write the lead [*sic*], Mr. Cornell the detail, and Mr. Hall the notes. . . . It seemed kind of quaint to leave a hick like me alone in the office to take care of their copy and all the other sport copy that would come in, while the three experienced guys went on a junket to Milwaukee for the simple reason that they were wild-eyed fight fans. Shroudy's instructions said I would have to watch my step, because the stuff would arrive by wire a piece at a time; I would have to figure out whose stuff was whose and keep it all straightened out. . . . Not even a broadcaster could have got things more messed up. Lead [*sic*], detail and notes were all jumbled together.[8]

As a "name" writer, Eckersall never had to work rewrite and likely benefited from talented colleagues on the *Tribune*'s desk. At a distance of more than a hundred years, it's impossible to know how much of Eckersall's writing was his own and how much was rewritten. But after early growing pains, Eckersall's voice became consistent and clear, with crisp facts in his game stories and more nuanced musings in his columns. Eckie's fingerprints were all over his newspaper stories, even if all the actual words may not have been his.

—

Although Walter Eckersall wasn't the first athlete to become a sportswriter, he stands out because of his prowess in both areas. Before Eckie, most stars-turned-writers simply dabbled in journalism. Camp wrote a weekly column; his day job as a corporate executive kept him too busy for regular newspaper work. High-profile coaches such as Fielding Yost and, later, Knute Rockne and Bob Zuppke similarly wrote columns on a part-time basis, nothing that would interfere with their coaching duties.

A handful of working journalists in Eckersall's era were former athletes, such as *New York Herald Tribune* columnist Grantland Rice, who played football and baseball at Vanderbilt, and *Boston Globe* writer Tim Murnane, a Major League Baseball player in the 1870s and 1880s. No one was nearly as prominent an athlete as Eckersall. His closest peer would be Robert Maxwell, Eckie's onetime Maroon teammate who made third-team All-American

27. Walter Eckersall at his *Chicago Tribune* desk, early 1920s. *Chicago Tribune*/TCA.

after he transferred to Swarthmore. Maxwell would become sports editor of the *Philadelphia Public Ledger* and a widely syndicated columnist.

From 1907 through 1909, Eckersall was almost exclusively a football writer. In January 1910 everything changed. Now, "By Walter H. Eckersall" was a year-round byline, and his output nearly tripled. This shift came shortly after daughter Betty's birth. Eckersall's increased *Tribune* workload, his short-term commitment to local writing assignments, and his retirement from semipro sports indicate that he tried to change his lifestyle to support his family. And even though Eckie would quickly abandon that family, he still had to pay alimony. Eckersall's long and significant career as a broad-based sports journalist may have jump-started because raising a child, even in 1910, was expensive.

—

In Eckie's day, sports editors Harvey Woodruff, Frank Smith, and Don Maxwell drew top-notch writers to the *Tribune*. Many of these names are long forgotten, but they were locally and nationally prominent back then: Sy Sanborn, Westbrook Pegler, Hugh Fullerton, Irving Vaughan, James Crusinberry. Two of Eckie's colleagues remain well known today: Lardner, who was a *Tribune* sportswriter on and off between 1909 and 1919, and Arch Ward, who joined the paper as a writer in 1925 and became sports editor in 1930.

Eckersall became the centerpiece of that sports staff. Over twenty-two-plus years on the *Tribune*, Eckie churned out more than 5,500 bylined articles, far outpacing his colleagues. Expanding beyond his original role as football specialist, he eventually covered just about everything. As the *Tribune* put it in a 1929 advertisement: "Walter Eckersall takes on a variety of assignments in half a hundred places."[9]

Football, boxing, and track would be Eckersall's main areas of focus, but he also covered swimming, bicycle racing, speed skating, and wrestling. He was the *Tribune*'s lead college baseball writer for three seasons. Among minor sports, he dabbled in motorcycle racing, rowing, fencing, polo, even ski jumping.

If people could compete in something, Walter Eckersall probably covered it.

Eckie had a reporter's nose for finding the best games, characters, and stories. In May 1911 Eckie joined a couple other *Tribune* reporters at an out-of-town auto race. Eckie knew next to nothing about auto racing; he only covered four such races throughout his career. He was only on location because he had covered a nearby boxing match the previous night.

But that day he witnessed history with the first running of the Indianapolis 500. Ray Harroun won the race, aided by a recent invention: the rearview mirror. Eckie's sense of amazement comes through as he tries to compare the relatively new sport of auto racing to sports that his readers would understand better:

> The race demonstrated that a little man—for Harroun weighs only 138 pounds—as a driver can have just as much success in these daredevil affairs as a man twice Harroun's strength. . . . He did not need a helper to look back to see which side of the track approaching cars were coming, for the thoughtful little driver had a mirror placed on his hood, and in this way he could see the cars coming from behind. He pumped his own oil and did everything else that other drivers had mechanicians do. . . .
>
> In baseball, football, basketball and other branches of sports, signals are used. . . . Harroun certainly had them today with his teammates who were in the pit. Every time Ray passed the pit some of the men would pick up a pair of pincers, a wrench, or some other article to let the driver know just what was doing and what he must do to stall off the attacks of the other pilots.[10]

Years later, Eckie stumbled upon another gem regarding hockey. He only occasionally wrote about the sport, covering just eighteen games in his career. But his friendship with a sports promoter garnered a huge scoop in 1926: Chicago would be receiving a National Hockey League franchise, which would become the Chicago Blackhawks.[11]

As a reporter, Eckie loved being close to the spotlight, covering big games, big stories, and big stars: a Big Ten football game with championship implications, a national AAU tournament, an Olympic trials in swimming or track. But he wrote about lesser events with equal passion, such as a track meet among Chicago bank employees; a Lutheran church–sponsored youth ice-skating tournament; a sparsely attended New Year's Day bicycle race over the icy streets of Chicago's South Side.[12]

When covering obscure sports and minor events, Eckie remained enthusiastic and informative. For example, from February 1911: "Playing with the dash and speed which has made him one of the best players in the country, Jim Mullins of the University club, yesterday defeated Edward Rogers of the Racquets and Tennis club of New York . . . for the western professional racquets championship. The match was featured by many stirring rallies, in which the ball zigzagged about the court in the most amazing manner. The players kept the ball low and hit hard, but the faster the going the better they seemed to like it."[13]

Never mind that few of Eckie's readers knew who Jim Mullins was or how to play racquets. Eckersall probably didn't know anything about Mullins or racquets until that morning, either. Yet, to Eckersall, the event he was covering on any given day was the most important to him and, by extension, to his readers.

As Don Maxwell, Eckie's sports editor for most of the 1920s, said, "He was just as eager to cover an unimportant wrestling match or a boresome track meet as he was to cover the Tunney-Dempsey fight in Soldiers' [*sic*] field."[14]

Eckie's colleagues occasionally poked fun at the way he embraced obscure events. In 1928 the *Tribune* published a mock dispatch of a horseshoe contest in a sleepy Northwest Side neighborhood: "Walter Eckersall, one of our young fellers trying to get ahead, whom we wish to encourage, respectfully submits an item to the effect that on July 4 William Gilbride beat William Phillips in a game of horseshoes at Portage Park, 21 to 19. It was refereed by Jack Lynch, and our correspondent deposes it was 'one of the best contested games ever witnessed in the history of Portage Park.'"[15]

—

Just as Eckersall covered a wide variety of sports, the types of stories he wrote were diverse: breaking news, opinion pieces, gossip columns, player profiles, general summaries of a week's events, previews of the following week's events, stories on emerging trends, nostalgic historical articles, stories about the intersection of sports with politics or the law.

Eckersall was at his best when writing about a game, a tournament, or a meet. Almost a quarter of his journalistic output consists of on-scene stories of an athletic event. He relished surprises and gleefully passed those on to his readers. For example, at the National AAU outdoor swimming championships of 1911, held at South Shore Country Club, Eckersall recorded how a sudden weather change affected athletes.

"As the men were preparing to swim to the mark large quantities of slag from the mills at South Chicago and Gary drifted into the course," Eckersall wrote. "Several of the swimmers were forced to withdraw from the competition because the slag cut their hands and feet in a manner which hindered their progress to such an extent that it was useless for them to continue. The first three men to finish the contest were so badly cut that they needed medical attention."[16]

Eckie would let a surprise speak for itself, rarely resorting to rhetorical tricks, which reflected his matter-of-fact writing style. See the first paragraph of his account of Notre Dame's football win over Army in 1924: "Using one of the most powerful running attacks seen in recent years, varied occasionally by delayed bucks into the line and an occasional forward pass, Notre Dame defeated the Army on the Polo ground here this afternoon, 13 to 7. It was the eleventh meeting of the two teams and today's victory gives Notre Dame eight victories. The Army has won twice while the struggle of 1922 resulted in a scoreless tie."[17]

Eckersall had churned out an information-packed lede, but it was dry and quickly forgotten. Not so the lede Rice wrote about the same game: "Outlined against a blue-gray October sky, the Four Horsemen rode again. In dramatic lore they are known as Famine, Pestilence, Destruction and Death. These are only aliases. Their real names are Stuhldreher, Miller, Crowley and Layden. They formed the crest of the South Bend cyclone before which another fighting Army football team was swept over the precipice at the Polo Grounds yesterday afternoon as 55,000 spectators peered down on the bewildering panorama spread on the green plain below."[18]

Rice's poetic lede is one of the most famous in sports journalism. But Eckersall succeeded in one area in which Rice fell short. While Rice dazzled with a lyrical quality, he fails to tell us that Notre Dame won. Eckersall, in contrast, informed his audience by getting right to the point of the story.

"I've always found that there is only one guiding principal [*sic*] in sports writing," a veteran Eckersall told younger *Tribune* writers. "Just tell 'em what happened."[19]

Unlike Rice or Lardner, Eckie never created enough punchy or poetic material to fill a "Walter Eckersall Reader." Yet, he was thorough, informative, and extremely diverse in both topic and format, and he had a front-row seat for some of the biggest moments of the Golden Age of Sports.

Eckersall was aware of his limitations. "I've thought it over many times," he told his colleague, *Bloomington (IL) Pantagraph* writer Fred Young, in the 1920s. "My chief regret nowadays is that I have such a poor command of the language. If I could do it over I would prepare myself better. Here I am supposedly an authority in sports and I doubt if I could secure a good grade in freshman college theme writing."[20]

—

Even though he put in nearly twenty-three years on the sports desk, the mechanics of writing never became easy for Eckersall.

"Writing was hard work for Eckie," said Eddie Jacquin, longtime sports editor of the *Champaign (IL) News-Gazette*, in 1930. "I remember journeying to the Western Union office in Philadelphia several years ago on that day when Grange ran through mud and snow to upset the four magicians of Penn. Tom Morrow of the *Illini* was with me. We had written our stories. But at 10 o'clock Ekie [*sic*] was still pounding away at his story."[21]

Eckersall sometimes struggled with accuracy. He misspelled names, and occasionally cited wrong years or misremembered sequences of events. When he covered a contest that he was also officiating, he might give only one or two examples of specific plays, with the rest of the story remaining fairly generic.

Tribune editor Keeley used to tell a story about a botched Eckersall detail, as Keeley biographer James Weber Linn later recalled:

> Eckersall wrote a story to the effect that "H.C. Lytton had sparred six rounds with [heavyweight champion Jack] Johnson in private, and the merchant had held his own." Now H.C. Lytton, owner of a State Street department store, was at the time some seventy years of age, and definitely fragile. His son George, however, was an amateur boxer of renown, and Eckersall of course referred to the son. Nevertheless the name appeared H.C. Lytton in the *Tribune*, and no sooner had Keeley seen it there than the editor of the sports department was summoned to Keeley's office. Pointing a stubby, capable forefinger at the headline he snapped:
>
> "Is that right?"
>
> "No, sir. It was George."
>
> "George, huh? If the man who wrote that story was drunk, fire him; and in any case, send H.C. a bill for one hundred dollars for the ad."[22]

This story is clearly spun to enhance the legend of Keeley as a hard-nosed editor. There's one major flaw: Eckersall did *not* write the H.C.-Lytton-as-boxer story. That article (which was not a recap, as Linn recalled, but rather a preview) carries no byline. This fact doesn't necessarily exclude Eckersall as author, but a close read shows that the author's voice doesn't even vaguely resemble Eckie's.

> Left and right swings, jabs and cross counters will be exchanged in what promises to be a great pugilistic "battle" this afternoon. There isn't to be any $1,000,000 purse or any big side bet, but one of the principals is to be none other than Jack Johnson, world's heavyweight champion. The match was arranged yesterday and Henry C. Lytton, clubman and State street merchant, will face the negro champion in an exhibition scheduled to go three rounds at a downtown gymnasium. Mr. Lytton,

> who for years has been considered some shucks as an amateur boxer, for long has been anxious to "mix it" in a little bout with Johnson.[23]

This clever, colorful introduction sounds nothing like an Eckie story. An Eckersall lede from the same week reads: "Jack Johnson, heavyweight champion, gave an interesting exhibition of boxing yesterday at O'Connell's gymnasium, when he boxed three fast rounds with his sparring partner, Walter Monahan, and two with Mickey Sheridan, an aspiring lightweight."[24]

There's no color, no cleverness, no "blue-gray October sky" in an Eckersall lede. Most likely, Keeley mixed up the details, years later, to make a point, and his most famous sportswriter ended up with some undeserved blame.

—

Though he may not have been a natural writer, the reporting side of the job came easily to Eckersall.

"The sports writer does not have to be a detective to get his stuff," Eckie told *Editor and Publisher* in 1927. "Ordinarily he forms many valuable friendships—ones which are continual sources of news to him."[25]

Eckersall's articles drip with familiarity. He's clearly close to his sources, in an era when such relationships were not only accepted but also encouraged. He frequently interviewed coaches he knew from his time as a player: Yost, Amos Alonzo Stagg, Minnesota's Henry Williams. Later, he befriended a new generation of coaches such as Illinois's Zuppke and Notre Dame's Rockne. As Eckersall's coverage expanded into other sports, he grew close to runners, boxers, swimmers, trap shooters, tennis players, and wrestlers, as well as promoters, gamblers, and bookies—anyone who could help tell the story.

Through it all, Eckie displayed the type of work ethic that typified his athletic career. As his editor, Don Maxwell, said:

> Walter Eckersall was the most energetic, hardest working fellow I ever knew. He never strolled into the office. He came rushing. And that was the way he continued day or night. Eckie was the first fellow to arrive at

> the ringside for a fight; the first official to report for duty at a football game; the first fellow back in the office after the game or the bout was over. Other writers might take their time, loaf a bit, fumble around before starting their pieces. Eckie tackled the job at hand. . . . Work was a fetish with him. Doing his job gave him more thrills than anything else. He didn't want a day off.[26]

Eckersall's output confirms Maxwell's statement. Yet even with this heavy workload, for most of his career, he pulled double duty. Beyond his writing, Eckersall traveled far and wide to work games as a football official.

17

The Official

On Thanksgiving Day 1906, just days after his last college football game, Walter Eckersall refereed a professional game between the Massillon Tigers and the Western All-Stars. During the game, a Massillon player piled on All-Stars quarterback Bunny Hare, a friend of Eckersall's from his playing days at Indiana. Instead of simply calling a foul, Eckie ran into the pile and punched the offending Massillon player. "The spectators crowded on to the field, cheering Eckersall and hissing the rowdy," read one news report.[1]

Today, an official who punched a player would be banned for life. Not so in the early 1900s. Instead, Eckersall's services were in great demand once he became an accredited game official in 1907.

—

Eckersall remembered his career as an official starting in October 1907, when Penn hosted the Carlisle Indian School. Nearly twenty years later, he recalled, "My first appearance as an official was almost by accident. In the fall of 1907 . . . [my editor] thought it would be a good thing for me to see the Pennsylvania-Indian game, to get a line on the Redskins. I went to Philadelphia, and about half an hour before the game started was asked to act as head linesman."[2]

Eckersall's memory of this game as his first professional officiating credit was faulty; he had refereed Indiana's win over DePauw three weeks earlier. But the Carlisle-Penn game made more of an impression, as the first of many Eckersall-officiated games to go down in football history. Carlisle was 6-0 and featured All-American end Al Exendine, with a skinny youngster named Jim Thorpe coming off the bench at halfback. Penn, which was 7-0, had four All-Americans. At this game, Carlisle coach Pop Warner unveiled his new "single-wing" offense, with an unbalanced line and one halfback shifted outside, and well behind, one of the ends. The formation puzzled Penn; Carlisle's effectiveness with the forward pass puzzled Penn even more. The Indians totaled more than 400 yards of offense in a 26–6 victory.[3]

For most of Eckersall's career, an officiating crew included four members: referee, umpire, field judge, and head linesman. The referee served as crew leader and was ultimately responsible for declaring whether a touchdown, field goal, or extra point was good. The umpire looked for penalties along the line of scrimmage and in the running game. The field judge watched for downfield possession, as well as ruling on punt returns, interference, and touchbacks. The head linesman marked distances in relation to yardage needed for a first down. Beyond their own spheres of influence, each official assisted the others, especially when another official was out of position to make an accurate call.

As a general rule, officials didn't work games involving their own colleges. Eckersall abided by this rule, with one exception. While he covered more than thirty games involving the Chicago Maroons as a reporter, the only one he officiated was a midweek game against a junior college during the war- and pandemic-shortened 1918 season.

As a former quarterback, Eckie gravitated toward the role of referee, the quarterback of an officiating crew. Eckersall was referee for more than 70 percent of the games that he officiated. He served as umpire, the second-most prominent crew member, almost 20 percent of the time.

The Penn-Carlisle game in 1907 and the Michigan-Penn game in 1910, which Eckie refereed and which ended in a 0–0 tie, were the highest-profile assignments of Eckersall's early officiating career. Overall, though, he only worked eleven college games in his first four seasons as an official. These weren't A-list games either; they involved Drake University, Beloit College, Lake Forest College, and Wabash College, as well as Notre Dame in the years before the Indiana school emerged as a national power. Even a former star like Eckersall had to pay his dues.

In 1911 Eckie's officiating career finally bloomed. He worked eleven games, traveling rapidly between the football field and the press box and from city to city, journeying as far as Houston. Ultimately, he would officiate at more than 230 football games, at all levels throughout the country.

—

Popularity could be fleeting for game officials. Fans of losing teams often felt the officials had cheated them out of victory. Aggrieved rooters would boo, threaten, and, in some cases, physically assault the officials who committed the perceived crimes.

Like any official, Eckersall received extensive verbal harassment. In 1911 Penn fans accused Eckersall of refusing to overrule a bad holding call that cost Penn a touchdown, and ultimately the game, in an 11–9 loss to Michigan. After a 1924 game between Illinois and Nebraska, the *Lincoln (NE) Star* ran a still photo that reportedly proved Eckersall had mistakenly awarded Illinois the game-winning touchdown ("the record . . . will stand regardless of the official's incorrect, if not unjust, ruling"). In 1928 fans of each team argued that Eckie flubbed the ending of a close Notre Dame–Army game, either cheating Army out of a down or granting Army an extra down, depending on which group of fans were asked.[4]

The greatest vitriol Eckie ever faced as an official came after the Michigan-Wisconsin game at Camp Randall Field in November 1923. In the second quarter, Michigan quarterback Tod Rockwell fielded a punt and was apparently tackled at midfield. Referee Eckersall was out of position for the call; the field judge, closer to the play, didn't think Rockwell was fully down. No whistle blew, so Rockwell sprang up and continued running for a touchdown, in a 6–3 Michigan victory that preserved a perfect season.[5]

Immediately after the game, angry Wisconsin fans rushed the field, trying to get a piece of Eckersall. While he hadn't made the ruling, Eckie was both the lead official and the best-known personality on the crew, so he drew the mob's anger.

Eckersall's newspaper colleagues in Wisconsin did nothing to calm tempers. "In Walter Eckersall, Michigan has a fine football team," wrote Bryn Griffiths of the *Madison (WI) Capital Times* the day after the game. "Eckersall's decision on the play, now the chief topic of discussion throughout the world will go down in gridiron history as the biggest hoax."[6]

Wisconsin players protected Eckersall, clearing a path through the angry fans to the officials' locker room. Still, Wisconsin's athletic director further stoked anti-Eckersall feelings, declaring: "Never again will Eckersall referee a game in which Wisconsin takes part." He wouldn't work another Badger game until 1929, his final season as an official.[7]

Eckie enjoyed a better reputation outside Madison. He was widely praised for his thorough knowledge of the rules, his fairness, and his control of the game.

"'Eckie' has been picked as one of the best football officials in the country," the *Detroit Free Press* declared in 1915. "That same darting speed which made him one of the greatest open field runners the game has ever known gets him on top of the plays and enables him to run off the game in a snappy manner."[8]

Similar praise poured out for Eckie throughout his career. In naming its All-America team for 1928, the *Los Angeles Evening Express* added All-American coaches and an All-American officiating crew. Twenty-two years after taking his last snap as a college quarterback, Eckersall was named the All-American referee.[9]

—

At roughly two-thirds of the games that he officiated, Eckersall pulled double duty by writing about the same games. While this arrangement is widely seen as a conflict of interest today, newspapers then had no problem with it. Since home schools paid travel, lodging, and meals for game officials, the arrangement kept a newspaper's expenses down.

Reporter-officials like Eckersall were essentially "double-dipping" by receiving both a newspaper salary and an officiating fee, $50 to $75 for a Big Ten game for most of Eckie's career. Other prominent reporters also worked as game officials, most notably Eckie's onetime Chicago teammate Robert Maxwell.

Eckersall officiated almost fifty Big Ten games during his career and an additional forty nonconference games involving Big Ten teams. If you include several Michigan games between 1907 and 1916, when Michigan had temporarily dropped out of the conference, more than half of the college games that Eckersall worked had a Big Ten connection.

Eckie also worked thirty Notre Dame games, more than any other individual team. The relationship started in 1908 and grew when Jesse Harper, Eckersall's backup on Chicago's championship team, was Notre Dame's coach between 1913 and 1917. Eckersall then became even more closely linked to Notre Dame under Harper's successor, Knute Rockne.

As a teenager growing up on the Northwest Side of Chicago, Rockne idolized the slightly older South Sider. Rockne, who claimed to have jumped the turnstiles at Marshall Field to see the Hyde Park–Brooklyn Poly Prep game in 1902, was spellbound by Eckersall's play: "Eckersall's sharp, staccato calling of signals; his keen, handsome face, and the smooth precision with which he drove and countered and drove again, handling his players with the rhythm of an orchestra leader, all this gave football a new meaning to me."

After Hyde Park's 105–0 victory, young Rockne lined up with a mob of other boys, trying to get close enough to meet Eckie. No dice.

"I had to go home without a handshake—yet, for the first time in a young and fairly crowded life, I went home with a hero," Rockne said.[10]

Rockne also claimed to have been in the stands for Chicago's 2–0 upset of Michigan in 1905, but he once again couldn't get close enough to meet Eckie. Later, when he was playing at Notre Dame, Rockne finally had the chance to meet his idol. As Rockne later recalled:

> Grasping his hand, I said, "I've been waiting years for this."
>
> "For what?" said Eckersall.
>
> "To shake your hand," I said, recounting how his brilliant performance for Hyde Park High had turned my mind seriously to football.
>
> "Stop, stop," said Eckersall in the middle of the recital, "or Notre Dame will be penalized five yards for speech making."[11]

With Rockne as coach, Eckersall worked an average of two Notre Dame games each season. Some historians later argued that Rockne tried to leverage friendships with favored officials like Eckie to gain competitive advantage. But there's a more logical explanation for Eckie's relationship with

Notre Dame: Much of Rockne's schedule was intersectional, and Eckersall loved a good matchup between teams from different regions.

—

The theme of intersectional competition runs throughout Eckersall's writing. Each year, he would discuss whether the Eastern or "Western" (encompassing the Midwest and Great Plains, but not the West Coast) brand of football seemed better that season.

Eckersall figured that the best way to compare regions was to travel. Starting with the Carlisle-Penn game in Philadelphia in 1907, he ventured frequently to big matchups in other regions: Arkansas versus LSU in 1910, Texas versus Texas A&M in 1911, Pitt versus West Virginia four times between 1917 and 1921, Georgia versus Georgia Tech in 1927. At most of these games, Eckie pulled double duty as a game official.

These games gave Eckersall a first-person view of football in different regions but didn't answer the question of which region was "better." Intersectional games were the best way to do so, and Eckersall loaded up on them.

This theory most explains why Eckersall officiated so many Notre Dame games. Notre Dame traveled widely, so Eckie followed along as Notre Dame played Army (a matchup that Eckie worked six times), Pittsburgh's Carnegie Tech (which he worked twice), Navy, Rutgers, Loyola of New Orleans, and USC. Eckie also worked intersectional games between Michigan and Penn five times and Ohio State–Princeton twice, and worked various intersectional one-offs like Rutgers-Nebraska, Detroit-Tulane, Gonzaga–West Virginia, Illinois-Penn, USC-Iowa, and Oregon-NYU.

Eckie already possessed a deep knowledge of football. With his increasing travels, that knowledge was growing broader as well. Over his career, he officiated games in twenty-one states, involving eighty-five different colleges.

"Mr. Eckersall will have officiated during 1915 in the east, middle west, and far west in contests between important teams," the *Chicago Tribune* wrote. "This close association with the football played in different sections of the country will give to his future writings on the gridiron game an intimate knowledge which could not be obtained in any other way. He also will have seen more varying football conditions than any other critic or official in the United States."[12]

All this coverage led the Tournament of Roses committee to invite Eckersall to the resumption of its annual football game in Pasadena, California. The game, now known as the Rose Bowl, was first held in 1902, when Michigan and Willie Heston drubbed Stanford 49–0. The game went on hiatus for fourteen years but resumed in 1916, with a matchup between Washington State and Brown.

Four days before kickoff, the committee sent an urgent telegram to Eckersall, asking him to drop what he was doing to come referee. Eckersall did, leaving immediately for the long train trip west. Washington State won 14–0, leading Eckie to voice an unpopular opinion: that Washington State was just as good as that season's widely acknowledged national champion, Cornell.

"There is not a better football team in the country [than Washington State]," Eckersall told the *Los Angeles Times*. Eckie could speak with relative authority; he had been field judge for Cornell's 34–7 win over Michigan in early November.

Eckersall returned to the Rose Bowl as referee in 1919 when the Great Lakes Naval Training Station squared off against the Mare Island Marines of Vallejo, California. George Halas, a Chicagoan playing for Great Lakes, hoped Eckersall would display some hometown bias.

"Paddy [Driscoll, Great Lakes' quarterback] threw a pass to me in the end zone," Halas wrote sixty years later. "It was short. I ran for it, bending low. My hands were only an inch off the ground. The ball came in and I held it. But the referee, Walter Eckersall, ruled that the ball had touched the ground. It had not. He cheated me out of a touchdown. And Walter from Chicago! I would have expected a little more civic cooperation."[13]

Eckersall became a fixture in Pasadena. He officiated Washington and Jefferson's scoreless tie with Cal in 1922, Notre Dame's 27–10 win over Stanford in 1925, and Alabama's 20–19 win over Washington in 1926. Even when he wasn't selected to officiate, Eckersall would go to the Rose Bowl anyway. He covered the game for the *Tribune* eleven times between 1916 and 1930.

—

28. Referee Walter Eckersall, center, follows the action as Alabama's Johnny Mack Brown, left, runs with the ball at the 1926 Rose Bowl. University of Alabama Museums, Department of Museum Research and Collections.

Eckersall's officiating ledger was decorated with the biggest games, best teams, and best players in college football history. These games featured dozens of Hall of Fame players, from Thorpe to George Gipp to Red Grange, and more than twenty-five Hall of Fame coaches.

Eckersall also gladly officiated obscure games. He worked six games involving tiny Lombard College of Galesburg, Illinois, and eight involving the "Little Giants" of Indiana's Wabash College. Several other small colleges in Illinois, Iowa, Wisconsin, and Michigan looked forward to at least an occasional visit from the country's most famous referee. Eckie simply loved being on the field, seeing good football, and uncovering little-known players. He even continued officiating high school games. These were mostly local affairs in Chicago, but he officiated the Iowa state championship game twice, along with several intersectional high school games.

As he reached middle age, Eckersall touted conditioning as an important side benefit of football officiating. "You'll be surprised," he told a fellow reporter in the 1920s, "but my weight is exactly the same as when I played football and that's 144 pounds stripped."[14]

(Walter Camp didn't believe Eckersall, noting in 1922: "Walter Eckersall, the star little quarter years ago of the Chicago team, [has] now grown considerably stouter of figure.")[15]

As Eckersall matured, he grew nostalgic about his officiating career. In 1929 Eckersall dismissed any talk of joining a threatened strike of Big Ten officials who were asking for a pay raise.

"The conference made me and I am going to stick," Eckersall said. "Why, I grew up with it. The only reason I officiate is for the love of the game, not the size of the fees. If the officials get the idea they are bigger than the sport, they should get that impression out of their heads."[16]

A few months earlier, when Woodruff, Eckersall's *Tribune* colleague, asked him if he still liked to officiate, Eckie sounded somewhat weary:

> Once I did, but it has grown to be rather a task. Rules are so complicated and involve so many questions of judgment that one feels heavy responsibility. So far as compensation goes, I'd willingly retire. But football is my favorite sport. It was good to me. I feel a responsibility, and officiating, of course, keeps me an even closer student and therefore better qualified to give service to those who read what I write about football. After you once start a thing you hate to give it up. I suppose that's the case with a majority of gridiron officials.[17]

Weary or not, Eckersall officiated football games for his entire adult life. Football would remain his favorite sport, and the one he wrote about most. Yet, Eckie would become known as more than just a football man through his extensive coverage of other sports, most notably boxing.

18

The Sweet Science

If a reader who knew nothing about Walter Eckersall pored over old editions of the *Tribune*, that reader might conclude that Eckie had been a boxer rather than a football player. Nearly 1,700 of Eckersall's articles, 30 percent of his total output, are about boxing, a close second to football among his favorite topics. Overall, Eckie actually covered more boxing matches than football games.

This fact holds a certain irony: For the vast majority of Eckersall's career, boxing was illegal in Chicago. In December 1900 a fixed fight at Tattersall's Arena on the Near South Side led the City Council to ban the sport. The state of Illinois soon followed Chicago's lead.[1]

Yet, due to logistical factors, Chicago remained a center for training boxers, promoting fights, and providing business support. It was a relatively short train ride from several cities where boxing was legal: Milwaukee and Kenosha in Wisconsin, East Chicago in Indiana, and Benton Harbor in Michigan. Organizers centralized their operations in Chicago, and boxers from all over the country moved to the city to work out and get noticed by promoters. Fighters who were based on the coasts or in Europe would temporarily relocate to Chicago when prepping for midwestern fights. Promoters used the city as the backdrop for signing contracts and initiating publicity efforts.

Once he expanded his writing interests beyond football, Eckersall was at the center of all the boxing action. And he loved it. "Chicago is a Mecca for fighters," Eckersall noted, without hyperbole, in 1912.[2]

The first boxer whom Eckie covered extensively was heavyweight Jack Johnson. Between 1910 and 1915, Eckersall wrote almost a hundred stories about Johnson, covering his frequent but brief visits to his adopted hometown of Chicago; his vaudeville act, which earned him more money than his fighting; his training regimen; the financial terms of his contracts; his impact on the Black community; even an article debunking the rumor that Johnson had died in a car accident.[3]

Along the way, Eckersall scored several interviews with the larger-than-life champion.

"It isn't right for fighters to be so unfriendly that they continually are calling one another names through the press and other sources," the gregarious Johnson told Eckersall in 1910 when he stopped by Eckie's *Tribune* office to send a "Happy Birthday" telegram to his upcoming opponent, Jim Jeffries.[4]

Was Johnson sincere, or was this gesture instead a bit of gamesmanship? Eckersall believed the former.

"The firmness with which he jabbed the pen into the telegraph blank demonstrated that the negro meant what he said," Eckersall reported.

Eckersall clearly put Johnson at ease, and vice versa. Johnson chatted in a friendly manner about his opponents, about why he enjoyed fighting overseas more than in the United States, and about the challenges of continuing to train hard as he aged.[5]

Only twice did Johnson speak to Eckersall on the issue of race. The first time, Johnson tried to ease fears that he might buy a home in a white neighborhood. "I know my place as a colored gentleman, and I do not intend to make enemies among the white people," Johnson declared.[6]

But the second time, Johnson was clearly upset when the chair of the New York State Athletic Commission denied him a boxing license. Johnson responded, "As an American citizen, why have I not the same right to box in New York as any one else? They allow fighters to work over there who are not even Americans. . . . Then why should not I be allowed the same privilege? I guess that's discrimination for you."[7]

—

Eckersall never covered a Jack Johnson fight in person, because the champ defended his title in faraway places including France, Argentina, and Cuba. So, Eckie found other fights to cover. By the time Johnson lost the heavyweight title to Jess Willard in 1915, Eckersall had established a foothold as a boxing writer.

Eckie wrote his first fight story in May 1910, on a lightweight bout in Milwaukee. His style mirrored his football writing, packed with description and action:

> In one of the fastest and fiercest fights seen in this city since the famous Ketchel-Papke battle Hugo Kelly of Chicago won by a shade over Eddie McGoorty of Oshkosh in their ten round bout at the Auditorium tonight.
>
> It was a rattling fight from start to finish. Kelly's experience in the ring stood him in good stead. . . . Kelly frequently feinted his man into openings and then jabbed him with straight lefts to the face and body. It was Kelly's blocking that won for him. The Badger fighter let loose with innumerable right and left hooks, only to have them land on the gloves of the clever Italian.[8]

The following year, Eckersall refereed his first fight, in Racine, Wisconsin. He didn't pull this double duty often, only refereeing a handful of bouts during his career. But Eckie frequently was the *Chicago Tribune*'s representative in the old Newspaper Decision system of determining winners.[9]

In the early twentieth century, newspaper writers would declare their opinions on the winner of a fight that went the distance. The writers would then be polled to come up with a consensus. The Newspaper Decision system was eliminated by state boxing commissions by the mid-1920s. In most states, a panel of judges would now award rounds to each boxer, and the boxer who won the most rounds won the bout. In some states, the referee had final say. Even after the system was reformed, Eckersall wasn't shy about sharing his opinion when it differed from the official one.

"While the decision of Referee Phil Collins of the west side met with the approval of the Mandell enthusiasts, to the unbiased spectator a draw would have been a fairer verdict, as Sammy's advantage was not big enough to justify taking a title away from a champion," Eckie noted after Sammy Mandell won a decision over Rocky Kansas in a lightweight title fight in July 1926. "It is true Mandell landed the counting punches with his left hand, but the fact must not be overlooked that Kansas was the aggressor and the holder of the title."[10]

—

Eckersall's fight stories received prominent space on the first sports page. But he did most of his reporting between bouts—in musty gyms, in promoters' and managers' offices, even in courtrooms or legislative hearings. Here, in a man's world run by powerful (and often shady) men, is where Eckie thrived as a reporter.

The boxing gossip that Eckersall gleaned fit well with his no-nonsense writing style. He strung together rapid-fire items that read more like bullet points than actual stories. In one such article, on May 4, 1911, Eckie packed his story with the following information:

Chicago Mayor Carter Harrison Jr. was considering allowing six-round boxing exhibitions in the city.

Middleweight contender Hugo Kelly needed to take a month off due to a hand injury.

Promoter Howard Carr, better known as "Kid Howard," was trying to arrange a slate of fights in Kenosha, Wisconsin, for Memorial Day.

A Cuban wrestler sparred with a heavyweight at O'Connell's Gym, was beaten badly, and ultimately decided to stick with wrestling.

A San Francisco promoter was in town hoping to exhibit "The Johnson-Jeffries Fight," a silent film of the previous summer's interracial heavyweight title fight that had been banned in much of the South.[11]

Eckie wrote dozens of similar columns over the years. Well into the 1920s, the *Tribune* based each column's headline on Eckersall's lead item. For example, the lead item in "Mandell Sees Busy Eve for Joe Burman," on

May 26, 1922, previews an upcoming lightweight title fight. But a headline-skimmer would have missed five other items of boxing gossip.

By 1926 Eckersall's *Tribune* editors began running his material under the headline "Eckersall's Gossip of the Boxers" or "Eckersall's Notes of the Boxers." Under those headlines, Eckie churned out more than sixty collections of items.

Eckersall liberally used nicknames, pseudonyms, adjectives, and appositives in connection with boxers, far more than in his other sportswriting. Indiana welterweight Gene Callahan was "Shuffle Callahan," not to be confused with New York welterweight "Mushy Callahan." Farrell Lacey, Bill Stribling, Maurice Billinghoff, and Jack Thompson all went by "Young." At least as many boxers went by "Kid." Navy veterans were known as "Sailor." Jewish fighters from Chicago's Maxwell Street neighborhood were "ghetto" boxers. And if you were a Jewish boxer who was also a navy veteran, you could be "Sailor Freedman, lightweight pride of the west side ghetto."[12]

Throughout all his boxing writing, Eckersall, though never a boxer himself, writes like an insider. His conversational style, use of nicknames, and direct approach made his *Tribune* readers feel like they, too, were in the know.

—

Eckersall favored Chicago-based fighters over those from other cities or regions. Even better if the Chicago-based fighter were also Chicago-raised, like lightweight Battling Nelson, from Hegewisch on the city's Southeast Side; middleweight Jimmy Clabby, who grew up just outside the city in Hammond, Indiana; and Logan Square resident Johnny Coulon, who held the world bantamweight championship for several years.

One of Eckie's favorite subjects was Packey McFarland, "Pride of the Stockyards." Eckersall wrote more than eighty items about McFarland and covered six of his fights while also noting the difficulty McFarland had in securing a shot at a world title. Between 1910 and 1913, McFarland arranged five separate championship bouts in both the lightweight and welterweight divisions. The only one that ever went through was a May 1912 fight with welterweight champ Ray Bronson. Packey won a ten-round Newspaper Decision, but he could only claim the title by knockout.[13]

Boxing historians would later name McFarland one of the best boxers of all time, and the best to have never won a championship, with 106 career wins against only one loss. Though he never got his title, McFarland received plenty of good press, much of it courtesy of Eckersall. That publicity turned into opportunities: The Pride of the Stockyards earned at least $200,000 during his career, a sum worth more than $6 million today.[14]

—

Eckie reported on several efforts to get the boxing ban in Illinois repealed, including a 1911 bill that passed the Illinois Senate but failed in the House; a similar 1915 effort; a 1919 law, which passed both chambers but was vetoed by the governor; a 1920 attempt that never came to a vote; and a 1923 bill, which passed the House but failed in the Senate.[15]

So, promoters skirted the law. Local authorities gave waivers to charity "exhibitions," benefiting survivors of the 1915 Eastland Disaster, or a wintertime coal fund for poor families, or a Catholic orphanage, or a relief fund for tornado victims. In reporting on these events, Eckie noted the generosity of Chicago's fight fans.[16]

But the charity angle was largely a ruse. A small percentage of funds found their way toward those causes, but most of the money went to the fighters and promoters, violating both the letter and spirit of Illinois law.

Another way promoters skirted the law was by staging fights on the USS *Commodore*, an aging naval ship moored in Lake Michigan at Randolph Street. As federal property, the boat was technically outside both city and state jurisdiction. Eckie covered several fights on the *Commodore* in the early 1920s, including one slate that the "Chicago Law and Order League" tried to break up. The reformers' efforts failed, but one investigator lamented the violence: "If this bout was a harmless boxing match, God help the poor prize fighter."[17]

Occasionally, promoters had to fool the authorities, and Eckersall was complicit. In 1914 he covered a slate of fights that was hastily moved fifteen miles when police were tipped off and prepared a raid. Another slate in 1923 was simply held at "a suburban club," with the actual location never revealed. Because boxing matches made good sports copy, Eckie wasn't spilling the beans.[18]

Beginning in 1921, two promoters openly defied the state's boxing laws and started hosting fights in Aurora, about forty miles west of Chicago. Michael Igoe, a boxing-friendly member of the Illinois House of Representatives, supported the organizers with a morally flexible argument: Since fighters negotiated a purse independent of the fight's result, modern boxing wasn't "prizefighting" but more of an "athletic contest," like a pro baseball or football game.

"So long as you continue to conduct athletic contests as you have in the past, I do not believe that you are violating the provisions of the law," Igoe said.[19]

Carried further, Representative Igoe's opinion could have opened all of Illinois to legalized boxing. But only Aurora dared test the waters. And Eckersall followed. Between 1921 and 1925, Eckie traveled to Aurora more than twenty times to cover fights. The small city wasn't super convenient for Chicago fans or reporters, but it was closer than Wisconsin.

In July 1925 Illinois finally repealed its boxing ban, allowing ten-round fights to a decision. Chicago voters legalized boxing the following April, in a referendum that passed by a 6-to-1 margin.

Eckersall was elated. "The boxing enthusiasts will not have to make the 100 mile trip to Milwaukee, the 40 mile journey to Aurora or the one to East Chicago or Michigan [C]ity," Eckie wrote. "They can remain at home while many of the contests will attract out of town fans, making business in general good for all concerned."[20]

On July 3, 1926, Chicago hosted its first legal prizefights in more than twenty-five years at Comiskey Park. The main event was a lightweight title fight between challenger Mandell and champion Kansas. Mandell won by decision, but because of a smaller-than-expected crowd, he had to pay Kansas $13,000 because his contract required him to cover any shortfall in the now-former champion's $50,000 guarantee.[21]

Eckie blamed rainy weather for the low attendance, but poor crowds continued. The first year of legal boxing in Illinois was disappointing and unprofitable.

"What is the matter with boxing in Chicago?" Eckie rhetorically asked in a June 1927 column. "Instead of being a great fight center, Chicago is now rated with those cities and towns which can not support the game. One by one the promoters are quitting and the survivors can not hope to make much money unless conditions are changed."[22]

Eckie made a couple suggestions to correct some of the issues: lower the boxers' guarantees, which Eckersall thought were too high; cut the state tax from 10 percent of gross receipts to 5 percent; and cut ticket prices, hoping that increased attendance would offset the marginal revenue surrendered. All solid ideas but fairly small ones.

As it turned out, the Chicago boxing scene was jump-started by one grand spectacle: the Dempsey-Tunney fight at Soldier Field.

—

Eckersall had covered two Jack Dempsey fights before, including his win over Willard in 1919 to capture the world heavyweight title. One of the iconic sports figures of the Roaring Twenties, Dempsey was champion for seven years but only defended his crown seven times.[23]

Gene Tunney had long been considered Dempsey's top challenger. In September 1926 Tunney claimed the title with a unanimous ten-round decision over Dempsey in Philadelphia. Dempsey fought his way back into contention with a knockout win over Jack Sharkey, a future champion in his own right, in July 1927. Immediately afterward, serious negotiations began for a second Dempsey-Tunney fight in Chicago. In one of his first articles on the buildup, Eckersall noted that if Soldier Field were at capacity, a promoter could clear more than $1 million in profit.[24]

The Dempsey-Tunney II contracts were quickly signed. In the six weeks leading up to the bout, Eckersall wrote thirty-one articles in anticipation of the big matchup. Other sportswriters also covered the fight extensively, but Eckersall uniquely positioned himself to get the inside scoop.[25]

Eckie embedded himself for a week at Dempsey's training quarters at Lincoln Fields, a horse-racing track thirty miles south of downtown Chicago. Eckersall then turned around and spent two weeks in Tunney's camp at Cedar Crest Golf Club in Lake Villa, fifty miles northwest of downtown. While embedded, Eckie focused on daily minutiae that fascinated readers:

Dempsey charged 500 fans $1.10 apiece to watch him spar.

Tunney suffered a minor eye injury from an over-aggressive sparring partner.

Dempsey's wife, Estelle, joined his entourage but wouldn't watch him train, since she couldn't stomach the sight of him taking a punch.

Tunney got a visit from politician and future Chicago mayor Anton Cermak.

Both fighters took several days off from training to play golf.[26]

A few days before the fight, Eckie became part of the story when he was listed as one of five finalists to be the Dempsey-Tunney referee. Experts argued the merits of the various candidates; Ed Hughes of the *Brooklyn Eagle* thought Eckie was the logical choice.

"He has developed the necessary poise and hair-trigger judgments essential to the competent arbiter," Hughes wrote in a September 20 column. "Eckersall's honesty is unquestioned and many believe he has the inside track for the job."[27]

Eckersall's limited experience as the "third man" in the ring kept him from serious consideration. Another candidate, Davey Miller, was dropped because of his reported ties to Al Capone, who had bet a hefty sum on Dempsey. Ultimately, the job went to veteran referee Dave Barry, whose handling of the fight is still discussed nearly a hundred years later.

Almost 105,000 fans packed Soldier Field on September 22, 1927, for a record-smashing gross of almost $2.7 million. At first, the fight didn't live up to the hype. Tunney displayed endurance and elusiveness, forcing Dempsey, better known for power punches than footwork, to chase him around the ring.

In the seventh round, Dempsey found a sense of urgency. In Eckersall's blow-by-blow account of the fight: "Dempsey came out of his corner with renewed confidence and looking for an opening. Tunney was short with a right cross. Dempsey put a left hook to the jaw followed by a right cross and Gene went down for the count of nine. Dempsey tore after him relentlessly. Tunney kept punching at Dempsey's stomach. Dempsey chased Gene

29. In the biggest sporting event Walter Eckersall ever covered, heavyweight champ Gene Tunney lies on the mat as referee Dave Barry motions Jack Dempsey to a neutral corner during the "Long Count" fight at Soldier Field in 1927. *Chicago Tribune*/TCA.

around the ring, but Gene held him off and went into a clinch. Gene is tiring. Dempsey motioned to him to fight."[28]

After the knockdown, Barry delayed the start of his ten-count until Dempsey had retreated to a neutral corner. Dempsey took his time, giving Tunney at least thirteen seconds between hitting the canvas and getting back on his feet. The *Tribune* devoted two front-page stories to Barry's now-famous "Long Count."

Tunney came back to win by unanimous decision. Besides his blow-by-blow account, Eckie also wrote an analysis of the fight: "It was Tunney's ring craft which enabled him to weather the seventh round, when he was sent to the mat by two left hooks followed by a right cross. Dempsey made a last ditch effort to win. The once great fighter had trained faithfully. He gave all he had, but his best was not quite enough."[29]

—

At the Dempsey-Tunney fight, Eckersall again had a front-row seat to history. The bout also put Chicago in the forefront of the boxing scene after a difficult first fifteen months back in the game.

The resurgence of boxing in Chicago reignited Eckersall's passion for the sport. In the sixteen years before boxing became legal in Chicago, Eckersall covered an average of about one boxing slate per month, almost all out of state. Over the next three and a half years, he covered three slates each month, with all but three of those taking place inside the Chicago city limits.

As a writer, Eckersall will always be most closely linked with football. But he proved to be a very good boxing writer, covering the sport with a tactician's insight and a reporter's ability to dig up gossip.

19

Football Goes to War

In April 1917 the United States entered World War I, the defining experience for a generation of Americans. The war's far-reaching effects on American culture, art, music, and literature are well known. In less obvious but no less real ways, the war would also radically transform American sports.

But in those first few months, the war threatened to grind American sports to a halt. Top athletes immediately volunteered for military service. Several colleges, including the "Big Three" of Harvard, Yale, and Princeton, suspended athletics. Major League Baseball considered canceling its season. There seemed to be no room for child's play in a world where real men were needed for fighting and killing.

As fall approached, Eckersall saw a way to keep football alive: by having military training camps play varsity-caliber football. He recalled a tournament held the previous winter among National Guard units in the Southwest, as well as games between naval crews in port, writing: "When the United States troops were on the border football was the favorite sport. There were several good players with the regiments and the struggles took on the color of real college games, only much rougher. When the fleets have been cruising in foreign waters games have been played between crews of the battleships. Officers of these crews for the most part were graduates of Annapolis who had played the game while at the navy school."[1]

Why not repeat those efforts, on a larger scale, in naval boot camps and the massive army cantonments that were hastily being built around the country?

By August Eckie noticed the buildup of football talent at a naval base in Newport, Rhode Island, and at Great Lakes Naval Training Station and the army's Fort Sheridan, both about thirty miles north of Chicago.

"Since most college teams have been weakened through the loss of star players who have joined the colors, it seems a certainty that elevens will be organized in the army and navy," Eckersall noted. "With so many college men in the new national army—players who have learned the game under the best coaches in the country—elevens will be developed which will be equal or superior to a majority of college aggregations."[2]

Within weeks, Eckie's prediction proved accurate. "As men are sent to different forts or camps, a Chicago man may get a chance to show his wares against a Yale player, a Michigan or Wisconsin star may have the opportunity to play opposite a Harvard or Princeton man, and so on," Eckersall wrote in mid-September. "If there was no war these men probably never would clash on the chalk lined field."[3]

Once these training camps started to play, Eckersall did free publicity work for the military, appealing to his *Tribune* readers' sense of both patriotism and fandom.

> Football fans are looking to the contests that have been arranged between different naval and camp elevens. These games are sure to be just as interesting as college combats, and should be a magnet for followers of the gridiron sport. . . . The game to be played at Stagg Field between teams representing the Great Lakes Naval training station and Fort Sheridan already is attracting a good deal of attention. It will be a replica of the Army-Navy game in the east. . . . The clean-cut way in which the games are conducted and the manner in which the players perform on the field make these spectacles worth any football fan's time or money.[4]

Beyond publicizing these games, Eckersall officiated them as well, spurning higher-profile college games to support the military version of the sport.

Half of the games Eckersall officiated in 1917 involved military teams. Most notable was Great Lakes–Fort Sheridan on Thanksgiving Day at Stagg Field, where Eckie was part of an all-star officiating crew that included Michigan coach Fielding Yost.[5]

To Eckersall, that first season of War Football was a success.

"During the football season just closed those who had the opportunities to see camp elevens in action saw battles which should have warmed the blood of even the most rank outsider," Eckersall wrote. "Football has made fighters out of players and it has made fighters out of the camp men who stood on the side lines and cheered themselves hoarse for their respective teams."[6]

—

By the end of the 1917 season, few Americans had shipped "Over There." That changed over the winter, as the United States began sending large numbers of troops overseas, including many athletes. In February 1918 Eckie began writing a series of features saluting these heroes. His subjects included his high school teammate Tom Hammond, who fought with the 42nd or "Rainbow" Division; West Point quarterback Horatio Hackett, who won the Silver Star during the Meuse-Argonne offensive; Birdie Gardner, former Carlisle end who played for and coached Camp Custer of Battle Creek, Michigan, in 1917 before fighting in Europe; and Jimmy Turner, an Englewood High School and Northwestern University player who was killed in the closing days of the war, one of at least a hundred former college players to die in combat.[7]

Eckersall saved his favorite subject for last. Sam Ransom had enlisted as a private with the all-Black 8th Illinois Regiment in 1917. Ransom was quickly promoted to lieutenant, and the regiment, rebranded as the 370th Infantry of the 93rd Division, fought with distinction under French command. In June 1918 Ransom earned a commendation for bravery under fire during a raid on enemy trenches.[8]

Amid this display of heroism from his peers, Eckersall never joined the military. Since he was over thirty when the United States entered the war, Eckersall was not subject to the initial rounds of the draft. When the draft expanded to include men up to age forty-five, Eckersall registered but wasn't called up by the time the war ended. Several sportswriting peers like Grantland Rice, who volunteered for the army, and Ring Lardner, who did a brief stint as a war correspondent, went overseas, but Eckersall seemed content to cover sports on the home front.[9]

—

The *Chicago Tribune* pared down its sports pages early in the war and reallocated space to war coverage, even though few Americans were involved in actual fighting at the time. Paradoxically, by the time American soldiers went overseas in large numbers in 1918, the *Tribune* expanded its sports coverage back to prewar levels, to give readers a necessary diversion.

But sports events were curtailed, since most top athletes had joined the service. Colleges and athletic clubs continued to hold games, meets, and matches, but with shoestring budgets and less-competitive lineups. Fortunately, Eckersall found fertile athletic ground just north of Chicago, at Great Lakes Naval Training Station.

Great Lakes' ambitious commandant, Capt. William Moffett, realized that sports were a great way to get into the news, so Great Lakes competed in *everything*, from basketball to ski jumping.

Eckersall followed it all. He covered intramural boxing matches and track meets among navy recruits. He wrote about Great Lakes' speed skating and ice hockey teams. He followed Great Lakes' championship-caliber swimming and track teams, which included two future Olympic gold medalists. Great Lakes hosted, and Eckersall covered, the Central and National AAU track meets. Eckie also covered Great Lakes' baseball team, which boasted at least sixteen former and future Major Leaguers, headlined by Hall of Fame pitcher Red Faber.

—

For the first sixteen months of the war, military athletics were a minor part of Eckersall's writing, totaling about 20 percent of his output. By the war's second football season in 1918, military sports crowded out everything else on Eckersall's schedule. Of his nearly one hundred *Tribune* bylines between mid-September 1918 and early January 1919, more than seventy-five were about military football. Ten of the twelve games Eckie covered in person that fall involved military teams.

Eckersall recognized the high quality of the 1918 military teams right away. Before the season opener between Great Lakes and University of Iowa, he noted, "Not only will the result have an important bearing on the two teams' prospects but it will determine the chances a young inexperienced team [Iowa] has against one composed of veterans, some of whom have played football for four and even six years. . . . The Great Lakes is a strong eleven and its showing today will determine whether it has prospects of . . . national consideration at the close of the season."[10]

Eckie covered Great Lakes football extensively that fall. Beyond the three Bluejacket games that he covered and officiated, Eckie wrote more than thirty midweek features about the team. His reviews weren't always glowing. After Great Lakes put up only 17 total points in its first two games, Eckersall criticized the sailors' failure to impose their will.

"Great Lakes' games with Iowa and Illinois do not warrant the sailor aggregation being considered any too powerful," he wrote on October 14. "On paper the team appears unbeatable, but it remains to be seen what it will do against a team of equal weight and experience. It has not been put to a test so far this season."[11]

Chicago had a second top-flight military team. The Chicago Naval Reserves at the city's newly built Municipal Pier (later renamed Navy Pier) had a level of talent similar to Great Lakes. Eckersall covered three Municipal Pier games that fall. After watching the team beat the University of Chicago, Eckersall wrote, "The pier aggregation is entitled to recognition as one of the strongest service teams in the west. There are not a few who believe the team is even stronger than the Great Lakes." The Chicago Naval Reserves would finish 1918 undefeated and untied.[12]

Eckie also covered four games involving Camp Grant of Rockford, in north-central Illinois. Camp Grant featured several former college stars, but Eckersall noticed one standout who hadn't yet played on a big stage. Center George Trafton had played on good teams at Oak Park High School but had only played sandlot football since graduating in 1915.

"Trafton . . . is much larger than when he went to the suburban school and has learned a lot of football," Eckersall wrote. College scouts noticed, too, and greater gridiron glory lay ahead for the future Hall of Famer, whose talents might have gone unnoticed if not for the war.[13]

Eckersall traveled to Cleveland with Camp Grant when they took on one of the best teams in the country, the Cleveland Naval Reserves. With Eckie as referee, Cleveland eked out a 14–6 win. The following week, the underdog Reserves scored the upset of the year in a 10–9 win over that season's college champion, the University of Pittsburgh. Eckie wasn't there though. He was 650 miles west in Des Moines, Iowa, covering and refereeing a game between Camp Dodge and the University of Iowa.[14]

That game turned out to be a fairly boring scoreless tie. But Eckie witnessed history that day, though he could hardly have known it at the time. Iowa's best player was freshman tackle Duke Slater, who would become a college and pro star before becoming only the second Black judge in Chicago. Slater lined up across from Omar Bradley, who went on to become America's top field commander during the liberation of Europe in World War II and the last of America's five-star generals.[15]

Meanwhile, Great Lakes traveled east to take on college football's best. On that trip, the Bluejackets—who hadn't lost yet but had tied twice—finally lived up to their hype. On November 16 Great Lakes thrashed previously undefeated Rutgers at Brooklyn's Ebbets Field, 54–14. The following week, against the undefeated Naval Academy in Annapolis, Maryland, the Bluejackets returned a fumble 90 yards for a touchdown in the closing minutes for a 7–6 victory. The two East Coast wins firmly established Great Lakes as one of the top teams of 1918.[16]

Great Lakes received an invitation to play in the Rose Bowl in Pasadena, California, on New Year's Day. Eckie accompanied Great Lakes on its four-day train trip from Chicago to California, sending dispatches full of gossip from whistle stops in Missouri, Colorado, and New Mexico. He noted that Great Lakes' Jimmy Conzelman passed the time by playing the ukulele, while players went through scaled-down drills in their Pullman cars. Eckersall commented, apparently without irony, both that "the players started card games" before the train even left Chicago and that "strict discipline was enforced throughout the trip."[17]

After arriving in California, Eckie sent back plenty of practice tidbits and quoted betting odds, which favored Great Lakes at 10-to-8 over the Mare Island Marines of Vallejo, California.

The Marines were beat up heading into the Rose Bowl, while Great Lakes, rested and refreshed, took in all the tourist attractions: the Southern California orange groves, the movie lots at the new Universal Studios, and the submarine base at San Pedro.[18]

Despite his status as an embedded reporter with the Great Lakes team, Eckersall was selected as Rose Bowl referee. Any question of potential bias ended up a nonissue, as Great Lakes dominated in a 17–0 shutout.

For Great Lakes, Paddy Driscoll had a tremendous all-around game with 34 yards rushing, 11 yards receiving, 77 passing yards and one touchdown on four completions, 115 yards on nine punt returns, six punts for a 44-yard average, and a 30-yard field goal. George Halas caught a 30-yard touchdown pass and ended a Mare Island scoring threat with an interception, which he returned 80 yards to the Marines' 10-yard line.

Decades later, Halas remembered, "Playing in the Rose Bowl was one of the greatest thrills of my life. That was the only game I ever starred in."[19]

At the time, there was no official Rose Bowl MVP award. Eckie wrote, "It would be hard to pick out a star on the Great Lakes eleven. Every man played a stellar game, including the substitutes." He finally settled on Driscoll as his MVP choice, adding, "George Halas was not far behind Driscoll. The former Illini was everywhere at the right time." Twenty-five years later, an expert panel flipped Eckie's choices, retroactively naming Halas the official MVP.[20]

In Eckersall's opinion, the Rose Bowl victory "gives the bluejackets the service championship . . . and a just claim to the national title." Walter Camp agreed, calling Great Lakes "easily the strongest football eleven in the country."[21]

—

After the war, the training camps demobilized quickly. A war-weary country quickly lost interest in military athletics. At camps that still sponsored sports, including Great Lakes, first-rate teams became also-rans, since their stars had been discharged back to civilian life.

For Eckie, as for most of America, the time had come to move on from war. But in 1919, the war remained alive in a surprising manner: through the way it jump-started the birth of organized professional football.

20

The Sunday Game

Walter Eckersall noticed the trend before just about anybody else. In 1919 millions of soldiers and sailors returned to civilian life, including thousands of football players. Most had already given up the sport they loved once, when they finished college. Through military football, their careers had been briefly extended. Now, they were once again players without teams.

But not for long. As they returned home, these players started to consider professional football as an option, to a much greater extent than before the war. Because these players were college-educated military veterans, they helped clean up the somewhat seedy image of professional football that had lingered before the war.

Eckersall was the first writer to notice the connection between military football and the professional game. "Men who left college when the United States entered the war . . . and received a taste of the game in the training camps, are eager to play this fall," he wrote in September 1919. "Professional football teams are being organized in all parts of the country and numbers in Chicago. These are composed . . . in a great many cases by service men who played in camps and cantonments."[1]

Just southeast of Chicago, the Hammond (Indiana) All-Stars were stocked with Great Lakes alumni, along with several other War Football veterans. The coach of the 1918 Chicago Naval Reserves at Municipal Pier was trying to organize a major pro team in Eckie's city. On the lower levels, the number of teams in the semipro Chicago Football League swelled that fall.

Eckersall welcomed this expansion of professional football but was wary of some rougher elements of the Sunday game.

"If professional football is to survive, *and there is no reason why it should not,* the players must conduct themselves like the men on the college elevens," Eckersall wrote. "The promoters of the contests can expect large crowds. . . . Those in charge of these teams can do a lot for professional football and the game in general if they make it imperative their players learn the rules and abide by the officials' rulings. This will do away with wrangling on the fields and subsequent fist fights."[2]

Eckersall himself had an on-and-off relationship with professional football, dating to his play for the eponymous Eckersalls in 1907. From then until 1917, he wrote about and/or officiated at only a handful of professional games. To Eckersall, prewar professional football was an afterthought.

That fit with the *Tribune*'s overall coverage. Autumn Mondays were light days for sports news, so the paper would run a few pro football items as filler. As an example, on October 30, 1916, the *Tribune* ran eleven brief items (out of forty-three total sports stories) on professional football games. None were more than two paragraphs long. Some consisted of only one sentence, such as "East Chicago Gophers won from the Mitchell A.C., 20–0, at East Chicago yesterday."

Pro football took a back seat to a bowling tournament; to a U.S.-versus-Sweden track meet; to a semipro baseball game, won by forty-nine-year-old pitching legend Cy Young; even to results from local pool halls. And of course to Walter Eckersall's fourteen-paragraph article about the implications of the previous Saturday's college football games. Nearly lost in the shuffle was Chicago native Knute Rockne's game-winning touchdown catch for the Massillon Tigers, buried on the bottom of the second sports page.[3]

But 1919 was different. Pro football remained behind the college game in terms of coverage but had made significant progress. The *Tribune* ran more stories, which were longer and more detailed. And the football itself was clearly superior to the prewar version.

Eckersall latched on to the best team in the area, the Hammond All-Stars. The team, founded by an ambitious yet overextended businessman named Paul Parduhn, signed nine former All-Americans, as well as Great Lakes end

George Halas. The All-Stars' starters averaged more than $100 per game in salary, leading the press to dub Hammond the "$20,000 football team."[4]

The All-Stars practiced in Hammond but played only one game there, in front of a meager crowd of 1,700. Parduhn thought he could sell more tickets at a big-city ballpark, so he leased Chicago's Cubs Park for the remaining six home games.

"The idea is to test the popularity of professional football in Chicago," the *Tribune* noted in October. "It's in the contract between the Chicago club and Manager Parduhn that the games must be clean and free from the rough stuff that has characterized some of the games between professional elevens in Chicago in previous years. . . . [To ensure this] Walter Eckersall has been selected to officiate as referee at all the games."[5]

Eckersall officiated six of Hammond's nine games that fall, including a matchup against Jim Thorpe's Canton Bulldogs. That game, which drew ten thousand fans to Cubs Park, ended in a 3–3 tie. (Eckie did not attend a hastily arranged Thanksgiving Day rematch, which Canton won; he had already committed to umpire a college game that day.)[6]

Curiously, Eckersall never wrote a bylined story about the Hammond team. The *Tribune* did run nonbylined articles on each game that averaged about five paragraphs, significantly longer than any prewar pro football coverage.

Soon after the season ended, Parduhn's checks started to bounce. The owner spent two nights in jail and, ultimately, lost control of his team. By that point, Eckersall had begun to sour on professional football.[7]

Shortly before Thanksgiving, Eckie wrote a column on the perceived abuses of pro football and its threat to the college game. Full of generalities, Eckersall offered no solid evidence and named no actual players or colleges.

> When a student develops into a football star, managers of the pro teams do not hesitate to offer him as high as $100 to play in one game. This is tempting. The player is told he can be payed [*sic*] under an assumed name and that no one will ever discover his identity. . . .
>
> There are so many teams playing in remote places that a well known player can easily slip out of town, play under an assumed name, and no

one will know the difference. If one player does this others will follow, and the practice should be curbed as soon as possible. . . .

[P]layers who are now making good coin playing pro football do not put forth their best efforts unless there is money wagered by the players on the result. . . . The spirit of a college game is lacking and the main thought of all is the pay envelope.[8]

College football was Eckersall's bread and butter, and after initially thinking that the college and pro versions could coexist, he changed his mind.

"Football is one branch of sport which belongs strictly to the colleges," Eckie declared in December 1919. "The growth of the game in pro ranks will be a reflection on the college game which will suffer accordingly."[9]

Eckersall gave pro football another brief chance. On October 3, 1920, he traveled to Decatur, Illinois, to referee a game between Halas's new Decatur Staleys and the Moline Tractors. This was the Staleys' first game after they became a founding member of the American Professional Football Association, later renamed the National Football League. The Staleys won, 20–0. But Eckie didn't write about the game, and the *Tribune* didn't cover it.[10]

That December, Eckie covered a Staleys game against the Akron Pros, this time in Chicago. Halas recognized, much as Parduhn had in Hammond, that pro football's potential was limited in a small city like Decatur. So, he moved the Staleys' last two games to Chicago's Cubs Park, a sign of a permanent move in 1921 and a rebranding as the Chicago Bears in 1922.

In his five-paragraph *Tribune* story, Eckersall noted that the players fought "with nearly the same spirit that featured their college careers." In a longer, repackaged exclusive for the *Akron Beacon-Journal*, Eckie called the game a "pleasing surprise . . . waged with all the vim and spirit of a college game . . . a super contest of football." On a slippery field in front of twelve thousand fans, the Staleys and Pros tied 0–0.[11]

After Eckersall's nearly fifteen-year relationship with pro football as a player, reporter, and official, this was the last pro football game that he covered. From then on, Eckie strictly dealt with amateur football. But he occasionally weighed in college football's superiority via his *Tribune* columns. These opinions came to the forefront in 1925, with the NFL debut of Red Grange.

—

Grange first caught Eckersall's attention as a high school junior in 1921, at the Illinois state track meet. Competing for small-town Wheaton High School, Grange won the long jump and the 100-yard dash, leading Eckie to call the seventeen-year-old a "classy young performer."[12]

As soon as he suited up for the University of Illinois in 1923, Grange was a media sensation. In his first college game, the sophomore earned the lede in Eckie's game recap: "Harold Grange, who learned to play football at Wheaton high school . . . was responsible for Illinois' victory over Nebraska here today by the score of 24 to 7." Grange scored touchdowns on an 8-yard run, a 20-yard catch, and a 65-yard punt return that day.[13]

His legend grew from there. Grange led Illinois to an 8-0 record and a claim to the national championship in 1923, while leading the Big Ten in scoring. As a junior in 1924, he led the conference in scoring again and won the *Tribune*'s inaugural Silver Football trophy as Big Ten MVP. He also had perhaps the greatest individual game in college football history, scoring five touchdowns and throwing for a sixth against Michigan.[14]

As Grange's accolades piled up, Eckersall took small but noticeable shots at the budding legend. He pointed out that Grange struggled on defense in Illinois's season finale against Ohio State in 1923, a curious comment not only because Illinois shut out Ohio State but also because Eckersall wasn't there. In October 1924 Eckie stated that "while so much is being said about Grange, the football world should grant a deal of credit to [Illinois coach Bob] Zuppke" for designing plays around Grange. The following month, after Grange had 272 yards of offense and two touchdowns in a win over Iowa, Eckie noted that "his success was made possible by some grand interference and blocking . . . it is the blocking which makes Illinois' attack so powerful."[15]

Readers noticed the slights. One complained:

> What's wrong with Walter Eckersall?
>
> We always thought Wallie was a good football player. We know now that he is a poor sport.

> His chief pastime seems to be to seek an alibi for any team that Illinois beats. For instance "Strong wind helps Illini defeat Iowa." Wallie was there because we saw him, so he must know that the same wind blew for Iowa as did for Illinois last Saturday.
>
> Now, we always thought Eckersall was great in his time and would like to see him take off his hat to a greater player and admit that the whole Illinois team is wonderful.
>
> Come on, Eckie, be a sport.[16]

In the end, Eckersall gave Grange his due, naming him first-team All–Big Ten, All-Western, and All-American during each of his three varsity seasons, accolades previously matched only by Eckersall. Shortly after Grange's last college game, Eckie stated, "Grange must be acknowledged as the greatest running back in the history of football."[17]

By then, Grange was making news in another way: as the highest-profile player to join the NFL. Grange went pro immediately after his final game for the Illini, making his debut with the Chicago Bears five days later.

"I'm afraid that Red Grange's turning professional will give the knockers of college athletics the other hammer," Eckersall said. "Football is being criticized too much now on the grounds of commercialism."[18]

That commercialism would only worsen. In Grange's first two and a half weeks as a pro, the Bears played ten games in eight cities, encompassing both the end of the NFL season and exhibitions against all-star squads. Predictably, Grange got injured, and Eckie wrote a lengthy "I told you so" column.

> Cracking of Red Grange under the strain of playing so many professional football games after his eight college contests this season is no surprise to close followers of the game or to those who have played it. The injury he received yesterday has been expected.
>
> Grange is competing solely for the money, and he knows that unless he continues to deliver his drawing power will diminish. This knowledge, that he must live up to his reputation every game, adds a great mental burden to the physical strain of playing. . . . In fact, it is small wonder Grange has not cracked before.[19]

After a two-week break, Grange and the Bears continued barnstorming, playing nine more exhibition games in the South and on the West Coast in just over a month. While the football was often lackluster, Grange's tour may have saved the struggling NFL.

Grange was a once-in-a-lifetime athlete and personality who symbolized the Golden Age of Sports. But Eckersall never covered the star as a pro. In drawing a hard line, Eckersall missed a huge opportunity to cover one of the great sports stories of the 1920s.

The *Tribune* followed Grange closely, with staff writers covering the entire barnstorming tour. By steering clear of Grange, Eckie cast his lot with traditional amateur principles—somewhat ironically, considering the rumors of professionalism that dogged him during college and his own experience as a semipro athlete.

Pro football flirted with Eckersall one more time. In February 1926 Grange's manager C. C. Pyle, thwarted in his attempt to become an NFL owner himself, announced plans to start a new American Football League, headlined by Grange. Pyle wanted Eckersall as league president, to give the organization some legitimacy. The AFL was prepared to offer Eckersall a $15,000-per-year contract, worth more than $260,000 annually today.[20]

Eckersall turned the AFL down. The league failed within a year, and Grange eventually returned to the Bears.[21]

While spurning the pros, Eckersall closely embraced amateur sports. He even served as an official with the Central AAU in the 1920s, a total about-face for someone who had openly battled the same organization during his playing days. This pivot, however, enabled Eckersall to get involved with the Olympic movement, which grew dramatically during his career.[22]

21

Chicago Goes for Gold

The modern Olympic Games were first held in Athens, Greece, in 1896, but you might have missed that in the Chicago newspapers. The *Tribune* ran a couple brief items from press wires, with minimal details. The 1900 Olympics were also largely overlooked in Chicago, although the *Tribune*'s Paris correspondent, an expat named Grace Corneau, wrote a lengthy article about track and field, in which Americans won sixteen of the twenty-three events.[1]

In 1904 Olympic coverage increased greatly. This growth was due partly to proximity, since the games (originally slated for Chicago) were held in St. Louis, and partly to the egalitarian nature of the American team. For the first time, American competitors came from across the country instead of just the East Coast, as well as from a diversity of backgrounds. Hurdler George Poage, the first Black athlete to represent the United States, won two bronze medals. Two medal-winning jumpers were Jewish. While most American athletes had attended college, a significant number were blue-collar laborers.

Several athletes also had Chicago connections: Eckie's high school foe Bill Hogenson, University of Chicago middle-distance runner Jim Lightbody, and Chicago-based distance runner Sidney Hatch all won medals. The *Tribune* took far more notice of these games than the previous two, running daily articles and highlighting the feats of Chicagoans.[2]

Starting with those 1904 Games, the *Tribune* covered the Olympics enthusiastically. The 1906 Intercalated Games in Athens (no longer considered an official Olympic Games) included regular dispatches from Hugo Friend, an assistant coach at the University of Chicago and a future judge who took bronze in the long jump. For the 1908 Olympics in London, Amos Alonzo Stagg, who helped coach the U.S. track team, telegraphed daily articles to the *Tribune*.[3]

—

Eckersall caught Olympic fever in 1908, too, but the *Tribune* didn't use any of his stories. Still a part-time football reporter, Eckersall earned no bylines in the *Tribune* that spring or summer. Other papers, such as the *Nashville* (TN) *American* and *Buffalo* (NY) *Courier*, picked up a handful of Eckie's Olympic-oriented stories in syndication.[4]

By the time of the Stockholm Games in 1912, Eckersall, now a full-time *Tribune* writer, participated in the PR machine that pushed the Olympics toward national and international prominence. Eckie began his 1912 reporting by setting high expectations: "Gathered at Stockholm will be a galaxy of stars to fight for the athletic honors of their respective countries. . . . The huge stadium, more than 1,000 feet long and 700 feet wide, built to accommodate a crowd of 75,000 persons, in which the games will be held, dwarfs into insignificance in everything except beauty the one at Athens. . . . Every contest in the 1912 games will be worth going miles to see."[5]

Eckersall talked up the prospects of American competitors and hyped Chicago's potential Olympians at every chance. "Chicago will contribute liberally to the organization of the American Olympic team which will compete in the world's games at Stockholm this summer," Eckersall wrote in March 1912. Twelve potential Olympians whom Eckie named made the team, and five Chicagoans would win medals.[6]

—

The city contributed in small but meaningful ways to the 1912 American team. Over the next several Olympic cycles, Chicago's presence would be much greater, fueled by the bustling rivalry between the Chicago Athletic Association and the Illinois Athletic Club. Eckersall covered both amateur clubs closely, weaving his stories on the rivalry into his broader Olympic narrative.

The CAA, founded in 1890 by prominent business leaders, built a headquarters on Michigan Avenue, across from today's Millennium Park. It would be known as the "Cherry Circle" club after its logo, an encircled red "C," which was later adopted by club member William Wrigley for his Chicago Cubs baseball team.[7]

At the CAA, titans of industry and political leaders might engage in some calisthenics or a swim, followed by a sauna or vigorous massage. The club also funded the sports activities of promising young athletes, allowing them to train at the CAA and sending them to regional and national competitions.[8]

Shortly after the 1904 Olympics, politician William Hale Thompson founded the IAC along with some three hundred members who had broken away from the CAA. The IAC built its own beautiful building a block south of the CAA and would be known as the "Tri-Color" club after its logo, a white *Y* with the arms of the *Y* separating wedges of purple, red, and yellow.[9]

The IAC and CAA squabbled frequently, and Eckersall recorded the juicy details. In 1911 the clubs avoided competing against each other for several months because of perceived poor sportsmanship on both sides. In 1918 the two argued which team had earned a "bye" for the National AAU water polo playoffs. In 1919 the IAC maneuvered, but ultimately failed, to have a CAA official removed from a key National AAU committee.[10]

This bitterness fostered tremendous competition, both locally and nationally. Throughout the 1910s, both teams performed well at National AAUs in track and swimming, but their athletes' chances at glory in the 1916 Olympics in Berlin were canceled due to World War I.

By 1920 a war-weary world was ready to focus on sports again, and on the upcoming Olympics in Antwerp, Belgium. So was Eckersall. In July 1920 Eckersall covered Olympic Trials in both swimming, held at Chicago's Lincoln Park Lagoon, and track, held at Harvard Stadium in Boston. Chicago athletes landed seventeen places on the American track team and five places on the swimming team. At the Antwerp Games, five CAA athletes medaled in track, with two winning gold. In swimming, the IAC's Norman Ross won two individual gold medals, while Ross teamed with the IAC's Perry McGillivray and two Hawaiian swimmers to capture gold in the freestyle relay.[11]

30. Illinois Athletic Club swimmer Ethel Lackie, winner of six National AAU titles and two Olympic gold medals, was one of the few female athletes that Walter Eckersall covered. SDN-068377, *Chicago Daily News* collection, Chicago History Museum.

As the 1924 Paris Olympics approached, Eckersall was again optimistic about U.S. chances. "America should again win the track and field competition of the Olympic Games," he wrote shortly after the trials. "The American team is unquestionably a much better balanced aggregation than that of any other nation. . . . Personal pride will be cast aside for a common cause, that of winning the honors in the track and field competition of the world's games."[12]

That summer, Eckersall had two big local Olympic interests. The first was the emergence of Chicago's female swimmers; the second was Johnny Weissmuller.

—

Eckie started covering the IAC's Sybil Bauer in 1921, when the seventeen-year-old backstroker won her first National AAU title. IAC freestyler Ethel Lackie was also seventeen when Eckersall first noticed her in 1924. Eckie

31. Walter Eckersall would cover races involving star Chicago swimmer Johnny Weissmuller, seen here in his Illinois Athletic Club uniform, twenty-two times between 1921 and 1928. SDN-063384, *Chicago Daily News* collection, Chicago History Museum.

wrote nearly twenty articles about the two swimmers, the first extensive coverage that he ever gave to women's sports. Eckersall highlighted Bauer as "one of the world's greatest women's swimmers," while noting Lackie's efforts to set new world records in the freestyle sprints. Bauer would win eleven national titles and an Olympic gold medal, and Lackie six national titles and two Olympic golds.[13]

Although Eckersall first wrote about Weissmuller in November 1921, the young swimmer had burst onto the scene earlier that year. In March the North Sider, only sixteen years old, came in second to IAC teammate Ross in the 500-yard freestyle at AAU indoor nationals at Great Lakes Naval Training Station. That August, Weissmuller beat Ross in the 100-yard freestyle at AAU outdoor nationals in Duluth, Minnesota. Weissmuller would go unbeaten in the freestyle for the remainder of his career.[14]

"Weissmuller is now considered the world's greatest swimmer," Eckersall wrote in 1922, shortly after Johnny's eighteenth birthday. "He is a product of Chicago and is an example for other boys to follow. He has gained the topmost rung in the ladder of swimming fame through sheer perseverance."[15]

Eckersall covered twenty-two races involving Weissmuller, who would win fifty-two national championships between 1921 and 1928. His AAU success translated into Olympic victories: three swimming gold medals, and a bronze in water polo, at the Paris Games in 1924 and two more swimming golds at the Amsterdam Games in 1928.[16]

—

Eckersall's Olympic coverage usually focused on CAA and IAC, but he also touted other Olympic hopefuls. Whenever Chicago hosted a National AAU meet, Eckie wrote about potential Olympians from other regions, including Newark, New Jersey, sprinter Loren Murchison, winner of track golds in 1920 and 1924; New York diver Helen Meany, who won gold in 1928; and Cincinnati swimmer Walter Laufer, who won individual silver and relay gold in 1928.[17]

Some figures seemed larger than life. Eckie covered Hawaiian swimming and surfing legend Duke Kahanamoku, winner of five medals over three Olympics, at National AAU meets in 1912, 1916, and 1920. But Eckie came to know Kahanamoku best in 1918, when Duke and two other Hawaiian swimmers spent a week in Chicago before an American Red Cross benefit at Lincoln Park Lagoon.[18]

Similarly, Eckersall befriended California sprinter Charley Paddock, winner of two golds and a silver in the 1920 Olympics and another silver in 1924. Eckie had covered Paddock at the 1920 Olympic trials in Boston and wrote a flattering profile in 1921. In 1923 Paddock visited with Eckersall in Chicago on his way to a meet in Europe, and Eckie returned the favor that winter, visiting with the sprinter while in California for the Rose Bowl and taking a long drive together through the San Gabriel Mountains.[19]

Occasionally, Eckersall crossed paths with foreign stars. In 1925 he covered two track meets featuring Paavo Nurmi, the "Flying Finn" who had already won eight gold medals in distance events and would add a ninth in

1928. Eckersall also covered races involving Nurmi's Finland teammate Willie Ritola, himself a five-time gold medalist, and German middle-distance runner Otto Peltzer, who would have been a 1924 contender if not for his country's postwar competition ban.[20]

Each year at the Big Ten track meet, Eckersall noted promising athletes who might make the national team. "When the western conference outdoor track and field championships are held at Northwestern university on May 25 and 26, the competing athletes will not only struggle to win points for the schools they represent but also for the right to win a place on the American Olympic team," Eckersall wrote in 1928, before giving the rundown on top contenders.[21]

In this way, he introduced his *Tribune* readers to decathlete and high jumper Harold Osborn of Illinois, long jumper DeHart Hubbard of Michigan, and sprinter Eddie Tolan of Ohio State. All would win Big Ten titles and Olympic gold.

Starting in 1921, when the NCAA held its first national track and field championships, Eckersall took detailed looks at competitors from other regions as well. Conveniently for Eckersall, the NCAA held its first twelve annual meets in Chicago, at either Stagg Field or Soldier Field. The NCAA meets helped Eckersall get the early dope on stars from all corners of the country, several of whom would go on to win medals for the United States.

—

In his coverage of Olympic sports, Eckersall didn't limit himself to swimming and track. In June 1920 he covered the road cycling Olympic trials, consisting of a ninety-mile race from Milwaukee to Chicago. Eckie was thrilled when Chicagoan Ernest Kockler won by less than a second. Kockler finished thirteenth at Antwerp in the event, which would be dominated by European cyclists for decades.[22]

Another non-marquee athlete whom Eckersall had long followed fared better in Olympic competition. Mark Arie, a shooter from Champaign, Illinois, often competed in Chicago, and Eckersall covered his tournaments at least seven times. Arie would win gold in individual trap shooting at Antwerp and also lead the United States to gold in the team clay pigeons.[23]

Winter sports didn't escape Eckersall's notice. In 1923 Eckie started covering a sixteen-year-old speed skater from the West Side.[24]

"O'Neil Farrell of the Alverno A.A. was easily the class of the racers in the boys' intermediate," Eckie wrote after one race. "He laid back with the field until there were two laps to go. He then jumped the pack, went to the front and increased his lead until he crossed the blue line twenty yards in advance. . . . Farrell is one of Chicago's most promising skaters."[25]

Eckersall wrote about Farrell's skating several times in the mid-1920s. In 1928, in the St. Moritz Winter Olympics, Farrell took bronze in the 500 meters, the only medal won by an American speed skater in those games.[26]

—

Eckersall wrote more than a hundred articles that previewed Olympic competition, and covered eleven different regional or national Olympic trials in four different sports. Yet, he never covered an Olympics in person. During Eckersall's *Tribune* career, all Olympic Games were held in Europe, and the paper never sent one of its sports reporters. In 1908 the *Tribune* hired Stagg as an Olympic correspondent, but he was going to London anyway, so the paper wouldn't have to pay his expenses. For Stockholm in 1912 and Antwerp in 1920, the paper's Olympic coverage was either provided by European stringers or taken off the press wires. In the 1920s, the *Tribune* would have European political correspondents cover the games. William Shirer, who later gained fame for his reporting from Nazi Germany, covered both the Winter Games in St. Moritz, Switzerland, and the Summer Games in Amsterdam in 1928, contributing twenty-one bylined stories to the *Tribune*.

As the *Tribune*'s lead sports reporter, Eckersall certainly would have covered the 1932 Winter Games in Lake Placid, New York, and the 1932 Summer Games in Los Angeles. His premature death precluded this.

Still, Eckie had a huge impact on amateur sports in America through his Olympic coverage. He had an even greater impact through his advocacy for youth sports, highlighted by the two great tournaments that he founded.

22

Silver Skates and Golden Gloves

As Walter Eckersall gained experience at the *Tribune*, his responsibilities expanded beyond simply reporting the news. Increasingly, Eckersall would be tasked with *making* the news, by creating events that he and his colleagues could cover.

Eckie's first effort was the "Tribune Ice Skating Carnival," a youth derby first held in February 1916. For two months, he wrote a stream of articles about the upcoming races. Much was mundane filler: Mayor William Hale Thompson had ordered the Chicago Fire Department to flood empty lots, to create practice space. Resourceful youth used roller skates to train on warm days. The *Tribune* would award gold buttons to winners of the preliminary events.[1]

The derby, held at Garfield Park on the city's West Side, drew five thousand fans for ten races in three age groups, plus two figure skating competitions. Eckersall proclaimed the event a success.

"It was a gathering for kids, and they rooted and cheered for their favorites the same as at a college meet," he wrote in his recap. "They were sincere in their cheering. . . . [It] came from the spot from which only kid enthusiasm is launched."[2]

Eckersall's problem became distinguishing the *Tribune* derby in a crowded marketplace. In the late nineteenth and early twentieth centuries, large numbers of northern European immigrants took their favorite wintertime recreation to the ponds and lagoons of Chicago's major public parks.

32. Art Staff of the Northwest Skating Club, winner of the inaugural Silver Skates derby in 1917. *Chicago Tribune*/TCA.

Many skating clubs were formed: the Mephistopheles Athletic Association, the Sleipner Athletic Club, the Norwegian Turners, the Scandinavian-American Athletic Union. Each club sponsored an annual derby, and the *Tribune* carnival featured the same races as all the others.[3]

As he planned his second derby in 1917, Eckie had another idea: Why not host a truly special event, a single long-distance race? The *Tribune* derby would go on as planned, but the following weekend Eckie would host a two-mile race, dubbed the Silver Skates.

"This is the first event of its kind attempted in the United States," Eckersall declared. "The thought reverts to 'Hans Brinker and the Silver Skates,' a book which nearly all of us have read at some time in our career. The intention is to make the Silver Skates race a classic in the skating world."[4]

At the inaugural Silver Skates, 141 athletes competed in one-mile heats to narrow the field down to fifteen finalists. Art Staff of the Northwest Skating Club won the finals, covering the two miles in five minutes and forty-two seconds.[5]

The Silver Skates soon became the premier wintertime sporting event in Chicago, and Eckersall took charge of all aspects of the race. Entry forms were directed to Eckie's desk at the *Tribune*. He organized dozens of volunteers, including his college teammate Wally Steffen, now a Cook County judge. He solicited help from the city's Bureau of Parks and Playgrounds and from the Chicago Police Department. He publicized the event, writing twenty to thirty preview articles each year. And he covered the race with long feature stories, big banner headlines, and large pictures of the action.

"Weeks ahead of the Derbies he began planning, carrying out details that to a lot of us would have been laborious and unpleasant work," wrote Don Maxwell, *Tribune* sports editor for most of the 1920s. "Most of us would have shoved the details onto someone else. That wasn't Eckie's way. He did the whole job himself."[6]

Initially, the Silver Skates consisted of one race to crown a single champion—or rather, a *male* champion. In 1919 Eckersall split the event into age groups. He added a Girls division in 1921, then split that division into age groups in 1922. In 1923 Eckie organized a "Champions Derby" of previous Boys Senior winners.

Although the competition was open to out-of-towners, most Silver Skates racers were homegrown. Of the sixty champions across all divisions, genders, and age groups between 1917 and 1930, fifty were from Chicago.

O'Neil Farrell, Boys Intermediate winner in 1924 and Boys Senior champion in 1925, later added international hardware to his trophy case, winning bronze in the 500 meters at the 1928 Winter Olympics. Eddie Murphy, the 1929 Boys Senior champion, won silver in the 5,000 meters at the 1932 Winter Olympics.

During Eckie's time, crowds at the Silver Skates averaged over thirty thousand. In the sincerest form of flattery, the *New York Daily News* copied Eckersall and launched its own Silver Skates in 1922.

Chicago Silver Skates, which continues today, thrived for decades. Several competitors went on to make the U.S. Olympic team, with at least two Silver Skates champions winning gold medals.[7]

—

Eckersall continued seeking good amateur events to sponsor. In 1918 he organized a *Tribune* youth track meet. In 1922 he launched the *Tribune* Bicycle Derby and the *Tribune* Water Carnival. The track meet lasted only a year, while the bicycle derby and water carnival fizzled out after six editions.[8]

In February 1923 Eckersall hit on the biggest idea of his career: an amateur boxing tournament, consisting of three-round bouts in every weight class.

The *Tribune*'s Hugh Fullerton announced the tournament publicly, and no contemporary article credits Eckersall as its founder. Later, Arch Ward would mistakenly be cited as the tournament's creator, but Ward—who wouldn't join the newspaper until 1925—gave credit to Eckie, sometimes alone and sometimes jointly with then sports editor Frank Smith.[9]

Whether the Golden Gloves idea was solely Eckie's or was born from a team effort, Eckersall was clearly in charge, and his fingerprints were all over the tournament. Entry forms, which readers could clip from the paper and return in the mail, were addressed to "Walter Eckersall, Tribune Plant." As with Silver Skates, Eckersall handled registrations, arranged brackets, publicized the event, and organized volunteers. Some of Eckie's assistants included future mayor Anton Cermak and future International Olympic Committee president Avery Brundage, both of whom had been athletes as Chicago youths.[10]

The tournament's mere existence was controversial. Boxing was still illegal in Chicago, although amateur fights were believed to be exempt from this ban. For several days, the *Tribune* solicited opinions. Big Ten commissioner John Griffith and Chicago Athletic Association general manager Martin Delaney spoke up in favor; the president of the Chicago Church Federation led the opposition.

The pros outweighed the cons by a 20-to-5 margin, although some opponents had harsh words for the *Tribune*'s sponsorship. One *Tribune* reader complained, "If you must do something barbarous and coarse to get the public eye, why don't you stage a bull fight or a bear match?"[11]

In an editorial, the *Tribune* defended its tournament on the grounds of virility. "We believe in giving [male youths an] outlet in rugged, wholesome sports, of which boxing is one," the paper opined. "If pale faces do not like it they are not compelled to subject themselves to it. If they do not like to have their noses hit or see other noses hit they are not required to. What we want is freedom for the other type which hasn't the inferiority complex and is not afraid if there is a bit of roughness."[12]

Applications poured in, as 424 boys signed up to compete. This positive response caused Eckie to double the length of the tournament; originally slated for three nights, it would now be held over six. Unlike other *Tribune* competitions, the boxing tournament would charge admission, with profits earmarked for disabled veterans.[13]

The inaugural tournament, held at the Ashland Boulevard Auditorium on the near West Side, netted $6,000. One favorite in the heavyweight class was Rip Miller, best known as one of the "Seven Mules" who blocked for the "Four Horsemen" of Notre Dame's football team. Miller advanced to the finals but was knocked out in the first round.[14]

"Nothing but favorable comment was heard in all quarters yesterday for the successful staging of the Chicago amateur boxing championships by the Tribune Athletic association," Eckersall wrote. "Following the last contest, boxers expressed satisfaction over their showings and all were unanimous in hoping the Tribune A.A. will stage a similar event next year."[15]

But in 1924, still concerned about the legality of amateur boxing in Chicago, the *Tribune* paused its tournament. Imitating the *Tribune* again, the *New York Daily News* launched an identical tournament at Madison Square Garden in February 1927. *Daily News* sports editor Paul Gallico gave his version a cool name that Eckersall probably wished he had thought of: the Golden Gloves, after a charm awarded to each division's winners.[16]

In May 1927, with all levels of boxing now unquestionably legal, Eckersall announced that the *Tribune* would restart its tournament the following spring. Since the "Tribune's Amateur Boxing Tournament" didn't exactly roll off the tongue, Eckie co-opted New York's "Golden Gloves" name.[17]

The 1928 Golden Gloves drew capacity crowds of up to five thousand over five nights at the Ashland Boulevard Auditorium. On the final evening, four thousand fans had to be turned away. The tournament raised $9,000 for disabled war veterans.[18]

Golden Gloves became a permanent fixture in Chicago each spring, and the show would continue even amid wars and a Great Depression. More

33. Walter Eckersall, right, presents a $9,000 check to Col. Albert Sprague, representing the profits of the 1928 Golden Gloves and earmarked for disabled veterans. *Chicago Tribune*/TCA.

than a hundred years after it was first contested, the Chicago Golden Gloves is still going strong.

After the 1928 Golden Gloves, the *Tribune* issued a challenge to the *Daily News*, offering to pit Chicago champions and runners-up against their New York counterparts. Eckie wrote nine preview stories leading up to the event, including profiles of several Chicago boxers. Lightweight champ Joe Kestian didn't make his high school football team because he was too small. Welterweight Nick Fosco was a product of Jane Addams's Hull House. Heavyweight Walter Radka had never gone to high school, instead building his muscles at a foundry. Light heavyweight champ Dave Maier had never lost a bout.[19]

The event drew a crowd of ten thousand to the Chicago Coliseum. New York and Chicago split the sixteen bouts evenly, earning a draw in the first of many Inter-City Golden Gloves championships.[20]

For the 1929 Chicago Golden Gloves, entries increased more than 60 percent. Eckie moved the event to the Coliseum, which could hold nearly twice as many fans as Ashland Boulevard. About twenty-five thousand fans attended the four-day tournament.

The 1929 Golden Gloves produced the tournament's first true star, a nineteen-year-old West Sider. "Barney Ross, another pupil of Jack Edmille's, took the title in the featherweight class," Eckersall wrote. "Ross is a two-fisted puncher who intends to turn professional after the intercity matches with New York."[21]

Ross would win his fight against New York featherweight champ Al Santora in the Inter-City Golden Gloves at Madison Square Garden the following month—a rare bright spot, as Chicago lost eleven of the sixteen fights. Ross went pro that summer and eventually won world titles in three different weight classes.[22]

For 1930, Eckie revised the Chicago Golden Gloves format. Regional competitions on the West, North, and South Sides would send four boxers in each weight class to the Chicago Finals at the Coliseum. They would be joined there by winners of satellite tournaments around the Midwest, including Fort Wayne, Indiana; Benton Harbor, Michigan; and Davenport, Iowa.[23]

Eckersall played up the city-versus-country aspect of the Chicago Finals, later rebranded as the "Tournament of Champions."

"Young Chicago is fighting mad," he wrote. "Called softies by lads from the farms, mines and mills, Pop Dearborn's soda jerkers, bellhops, and whatnots are ready to show 'em."[24]

As in previous years, Eckie handled registrations, organized volunteers, and publicized the tournament. Due to illness, though, Eckie didn't cover the fights in 1930. His *Tribune* colleague French Lane reported on the three regional preliminary rounds, while Lane and Maxwell teamed up to cover the four-night finals at the Coliseum, where Chicago fighters took six of the eight divisions against their "country cousins." Gross receipts exceeded $40,000, with profits again earmarked for disabled veterans.[25]

Eckersall was back on the beat for Inter-City Golden Gloves. More than twenty-two thousand fans, which both the *Tribune* and the *New York Daily News* claimed was a record for an indoor boxing event, packed Chicago Stadium on the city's Near West Side. Chicago won its first Inter-City title, beating New York eleven bouts to five. Eckie wrote a detailed blow-by-blow account of each of those sixteen fights.[26]

The 1930 Inter-City Golden Gloves would be the last sporting event that Walter Eckersall covered. Perhaps that is fitting, since the tournament was largely his creation.

The Chicago Tournament of Champions would launch the boxing careers of several fighters from other midwestern cities: Detroit's Joe Louis, light-heavyweight champ in 1934; Cincinnati's Ezzard Charles, middleweight champ in 1939; Sonny Liston of St. Louis, heavyweight champ in 1953; and perhaps the most famous boxer of all time, Muhammad Ali of Louisville, Kentucky, winner of the light-heavyweight title in 1959 and the heavyweight title in 1960.[27]

The Golden Gloves continue today, and the tournament has remained relevant long after its founder was more or less forgotten.

23

Color Lines

"Stick to sports" goes the modern adage, whenever a prominent athlete supports a political or social cause in an outspoken way. In reaction, sportswriters either parrot the detractors' "stick to sports" line or defend the athletes' First Amendment rights.

The idea of politically engaged athletes, or sportswriters, didn't emerge until the 1960s. Throughout much of the twentieth century, athletes did truly stick to sports, at least publicly. For the most part, so did Walter Eckersall. In 5,500 bylined articles over twenty-three years, he never revealed any controversial political or social opinions whatsoever, with one key exception: Eckie stood firmly and consistently against racism.

Eckersall's stance stems from his early friendship with his Hyde Park teammate Sam Ransom. In surviving pictures of Hyde Park's baseball and football teams, Eckersall and Ransom are frequently seen side by side, friends and teammates sticking together.

Ransom could certainly use the support. High schools in Chicago were never formally segregated, and neither were their sports; Englewood High School had an African American baseball player as far back as 1892. But the Great Migration from the South wouldn't start in earnest until 1916, at which point Chicago was only 2 percent Black. This lack of diversity was magnified by restrictive real-estate covenants, which made segregation a fact, if not an actual law, in daily Chicago life.[1]

34. Sam Ransom as a Hyde Park athlete. Walter Eckersall's lifelong friendship with Ransom would shape his progressive stances on race relations and equal opportunity. SDN-001508, *Chicago Daily News* collection, Chicago History Museum.

Athletically, there was much to admire about Ransom. "He was hard as nails and a fairly fast runner," Eckersall remembered. "He was quick and agile and one of the best backs I ever fed a football to. Not alone was he a valuable man on the offense, but he was a tower of strength on the defense. . . . He was a reliable performer in any branch of sport, and a lot of Hyde Park's athletic showing in those years is due to him. . . . [He is] one of the greatest all around athletes ever developed by a Chicago preparatory school."[2]

In the fall of 1903, when Eckersall was a freshman at Chicago, he served as a volunteer coach at Hyde Park to help out Ransom, who still had one more season of high school eligibility. After Ransom enrolled at tiny Beloit College in southern Wisconsin, Eckersall pointed out the injustice that kept Ransom from playing at one of the Big Nine schools.[3]

"It was only his color that kept him from making one of the big elevens," Eckersall lamented. "He went to Beloit, and was the mainstay of the football and baseball team. . . . Unfortunately he did not have much support, and he could not make the same name for himself as he did in high school."

(The great irony here was that Ransom was far more academically prepared for a Big Nine education than his Hyde Park teammates. Unlike Ransom, neither Eckersall nor Tom Hammond graduated from high school.)

Eckie would later recall of those days: "I had the pleasure of learning to know a Negro whose friendship I hold in high esteem. He was well liked by all the students . . . [and] had the respect not only of the high school body, but of his opponents as well, and always conducted himself, on and off the field, in a most gentlemanly way. He was branded as a true sportsman by all."[4]

—

Eckersall's friendship with Ransom clearly helped him feel more at ease among African Americans than many of his peers did. Starting in 1910, he traveled frequently to the "Black Belt," the African American neighborhood that centered on Thirty-First and State Streets, to interview heavyweight boxing champion Jack Johnson. When Johnson was defending his title out of town, Eckersall would return to the Black Belt to interview Johnson's neighbors.[5]

The writer sought to humanize an athlete whom much of the press called "brute," "black brute," "black giant," and worse, especially in the South. By contrast, Eckie had a friendly relationship with Johnson and gave examples of the boxer's kindness and humility in his articles. Eckersall also passed on statements from Johnson about sportsmanship and fair play.[6]

Eckie took the boxer's side in various disputes, exposing the injustices that Johnson faced, including the refusal of various white contenders to enter the same ring as Johnson. Conversely, he relayed the ambitions of various "Great White Hopes" to reclaim the heavyweight title in the name of racial superiority. Eckie also reported on the New York State Athletic Commission's denial of a boxing license for Johnson based on his race, and Johnson's ban from training at O'Connell's Gym in downtown Chicago, where he had once regularly sparred, for the same reason.[7]

35. Walter Eckersall sought to humanize the often-maligned boxer Jack Johnson, world heavyweight champion from 1908 to 1915. SDN-065687B, *Chicago Sun-Times/Chicago Daily News* collection, Chicago History Museum.

"I found it necessary to tell Johnson to stay away from my place, because his presence was hurting my business," gym owner Bill O'Connell told Eckersall in a half explanation, half apology. "After his appearance in the gym on Wednesday several of my pupils protested and said they would quit if Johnson was permitted to train there. So it was necessary for me to take action."[8]

Eckie noted racially motivated slights to other African American athletes. As one example, in 1911 Harry Fitzpatrick of the New Orleans Athletic Club refused to compete in the National AAU track meet in Chicago unless his Black opponent, Frank Holmes, was barred. "Either he goes or I go" was Fitzpatrick's ultimatum.

For the AAU officials, this decision was easy. "I believe in giving everybody a chance, regardless of color or religion," National AAU president Everett Brown told Eckersall, "and as long as Holmes is an American citizen I cannot see any reason why he should not be allowed to pit his skill on the athletic field against other men."[9]

Holmes—a 1908 Olympian who ironically competed for the Illinois State Gaelic Athletic Association, founded by athletes of Fitzpatrick's Irish ethnicity—got to compete. Fitzpatrick stayed behind in the South.

Several years later, Eckersall feared a similar boycott in a football game between Camp Dodge of Des Moines, Iowa, and the University of Iowa, which featured star African American tackle Duke Slater. Eckie was pleasantly surprised at the outcome this time:

> In former years games have been called off because southern players refused to play against teams including one or two Negro players. . . . The Dodge team had Maj. Bradley of the regular army playing right tackle, while opposed to him was Slater, the giant Negro tackle of the Hawkeye team.
>
> Maj. Bradley hails from a town in the southern part of Missouri. He had been born and brought up along the strict southern lines of relationship between whites and Negroes. Before the game started Maj. Bradley was asked if he cared to play against Slater, and replied in the affirmative.
>
> The writer was an official in this contest and was warned beforehand to be on the alert for foul tactics. A few plays was enough to convince anyone that the best of feeling existed between the pair. On several occasions, Maj. Bradley helped Slater to his feet when the latter was handled roughly.[10]

Although Maj. Omar Bradley had been a backup lineman on West Point's undefeated national championship team in 1914, he is best known today for his role in liberating Europe during World War II. As U.S. Army chief of staff in 1948, Bradley was tasked with carrying out President Harry Truman's order to desegregate the armed forces. One can only wonder if the foundation of Bradley's efforts was laid on that November afternoon in 1918, when under Eckersall's watchful eye he agreed to play fairly with Duke Slater.

—

Perhaps Eckie best advanced the cause of racial justice simply by highlighting the achievements of African American athletes. Many reporters, whether bigoted themselves or afraid of provoking reactions among their readers, simply skirted the issue of race.

In Eckie's time, the few Black football players at integrated institutions were largely marginalized. Frequently, newspapers simply ignored those players. "African Americans made slow but steady gains on football fields, yet remained nearly invisible in popular representations of the game," wrote NFL player turned college professor Michael Oriard in *King Football*, his comprehensive examination of football media coverage from the 1920s to the 1950s.[11]

When ignoring a player like a high-scoring back was impossible, he might be presented as either a curiosity piece or as the butt of a joke. "The 'joke' was simply that blacks could not possibly understand a game so complex as football," Oriard wrote.[12]

After playing three sports with Ransom in high school, and playing football against Bobby Marshall and baseball against Rube Foster, Eckersall knew better. He treated Black athletes not as curiosities but with dignity, as athletes and as men.

Two African American football players whom Eckie highlighted would eventually make the Pro Football Hall of Fame, the only two from that era to do so. Eckersall first covered Fritz Pollard as a track athlete at Chicago's Lane High School back in the spring of 1911, then as a football player for Lane that fall, and was impressed with the young halfback's elusiveness.[13]

Eckie covered Pollard again in the 1916 Rose Bowl, when he played for Brown University: "The game was all Brown's in the first half, with Pollard, the Negro half back, making yardage on end runs and forward passes." Although Brown lost the game, Pollard had again caught Eckersall's eye, and he named Pollard second-team All-American the following season.[14]

He would cover Pollard once more, noting that the halfback ran the ball well for the Akron Pros in a 0–0 tie with George Halas's Decatur Staleys during the NFL's inaugural season of 1920. In 1954 Pollard entered the College Football Hall of Fame but had to wait more than fifty additional years until he was posthumously elected to the Pro Football Hall of Fame.[15]

Eckersall would become even more familiar with Slater. In 1914 Eckie officiated the Iowa high school championship game between Clinton High School, whose star was Slater, and West Des Moines, whose sibling tandem of Aubrey and Glenn Devine would later team with Slater at Iowa. A few years later, Eckie was the umpire in Slater's first college game, against Halas's Great Lakes Naval Training Station team. Late in the second quarter, with the ball on the Great Lakes 20, Iowa deployed Slater as a secret weapon.[16]

"At this point Slater, the giant Negro tackle, was called back five yards from the line of scrimmage," Eckersall wrote. "The big lineman tore through the bluejacket line like a wild bull and the ball finally rested on the sailors' five yard line with only a minute left to play. Slater was again called back to make three yards on a fourth down, but the pass went wide and Iowa lost the ball on downs."[17]

Slater made a great first impression, even though Iowa would lose that game. Eckie covered five more Iowa games during Slater's career and consistently had high praise: "[Slater] is about the best lineman any football follower will see in the conference this year"; "Slater, the giant colored tackle of Iowa, is undoubtedly one of the best linemen in the west this year. He is big and powerful"; "He is so powerful that one man cannot handle him and opposing elevens have found it necessary to send two men against him every time a play was sent off his side of the line."[18]

Eckie named Slater first-team All–Big Ten three times, and first-team All-American in his senior season of 1921, when Iowa went undefeated and earned a claim to the national title. Slater later went on to a ten-year career in the NFL, fitting in football practice around law school studies; he eventually became a judge. When the College Football Hall of Fame was founded in 1951, Slater was the only African American inductee. Almost seventy years later, he was posthumously elected to the Pro Football Hall of Fame.

In track, Eckie highlighted the type of Black athletes who were increasingly emerging as stars. One Eckersall favorite was University of Chicago middle-distance runner Binga Dismond, a ten-time Big Ten champion and future medical doctor who would have been a top contender for the 1916

36. Walter Eckersall highlighted the achievements of Black athletes like Michigan's DeHart Hubbard, a three-time NCAA champion and the first African American to win individual Olympic gold. BL001111, Bentley Historical Library Image Bank, University of Michigan Library Digital Collections.

Olympics in Berlin had World War I not interfered. "Binga Dismond was the shining light for Chicago," Eckie noted after one race.[19]

Another favorite was sprinter and long-jumper Sol Butler of Dubuque College (today's University of Dubuque): "Butler came east to break the [American long jump] record and he accomplished his purpose, thereby making his selection for a place on the Olympic team a certainty," Eckersall wrote in 1920. Butler was injured in the prelims at Antwerp and finished a disappointing seventh.[20]

In 1924 DeHart Hubbard of the University of Michigan won Olympic gold in the long jump, the first Black athlete to take the top prize in an individual event. The following year, Hubbard won both the 100-yard dash and the long jump at the NCAA track championships at Stagg Field, setting a world record in the latter. Eckie's writeup the next day dedicated eight paragraphs to Hubbard's performance.

"It had been frequently predicted that Hubbard would smash the world's record in his favorite event before the end of his college career," Eckersall wrote. "And so it was yesterday that on his last jump and in his last intercollegiate competition, Hubbard accomplished the goal of his ambitions."[21]

Eckie also took notice of a local African American sprinter. "Ralph Metcalfe of Tilden High, Chicago, hung up one of the best performances of the games when he won the 100 yard dash in :09 9-10," Eckersall wrote in 1928 after a meet in Milwaukee. "This performance set a meet record and the Tilden athlete won without being pushed." Weeks later Metcalfe, just a high school sophomore, ran the 100 in 9.8 seconds to break Eckie's twenty-five-year-old Illinois state meet record. He would ultimately win nine Illinois state titles, six NCAA titles while running for Marquette, and four medals over two Olympics (including a relay gold, teaming with Jesse Owens, in 1936), before embarking on a long political career.[22]

Besides Jack Johnson, Eckie highlighted several other top African American boxers. He wrote about heavyweights Sam Langford and Harry Wills, who combined to hold the so-called "World Colored Heavyweight" title for all but seven months between September 1910 and November 1926. Eckie was supposed to cover a fight between Langford and an Italian boxer in Kenosha, Wisconsin, in May 1911, but the Wisconsin governor canceled that bout. Officially, the governor said the fight violated a Wisconsin law that permitted "exhibitions" but barred "prizefights." In reality, the governor wanted to avoid the sorts of racial unrest that followed Jack Johnson's victory over white boxer Jim Jeffries the previous summer.[23]

That was the closest Eckie came to covering a fight involving either boxer. Frustratingly, neither ever got a chance to compete for the heavyweight title. First, Jack Johnson denied Langford a title shot, mainly because he could earn more money by fighting white opponents. In the 1920s heavyweight champ Jack Dempsey toyed with the idea of boxing Wills in a title fight but ultimately dodged his Black challenger.

Eckie reported on various behind-the-scenes maneuvers to arrange these interracial title fights, as well as on those efforts falling through. In 1925 Eckersall interviewed retired boxing coach George Dawson about Wills's chances in a hypothetical bout against Dempsey. Dawson's thoughts were provocative, especially considering Dempsey's extreme popularity at the time.[24]

"Harry Wills, whom I consider the best heavyweight of the last ten years, would have whipped Dempsey," Dawson said. "Wills is the more scientific of the two men. Dempsey is strictly a puncher, while Harry is a puncher and a boxer."[25]

Ultimately, no Black heavyweight would get a title shot from the time Johnson lost the crown in 1915 until Joe Louis won it in 1937. But African Americans did win titles in several other weight classes. One such champion was middleweight Tiger Flowers.

"Flowers is of the boxer type," Eckie wrote in 1925 on the eve of a fight in Aurora, Illinois. "In fact, he is more of the combination of fighter and boxer than most of the fighters seen in Chicago this summer. He can hit and he can box."[26]

Eckie covered three bouts involving Flowers. At one of those fights, Flowers lost his middleweight title, controversially, to Mickey Walker at the Chicago Coliseum. Eckie hinted that the referee's decision was rooted in racism, without writing those words:

> To those around the ringside it looked as if the champion was entitled to the verdict by a wide margin. Tiger forced the milling, landed the scoring punches, and on only a few occasions was in danger of defeat. . . . Even the members of the boxing commission looked upon the verdict with surprise, although none of them would venture an opinion. Around the ringside some of the spectators thought Referee Yanger had made a mistake and held up the wrong fighter's hand, but when the real truth of the decision was known the fans filed out of the building expressing their disgust and asserting the boxing game . . . will not survive if similar decisions are rendered.[27]

—

Eckersall never used the "N-word" in print, which even a Northern, formerly abolitionist paper such as the *Tribune* used surprisingly often, about once a week during Eckersall's career. He did use some language that we now consider racially charged, words like "colored," "Negro," "dusky," and so on, but those terms were considered acceptable in Eckersall's time.

Acceptable, at least, to white people. In 1912 one African American reader took note of Eckersall's language. The reader complained not to Eckie's editor but to the editor of the nation's leading Black newspaper, the *Chicago Defender*.

> Did you ever see such a change as has come over "Eckie"? When he was in school he would fight for his pal, Sam Ransam [*sic*], but since he got to be a reporter the meanest things he can say about the race seems not so good. Not long since I saw him eat dinner at the table with Jack Johnson . . . the next morning in the Tribune we would read under his caption, "Jack Johnson, the Negro champion." The point, Mr. Editor, I want to bring home is this: Aren't the Americans aware of Jack's race, or is there a white champion by the same name? Please let us know.

The *Defender*'s sports editor demurred in his reply. "Mr. Eckersall is forced to write his article the way he does because the policy of the Tribune is to down the Negroes . . . so don't think hard of 'Eckie,' for if he did not please his editor-in-chief, as well as follow the policy of the Tribune, he would be canned."[28]

A greater point here: Eckersall was one of the few white reporters to highlight Black athletes for a mainstream newspaper. In a sense, Eckersall was still fighting for his friend Sam Ransom, who had largely faded into obscurity since his Hyde Park High School days.

Yet, Eckersall was no social justice warrior. After high school, Eckersall never had a Black teammate. If the benign neglect of his college coach, Amos Alonzo Stagg, or the vicious racism of his semipro baseball manager, Cap Anson, bothered him, he never said anything publicly.

Similarly, Eckie never spoke up specifically against Major League Baseball's color line. Then, during Chicago's race riots in the summer of 1919, Eckie simply went about his business, writing previews of two different track meets, covering a swim meet, and writing a story on college football's prospects for that fall, even as much of the Black Belt, where he had once visited so comfortably, lay in turmoil.[29]

Though clearly progressive on race issues, Eckersall occasionally gave in to the perceived desires of his overwhelmingly white readership by poking fun at the expense of African Americans.

"Among many interesting features to the program, the contest which attracted most attention, was the quarter mile race for colored persons who made affidavits that they had never been on skates before, and that they were born south of the Mason and Dixon line," Eckie wrote after a 1911 ice-skating derby. "The crowd sat up and took notice when the contestants came out on the track with the well known policy [an illegal organized crime–sponsored lottery, popular in Black neighborhoods] numbers, 23, 7, 18, 11, and 44 placarded on their backs."[30]

A few years later, Eckie reported on "an old fashioned battle royal between five Negroes in which Linnie Banks survived." Decades later, in his novel *Invisible Man*, author Ralph Ellison captured the humiliation and degradation of his protagonist fighting a similar battle royal in front of a similar white audience. Yet, Eckersall relayed this situation as a humorous anecdote, either not realizing or intentionally ignoring how the Black contestants must have felt.[31]

—

These lapses, while abhorrent, were few. In most respects, Eckersall was far ahead of his time on race relations. He publicized the achievements of African American athletes, advocated for a level playing field, and called out injustices when he saw them. This attitude remained consistent throughout Eckie's career.

Eckersall's empathy is perhaps best illustrated by an article that he contributed in 1918 to *The Ann Arbor (MI) Negro Year-Book*. The yearbook's editor asked both Walter Camp and Walter Eckersall for some comments about the best Black football players each had seen.

Camp wrote a two-sentence, sixty-word reply, mentioning Harvard's William Henry Lewis and Brown's Fritz Pollard. Camp then goes on to say that "[Paul] Robeson who played end at Rutgers this year, is, however, the best I ever saw."

In contrast to Camp's telegram-length statement, Eckersall wrote a 650-word essay.

"Having seen and played against a number of colored football players, I will not hesitate a moment to name Bob Marshall, of Minnesota, Fred Pollard, of Brown, and Sam Ransom, of Beloit, as the three best colored warriors who ever donned the moleskins," Eckersall said. (Slater, whom Eckie would eventually rate as the best African American football player, wouldn't matriculate at Iowa until that fall.)

Eckie repeated his long-standing contention that Ransom was a "player of great possibilities but who did not have the opportunities. . . . [He] went to Beloit college where he practically had to play the whole game because his teammates were of inferior ability. Despite the fact he was a marked man in every game, his opponents knew they had been in a game when the final whistle blew."

His college opponent, Bobby Marshall of Minnesota, earned similar praise. "[Marshall] was a powerful built man, being six feet in height and weighing in the neighborhood of 200 pounds," Eckersall wrote. "He was fast and had football intuition. He was a remarkable kicker and it was his ability to kick goals from the field that resulted in the defeat of Chicago in 1906 by the score of 4 to 2. I was captain of the Maroon team at that time and well know the game he played against us. He certainly was a remarkable player."

Eckie also had high praise for Pollard: "I think Fred Pollard, last year's halfback on Brown university was as good a football player, as the colored race has produced."

As far as the original question was concerned, Eckersall had completed the assignment. But as an ally, he felt the need to go beyond.

> In every line of athletic endeavor in which teams are organized there are players of different nationalities and colors and although discrimination has been shown by some colleges in regard to the latter, the general opinion of unfairness has been manifested many times.
>
> In my twenty years of athletic experience as a player and writer of sports, I have met colored athletics who, to my mind, were the superiors of their white teammates. In every case, the colored athletic has conducted himself on and off the field in a manner which could not help but command the respect of all.[32]

In three short sentences, Eckersall not only editorialized about the plight of the Black athlete in America but also signaled to African American readers that he stood with them in their struggle.

24

The Seedy Side of Sports

During Walter Eckersall's playing days, newspapers linked him to many scandalous rumors: That he was secretly receiving money and other perks. That he was a student in name only. That he had faked an injury to get Michigan's Joe Curtis ejected from the 1905 Chicago-Michigan game, essentially cheating his way to his greatest victory.

One would have understood if Eckie, once he became a newspaper writer, avoided the types of rumors and gossip that had followed him as an athlete. Instead, Eckersall delved into the dark corners of the sporting world, exposing anything shady he saw.

Even an old favorite like Jack Johnson wasn't spared from scrutiny. "If reports are true that Jack needs money there is a chance he may be bought off," Eckersall quoted one observer before Johnson's 1915 title bout with Jess Willard. "I understand the syndicate which is to stage the fight has enough money to offer Johnson a substantial sum to 'flop.'"[1]

Eckersall's later reporting indicated that the fight was fair; Willard won the title with a twenty-sixth-round knockout. But four years later, Johnson, who had been found guilty of violating the Mann Act in 1913, claimed he had thrown the fight in exchange for a suspended prison sentence, and Eckie passed along Johnson's statement. Some experts believed Johnson; others thought he was simply making excuses for losing. More than a hundred years later, the truth remains unclear.[2]

Eckie also probed the integrity of another favorite, Packey McFarland, when a referee accused Packey's opponent of taking a dive in a 1911 bout. In a 1927 fight that he covered, Eckie wondered whether a middleweight from Philadelphia had thrown a fight: "The blow did not appear to carry enough power to upset any fighter," Eckersall noted. "Many declared it looked like he went into the ring to take a dive."[3]

Eckie felt an almost religious duty to defend sporting integrity. Beyond the possibility of thrown fights, Eckersall reported on shakedowns of boxing promoters by greedy politicians; on the sheriff of Peoria, Illinois, canceling a fight based on word of a potential frame-up; and on rumors that "hoodlums" might try to poison or kidnap lightweight champ Sammy Mandell before a title fight in 1929.[4]

The writer also shone his light on professional wrestling. Originally an authentic sport, pro wrestling had already become a theatrical spectacle by Eckie's day. He covered flamboyant fan favorites like the Masked Marvel and Strangler Lewis, and insisted that Lewis could beat Jack Dempsey in a fight. Yet as early as 1919, Eckie also relayed the then-shocking news that pro wrestling might be fake. He reported that gamblers lost as much as $4,000 on matches whose outcomes had been prearranged and noted later efforts by the Illinois Boxing Commission to ban pro wrestling due to this fraud.[5]

Eckie publicly condemned anything that even hinted of scandal among current athletes. But at the same time, he gleefully recounted tales of anonymous nineteenth-century athletes and gamblers who used every trick in the book to gain competitive advantage.

These old-time legends included: How a Texas ranchman in the 1870s brought in a ringer from the East to beat the local sprinting champ, winning $6,000 but getting run out of town in the process. How sprinters in the 1880s would travel rural Canada, betting the locals that they could run 100 yards in less than ten seconds, then using a trick tape measure to cut the course short and guarantee victory. How in 1892 a hotel clerk in Michigan ("whom we will call Smith, because he did not want his name used") had doped a sprinter's coffee to fix a race, helping a gambling syndicate win $18,000.[6]

The way these stories are relayed, a reader can't quite tell if Eckersall is condemning the cheaters or celebrating them. Either way, he highlighted the people who made cheating profitable: the gamblers who flocked to the *Tribune*'s sports pages for inside information.

Eckersall obliged them. He packed his midweek football articles with tidbits, gleaned from interviews and from his open access to practices. He hung around boxing gyms and talked to promoters, trying to get a line on favorites for upcoming fights. He vetted tips on injuries that might sway a betting man's decision and refuted false rumors. He offered expert picks on football games, boxing matches, and track and swimming meets.

And he talked to bookies. Lots of bookies.

—

In February 1912 Eckersall first quoted betting odds on a boxing match, listing McFarland as a 10-to-7 favorite in a lightweight bout. McFarland won, and soon Eckie reported boxing odds whenever he could get them.[7]

Eckie had an even longer history of listing odds in football, though he didn't quote football odds as frequently. In 1907 he noted that Carlisle was a 3-to-2 favorite over Big Eight champion Chicago. Carlisle won 18–4, returning $150 to a gambler who had risked $100. In 1908 Eckersall reported 5-to-4 odds on Chicago over Minnesota, a game that Chicago would win; 3-to-2 odds on Cornell over Chicago, which would end in a tie; and 2-to-1 odds on Chicago over Wisconsin, which Eckie thought was too generous but which would ultimately pay off when Chicago won. In 1909 and again in 1910, Eckie reported Minnesota as a slight favorite over Michigan, but the underdog would win both of those games.[8]

What those first few games all had in common: Eckie was strictly in the press box, not on the field as an official. Eventually, though, he started quoting odds on games that he was also working. The first game for which he both quoted odds and officiated seems to be the 1919 Rose Bowl, where he listed Great Lakes as a 10-to-8 favorite over the Mare Island Marines.[9]

A few years later, Eckie would quote California as a 5-to-1 favorite over Washington and Jefferson in the 1922 Rose Bowl. In a major twist from gambling convention, Eckie also reported Cal as a 2-to-1 favorite to win by

21 points or more. While this quote doesn't quite qualify as a point spread (which would imply even odds after points are added), it's an example of creative bookmaking, and a step toward the point-spread system that would become ubiquitous by the 1950s. Either way, Cal was a big favorite, and Eckie was on the sideline as field judge when Washington and Jefferson pulled off the "upset" with a 0–0 tie.[10]

Eckie usually didn't quote odds for games that he officiated, but he did so often enough to be noticeable. Even more so because these tended to be big games. Eckersall quoted Notre Dame as an 8-to-5 favorite over Stanford in the 1925 Rose Bowl; Notre Dame as a 6-to-5 favorite over USC in 1927; and USC as a 2-to-1 favorite over Carnegie Tech in 1929.[11]

Stepping away from his more familiar roles as referee or umpire, Eckie was head linesman for the first two games, and field judge for the third. Perhaps he felt more comfortable quoting odds in these roles, in which he was less likely to affect the outcome. But by providing odds on games that he was also officiating, Eckersall was playing a dangerous game, even if the practice didn't lead to any backlash in the 1920s.

—

Athletes, managers, promoters, and bookies weren't the only sporting figures associated with bad behavior. Unruly crowds had always been part of the equation.

The fans in the stands were always a part of Eckersall's stories. He noted attendance numbers, the presence of any celebrities, and whether factors like poor weather may have kept spectators away. Usually, Eckie celebrated the crowd's spirit and energy in supporting the home team or a fan favorite. Sometimes, he noted a crowd's silence after the tide had turned in favor of the visitors.

Occasionally, crowds crossed a line, and Eckie relayed those episodes to his readers. He noted several near-brawls at boxing matches, such as a 1911 middleweight fight in Gary, Indiana. When ticket sales didn't cover Eddie McGoorty's $400 guarantee, he refused to come out of the dressing room, which caused the crowd to nearly riot. Eckersall reported shouts of "Give us our money back!" and "Never again!" coming from spectators, while editorializing, "If the fight had not taken place the game would have been killed in this city." Eventually a hat was passed, collecting enough money to lure McGoorty into the ring and settle things down.[12]

Unruly spectators also appeared in Eckersall's wrestling stories. "As the match wore on the crowd booed the men and shouts of 'fake' rent the air," Eckie noted after a 1922 match at the Chicago Coliseum. At another bout in which Strangler Lewis beat Stanislaus Zbyszko at Dexter Park Pavilion: "Admirers of Zbyszko immediately shouted foul, and rushed toward the ring. They charged Lewis and [referee Pat] McGill with 'funny' work. . . . It was necessary for police and firemen to escort Lewis and McGill through the angry mob to the dressing rooms."[13]

Often, crowds turned unruly simply because they thought athletes weren't trying hard enough. "Sailor [Freedman] was booed for holding during the first five rounds but he was compelled to stay close to avoid punishment," Eckie wrote after a middleweight fight in East Chicago. "In the seventh, eighth and ninth rounds the boxers held on and wrestled so much that the crowd booed them," he reported from a featherweight bout in Aurora. "In the fifth Referee Jimmy Gardner warned [light heavyweight Ad] Stone about pulling his punches," Eckie wrote after another East Chicago fight. "The small crowd of 1,800 fans was aware of the effort and booed the fighters continually."[14]

Eckie also noted another negative effect of boxing crowds: the presence of pickpockets, muggers, and other outright criminals.

"Toledo returned to quiet life this morning," Eckersall wrote after Dempsey beat Willard in Toledo, Ohio, to claim the world heavyweight title in 1919. "Today a person can walk along the streets without being relieved of his valuables and money."[15]

—

Eckie's reporting also occasionally brought him uncomfortably close to organized crime.

In 1921 the Illinois High School Association asked Eckersall to draw the random matchups for its state basketball playoffs. He was joined by the *Tribune*'s crusading crime reporter, Jake Lingle. Almost a decade later, Lingle was gunned down in downtown Chicago. Initially hailed as a martyr slain for his anticrime reporting, Lingle was soon revealed to be on the mob's payroll himself, killed in retaliation for some sort of double-cross.[16]

In 1923, with boxing still illegal in Illinois, two rival promoters scheduled competing charity exhibitions for the same night. Eckersall attended a meeting to settle this "local boxing war." One of the promoters brought a special negotiator to the conference: Johnny Torrio.[17]

The *Tribune* had loosely linked Torrio to organized crime for several years, as the owner of a bar where mobsters hung out and as a person of interest in the 1920 murder of crime boss "Big Jim" Colosimo. But to Eckie, who had covered a handful of bouts involving fighters that Johnny managed, he was simply "Torrio, a real sportsman and lover of boxing."[18]

With mob muscle in the conference room, the tone of the boxing war changed. "We set our show back a day for the good of boxing," the rival promoter told Eckersall. "I am sure Johnny Torrio, who is interested . . . in the promotion of the Monday night show, would have done the same thing. . . . It was up to either of us to swallow his pride and give way. In neither case, however, has any one backed down."[19]

That face-saving statement was clearly not true. With Eckersall as a witness, Torrio's rival caved but likely saved his kneecaps in the process. Within months, the *Tribune* named Torrio "the accredited leader of the beer running syndicate" in Chicago. Torrio later merged competing crime organizations into a cartel known as the National Crime Syndicate.[20]

A month after the Johnny Torrio incident, another charity exhibition brought Eckie close to another mobster—but this time, the mobster was an athlete. At a May boxing benefit for a Catholic grammar school, Eckie noted an undercard bout between "two welterweights, Glen Milligan of Iowa and Jack McGurn of the west side."[21]

McGurn, a Sicilian whose real name was Vincenzo Gibaldi, adopted the pseudonym because he thought Irish boxers could book better fights. Several months later, in his "Notes of the Boxers" column, Eckersall wrote, "Jack McGurn, promising 20 year old local boxer, has started active training for welterweight bouts. He has a following among Italian fight fans."[22]

One of those Italian fans would have been McGurn's boss, Al Capone, who was already using "Machine Gun Jack McGurn" as an enforcer and hit man. McGurn would later be credited with slaying Capone rival Hymie Weiss, stabbing singer Joe E. Lewis in a contract dispute, and helping plan the St. Valentine's Day Massacre of 1929.

—

Before any of these close encounters with infamous criminals, Eckie's reporting accidentally helped uncover the greatest scandal in sports history.

Eckersall didn't write much about professional baseball; he only covered one Major League game during his career. But as the 1919 World Series between the Chicago White Sox and the Cincinnati Reds approached, the *Tribune* needed extra hands to write background stories. So, Eckie wrote about the dark corners of the national pastime.

His first two stories dealt with ticket scalpers. Eckie's third story addressed the gambling scene and the movement of money in betting circles. Although the White Sox had been heavy favorites heading into the World Series, Eckie reported that the odds shifted significantly after the Reds won the first game.

"The decisive victory of Cincinnati over Chicago's White Sox in the opening game of the world's series has made the Reds a 6 to 5 favorite in the series at most places where the gambling fraternity congregate," Eckersall reported. "In fact, there is plenty of Cincinnati money here, as was shown yesterday, when several thousand dollars changed hands."[23]

Eckie noted innocently—at least, as innocently as one hanging around gambling dens could—that after the Sox tied the score in the second inning of Game 1, one gambler eagerly covered a Sox fan's $2,500 bet on the remainder of the game, at even odds. By then, anyone in the conspirators' circle would have known the fix was in. Eckersall further noted heavy gambling in the Stockyards district, and that "the tip went out through the yards that [White Sox pitcher Eddie] Cicotte was not in his best form." Cincinnati went on to win that first game 9–1, costing the unwitting Sox fan about $45,000 in today's dollars.

There's no indication that Eckersall suspected collusion between eight White Sox players (including Cicotte) and a New York–based gambling syndicate to throw the 1919 World Series. Eckie didn't cover the rest of the

Series, since college football season started three days later. But his reporting alerted other writers, including his off-and-on *Tribune* colleague Hugh Fullerton, that things might not be on the square. Under heavy scrutiny, the Sox lost, five games to three. Within a year, the "Black Sox Scandal" was exposed, and while the players were acquitted in court, Baseball Commissioner Kenesaw Mountain Landis would permanently ban all eight from baseball.[24]

—

Over the years, Eckersall loved exploring the seedy side of sports, writing about topics ranging from poor sportsmanship to outright cheating, to the world of gamblers and bookies, to the intersection of sports with the underworld.

That seedy side still accounted for a fairly small percentage of Eckie's output. As he covered a growing variety of sports, developed extensive networks of sources, and traveled widely in search of the biggest games and events, Eckersall evolved into a true authority on the sporting world.

25

The Authority

"Eckersall was not a great writer," his friend Eddie Jacquin, sports editor of the *Champaign (IL) News-Gazette*, stated bluntly. "But he was an authority."[1]

The *Tribune* began marketing Eckie as its "football expert" by 1909, before he was even a year-round employee. In his first public debate as a pundit, Eckersall championed the open game that had started to emerge during his senior season at Chicago. This advocacy placed him at odds with the Father of American Football, Walter Camp.[2]

Eckie urged Camp to get with the times, writing: "American football is in better condition this fall than it ever has been. The open game of last season won the hearts of the American people generally, and many of those who were bitterly opposed to football a year ago are now its strongest supporters."[3]

Open football was better not only for safety, Eckersall argued, but also because it was more interesting. As an added bonus, the open game leveled the playing field between big and small colleges, rewarding innovative coaches and risk-taking teams.

Camp continued to fight the forward pass, engaging in a philosophical battle with both Eckie and his mentor, Amos Alonzo Stagg. In February 1912 Eckie reported on a pending showdown at a Rules Committee meeting, where Camp would propose banning the forward pass after a six-season experiment. Stagg and others outmaneuvered Camp, removing a couple significant restrictions on passing while granting teams four downs, instead of three, to gain first down. (At the same meeting, touchdowns were increased in value from 5 to 6 points.)[4]

To Camp's chagrin and Eckie's satisfaction, modern football was here to stay.

—

While Eckie disagreed with Camp on how football should be played, he imitated the Father of American Football in one important way. After the 1907 season, Eckersall started naming his own all-star teams. Curiously, Eckie's first All-America team, like most of Camp's teams, was made up entirely of Eastern players.[5]

For the next six years, Eckie didn't name an All-America team, sticking with All-Conference and All-Western selections. After Eckersall resumed picking All-Americans in 1914, his teams better reflected the country. In 1915 almost half of his selections came from the Midwest. In 1916 Brown's Fritz Pollard became the first Black player to make Eckie's All-America team, followed by Iowa's Duke Slater in both 1919 and 1921. In 1917 Eckie named the first Southern college players to his All-America team . . . or so it appeared.[6]

On first glance, nothing seemed wrong with Eckie's teams, which included eight well-known players from the Big Ten and twelve from the East. To round out his first team, Eckie included two names from Atlanta's Georgia Tech. Coached by John Heisman, Tech was widely regarded as the national champion for 1917. But the *Tribune* hadn't covered Georgia Tech at all, not even through wire stories. The one game that might have earned some coverage, a 32–0 win over Penn in October, was crowded off the *Tribune*'s sports pages by coverage of the White Sox in the 1917 World Series. Georgia Tech and its players were a total mystery to *Tribune* readers.

Eckie had the *Tribune*'s newspaper "morgue" of out-of-town clippings and his personal contacts, which he could leverage to find names for Georgia Tech's best players. But then, Eckie got sick. On Monday, December 3, shortly after returning from a game in Nebraska, Eckie collapsed in his downtown office. He was rushed to the hospital in grave condition. Eckersall remained in the hospital for more than a week and wouldn't return to his reporting duties for almost three weeks.[7]

But his All-American picks, scheduled to appear in the *Tribune* and in syndication in mid-December, were due. Eckie likely had roughed out an article, perhaps with a note like "Georgia Tech players," without names. With Eckersall incapacitated, his colleagues scrambled to finish his story. That's how Georgia Tech linemen Harvey McCord and Sid Sault made Eckie's 1917 All-America team.[8]

Within a couple days, the flaw was exposed: McCord and Sault were *not* Georgia Tech players but rather played for Atlanta's Tech High School.

Eckie was mocked, then and for decades thereafter. "The football fans of this city are today enjoying a loud guffaw at the expense of Walter Eckersall, Chicago football 'expert,'" came one report, which was picked up in syndication. These selections became a cautionary tale, as later sportswriters imagined Eckersall blindly grabbing a couple of random names while combing through clippings.[9]

In real time, only the *New Brunswick (NJ) Home News* connected the dots to figure out the reason for the mistake: "Coincident with the news that Walter Eckersall, the famous Chicago quarterback, has recovered from his recent illness, comes his annual All-American selections. As we gaze over the two elevens we cannot believe that they really were the work of Eckersall. . . . The naming of 'McCord' and 'Gault' [*sic*] is not a typographical error, for in discussing the selections Eckersall—or, more likely, the man who got up the selections for Walter—mentions both names and tells about their remarkable ability."[10]

Eckie never threw his ghostwriter (or, as the *Home News* called him, "Eckersall's pinch hitter") under the bus. His reputation recovered, and his all-star teams became an annual staple, devoured by fans around the country.

Eckie placed an actual Southern college player, tackle Josh Cody of Vanderbilt, on his 1919 All-America team. In 1921 he added his first West Coast player, Cal tackle Dan McMillan. Spurred in part by his trips around the country, Eckersall eventually named more than fifty Southern and West Coast players to his All-America teams. By contrast, Walter Camp only named forty such players to his teams, even though Camp made All-American selections for twice as long as Eckersall did.[11]

Beyond geographic diversity, Eckersall highlighted players from small and medium-sized colleges. His All-Western teams regularly included players from schools that were not traditional powerhouses: Wabash, Lombard, Beloit, Coe, Xavier, Grinnell. In 1920 Eckie's first- and second-team All-American quarterbacks both hailed from small schools: Bo McMillin of Centre College in Kentucky and Benny Boynton of Williams College in Massachusetts. Both would later make the College Football Hall of Fame.[12]

—

Although Eckersall and Camp differed on football philosophy, they had much in common as ambassadors for the sport. As editor of the premier annual football yearbook, *Spalding's Official Foot Ball Guide*, Camp solicited writers like Eckie for articles on football in various parts of the country.

Starting in 1910, Eckersall contributed his observations on regional football for Camp's national audience. He took this role seriously, writing articles that were three or four times longer than the ones that Camp had previously run. Recognizing that the typical Eastern or Southern reader wouldn't know much about Midwest football, Eckie went into extensive detail about the best players, teams, and games.

Eckersall's Midwest football review became a staple of the *Spalding Guide* for the rest of his career. Through these longer features, Eckersall was able to go in-depth on players and teams in ways that he rarely could in his daily *Tribune* write-ups.

From the start of his reporting career, even though he was in his early twenties, Eckersall spoke like an elder statesman about football. Back in 1907, he started an interactive "Football Queries" column, in which fans could ask him questions about strategy, history, and specific game scenarios. After that first season, Eckie dropped his byline from the column, which he continued to write through at least 1911.[13]

Eckersall would also imitate Camp's *How to Play Foot Ball* book by twice writing his own series of articles. Unlike Camp, he didn't farm out any of his work, writing the entire series himself. In 1912 he wrote ten separate "How to Play Football for Beginners" articles, on topics ranging from the rudiments of football to the fundamentals of various positions. In 1928 Eckersall reprised and expanded the series, publishing fifteen articles and ten diagrams over six weeks. The *Tribune* reprinted Eckie's work in booklet form, selling copies for ten cents each.[14]

Periodically, Eckersall looked back at football history the way a pundit would. In 1923 he published a series of "The Greatest" articles on the top players at various programs, many of whom Eckersall had played against or written about. These included Michigan's Willie Heston, Iowa's Aubrey Devine, Ohio State's Chic Harley, and Notre Dame's George Gipp.[15]

For the University of Chicago, Eckersall named his childhood hero, quarterback Walter Kennedy, as best in program history, with Wally Steffen a close second. Eckie's *Tribune* editors vetoed this decision, stating loudly and clearly: "Walter Eckersall was the greatest football player who ever wore the Maroon of Chicago."[16]

—

Occasionally, Eckersall's public stances as a pundit were tone-deaf.

In 1909 Eckie gave his take on the case of Wisconsin quarterback Keckie Moll, who had been suspended for a hazing incident in which he knocked out another student's teeth. A group of Wisconsin players and alumni protested and called for a general student strike until Moll's suspension was lifted.[17]

Eckersall headed to Madison to cover the story, but Moll had been reinstated by the time he arrived. Eckie's reaction was one-sided:

> There is great rejoicing in Madison tonight. Keckie Moll, Wisconsin's star quarter back, has been reinstated in college, and with this action on the part of President Van Hise Badger football stock has gone up many per cent. Probably never in the history of the institution has a thing happened which has caused so much bitter feeling towards the faculty as the Moll case. . . .
>
> But the students and townspeople here have secured their revenge. The unanimous opinion here is that the faculty had to back down and for once listen to the appeals of those who are fighting hard to regain Wisconsin's old rank in western athletics. On every side is heard the victory of the students over the faculty. . . . *It is rather a pity that an*

institution with such grand athletic spirit should be continually handicapped by faculty restrictions.[18]

The Keckie Moll case again raised the fundamental question: Who should be in charge of college sports—faculties or athletic departments? In Eckersall's now-expert opinion, athletic departments should rule, and faculties should butt out.

Eckersall had similar bad takes on player safety. Since he had avoided injury so skillfully himself, Eckie reasoned that all players should be able to do the same. He would frequently blame the victims for head and neck injuries that continued to loom over the sport.

"The only thing that marred the season was the number of deaths and serious injuries," Eckersall wrote in 1915, when fifteen football-related fatalities were reported. "Most of the fatalities occurred on teams which were not properly trained or coached. In most places the players were not subjected to a physical examination, and if this had been done some of the deaths could have been avoided."[19]

As if a good, thorough physical could negate a hard blow to the head.

At times, Eckersall mimicked the language of Social Darwinism, played out on the football field. "Football always has and always will be a dangerous sport, and if it were not for the danger element it would not be so popular with the American boys," he wrote. "Football is not a parlor game. Fatalities will happen the same as in any other line of sport."[20]

One of Eckersall's more callous statements came after Ralph Wilson of Wabash College died in October 1910, the day after suffering a head injury during a game. Wabash, 4-0 at the time of Wilson's death, canceled the rest of its season. Now Eckie expressed sadness, but not so much because of the death.

"The death of Half Back Davis [*sic*] of the Wabash College eleven is an accident to be regretted," Eckersall wrote. "The subsequent abolishment of football at Wabash for the year will deprive followers of the sport from seeing a number of good, clean battles. Wabash was rated as having one of the strongest teams in the minor colleges and this unforeseen accident will rob western football of one of its best teams."[21]

Eckersall seemed sadder about the loss of a contending team than about the sudden, shocking death of one of its players—whose name Eckie didn't even get right. Again, tone-deaf.

—

Occasional bad takes aside, Eckersall continued to grow in influence as a leading national voice on college football. After Camp's death in March 1925, Eckersall became the sport's most prominent expert.

In 1927 the Football Rules Committee invited Eckersall to serve on an officials' advisory committee at the annual meeting in New York. Eckie returned east, this time to Philadelphia, in the same capacity for the 1928 meeting.[22]

Other organizations sought Eckersall for full-time roles. In 1923 he was offered the post of commissioner of the newly organized Tri-State Athletic League, comprising small colleges in Illinois, Iowa, and Wisconsin. In 1926 the upstart American Football League sought Eckie's services as league president. In 1929 Eckersall was on a short list of candidates for commissioner of the Pacific Coast Conference. Also in 1929, Governor Louis Emmerson offered Eckersall a spot on the three-member Illinois Boxing Commission.[23]

Eckersall never took any of these jobs, content to remain on the sports desk at the *Tribune* as well as on the football field as a game official. He did, however, accept a couple of part-time roles.

In 1928 he joined a committee that would organize sporting events tied to Chicago's Century of Progress World's Fair in 1933–34. The financial crunch caused by Great Depression halted these events, with the lone exception of Major League Baseball's inaugural All-Star Game. In any case, Eckersall would die before the World's Fair opened.[24]

In 1924 Eckersall became publicity chair of the Central AAU, the same organization he had battled during college. Like his dual role as a sportswriter–game official, Eckie's dual role as a sportswriter-publicist caused no controversy in its time.[25]

Eckersall did his duty for the AAU, covering at least eighteen AAU events and writing twice as many background stories about those events. These competitions were big news involving big names, so Eckersall would have covered them anyway. He fulfilled his AAU volunteer commitment simply by doing his job.

A reform-minded observer might have expected Eckersall to pull his punches when writing about the same organization for which he was volunteering. In fact, the opposite happened. Eckersall didn't mince words when he felt the AAU deserved criticism.

In an exclusive interview from California, Eckersall took the side of Olympic sprinter Charley Paddock in the latter's beef with the AAU before the 1924 Olympics. The previous summer, Paddock, with the NCAA's blessing, had competed at a meet in Europe. The AAU suspended him not for professionalism but for failing to secure AAU permission as well.

"The actions of certain A.A.U. committees were unjust and arbitrary and not to the best interest of the athletes," Paddock told the world, through Eckersall. The AAU and Paddock reconciled before the Olympic trials.[26]

Similarly, in April 1928, Eckie aired a series of grievances against the AAU in the buildup to the Amsterdam Olympics. Exposing what Eckie termed the AAU's "domineering tactics," he extensively quoted Big Ten Commissioner John Griffith, who labeled AAU officials "cheap politicians."[27]

Eckie continued to air Griffith's criticisms of the AAU. He passed along charges that compared the AAU's inner workings to those of organized labor. He accused the AAU of rewarding loyal soldiers with free Olympic trips for little actual work. And he called out the disproportionate influence the AAU had in selecting Olympic track athletes and coaches: The AAU had forty-one votes, while the NCAA and its two most influential member leagues had only seven.[28]

This appearance of balance, at a time when journalists really weren't held to that standard, in Eckie's AAU coverage seems admirable. But consider Eckersall's competing interests before declaring him "objective." By taking issue with the AAU, Eckie was standing up for the Big Ten—which gave Eckersall officiating assignments, putting real money in his pocket.

—

Eckersall's status as a sporting authority grew steadily as his career went on. The trade journal *Editor and Publisher* cited Eckersall as "a famous football expert," listing him alongside sports authorities such as Grantland Rice and Damon Runyon. It also ran a lengthy, overwhelmingly positive feature on Eckersall in 1927, in honor of his twentieth year at the *Tribune*.[29]

His extensive reach through syndication perhaps best reflects Eckersall's status as an authority. His articles had been syndicated since the beginning of his career: The fifth article that he wrote for the *Tribune* was picked up the following day in the *Pittsburgh Press*. By the 1920s, Eckersall's byline regularly appeared in the *New York Daily News*, along with many small-town newspapers and as far away as Hawaii. His 1928 *How to Play Football* series was carried by more than a dozen newspapers. Eckie's final All-America team was published in the *Los Angeles Times*, the *Baltimore Sun*, and everywhere in between.[30]

Perhaps the *Chicago Tribune* was premature in calling Eckersall a "football expert" back in 1909. But by the close of the 1920s, the *Tribune* could rightly tout its star writer as "America's Greatest Football Authority."[31]

26

The Friend

For a man who spent three decades in the spotlight, few details about Walter Eckersall's private life were widely known during his lifetime. A century later, those details remain elusive.

During his playing days, writers occasionally referenced some of the star's personal attributes. In 1904 the *Tribune*'s Hugh Keough noted his strong family ties: "And what makes us admire Eckersall more is that he is awfully good to his folks." That's it . . . a one-sentence item portraying Eckie as a nice guy, in the "gee-whiz" tradition once common in sports journalism.[1]

In the not-so-nice category, some writers hinted that the young athlete was a prima donna, perhaps best exemplified by his stubbornly delayed apology to coach Amos Alonzo Stagg for missing curfew in 1905. Newspapers around the country ran stories about Eckersall's 1907 theft from a downtown Chicago tailor.[2]

But at the time, reporters didn't expose his University of Chicago expulsion, or the juicy charges of loose morals, bad debts, and questionable friendships. The University of Chicago was complicit, burying Eckie's flaws for decades.[3]

After his playing days were over, the already-thin details on Eckersall's personal life dropped out of the daily press, of which Eckersall was now a member. Eckie successfully concealed the shotgun nature of his wedding. His divorce, and Jappy's accusations of drunkenness and abuse, were only lightly covered by the newspapers. He was never publicly tied to a woman again. After 1915, when Jappy took Eckie to court for overdue alimony, information on his personal life disappears from the news entirely.

To his *Tribune* readers and to the sports-loving public, Walter Eckersall was all work, all the time. To his friends, the adult, mature Eckersall was no longer the college-age prima donna or the volatile drunk, but a nice guy and generous soul.

"When a fellow needed a friend, there was none to be found more satisfactory than Eckie," Ring Lardner wrote. To illustrate his point, Lardner recalled his own near-firing by the *Chicago Examiner* after a botched rewrite job in 1908. Upon his return to the *Examiner*'s office, fully expecting to be fired, Lardner was instead forgiven.

"This pleasant surprise, however, was a double play in which Eckie ought to be credited with an assist," Lardner recalled. "I learned long afterward that [Eckersall] had pleaded my cause for hours and had even gone to his own boss, Harvey Woodruff, of the *Tribune*, and persuaded him to make room for me in the event I got the air from the *Examiner*."[4]

University of Michigan track star DeHart Hubbard recalled another specific act of kindness by Eckie. In 1925, after Hubbard set a world record in the long jump at Stagg Field, he rushed to notify his family but found himself short of the cash needed to send a telegram. Eckersall noticed and gave Hubbard the fee, allowing one of his favorite athletes to wire his one-year-old daughter: "Daddy presents you with a world record on your birthday."[5]

Bert Demby, a Chicago-based United Press correspondent, noted how generous Eckersall was with his time, especially while mentoring new reporters. "The best thing about Eckie was his quiet attitude of friendship," Demby wrote. "No matter how young you were and how hard pressed he was to get his story into the Chicago Tribune, his paper, he always had time to help a fellow out. If you didn't know the whys and wherefores of any given thing the rule was 'Ask Eckie.'"[6]

Eckersall also fostered a sense of allegiance among his Golden Gloves and Silver Skates volunteers. As *Tribune* sports editor Don Maxwell recalled: "Almost without exception this original band stuck with Eckie through the years. No matter how tired they might be after their day's work, if Eckie needed them they responded. No matter how trivial or how uninteresting

37. Formal portrait of Walter Eckersall in the 1920s. In his later years, Eckersall was shy, very private, and extremely well liked by his sportswriting peers. University of Chicago Photographic Archive, apf1-05920, Hanna Holborn Gray Special Collections Research Center, University of Chicago Library.

the job he wanted them to perform, they did it because they wanted to please Eckie. They were loyal to him because he was loyal to them."[7]

—

Besides his friendliness and generosity, Eckersall exhibited a few other consistent personality traits. For one, he was an insomniac, much like Lardner. "I was the only person he knew who shared his horror of going to bed," Lardner wrote. "Night after night, until it was almost the next night, we would sit and just talk, nearly always on one subject—football."[8]

In one-on-one conversation, Eckersall was engaging. He thrived in personal interactions and small-group settings.

"Whenever we heard his voice something happened to us," remembered his 1905 Chicago teammate Merrill Meigs. "It electrified us. Our spirits seemed to soar and nothing was impossible."

Yet paradoxically, Eckersall was quiet and withdrawn in large groups. "A dynamo on the playing field, he was gentle, modest, retiring—almost shy—on the campus," Meigs said.[9]

Eckersall could bark out orders and take charge of ten teammates, but he clammed up in front of a crowd, to the point where the few speeches he gave were newsworthy events.

"If you know Eckie, you know that speech making isn't his recreation," Maxwell wrote after the Inter-City Golden Gloves at Madison Square Garden in 1929. "He dodges every meeting where he suspects he might be introduced. But Walter was different today. He had something to tell these champions."

Eckie got up and inspired the team. "'Now fellows,' and I'll swear there was a break in Eckie's voice, 'Let's do it,'" Maxwell recalled, then added as an aside to his readers, "I wish you had been there. You would have felt a tingle, too."[10]

(The speech didn't achieve its intended result, as Chicago lost eleven of the sixteen fights.)

Intimate gatherings were a much better fit for Eckersall's personality than large speaking engagements. In July 1928 Eckie hosted a homecoming luncheon for aviator Amelia Earhart, who had supplanted Eckersall as Hyde Park High School's most famous product. Fittingly for two shy people who had been the subject of much public adulation, the Eckersall-Earhart luncheon was small, unlike the lavish banquet in Earhart's honor that same evening, which was attended by hundreds and featured twenty speakers, including Coach Stagg.[11]

Beyond his shyness, Eckersall was publicly modest. When writing retrospective articles, he would understate his accomplishments, like, "The writer was a member of the Chicago eleven," not that he was captain or an All-American. In recalling the Chicago-Michigan game of 1904, he wrote that "Heston fumbled the ball, resulting in a touchdown for Chicago," failing to mention that Eckersall himself scored that touchdown. When writing about his Hyde Park or University of Chicago teams, Eckie consistently downplayed his own contributions.[12]

"I feel that as a player his predominate characteristic was modesty," Coach Stagg said. "He was very unselfish and unassuming. I never saw anything but that in him in his four years at the university. He did not care for fulsome praise."[13]

Lardner recalled having hundreds of conversations about football with Eckersall: "I want to testify that never did I hear him brag of his own skill at that sport, skill equaled—in my opinion and that of other experts who have visited or dwelt in the wilderness west of the Hudson River—only by Jim Thorpe, of Carlisle, and George Gipp, of Notre Dame."[14]

Demby remembered Eckersall as "a man without an ego." Maxwell recalled similarly: "He never lost a diffidence, a modesty, that was almost embarrassing to his friends."[15]

—

As for living arrangements, Walter Eckersall dwelled with his family of origin for most of his life.

Although he lived with Jappy for at least part of their brief marriage, the two were living apart by census time in April 1910, when Walter—listed, probably incorrectly, as twenty-six years old—was back with his parents and sisters in the house on Sixty-Fifth Street. Between 1910 and 1914, that house was torn down to make way for an apartment building. The family moved temporarily to Dante Avenue just north of Sixty-Fourth Street, still in Woodlawn. That building has since been torn down, and the site is now a parking lot for Mount Carmel High School—which, coincidentally, is a football powerhouse.[16]

In 1914 the Eckersalls paid $2,000 to build a 1,400-square-foot, one-and-a-half-story stucco house in Chicago's South Shore neighborhood, about three miles southeast of the original family home. This house, at 7331 S. Kingston Avenue, still stands today.[17]

Before construction was completed, Walter Sr. died in November 1914, at age sixty-six. The cause of death was then called "dropsy" but was most likely the result of congestive heart failure. Walter Sr. had a brief funeral service at the Dante Avenue house and was buried at the same Oak Woods Cemetery where he had worked more than forty years earlier.[18]

A few months later, Eckie's younger sister, Jessie, got married at age twenty-six. This marriage set up the new family dynamic: Widowed mother Minnie, divorced son Walter, and never-married daughter Etta, sharing the modest house on Kingston. According to friends, Eckie remained "exceptionally loyal to his widowed mother" for the rest of her life.[19]

Etta, a Chicago grammar school teacher, recalled her brother in much the same terms as his sportswriter friends. "The thing I remembered best about Walter, aside from his great football performances, was his personal qualities," Etta said. "He was so generous and fair."[20]

Life in the Kingston Avenue home allowed Walter to engage in one of his few documented leisure activities that did not revolve around sports: Eckie was a fire fan. He hung out at firehouses, playing cards, absorbing the fraternal atmosphere, and helping with minor tasks at large fires. Conveniently, shortly after Minnie's new house was completed, the Chicago Fire Department built a firehouse on Kingston Avenue, just 150 feet north of the Eckersall home.

"Eckie was a frequent visitor at the fire house," the *Tribune* reported. "The former football hero got his greatest thrills out of going to a fire. He made many daylight and night trips to the scene of a conflagration on the fire trucks and in the fire wagons."[21]

Minnie Eckersall died in November 1928, at age seventy-eight. Her funeral was held at her longtime church, Holy Cross, and she was buried next to Walter Sr. at Oak Woods. Shortly after Minnie's death, Eckie moved into a suite of rooms at the Chicago Athletic Association, less than a mile from his *Tribune* office, though he kept his legal address with Etta at the Kingston Avenue house.[22]

As for Eckie's other family, he doesn't appear to have had much to do with daughter Betty after his 1912 divorce from Jappy.

Eckie's ex-wife married at least once more, to a man with the last name Bateman, but that marriage also ended in divorce. Jappy kept her second husband's last name through at least 1930, but at some point in the 1930s, she changed her name back—not to Jahn but to Eckersall. During one interview late in her life, Jappy referred to herself as Walter's widow, conveniently omitting the fact that they had divorced.[23]

Jappy and Betty eventually settled in Garfield Park on Chicago's West Side, sixteen miles from Eckie's South Shore home, though only six miles from his later residence at the CAA. In the spring of 1929, shortly after graduating from Austin High School, Betty got into a car accident, injuring her right hand and totaling Jappy's car. A post-accident article in the *Decatur (IL) Herald* was the first news story since 1915 to acknowledge that Walter Eckersall was a father.[24]

When Betty was a teenager, Eckie made some efforts to rebuild the relationship, centering on the football field. "He took me to all the football games he attended either as an official or a reporter, and he insisted that I diagram as many plays as I could," Betty told a *Los Angeles Times* reporter. "Father always impressed upon me the necessity of being able to write sport stories from a player's point of view, rather than from a spectator's."[25]

These insights served Betty well when she became a *Tribune* writer herself, mainly covering women's sports. She acknowledged once that "I got in on my name." But in her own articles, she never wrote about her famous father and never mentioned any memories of or relationship with him.[26]

Yet, Betty kept the Eckersall name alive. After she gave birth to her only child in 1936, Betty gave her daughter, Gay Gordon, the middle name "Eckersall." And after Betty married and divorced twice, she reverted to her original last name. For the last two decades of her life, she once again went by "Betty Eckersall."[27]

—

Although his shyness steered him away from radio appearances or public speaking, Eckersall found another way to earn a few extra bucks.

Product endorsements by athletes, especially baseball players, were nothing new. New York Giants pitcher Christy Mathewson hawked Tuxedo tobacco, while his manager John McGraw endorsed Coca-Cola. Detroit Tigers star Ty Cobb appeared in ads for the patent medicine "nuxated iron." New York Yankees slugger Babe Ruth pitched everything from candy bars to underwear.[28]

Eckersall didn't enter the celebrity endorsement market until the 1920s, but he ultimately tied his image to several products: Munsingwear union suits, Mennen shaving cream, the wheat-based hot drink Postum, the "Walter Eckersall Health Belt" weight-reduction device, and a board game dubbed "Eckersall's Indoor Football Game."[29]

One of those endorsements raised eyebrows. In 1927 the American Tobacco Company began a three-year national campaign featuring celebrity testimonials about why they smoked Lucky Strikes. The fees varied based on how brightly each star shone, but Notre Dame football coach Knute Rockne reportedly turned down a $2,000 offer for a Lucky Strike ad.[30]

Most celebrities in the series have been long forgotten, but some are remembered today: aviator Amelia Earhart, actor and singer Al Jolson, Broadway star George M. Cohan, politician James A. Farley, and vaudeville entertainer Eddie Cantor.[31]

Eckie's ad ran in newspapers on December 6, 1928. In the copy, Eckersall credits cigarettes with keeping him in good enough shape to run up and down the football field, declaring: "Football is a supreme test of physical fitness and mental alertness. At every game, Luckies help me through. I can't afford to get fat—no sweets, no over-rich deserts [*sic*] for me. I light a Lucky instead. Throughout the athletic world, I find Luckies the reigning favorites—during intermissions at the games, other officials who pride themselves on keeping fit, always ask for Luckies from my supply—that toasted flavor can't be equaled."[32]

This endorsement had the potential to disappoint Coach Stagg, a vocal critic of both drinking and smoking for his entire life. Later authors speculated that Stagg must have been displeased by Eckersall's public promotion of such a vice. If Stagg voiced any concerns at the time, they were not recorded, however. It's not entirely certain that Stagg even knew about the ad. While the celebrity "Lucky Strike" endorsements regularly ran in the *Chicago Tribune*, Eckersall's didn't appear there, or in any Chicago newspapers.

—

Throughout the years, Eckersall regularly kept in touch with pals from his football-playing days. From Hyde Park, he remained lifelong friends with Sam Ransom, who had settled in St. Paul, Minnesota, and Tom Hammond, who embarked on a business career in Chicago. He stayed close to Chicago teammates Hugo Bezdek, Wally Steffen, and Jesse Harper, who all became coaches, and Robert Maxwell, who settled in Philadelphia and followed Eckie's path by becoming both a sportswriter and a game official.

38. Walter Eckersall's "Lucky Strike" cigarette ad, which ran as part of a three-year celebrity endorsement campaign. *New York Daily News*, December 6, 1928.

Notre Dame coach Knute Rockne would become a close friend. Shrugging off potential concerns about impartiality, Eckersall and Rockne maintained a frequent correspondence, trading at least forty-six letters and telegrams between 1924 and 1929. The pair occasionally shared taxicabs while traveling from hotels to stadiums on game days.[33]

But the old relationship that mattered most to Eckersall was the one with Stagg, which ran hot and cold throughout his adult life but always loomed in the background.

Eckersall clearly saw his old coach as his chief mentor. "I cannot tell you how great a privilege it has been to spend four years under Coach Stagg," he noted on the eve of his final college game in 1906. "I owe what success I have had to him. He not only trains his men in athletics but he trains their character."[34]

During Eckie's journalism career, Stagg was his most reliable source. Whenever he needed a quote or a midweek filler story, Eckersall could call on Stagg, who was certainly happy for the publicity. Eckie also attended Stagg's games regularly, covering thirty-six during his career, more than any other individual team.

When critics harped on Stagg for having a poor year in 1916 and suggested the game had passed him by, Eckie reminded those critics that Stagg had fielded an undefeated championship team just three years earlier. When pundits assumed that Illinois's Red Grange would run all over Stagg's Maroons in 1924, Eckersall predicted Stagg would keep the game close—and indeed, Chicago tied Illinois 21–21, en route to Stagg's seventh and final conference title.[35]

During his first few years on the *Tribune* staff, Eckie would violate all journalistic norms by helping Stagg out at practice. Later, Eckersall championed the renaming of Chicago's renovated stadium as Stagg Field.[36]

Occasionally, Eckersall took shots at his old coach. In 1907, when Stagg experimented with a meatless diet for his players, Eckie mocked "Stagg's vegetarians." He pleaded with Stagg to *not* use his top track runner, Ira Davenport, as a halfback in 1911, perhaps remembering how football hastened the end of Eckie's own track career. (Davenport did get hurt, but this injury ironically helped him; his broken collarbone early in the football season gave him ample time to recover for the 1912 track season, when he won two conference track titles and a bronze medal at the Olympics.)[37]

In the 1920s the relationship between Eckersall and Stagg cooled. Reportedly, Stagg loaned Eckersall $20—worth more than $300 today—which Eckie never paid back. Stagg also complained to his wife that his former athlete "has given me the go bye for years." On the surface, this statement doesn't quite ring true: Eckie continued to cover Chicago football practice extensively and continued to use his old coach as a source.[38]

The writer did, however, stop attending Chicago games. He only covered three Maroon games after 1916, and none after 1921. Stagg may have felt hurt by this perceived slight. Two factors, however, explain Eckie's absence. First, the writer was in growing demand as a game official, and he couldn't officiate Chicago games. Also, Maroon football was on the downslide through much of the 1920s. As the *Tribune*'s lead football writer, Eckie covered teams and games that meant something, and in the late 1920s, the Maroons simply didn't matter much anymore.

Although the relationship ran cold at times, Stagg always maintained a paternal type of affection and concern. After Eckersall collapsed at his *Tribune* office in 1917, Stagg rushed to Eckie's bedside at St. Luke's Hospital, where he counseled his protégé about his drinking in a fatherly way.

"He was in very great danger of dying as the result of a very severe heart dilation brought on as a result of dissipation," Stagg recalled several years later. "I said to him, 'Eckie you are going to turn over a new leaf now, aren't you?' and he said 'Yes, Mr. Stagg, I am.' . . . Eckie has been true to his word. He hasn't touched liquor since his hospital experience and he has become a dependable and good citizen."[39]

Despite the occasional tension, the pair had a deep and enduring affection. In December 1929 Stagg ran into Eckersall at a USC–Carnegie Tech football game in Los Angeles. Eckie was pulling his usual double duty, writing about the game for the *Tribune* and officiating as field judge, while Stagg was in town to support another protégé, Carnegie coach Steffen.

"He seemed to be in splendid condition, both physically and mentally," Stagg recalled. "He got me a ticket for the game at Pasadena [the 1930 Rose Bowl between USC and Penn State, two weeks later] at that time."[40]

That pleasant encounter would be the last one between the former star and his mentor.

27

—30—

March 24, 1930, was shaping up as a slow day in Chicago sports. Inter-City Golden Gloves, which Team Chicago had won for the first time, wrapped up a few days earlier. Both of the city's Major League Baseball teams were away at spring training: the Cubs in Southern California and the White Sox in Texas. The Chicago Blackhawks were heading to Montreal for a Stanley Cup playoff game the next day. Northwestern was hosting Stanford that night in a dual swim meet, and a boxing slate was scheduled for White City Arena on the South Side. Otherwise, there wasn't much happening on the local sports scene.[1]

Walter Eckersall took advantage by getting in a morning workout at the Chicago Athletic Association's gym, downstairs from the rooms he had rented for the last sixteen months. After a few minutes of exercise, Eckie complained of a headache. He reclined in the locker room for a bit, then headed upstairs to his suite.

Around 1 p.m., AP sportswriter Charles Dunkley paid Eckersall a visit. Dunkley found his friend barely conscious and clearly dying. According to one version of the story, Eckie remained in bed and whispered something about making a 20-yard gain. According to another version, Eckie stood up, thinking he would feel better if he simply got back on his feet. Either way, Walter Eckersall died in his room at 2:30 p.m., before a doctor could arrive.[2]

No formal autopsy was conducted, but Dr. Lewis Eastman, Eckie's physician who had previously worked on the Cook County Coroner's staff, listed the cause of death as organic heart disease.[3]

How could such an active, vibrant person have died so young? Eckersall, most likely forty-four or forty-five years old, had officiated ten college football games the previous season. He journeyed to California for three games on his annual New Year's trip, and he had traveled to Minneapolis to cover the Big Ten indoor track championships just a couple weeks before his death. Already that year he had organized and hosted Silver Skates, Golden Gloves, and Inter-City Golden Gloves. Until the end, he worked at a furious pace, contributing sixty-seven bylined stories to the *Tribune* in the first eighty days of the year.

But his closest friends knew Eckersall was ailing. In the fall of 1929, Eckie was out of the office for two weeks and missed two football games with what was described as the flu, but it was probably cardiac-related. He soon returned to his duties, but as Harvey Woodruff noted, "Eckersall failed to regain his accustomed vigor, although to intimates he insisted he was in 'tiptop' condition."[4]

During Inter-City Golden Gloves on March 19, Eckie felt poorly enough to seek Dr. Eastman's help. Eastman, a friend who regularly volunteered at Silver Skates and Golden Gloves, prescribed rest. Eckersall took it easy for a few days but not until after he filed what turned out to be his final *Tribune* story, which ran on March 21.[5]

Despite his public image of vigorous good health, Eckersall was frequently ill. Throughout his career, he had five extended absences from the *Tribune*. One was extremely public: His December 1917 collapse in his *Tribune* office, which led to an extended hospitalization and a morbid national death watch.[6]

In the mid-1920s, when he was around forty, Eckersall was diagnosed with heart trouble. United Press football writer Bert Demby said that Eckie had "beat off the heart attack" several times through a combination of sheer willpower and by simply standing up long enough to help his blood flow better. (Demby clearly had not studied cardiology.) While under Dr. Eastman's care, Eckersall's blood pressure had risen far above normal.[7]

Demby recalled a conversation the two had a couple years earlier about Walter Camp, who had died of a heart attack at age sixty-five. "Gee, he went out like a light, didn't he? That's the way I want to die. . . . He has my envy. I want to die that way because there have been so many of us in the world who were stopped by a heart which refused to beat any longer. Perhaps that is a queer feeling but then we all must die so what the hell? Camp was lucky. If I am that lucky I'll thank whatever gods there are, for when you drop dead you beat a lot of suffering."[8]

—

One theory about Eckersall's heart problems quickly made the rounds. "His passing will again, no doubt, revive discussion of the effect of athletic training upon the life span," the *Milwaukee Sentinel* speculated. "It has been held by many physicians that the heavy training incidental to athletic competition puts such a strain on the heart muscles that, as middle life comes on, the organ becomes too weak to do its work and premature death results."[9]

This once-common belief has been debunked. If anything, the type of training Eckersall engaged in as a youth improves cardiac function. Former athletes who gain weight or lapse into a sedentary lifestyle do face increased cardiovascular risk, but neither of these problems plagued Eckersall. Overtraining seems an unlikely explanation for his early death.[10]

Another culprit was grief. "The death of his mother last Fall broke his heart and his will to live was hardly that of the 145-pound football player who used to blast through ponderous lines," an AP reporter wrote. Decades later, the *Biographical Dictionary of American Sports* echoed that Eckersall was "loyal to his widowed mother. Her death in 1929 profoundly affected him and caused his health to fail. Within a year, he died."[11]

But this theory gets the timeline wrong: Minnie Eckersall died in 1928, not 1929. Although Walter took a week off work after her death, he quickly returned to his routine, traveling to New York less than a month later and to San Francisco less than a month after that. He even took his first airplane flight that March, four months after Minnie's death. Instead of an intense and prolonged period of mourning, Eckie hardly missed a beat.[12]

Another logical explanation is genetics. Walter Sr. died from what was likely congestive heart failure, so Walter Jr. was probably predisposed to heart disease himself.

Cigarette smoking, which more than doubles the risk of heart failure, also could have contributed. However, there's no evidence that Eckersall was a smoker, other than his (paid) testimony that he preferred Lucky Strikes to sweets. No known pictures of Eckie with a cigarette exist. Eckersall may have smoked, or he may have simply *said* that he smoked to collect endorsement money.[13]

Another theory, ignored for decades, has recently gained traction: that alcohol abuse compounded Eckersall's health problems.

During his lifetime, only one public reference was ever made to Eckersall's drinking, but it was a very damning one: Jappy's 1912 accusation that "I have seldom seen him sober." A few years after Eckie's death, James Weber Linn, who taught English at Chicago while Eckersall was a student, noted more mildly that he displayed "occasionally careless habits of drinking." Decades later, Amos Alonzo Stagg biographer Robin Lester uncovered a memo, written by Stagg sometime in the 1920s, that identified Eckersall as a reformed drinker who had been sober for several years.[14]

It's worth noting that, for the last ten years of Eckersall's life, the Eighteenth Amendment made alcohol consumption illegal in the United States. In a wide-open town like Chicago, Prohibition rarely proved a hindrance for drinkers. In 1926 federal agents seized thirteen and a half cases of liquor from Eckie's own physician, though Dr. Eastman insisted the alcohol was strictly medicinal. Chicago newsrooms, in particular, had a reputation, bolstered by figures like reporter-turned-playwright Ben Hecht, for free-flowing booze.[15]

From assorted strands of evidence, some recent writers state that Eckersall died after "a long struggle with alcoholism." Unfortunately, these assertions come either without references, or with references that do not actually cite alcohol as his cause of death. Recently, free-content online encyclopedias such as Wikipedia have claimed, without evidence or references, that Eckersall died of cirrhosis. A 2019 biography of Stagg begins with a vivid, touching scene of the coach visiting his jaundiced former star in a hospital room; yet, this exchange is purely conjecture, based on Stagg's brief, undated memo.[16]

Walter Eckersall clearly had a drinking problem as a young adult, at the very least. But after almost a hundred years and with scant evidence from primary sources, it's impossible to directly link alcohol abuse with either his heart problems or his early death.

Another theory, hinted at but never fully explored: The writer may have simply worked himself to death.

Overwork was the public explanation for his 1917 collapse. After that episode, Eckersall slowed down only briefly. Within weeks, he was organizing Silver Skates and covering pro wrestling matches, hockey games, and swim meets. He covered more than eighty live sporting events in 1918 and kept up a similar pace for the rest of his career.

Covering these events led to a lot of travel. During his sportswriting career, Eckie made thirteen trips to California; twelve to New York City; twelve to Lincoln, Nebraska; six to Pittsburgh; six to West Virginia; six to Lawrence, Kansas; five to Philadelphia; four to Boston; plus, a trip or two each to Atlanta, New Orleans, Denver, Houston, and Arkansas. Filling the gaps between these longer trips were frequent visits around the Midwest: twenty-five trips to Ann Arbor, Michigan; sixteen to Minneapolis; twelve to Madison, Wisconsin; and eleven to Columbus, Ohio. All that travel meant living out of a suitcase and spending lots of time on trains and in hotels, eating meals on the run, making transfer connections late at night, and basically being always on the go.

"Work was a fetish for him," Eckersall's friend and editor Don Maxwell wrote on the day he died. "Doing his job gave him more thrills than anything else. He didn't want a day off."[17]

Maxwell meant that as a compliment. He probably didn't consider that the same work ethic may have hastened Eckersall's demise.

Most likely, Eckie's heart attack came from a combination of factors, including genetics, overwork, and possibly alcohol abuse. In tandem, they created a fatal combination.

—

The *Chicago Tribune* devoted nearly a full page on March 25 to coverage of Eckersall's death. Over the next couple days, condolence telegrams arrived from the likes of Ring Lardner, Jack Dempsey, and George Halas. Knute Rockne was recuperating from illness in Miami and unable to travel for the funeral but issued a brief statement that he later expanded on in a column: "Quiet and reserved, he was a real friend. He never hurt anyone, but was always ready to lend a helping hand. His passing is a great loss to football."[18]

Stagg gave a lengthy interview about his fallen star, and the *Tribune* printed more than 1.200 words full of sadness and surprise at Eckie's sudden death, nostalgia for the good old days of Maroon football, and praise for the greatest player Stagg would ever coach.[19]

Eckersall lay in state on Wednesday, March 26, at the Kingston Avenue house. His old firefighter neighbors cleared the snow for several surrounding blocks so that hundreds of mourners could pay their respects to siblings Arthur, Elmer, Etta, and Jessie. Twelve surviving members of Chicago's 1905 championship football team delivered a signed condolence message.

At the same time as the wake, the Chicago City Council passed a resolution honoring Eckersall, which read, in part: "The life of Walter H. Eckersall as an active athlete, as a sports writer and as a sports official was representative of the highest standards of true sportsmanship, and was such as to command the admiration and respect of all with whom he came in contact, and will live as an inspiration to the youth of our country."[20]

Eckie's funeral took place on Thursday, March 27, at Holy Cross Catholic Church. Four priests—the type of showing usually reserved for a bishop, politician, or business leader—concelebrated the Mass, which drew an overflow crowd of 1,500 mourners. His pallbearers included a who's who of the Chicago sports scene: longtime *Tribune* colleague Harvey Woodruff, Maroon teammate Wally Steffen, Big Ten commissioner John Griffith, and AAU and Olympic official Avery Brundage. Stagg, now 67 years old, was an honorary pallbearer; already known as the Old Man for more than thirty years, he would live to age 102.

After the funeral, Eckersall's body was taken to Oak Woods Cemetery and buried next to his parents. Newspapers noted that Walter Eckersall would rest for eternity near the same gridiron where he had achieved his

39. Pallbearers carry Walter Eckersall's casket out of Holy Cross Church. From left: Judge Wally Steffen, *Tribune* colleague Harvey Woodruff, AP sportswriter Charles Dunkley, football official Joe Lipp, *Tribune* colleague Frank Schreiber, and Big Ten commissioner John Griffith (face obscured). Honorary pallbearer Amos Alonzo Stagg is on the left, visible between Steffen and Woodruff. *Chicago Tribune*/TCA.

greatest glories. That was true only in a very general sense: Oak Woods was about two miles away from Stagg Field, which had been rebuilt and renamed since Eckersall last played there. But the cemetery bordered on the Woodlawn neighborhood where Eckie had grown up, and was within half a mile of his childhood home, his grammar school, and the vacant lots where he and friends had first learned how to kick a football. In both a figurative and a literal sense, Walter Eckersall had come home.[21]

28

Legacy

For fifty years after he took his last college snap, Walter Eckersall remained just about everybody's All-American. Walter Camp, Grantland Rice, Fielding Yost, Jim Thorpe, Red Grange, John Heisman, and Arch Ward all named him the All-Time All-American quarterback. Polls of college coaches conducted in 1920, 1924, and 1931 selected Eckersall as All-Time quarterback, as did a 1951 national AP poll of sportswriters and broadcasters.[1]

Eckersall received the highest praise from his former teammates. "Eckersall was the finest all-around back I ever saw," said Sam Ransom in 1942. "He possessed a brilliant football mind, and as quarterback, was like having a coach directing the team on the field. Eckie was faster and more elusive than Grange. . . . He had the courage and poise to always deliver in the clutches, too."[2]

College teammate Merrill Meigs echoed those sentiments. In a 1947 article, Meigs laid out the case that Eckie was the greatest player ever, at any position.

> That's a flat statement, without reservations. It's not wishful thinking. The record bears it out. I've been waiting 40 years, with an open mind, to see his equal. I haven't yet . . .
>
> He had more speed than any of your modern greats. He could have been the "fastest human" if he'd devoted the same attention to sprinting he did to football. . . . He could spin and turn and reverse his field like a

> jackrabbit. . . . He was a vicious, deadly tackler with a heart that didn't know when to quit. . . .
>
> He was tops in all departments. And he had something else, something that made him more than a football player. He had the power to lift a whole team from mediocrity to the greatness of which he himself was capable—with the most inspiring voice the gridiron ever knew![3]

When the College Football Hall of Fame was founded in 1951, Eckersall was one of fifty-three charter members. One of his classmates was Amos Alonzo Stagg, then still actively coaching even as he neared age ninety.[4]

In 1969, in honor of college football's centennial, the Football Writers Association of America named an All-Time All-America team. With the development of the passing game, the FWAA felt that it couldn't place a running quarterback first any longer. So, the organization named "Early Days" and "Modern Days" teams, with 1919 as the dividing line. Eckersall easily won honors as top "Early Days" quarterback.[5]

—

A few weeks after Eckersall's death, the Drake Relays created a Walter Eckersall Trophy for the two-mile relay champion. Notre Dame won in 1930, but the Eckersall Trophy was discontinued after that first year. The following winter, the Silver Skates created a Walter Eckersall Trophy, for the team that scored the most points across all Silver Skates age and gender divisions. That trophy was awarded through 1955.[6]

In 1940 the Chicago Board of Education built two football stadiums for Chicago Public League football and track: one on the city's Northwest Side and the other on Eighty-Second Street in the South Chicago neighborhood, near the U.S. Steel South Works. The South Chicago site was dubbed Yates Stadium, after the street on its western border.

In November 1948 the Board of Education voted to rename Yates Stadium in Walter Eckersall's honor. Eckersall Stadium was dedicated in September 1949, with siblings Elmer, Etta, and Jessie in attendance (Arthur had died in 1939) and with Ward and Meigs among the speakers. Over the next

40. Dedication of Eckersall Stadium. From left: Chicago Public Schools superintendent Herold Hunt, sister Jessie Eckersall Anderson, nephew Walter G. Eckersall, brother Elmer Eckersall, sister Etta Eckersall, Big Ten commissioner Tug Wilson, and *Tribune* colleague Arch Ward. *Chicago Tribune*/TCA.

few years, the Chicago Park District acquired three adjacent acres of land and named that space Eckersall Park in 1955.[7]

When the city of Chicago hosted the Pan-American Games in 1959, a delegation from Venezuela commissioned a bronze plaque in Eckersall's honor. In a brief ceremony, the plaque was dedicated in the sports department at Tribune Tower on Michigan Avenue, near Eckie's old desk. The fate of that plaque is unknown.[8]

No such memorial was ever created at the University of Chicago. Within days of Eckie's death in 1930, his friend John Messmer, a former football captain at Wisconsin, called for a permanent monument on Chicago's campus, perhaps a bronze bust or a plaque. Messmer said that he was in contact with university officials, but his proposal simply died.[9]

Messmer's timing was poor. Chicago's new president, Robert Maynard Hutchins, was actively steering the school away from competitive sports, and likely didn't want to grant such an honor to someone who had been expelled. Eckersall would receive no formal honors from the university until its Athletic Hall of Fame was founded in 2003, with Eckie as a charter member.[10]

—

Eckersall Stadium and Eckersall Park are the athlete's only lasting public memorials. Eckie's influence, however, remains alive in a couple very real ways.

The Silver Skates tournament, which Eckersall created in 1917, continues today. For decades, the citywide final was the premier wintertime athletic event in Chicago, with tens of thousands of fans cheering hundreds of skaters at one of the city's grand public parks. Several champions would compete in the Winter Olympics, and at least five would win Olympic medals.

The *Chicago Tribune* turned the event over to the Chicago Park District in 1974. Silver Skates has since declined in size and scale, and the finals have moved indoors. The longest current race is a thousand meters rather than two miles, as crowds in the hundreds cheer on fewer than a hundred competitors. It's a far cry from the event's heyday in Walter Eckersall's time.[11]

Eckie's Golden Gloves tournament also continues, but it has thrived, growing in both size and scale. Golden Gloves currently includes thirty regional tournaments and a six-day national final. Both the local and national Golden Gloves competitions have served as a launching pad for several Olympic and world champion boxers over the years.

Despite the success of Golden Gloves, Eckie's contributions have been forgotten. Ward is frequently credited—by the *Tribune* and the Golden Gloves Association, along with many other sources—with founding the tournament as sports editor in 1923. But Ward didn't arrive at the *Tribune* until 1925 and didn't become sports editor until 1930. Ward was posthumously inducted into the Golden Gloves Hall of Fame in 1971, but Eckersall, its actual founder, has never been so honored.[12]

—

During his career, Walter Eckersall helped turn *Chicago Tribune* sports from an afterthought into one of the newspaper's major draws. By 1918 the *Chicago Tribune* took the circulation lead among the city's five major dailies. For decades thereafter, the *Tribune*, and *Tribune* sports, thrived.

In April 1930 sports editor Don Maxwell was promoted to news editor, the next step on a career path that would see him succeed Robert R. McCormick as editor and publisher. Ward replaced Maxwell as sports editor and reigned over *Tribune* sports for twenty-five years.

Ward created sports news much as Walter Eckersall had done. His most enduring legacy remains the Major League Baseball All-Star Game, first held at Comiskey Park in 1933. In 1934 he created an annual football game featuring NFL champions versus college all-stars, held at Soldier Field, which lasted until 1976. Ward also organized the All-America Football Conference, with competition starting in 1946. The AAFC opened new markets, reintegrated major professional football, and introduced several strategic and technological innovations. The league would last four seasons until financial difficulties forced a merger with the NFL.[13]

Ward and his successors continued to produce a highly regarded sports section. Under editor Wilfrid Smith in the 1960s, the *Tribune* boasted that it had the largest sports department in the country; later, under Cooper Rollow in the 1970s, it would make the more modest claim of "the Midwest's largest sports staff." The section took up six to eight pages on weekdays, with feature-packed sections of up to twenty pages on Sundays.[14]

Tribune sports covered it all: the demise of University of Chicago football in the 1930s; the glory years of the Chicago Bears in the 1940s and the team's resurgence with a roster of folk heroes in the 1980s; decades of futility by the city's two Major League Baseball teams, ending with long-awaited titles by the White Sox in 2005 and the Cubs in 2016; the state of Illinois's lone NCAA basketball championship, won by Loyola University of Chicago in 1963; the emergence of the consensus no. 1 basketball player in history, the Chicago Bulls' Michael Jordan, in the 1980s and 1990s; and stellar high school athletes and teams throughout.

The *Tribune* remained atop the Chicago market after the field thinned to just two major dailies in 1978. The emergence of the internet, and the related industrywide drop in print circulation, led to major challenges by the early twenty-first century. A series of ill-timed ownership changes led to rising debt, just as advertising revenues dropped. The size of the paper and its sports section were slashed. A typical sports section now takes up six pages in the Sunday paper, less than during Walter Eckersall's heyday a hundred years ago. The *Chicago Tribune* continues to publish but with an uncertain future for both the paper and its sports.

—

In 1938 James Peterson, a business executive and football fan, began hosting an annual luncheon to coincide with Ward's game of college all-stars versus NFL champions. Starting in 1954, Peterson used the luncheon to release a self-published book about an old football star, such as Jim Thorpe, George Gipp, Duke Slater, or Red Grange.[15]

Eckersall of Chicago, released in 1957, was the fourth volume in Peterson's series. As both biography and history, it's an amateur effort. With thirty-seven pages of text, the nonpaginated work is hardly book-length. More than half of the book is context, about the founding of the University of Chicago, football's then-prevailing rules, and Coach Stagg. When Peterson does discuss Eckersall, he only writes about him as an athlete, with nothing about his personal life or his postcollegiate careers as a sportswriter and official.[16]

Still, Eckie's teammates welcomed this opportunity to remember their friend. Leo DeTray, Merrill Meigs, and Fred Walker, now all in their seventies, attended the book release luncheon. Stagg, almost ninety-five years old and living in California, made a guest appearance via speakerphone.[17]

For sixty-eight years, *Eckersall of Chicago* would remain the only biography of Walter Eckersall, until the appearance of this book. Feature articles about Eckie and his 1905 team occasionally appeared in print. But for the most part, the greatest player of his era faded away.

His reputation receded, too. After his "Early Days" quarterback nod in 1969, Eckersall never drew serious consideration for all-time honors. Occasionally, stories about "The Greatest" or about an "All-Time Team" mentioned something like "Apologies to Walter Eckersall . . . ," then listed another player, or several others, ahead of him. In 1999 he made the Illinois High School All-Century team not as a quarterback but as a kick returner.[18]

At some point, Eckersall became irrelevant to a modern audience. The football pantheon no longer had room for the dazzling runner who could twist, stop on a dime, and corkscrew through a crowded field; the undersized tackler who overcame his small stature with blazing speed and perfect form; the threat to drop-kick up to 50 yards at a moment's notice; the booming, coffin-corner punter; the coach on the field, who read defenses and called plays and mastered the psychological game of football.

Eckersall's skills made a perfect all-around package for the early 1900s. But in the modern era of hundred-man rosters, unlimited substitution, a high degree of specialization, and control of all details by large coaching staffs, Eckie had become an anachronism.

—

First, Eckersall's reputation faded; later, it became tarnished.

In 1993 Murray Sperber published *Shake Down the Thunder*, a critical look at the lengths coach Knute Rockne went to in order to guarantee victory.

Sperber imagines the relationship between Rockne and Eckersall as a corrupt bargain. In Sperber's view, Rockne hoped that by hiring Eckersall as a game official, Eckersall would favor Notre Dame in his on-field judgments, give the Irish extra publicity, and regularly select Notre Dame players to his All-America teams. Eckersall obliged, at least subconsciously, since he depended on Rockne for officiating fees and information for his columns. Rockne further sweetened the pot by giving Eckersall free tickets, to either distribute to friends or profit from on the resale market.[19]

Perhaps most damningly, Rockne hired Eckersall to publicize Notre Dame's 1927 game against USC at Chicago's Soldier Field. The $250 publicity fee—for a game that Eckersall was going to publicize anyway—was a clear ethical violation even by the loose standards of the day.

Around the same time, the New York–based Carnegie Foundation for the Advancement of Teaching investigated this practice. "The statement was made frequently to members of the staff that the newspaper publicity accorded to many coaches was bought or paid for in cash or in kind," the Carnegie investigators wrote. "In view of the seriousness of the charge, special steps were taken to study it. . . . No such accusation was clearly substantiated."[20]

Yet, Eckie and Rockne were clearly guilty of this "serious charge" at least once. No wonder Rockne asked Eckersall to keep the arrangement secret.

Two years after Sperber's book, Robin Lester published *Stagg's University*, a scathing look at Maroon football. Lester writes about Stagg's triumphs but also exposes recruiting violations, academic fraud, and the hypocrisy of a coach so often held up as a moral paragon.

While Stagg is Lester's primary target, he covers the shady recruiting of Eckersall and outlines his academic troubles. Lester was the first writer to discover Eckersall's expulsion. He also revealed Eckie's heavy drinking in his young adulthood and an apparent rift in his relationship with Stagg in the 1920s. In Lester's narrative, Eckersall serves as a cautionary tale about the excesses of big-time athletics.[21]

In this author's opinion, Lester's criticisms are fair. Walter Eckersall was not academically suited for the University of Chicago, and probably didn't belong in college at all. He also displayed deep personal flaws such as lying, theft, alcohol abuse, and abandonment of his wife and child. Lester not only exposes some long-hidden facts but also portrays Eckersall as much more human than the "gee-whiz" journalists of his era ever portrayed.

Sperber's criticisms, however, seem excessive. Sperber calls the journalist-official model "corrupt and corrupting," but in doing so, he views the 1920s through a 1990s lens. He chides Rockne's relationship with "his new 'friend'" and asserts that the Rockne-Eckersall relationship was based on "quid pro quo," in which Rockne gave Eckersall inside information in exchange for good press.[22]

In reality, Eckersall received similar information from many coaches, who were very willing to share. The information was usually benign, anyway. Then, as now, coaches rarely gave up any competitive advantage via the press. And any publicity received by Notre Dame was well deserved, since the team had five undefeated seasons during Rockne's thirteen years as coach.

A corrupt bargain between Rockne and Eckersall makes an interesting theory. But the record doesn't reflect such a conspiracy. Visiting coaches had the right to reject potential officials, and they would have sniffed out any pro-Rockne bias over time.

Eckersall was one of the most widely respected, in-demand officials in the country, and he knew that. He was also one of the most widely respected football writers in the country, and he knew that, too. Any lapses would have risked his reputation in both areas. In the end, outside of accepting that publicity fee in 1927, Eckie seems to have approached his roles as both journalist and game official with integrity.

It's worth noting that Notre Dame fared significantly worse with Eckersall officiating than it did overall. The Irish went 17-5 in games that Eckersall worked during the Rockne years. That's an impressive .773 winning percentage but far behind Rockne's overall .881 percentage. Put another way, Eckersall officiated at 18 percent of Rockne's career games, but at 42 percent of his losses.

After hinting at conspiracy, Sperber punts: "No evidence exists, however, that Eckersall ever 'threw' a game for Notre Dame."[23]

No matter how fair a Walter Eckersall might have been, the sportswriter-official model had the potential for the kind of corruption Sperber envisioned. Gradually, the model (which wasn't rare, but was never as ubiquitous as Sperber suggests) faded away, disappearing entirely by 1950.

—

By joining the staff of the *Chicago Tribune*, Walter Eckersall became an unwitting pioneer of another now-widespread archetype: the sports star turned sports journalist.

Other stars had dabbled with journalism before but usually only in a weekly column. A few former athletes preceded Eckersall as working sportswriters, but none had been stars themselves.

Eckie paved the way for generations to follow. At first, he had few peers. The only All-Americans from the era to turn into productive sportswriters were Eckersall and Robert Maxwell. Georgetown quarterback Harry Costello and Chicago Cardinals lineman Wilfrid Smith, both slightly younger than Eckie, would become ace sportswriters, but neither had a playing record that approached Eckersall's.

The emergence of radio changed the landscape drastically. Soon a new position emerged: the expert commentator, who provided insight and context to listeners.

Early sports broadcasts were mainly hosted and conducted by seasoned newspaper reporters. The thought of paying a former star athlete to give an expert's view over the airwaves didn't initially cross anyone's mind. That changed when Red Grange came along.

In 1934, Grange's last season as an NFL player, he began hosting "Football Forecasts" for CBS Radio. In his initial season, Grange earned $500 a week for three fifteen-minute shows, at a time when the average family income was about $1,000 per year.[24]

After retiring as a player, Grange continued his broadcasts. In 1940 he started announcing college games in the role of what is now known as color commentator; added NFL games in 1946; and transitioned into television in 1949. Grange would continue broadcasting until 1963, interjecting opinions on strategy, making points about game flow, and dissecting specific plays, all while making his audience feel like football "insiders." Basically, Grange did on radio and television what Walter Eckersall had done in print decades earlier.[25]

Eckie pioneered the role of sports star turned sportswriter; Grange shifted the model to sports star turned broadcaster. Together, they paved the way for the hundreds of star athletes who went on to become media personalities.

—

In 2008 Walter Eckersall's name resurfaced in a historical exercise conducted by *Sports Illustrated*, which posed the question: Who would have won the Heisman Trophy between 1900 and 1934, had such an award existed? The magazine determined that Eckie would have won the Heisman in both 1905 and 1906.

For 1905, *Sports Illustrated* wrote, "The man who helped to end Michigan's 56-game streak without a loss—that's what was on the minds of voters when they picked Eckersall." For 1906, the magazine wrote, "Eckersall capped a magical career at Chicago with a senior season in which he was equally valuable as a kicker, passer and rusher, thanks to Stagg's brilliant football mind."[26]

In 2019 college football celebrated its 150th anniversary, giving pundits another chance to honor players who had influenced the sport. Unlike in 1969, Walter Eckersall was ignored by most of those experts.

Then again, so was everybody else from football's early days. The fifty members of ESPN's 150th Anniversary All-Time All-America team include only one player who took the field before 1940, Minnesota's Bronko Nagurski. CBS Sports' team suffers even more from recency bias; that fifty-four-man team has no pre-1940 members and only one, Penn's Chuck Bednarik, from before 1950.[27]

The Walter Camp Foundation named a much larger 150th Anniversary team with 130 players, including nine quarterbacks. But Eckersall is missing from that list, too. With 16 players from the game's first eight decades and 114 from the following seven, the Walter Camp team can hardly be considered representative.[28]

The Athletic took a more comprehensive approach for its 150th Anniversary team. By self-imposed rule, *The Athletic* chose at least three players from each of college football's fifteen decades for either its first or second teams. Florida's Tim Tebow was named first-team quarterback and TCU's Sammy Baugh made the second team, but Walter Eckersall cracked *The Athletic*'s lineup as first-team punter.

"Eckersall quarterbacked the peak of the storied Amos Alonzo Stagg era at Chicago," *The Athletic* college football editor Matt Brown wrote. "He starred as an open-field runner, threw the ball as a senior following the legalization of the forward pass and made plays as a defender. As important as anything in the early 1900s was his punting ability, which even led to the winning safety in the 2–0 national championship victory against Michigan on Thanksgiving 1905."[29]

Eckersall, along with Willie Heston, made *The Athletic*'s all-1900s team. The 1905 Chicago team ranked as fourth-best of the decade, while Heston's 1901 Michigan team ranked second. *The Athletic* also named the 1905 Chicago-Michigan game the decade's best football game.[30]

—

In the end, Walter Eckersall was a man full of paradoxes and contradictions:

He was a lazy, indifferent student who never graduated high school and often skipped his college classes. But he had a tenacious work ethic as a young athlete and, later, as a writer and game official.

He was a rumored "pay-for-play" athlete who spent most of his college career under AAU suspension, and started playing pro sports within months of leaving school. But in the 1920s, he became an ambassador for amateur sports and an AAU official, and frequently railed against the evils of professionalism.

He performed in front of huge crowds as an athlete, officiated games in front of even larger crowds, and wrote for an audience of millions. Yet, he was extremely shy in public, preferring gatherings with, at most, a few people.

He was nominally Catholic but never discussed religion, and politically neutral though he spent his adult life working for a Republican newspaper. Yet, in the one firm moral stance he publicly took, he was an outspoken and consistent champion of equality for African Americans.

He was extremely generous with his time, gladly mentored younger reporters, and got his friend Ring Lardner out of a serious jam once. But he also ran up debts that he never repaid, and very publicly got caught stealing.

He was a champion of youth athletics, founding the Silver Skates speedskating tournament and the Golden Gloves boxing tournament. Yet, he appears to have had little relationship with his own daughter, whom he abandoned in her infancy.

As an athlete, Eckersall was one of the all-time greats. Later, through his officiating and newspaper work, he stayed on top of the sporting world long after his competition days were over. For thirty years, Eckie was synonymous with Chicago sports. And for those same thirty years, Chicago sports grew tremendously, largely through his influence.

As the city's first true prep superstar at Hyde Park High School, Eckie garnered previously unknown levels of attention and paved the way for generations of future stars. Under Coach Stagg, Eckie turned University of Chicago football from a regional player into a national power, winning a championship for the ages and earning his place as the city's first college football hero. As the *Chicago Tribune*'s lead sportswriter, Eckie became the lens through which a generation of readers came to understand and appreciate their sports. He became the nation's leading expert on football; lobbied for the re-establishment of legalized boxing in Chicago; and introduced his readers to Olympic sports and athletes. Along the way, Eckie wound up right in the middle of some of the biggest moments in the Golden Age of Sports.

From its humble beginnings in the late nineteenth century, Chicago rose to a premier position in the national sporting conversation by the time of the Dempsey-Tunney fight at Soldier Field. Through his three distinct but interrelated roles over the course of thirty years, Walter Eckersall became the most pivotal figure in the rise of Chicago sports.

APPENDIX

WALTER ECKERSALL'S FOOTBALL RECORD

Notable plays by Eckersall, including all credited scoring plays, appear beneath the score line.

1900	Hyde Park High School (5-4-3; 4-3-2 versus high schools; 2nd in Cook County League).
September 15	University of Chicago 5, Hyde Park 0. At Marshall Field.
September 29	Hyde Park 0, University of Chicago JV 0. At Marshall Field.
October 9	Hyde Park 5, Marshall Field Warehousemen 0. At Marshall Field.
October 10	Lake Forest Academy 5, Hyde Park 0. At Lake Forest.
October 17	Hyde Park 0, North Division High School 0. At Washington Park.
October 24	Hyde Park 11, English and Manual Training 6. At Washington Park.
October 27	Hyde Park 6, Englewood 6. At Marshall Field.
November 3	Hyde Park 6, South Division 0. At Washington Park.
November 10	Hyde Park 17, Evanston 0. At Marshall Field. *35-yard run.*

November 17	Hyde Park 16, Austin 6. At Oak Park.
November 24	East Aurora 16, Hyde Park 5. At Aurora. *60-yard punt return touchdown.*
November 30	North Division 6, Hyde Park 5. At Marshall Field. *105-yard kickoff return touchdown.*
1900 scoring	2 touchdowns—10 total points.
1901	Hyde Park High School (10-3-1; 8-0-1 versus high schools; 1st in Cook County League).
September 25	Hyde Park 6, Chicago 0. At Marshall Field. *35-yard run to set up the game's only touchdown.*
September 28	Hyde Park 0, East Aurora 0. At Aurora. *30-yard punt return as time expired.*
October 5	Wisconsin 63, Hyde Park 0. At Camp Randall Field, Madison, Wisconsin.
October 9	Hyde Park 17, Chicago JV 5. At Marshall Field. *30-yard field goal.*
October 12	Hyde Park 6, North Division 0. At Marshall Field. *1 extra point.*
October 16	Hyde Park 16, South Side Academy 0. At Washington Park.
October 19	Hyde Park 18, South Division 0. At Washington Park.
October 23	Chicago 17, Hyde Park 0. At Marshall Field.
October 30	Chicago Dental School 11, Hyde Park 6. At Washington Park.
November 9	Hyde Park 29, Evanston 5. At Marshall Field. *Touchdown run.*
November 16	Hyde Park 33, Englewood 0. At Marshall Field. *50- and 30-yard runs.*
November 23	Hyde Park 10, Elgin 0. At Elgin.

November 30	Hyde Park 57, West Division 0. At Marshall Field. *85-yard kickoff return touchdown, field goal. Also, 80-yard kickoff return and 55-yard run.*
December 7	Hyde Park 11, North Division 0. At Marshall Field. *60-yard punt return touchdown, 40-yard field goal.*
1901 scoring	3 touchdowns, 3 field goals, 1 extra point—31 total points.
1902	Hyde Park High School (5-3; 5-0 versus high schools; 1st in Cook County League; claimed national championship).
September 24	Chicago 6, Hyde Park 5. At Marshall Field.
September 27	Chicago JV 5, Hyde Park 0. At Marshall Field.
October 4	Wisconsin 24, Hyde Park 5. At Camp Randall Field, Madison, Wisconsin. *50-yard run off a fake punt.*
October 11	Hyde Park 72, South Division 0. At Marshall Field. *110-yard kickoff return touchdown, 1 extra point.*
October 18	Hyde Park 28, North Division 0. At Ravenswood Field. *50-yard touchdown run off a fake punt, 20-yard field goal.*
November 8	Hyde Park 74, West Division 0. At Washington Park. *6 touchdowns, including two 80-yard kickoff returns and 50-yard punt return; 25-yard field goal; 2 extra points.*
November 22	Hyde Park 57, Englewood 0. At Marshall Field. *60-yard touchdown run, 15-yard field goal.*

December 6	Hyde Park 105, Brooklyn Poly Prep 0. At Marshall Field. *90-yard punt return touchdown, 85-yard kickoff return touchdown, 60-yard touchdown run. Missed final eleven minutes with a broken collarbone.*
1902 scoring	12 touchdowns, 3 field goals, 3 extra points—78 total points.
Career high school scoring	17 touchdowns, 6 field goals, 4 extra points—119 total points.

1903	University of Chicago (12-2-1; 10-2-1 versus colleges; 4-1-1 in Big Nine, 4th place).
September 17	Chicago 40, Englewood High School 0. At Marshall Field.
September 19	Chicago 34, Lombard College 0. At Marshall Field. *45-yard kickoff return.*
September 23	Chicago 33, North Division High School 0. At Marshall Field.
September 26	Chicago 23, Lawrence University 0. At Marshall Field. *70-yard kickoff return, 50-yard rush.*
September 30	Chicago 108, Monmouth College 0. At Marshall Field.
October 3	Chicago 34, Indiana 0. At Marshall Field. *75-yard punt return touchdown, 75-yard kickoff return touchdown, 45-yard field goal.*
October 7	Chicago 23, Cornell College 0. At Marshall Field.
October 10	Chicago 22, Purdue 0. At Marshall Field. *Recovered a fumble.*

October 14	Chicago 40, Rush Medical College 0. At Marshall Field. *Did not play.*
October 17	Chicago 0, Northwestern 0. At Marshall Field.
October 24	Chicago 18, Illinois 6. At Marshall Field. *60-yard punt return touchdown.*
October 31	Chicago 15, Wisconsin 6. At Camp Randall Field, Madison, Wisconsin. *3 field goals.*
November 7	Chicago 17, Haskell 11. At Marshall Field.
November 14	Army 10, Chicago 6. At The Plain, West Point, New York.
November 26	Michigan 28, Chicago 0. At Marshall Field.
1903 scoring	3 touchdowns, 4 field goals—35 total points.

1904	University of Chicago (10-1-1; 8-1-1 versus colleges; 5-1-1 in Big Nine, 3rd place).
September 17	Chicago 40, Lombard College 5. At Marshall Field. *4 extra points.*
September 22	Chicago 72, Englewood High School 0. At Marshall Field. *42-yard field goal, 4 extra points.*
September 24	Chicago 29, Lawrence University 0. At Marshall Field. *2 extra points.*
September 28	Chicago 18, North Division High School 0. At Marshall Field. *1 extra point.*
October 1	Chicago 56, Indiana 0. At Marshall Field. *25-yard fumble return touchdown, 1 extra point.*

October 8 — Chicago 20, Purdue 0. At Marshall Field.
33-yard field goal.

October 15 — Chicago 39, Iowa 0. At Marshall Field.
90-yard kickoff return touchdown.

October 22 — Chicago 32, Northwestern 0. At Marshall Field.
5-yard touchdown run, 2 field goals, 1 extra point, more than 200 all-purpose yards.

October 29 — Chicago 6, Illinois 6. At Marshall Field.

November 5 — Chicago 68, Texas 0. At Marshall Field.
100-yard fumble return touchdown, 40-yard field goal, touchdown-saving tackle.

November 12 — Michigan 22, Chicago 12. At Ferry Field, Ann Arbor, Michigan.
40-yard fumble return touchdown.

November 24 — Chicago 18, Wisconsin 11. At Marshall Field.
105-yard kickoff return touchdown.

1904 scoring — 6 touchdowns, 5 field goals, 13 extra points—63 total points.

1905 — University of Chicago (11-0; 10-0 versus colleges; 7-0 in Big Nine, 1st place; claimed national championship).

September 16 — Chicago 26, North Division High School 0. At Marshall Field.
38-yard field goal, 1 extra point.

September 23 — Chicago 33, Lawrence University 0. At Marshall Field.
1 extra point.

September 30 — Chicago 15, Wabash College 0. At Marshall Field.
23-yard field goal.

October 4 — Chicago 38, Beloit College 0. At Marshall Field.
Did not play.

October 7	Chicago 42, Iowa 0. At Marshall Field. *70-yard punt return touchdown.*
October 14	Chicago 16, Indiana 5. At Marshall Field. *20-yard field goal.*
October 21	Chicago 4, Wisconsin 0. At Camp Randall Field, Madison, Wisconsin. *25-yard field goal, 50- and 40-yard runs off fake punts, 5 punts of more than 50 yards.*
October 28	Chicago 32, Northwestern 0. At Northwestern Field, Evanston, Illinois. *15-yard field goal.*
November 11	Chicago 19, Purdue 0. At Marshall Field. *45-yard field goal, 15-yard field goal.*
November 18	Chicago 44, Illinois 0. At Marshall Field. *5 field goals, 30-yard touchdown run, punts of 50, 65, and 70 yards.*
November 30	Chicago 2, Michigan 0. At Marshall Field. *20-yard run off a fake punt to halt Michigan's best scoring threat; 55-yard punt resulted in the game-winning safety.*
1905 scoring	2 touchdowns, 12 field goals, 2 extra points—60 total points.

1906	University of Chicago (4-1, all versus colleges; 3-1 in Big Nine, 4th place).
October 20	Chicago 39, Purdue 0. At Marshall Field. *25-yard touchdown run, 65-yard punt return touchdown.*
October 27	Chicago 33, Indiana 8. At Marshall Field. *45-yard field goal, 70-yard punt return to set up a touchdown.*
November 10	Minnesota 4, Chicago 2. At Marshall Field. *45-yard punt return.*

November 17	Chicago 63, Illinois 0. At Marshall Field. *85- and 40-yard touchdown passes, 30-yard touchdown run, 20-yard field goal, touchdown-saving tackle, nearly 300 yards of total offense.*
November 24	Chicago 38, Nebraska 5. At Marshall Field. *98-yard touchdown pass, 5 field goals.*
1906 scoring	3 touchdowns, 7 field goals—43 total points. Also threw 3 touchdown passes for 15 points.
Career collegiate scoring	14 touchdowns, 28 field goals, 15 extra points—201 total points. Also threw 3 touchdown passes for 15 points.

1907–9	Eckersalls (Chicago Football League, 1907; Independent, 1908–9, 12-0-2).
October 6, 1907	Eckersalls 10, Englewood A.C. 0. At Anson's Park.
October 13, 1907	Eckersalls 34, Aurora Tigers 0. At Anson's Park. *4 field goals, 3 extra points.*
October 20, 1907	Eckersalls 22, Waukegan 0. At Anson's Park. *3 field goals.*
October 28, 1907	Eckersalls 5, Morris A.C. 0. At Anson's Park. *Did not play.*
November 3, 1907	Eckersalls 27, Starbucks 0. At Anson's Park. *Did not play.*
November 10, 1907	Eckersalls 18, Woodstock A.C. 0. At Anson's Park. *Did not play.*
November 17, 1907	Eckersalls 25, South Chicago 0. At Anson's Park. *3 extra points.*
November 24, 1907	Eckersalls 39, Calumets 0. At Anson's Park. *4 extra points.*

November 28, 1907	Eckersalls 11, All-Suburbans 6. At Anson's Park. *1 extra point.*
December 1, 1907	Eckersalls 6, Thistles 0. At Anson's Park. *40-yard field goal.*
December 8, 1907	Eckersalls 0, Mohawks 0. At West Side Park, Chicago.
December 22, 1907	Eckersalls 6, First Regiment 0. At Anson's Park. *35-yard touchdown pass, 1 extra point.*
November 26, 1908	Eckersalls 4, Minneapolis Deans 4. At Nicollet Park, Minneapolis. *1 field goal.*
January 1, 1909	Eckersalls 12, St. Louis All-Stars 4. At St. Louis Coliseum. *3 field goals.*
Career semipro scoring	0 touchdowns, 12 field goals, 12 extra points—60 total points. Also threw 1 touchdown pass for 5 points.

NOTES

PREFACE

1. Brad Kelly (@CoachBKelly), Twitter (now X), February 19, 2020, twitter.com/CoachBKelly/status/1230320754862043139, retrieved on November 10, 2022.
2. Brad Kelly (@CoachBKelly), Twitter (now X), November 9, 2019, twitter.com/CoachBKelly/status/1193363767830163457, retrieved on November 10, 2022.
3. Midwest (@Midwest_ern), Twitter (now X), November 9, 2019, twitter.com/Midwest_ern/status/1193365434843709441, retrieved on November 10, 2022.
4. Brad Kelly (@CoachBKelly), Twitter (now X), November 9, 2019, twitter.com/CoachBKelly/status/1193365901745250305, retrieved on November 10, 2022.

1. WOODLAWN

1. Kitagawa and Taueber, *Local Community Fact Book*, 99.
2. USCR for Walter and Minnie Eckersall and family, 1900, and for Walter and Mary Eckersall and family, 1910; CCMI for Walter Herbert Eckersall and Minnie Killerlain, September 22, 1871; "Walter Eckersall Sr. Dies," *Chicago Tribune*, November 15, 1914; "Mrs. Eckersall, Mother of Noted Writer, Is Dead," *Chicago Tribune*, November 10, 1928.
3. Grossman et al., *Encyclopedia of Chicago*, 886.
4. "Situations Wanted—Males," *Chicago Tribune*, March 20, 1872.
5. USCR for Walter and Minnie Eckersall and family, 1900, and for Walter and Mary Eckersall and family, 1910.
6. "Walter Eckersall Sr. Dies"; "Pedestrianism," *Chicago Inter Ocean*, October 6, 1879; United States Patent Office, *Official Gazette*, 353.
7. USCR for Walter and Minnie Eckersall and family, 1900; "Walter Eckersall," College Football Hall of Fame, accessed February 27, 2024, www.cfbhall.com/inductees/walter-eckersall-1951; WWIDR for Walter Eckersall, September 12, 1918; ISMI for Walter Herbert Eckersall and Elizabeth Louise Jahn, August 18, 1909; ICOD for Walter H. Eckersall, filed March 26, 1930.
8. Grossman et al., *Encyclopedia of Chicago*, 23, 898–902; Chernow, *Titan*, 315.
9. "Building Operations of a Month," *Chicago Tribune*, February 5, 1893; "Classifieds," *Chicago Tribune*, July 16, 1893.

10. Edward Burns, "Eckersall . . . Football Immortal," *Chicago Tribune Grafic*, November 24, 1946.
11. Harvey Woodruff, "Heart Attack Takes Walter Eckersall," *Chicago Tribune*, March 25, 1930; "Eckersall Laid to Rest Near Old Grid Field," *Chicago Tribune*, March 28, 1930; "L.C. Wagner Called from Retirement to Head Midway Bank," *Chicago Tribune*, September 16, 1928.
12. "Calumet Boys Will Kick," *Chicago Chronicle*, September 23, 1895; "Cadets Meet Englewood Unions," *Chicago Tribune*, October 24, 1896; "Many Entries for Athletic Carnival," *Chicago Inter Ocean*, March 25, 1902; "With the Amateurs," *Chicago Inter Ocean*, September 20, 1897; "Today's Long Road Race," *Chicago Tribune*, September 4, 1899; "Collier Brothers the Winners," *Chicago Tribune*, July 30, 1899; "Breaks Arm, but Skates On," *Chicago Tribune*, January 3, 1906; "Women Give Entertainment," *Boston Globe*, April 29, 1910.
13. Walter Eckersall, "My Twenty-Five Years of Football," pt. 1, *Liberty* 3 (October 16, 1926): 23.
14. Eckersall, "My Twenty-Five Years of Football," pt. 1, 23, 27.
15. Eckersall, "My Twenty-Five Years of Football," pt. 1, 27.
16. Lester, *Stagg's University*, 55.

2. PRE-1900 HIGH SCHOOL SPORTS

1. Pruter, *Rise of American High School Sports*, 4–5.
2. Pruter, *Rise of American High School Sports*, 13–14; "The High-School League," *Chicago Tribune*, April 26, 1890; "Evanston High School, 8; Chicago, 1," *Chicago Tribune*, June 8, 1890.
3. "High School Athletes," *Chicago Inter Ocean*, July 3, 1889.
4. Pruter, *Rise of American High School Sports*, 26; "Illinois High School Athletes," *Chicago Tribune*, May 21, 1893; "Boys Track and Field Records & History," Illinois High School Association, accessed February 27, 2024, www.ihsa.org/Sports-Activities/Boys-Track-Field/Records-History.
5. Pruter, *Rise of American High School Sports*, 17–19.
6. "A Football League," *Chicago Tribune*, September 28, 1889; "Hyde Park Wins the Championship," *Chicago Tribune*, November 1, 1889; "High-School Foot-Ball Champions," *Chicago Tribune*, April 19, 1890.
7. "Football at Jackson Park," *Chicago Tribune*, November 21, 1890; "Found the Charges True," *Chicago Tribune*, December 11, 1890; "High School League's Rules," *Chicago Tribune*, February 19, 1898; "Ready for the Games," *Chicago Tribune*, September 7, 1896.
8. Pruter, *Rise of American High School Sports*, 29.
9. Walter Eckersall, "My Twenty-Five Years of Football," pt. 2, *Liberty* 3 (October 23, 1926): 59.
10. "High School Football League Competition Becoming a Farce," *Chicago Tribune*, November 7, 1896.

11. "High Schools to Line Up," *Chicago Chronicle*, September 16, 1896.
12. Pruter, *Rise of American High School Sports*, 73–74; "High School League Formed," *Chicago Tribune*, February 5, 1898; "Divisions to Play First," *Chicago Inter Ocean*, September 11, 1898.

3. HYDE PARK HIGH SCHOOL

1. "Pride in Its School," *Chicago Tribune*, May 19, 1894.
2. Walter Eckersall, "My Twenty-Five Years of Football," pt. 2, *Liberty* 3 (October 23, 1926): 60.
3. "University School Beats Hyde Park," *Chicago Tribune*, January 21, 1900; "Hyde Park High School Meet," *Chicago Tribune*, April 1, 1900.
4. "Ten High School Nines," *Chicago Tribune*, April 15, 1900; "Hyde Park, 12; West Division, 4," *Chicago Tribune*, June 9, 1900; "Austin Team Beats Hyde Park," *Chicago Tribune*, June 17, 1900; "All-High-School Team," *Chicago Inter Ocean*, June 22, 1900.
5. Brown, *How Football Became Football*, 9, 11–13, 38–39, 61, 68, 358.
6. "Football Season Is On," *Chicago Tribune*, September 16, 1900; "Chicago Played Close by Knox," *Chicago Tribune*, September 30, 1900; "Hyde Park Beats Merchants," *Chicago Tribune*, October 10, 1900.
7. "Lake Forest Academy, 5; Hyde Park, 0," *Chicago Tribune*, October 11, 1900; "Neither Team Could Score," *Chicago Inter Ocean*, October 17, 1900; "Games at Washington Park," *Chicago Tribune*, October 25, 1900; "Englewood and Hyde Park," *Chicago Tribune*, October 28, 1900; "Hyde Park, 6; South Division, 0," *Chicago Tribune*, November 4, 1900; "Boys Play Football," *Chicago Daily News*, November 10, 1900; "Hyde Park High Trims Austin," *Chicago Tribune*, November 18, 1900.
8. "East Aurora, 16; Hyde Park, 5," *Chicago Tribune*, November 25, 1900.
9. "North Division Beats Hyde Park," *Chicago Tribune*, December 1, 1900; "Hyde Park Is Beaten," *Chicago Inter Ocean*, December 1, 1900; "Stands by Timekeeper," *Chicago Tribune*, December 5, 1900.
10. "Game Ends in the Usual Wrangle," *Chicago Tribune*, March 10, 1901.
11. "Englewood Wins Meet," *Chicago Tribune*, May 19, 1901; "High School Track Meet," *Chicago Tribune*, June 16, 1901.
12. "Hyde Park, 13; Aurora [*sic*], 9," *Chicago Tribune*, April 21, 1901; "High School League Games," *Chicago Tribune*, May 5, 1901; "High School League Games," *Chicago Tribune*, May 12, 1901; "Hyde Park Defeats Austin," *Chicago Tribune*, June 20, 1901.
13. "Hyde Park Is Champion," *Chicago Tribune*, June 23, 1901.
14. "Hyde Park Team Beats Maroons," *Chicago Tribune*, September 26, 1901.
15. "Aurora Ties Hyde Park," *Chicago Tribune*, September 29, 1901.
16. "Badgers Bury Hyde Park," *Chicago Tribune*, October 6, 1901; "Hyde Park, 17; Varsity Scrubs, 0," *Chicago Inter Ocean*, October 10, 1901.
17. Walter Eckersall, "Sam Ransom Fearless in War or Sport," *Pittsburgh Post*, July 21, 1918.

18. "Hyde Park Beats North Division," *Chicago Inter Ocean*, October 13, 1901; "Hyde Park, 16; South Side, 0," *Chicago Inter Ocean*, October 17, 1901; "Hyde Park, 18; South Division, 0," *Chicago Tribune*, October 20, 1901.
19. "Varsity Defeats Hyde Park," *Chicago Inter Ocean*, October 24, 1901; "Dentists Beat Hyde Park," *Chicago Tribune*, October 31, 1901; "Hyde Park Beats Evanston," *Chicago Tribune*, November 10, 1901.
20. "Hyde Park High Beats Englewood," *Chicago Inter Ocean*, November 17, 1901; "Hyde Park, 10; Elgin, 0," *Chicago Inter Ocean*, November 24, 1901; "Hyde Park Wins Easily," *Chicago Tribune*, December 1, 1901.
21. "School Teams Battle Today," *Chicago Tribune*, December 7, 1901.
22. "Hyde Park Wins Brilliant Game," *Chicago Tribune*, December 8, 1901.
23. "Pick of Cook County," *Chicago Daily News*, December 9, 1901.
24. "Hyde Park's Great Leader," *Chicago Inter Ocean*, December 1, 1901.
25. "Hyde Park Wins Dual Meet," *Chicago Tribune*, February 2, 1902; "Hyde Park Wins Banner," *Chicago Tribune*, February 16, 1902; "Hyde Park Makes Good Record," *Chicago Tribune*, February 23, 1902; "Hyde Park, 77; Lake View, 23," *Chicago Inter Ocean*, March 16, 1902; "Hyde Parks the Victor," *Chicago Tribune*, March 23, 1902; "Exciting Track Meet at Armory," *Chicago Inter Ocean*, March 30, 1902; "South Division to Go East," *Chicago Inter Ocean*, April 20, 1902; "Badgers Down Hyde Park Team," *Chicago Tribune*, May 2, 1902.
26. "Ransom Re-Elected Captain," *Chicago Tribune*, March 3, 1903; "Stagg's Men Defeat Hyde Park," *Chicago Inter Ocean*, March 26, 1902; "Hyde Park Boys Meet Defeat," *Chicago Tribune*, May 1, 1902; "Hyde Park, 8; Varsity Scrubs, 7," *Chicago Inter Ocean*, April 6, 1902; "Hyde Park, 3; Maroon Scrubs, 2," *Chicago Inter Ocean*, April 13, 1902; "Union Giants, 13; Hyde Park, 6," *Chicago Tribune*, April 16, 1902.
27. "Hyde Park May Lose the Banner," *Chicago Tribune*, April 18, 1902.
28. "Hyde Park High Wins," *Chicago Inter Ocean*, April 27, 1902.
29. "Hyde Park Teams Suspended," *Chicago Tribune*, May 14, 1902; "Hyde Park Baseball Team, Disbarred from League Games by Board of Education," *Chicago Tribune*, May 21, 1902.
30. "Hyde Park Will Not Compete," *Chicago Tribune*, May 16, 1902; "Easy for Chicago Lads," *Chicago Tribune*, May 18, 1902; "High-School Athletes Compete," *Chicago Inter Ocean*, June 15, 1902.
31. "Plead for a Reinstatement," *Chicago Tribune*, May 20, 1902; "Hyde Park 12; North Division 1," *Chicago Inter Ocean*, May 25, 1902.

4. HIGH SCHOOL SUPERSTAR

1. "School Teams at Work," *Chicago Tribune*, September 7, 1902.
2. "School Elevens at Work," *Chicago Tribune*, August 31, 1902; "Pick Hyde Park to Win," *Chicago Tribune*, November 22, 1902.
3. "Maroons Beat Hyde Park 6 to 5," *Chicago Tribune*, September 25, 1902.
4. "Scrubs Outdo the Varsity," *Chicago Tribune*, September 28, 1902.

5. "Hyde Park Boys Tally," *Chicago Tribune*, October 5, 1902.
6. "Hyde Park Makes a Big Total," *Chicago Inter Ocean*, October 12, 1902.
7. "Hyde Park Beats North Division," *Chicago Inter Ocean*, October 19, 1902.
8. "Big Score for Hyde Park Team," *Chicago Tribune*, November 9, 1902.
9. "Hyde Park Defeats Englewood 57 to 0," *Chicago Inter Ocean*, November 23, 1902.
10. "Hyde Park the Champions," *Chicago Tribune*, November 26, 1902.
11. "Southerners Bar Ransom," *Chicago Tribune*, November 24, 1902.
12. "Alumni Stand by Ransom," *Chicago Tribune*, November 25, 1902.
13. "High School Turns Table on Manual," *Louisville (KY) Courier-Journal*, November 28, 1902.
14. "Schoolboy Football Match," *New York Times*, December 2, 1902.
15. Walter Eckersall, "My Twenty-Five Years of Football," pt. 2, *Liberty* 3 (October 23, 1926): 62.
16. "St. Paul's School Defeats Poly Prep," *Brooklyn Daily Eagle*, November 9, 1902; "Erasmus Hall Wins from Poly Prep," *Brooklyn Daily Eagle*, November 20, 1902; "Poly Prep Vanquishes Her Old Time Rival," *Brooklyn Daily Eagle*, November 28, 1902.
17. "Brooklyn Team Arrives Today," *Chicago Tribune*, December 5, 1902.
18. "Football Team Leaves," *New York Times*, December 5, 1902.
19. "Brooklyn Team Arrives Today"; "Sketch of the Eastern Team," *Chicago Tribune*, December 5, 1902.
20. "Hyde Park Eleven Overwhelms Poly Prep," *Brooklyn Daily Eagle*, December 7, 1902.
21. "Hyde Park, 105; Brooklyn Poly, 0," *Chicago Tribune*, December 7, 1902.
22. "Officials Praise Hyde Park," *Chicago Tribune*, December 7, 1902.
23. "All Star School Team. Hyde Park Lands Ten of the Eleven Best Players," *Chicago Tribune*, November 30, 1902.
24. "Track Athletes at Indoor Meet," *Chicago Tribune*, February 6, 1903; "Maroon Freshmen Beat High Schools," *Chicago Inter Ocean*, February 1, 1903; "Clean Sweep by Chicago Teams," *Chicago Tribune*, February 27, 1903; "High School Boys Fast," *Chicago Tribune*, March 1, 1903; "First Regiment Wins Big Meet," *Chicago Tribune*, March 8, 1903; "Chicagoans First in Athletic Meet," *St. Louis Republic*, March 22, 1903.
25. "Hyde Park Wins Honors," *Chicago Tribune*, April 19, 1903.
26. "Michigan Wins Four-Mile Relay Race from Old Eli at Penn's Big Carnival," *Philadelphia Inquirer*, April 26, 1903.
27. "Hyde Park High Wins Track Meet," *Chicago Inter Ocean*, May 3, 1903.
28. "Hyde Park Boys Are Champions," *Chicago Tribune*, May 17, 1903.
29. "Calls Cook County Meet Off," *Chicago Tribune*, June 3, 1903; "Anti-Cigaret League Meet," *Chicago Tribune*, June 27, 1903; "Lewis Wins by One Point," *Chicago Tribune*, June 7, 1903.
30. "School Season Is Ended," *Chicago Tribune*, June 28, 1903.

31. "Hyde Park, 14; West Division, 4," *Chicago Tribune*, May 6, 1903; "Hyde Park, 14; North Division, 8," *Chicago Tribune*, May 30, 1903; "Hyde Park, 8; Goshen, 2," *Chicago Tribune*, May 31, 1903; "Hyde Park, 11; English High, 9," *Chicago Inter Ocean*, June 12, 1903.
32. "Hyde Park High Wins the Pennant," *Chicago Inter Ocean*, June 20, 1903.
33. "Hyde Park, 13; Delavan, 2," *Chicago Tribune*, June 21, 1903.

5. HIGH SCHOOL SPORTS AFTER ECKERSALL

1. "Easy Prey for North Division," *Chicago Tribune*, November 29, 1903; "Champions of United States," *Seattle Star*, January 2, 1907.
2. "Englewood Team Wins Butte Game," *Chicago Tribune*, December 20, 1908; "Englewood Loses to Longmont, 13–0," *Chicago Tribune*, December 26, 1908; "Trip Stirs School Board," *Chicago Tribune*, December 19, 1908.
3. "Urion Says No Junkets," *Chicago Tribune*, December 15, 1909.
4. "Oak Park Beats Rivals on Coast," *Chicago Tribune*, December 27, 1910; "Oak Park Beats Portland, 6 to 3," *Chicago Tribune*, January 1, 1911; Walter H. Eckersall, "'Prep' Champions of West Humble St. John's by 17–0," *Chicago Tribune*, December 3, 1911; "Oak Park Eleven Crushes Everett in Clash for Title," *Chicago Tribune*, December 1, 1912.
5. Robert Pruter, "A Century of Intersectional and Interstate Football Contests," Illinois High School Association, accessed February 15, 2024, www.ihsa.org/archive/hstoric/football_intersec.htm.
6. "Trouble at South Division," *Chicago Tribune*, October 11, 1901; "Expels South Division," *Chicago Tribune*, October 18, 1901; "Plead for a Reinstatement," *Chicago Tribune*, May 20, 1902.
7. "Clash in Cook County League," *Chicago Tribune*, November 21, 1900.
8. "New Athletic School League," *Chicago Tribune*, October 7, 1902; "High School Boys Disband," *Chicago Tribune*, October 16, 1902.
9. Pruter, *Rise of American High School Sports*, 77, 89–97.
10. Robert Pruter, "Chicago High School Football Struggles, the Fight for Faculty Control and the War Against Secret Societies, 1898–1908," Illinois High School Association, accessed February 27, 2024, www.ihsa.org/archive/hstoric/fraternities.htm; "Eckersall Has Broken Rib," *Chicago Tribune*, May 7, 1903.
11. "High School Fraternities," *Chicago Tribune*, January 8, 1905.
12. "New Rules Are Disliked," *Chicago Tribune*, March 13, 1904.
13. "School 'Frats' May Go," *Chicago Tribune*, May 26, 1904.
14. "Rule Passed to Crush High School Fraternities," *Chicago Tribune*, June 7, 1904.
15. "'Greeks' in Arms to Save 'Frats,'" *Chicago Tribune*, May 27, 1904; "Fraternity Boys Appeal to Courts," *Chicago Inter Ocean*, September 28, 1904; "School Boys Win Legal Battle," *Chicago Tribune*, October 25, 1904; "Hyde Park Jubilant," *Chicago Inter Ocean*, October 26, 1904.

16. "Anti-Frat Rule in Full Effect," *Chicago Tribune*, May 10, 1906; "Havoc by Anti-Frat Rule," *Chicago Tribune*, November 23, 1906; "Court Is Cold to Frats," *Chicago Tribune*, November 24, 1906; "Fraternities Lose Appeal," *Chicago Inter Ocean*, March 7, 1908.
17. "'Frat' Boy Loses in Legal Fight," *Chicago Tribune*, November 12, 1907.
18. "Frats Outlawed; Sept. 1 Dead Line," *Chicago Tribune*, March 12, 1908; "Frats Defy Rule of School Board," *Chicago Tribune*, September 8, 1908.
19. "Spanking as Cure for 'Frat Evil,'" *Chicago Tribune*, September 16, 1908.
20. "Judge Rules Against Frats," *Chicago Tribune*, October 4, 1908.
21. "New Rules Are Disliked," *Chicago Tribune*, March 13, 1904; Pruter, *Rise of American High School Sports*, 150, 157, 160.
22. "Prep League Lets Down Bar," *Chicago Tribune*, September 19, 1911; "Fourteen Teams in Prep League," *Chicago Tribune*, September 26, 1911; Prep, "St. Phillip's Nine Pennant Winner," *Chicago Tribune*, June 18, 1912.
23. "Catholics to Form League," *Chicago Tribune*, October 3, 1912.
24. Prep, "Chicago 'Preps' Break Up League," *Chicago Tribune*, May 22, 1913; "'Prep' Athletics Show Gain During the Season of 1913," *Chicago Tribune*, December 28, 1913; "High School Baseball," *Chicago Tribune*, April 30, 1970.
25. "Boys Track and Field Records & History," Illinois High School Association, accessed February 27, 2024, www.ihsa.org/Sports-Activities/Boys-Track-Field/Records-History; "Four Quintets Survive in Central States Tournament," *Chicago Tribune*, March 14, 1914; "Basket Title to Evanston," *Chicago Tribune*, March 15, 1914; Prep, "Honors Divided in 'Prep' Games," *Chicago Tribune*, December 27, 1914; "Oak Parkers Seek Battle," *Chicago Tribune*, November 25, 1913.
26. "Hyde Park Will Play 'U' High," *Chicago Tribune*, November 26, 1913; Wilfrid Smith, "Mount Carmel Wins City Prep Grid Title," *Chicago Tribune*, December 4, 1927.
27. Edward Burns, "Austin High Conquers Leo, 26 to 0, Before Record Crowd," *Chicago Tribune*, November 28, 1937.
28. "Prep Bowl History," Chicago Public League, accessed February 27, 2024, https://assets-rst7.rschooltoday.com/rst7files/uploads/sites/173/2023/12/15122628/CPS-Prep-Bowl-History-Page-cpsathletics.com_pdf; Tina Akouris, "If a Football Squad Wanted Bragging Rights in Chicago, the Prep Bowl Was What Mattered," *Chicago Tribune*, November 27, 2020.
29. "State Teachers Have Busy Day," *Chicago Tribune*, December 28, 1900; Pruter, *Rise of American High School Sports*, 81; "A Brief History of March Madness," Illinois High School Association, accessed February 27, 2024, https://www.ihsa.org/Sports-Activities/March-Madness-Experience/March-Madness-History.
30. "6 Chicago High Schools Join Illinois Ass'n," *Chicago Tribune*, March 30, 1926.
31. "Bars Girls from Basketball," *Chicago Tribune*, November 3, 1907.
32. Jerry Shnay, "Catholic League to Join IHSA; Cites Competition," *Chicago Tribune*, January 31, 1973; "Football Records & History," Illinois High School Association,

accessed February 27, 2024, www.ihsa.org/Sports-Activities/Football/Records-History.

33. "Future Is Dim for Prep Bowl," *Chicago Tribune*, August 12, 1985; Akouris, "If a Football Squad Wanted Bragging Rights."
34. "Boys Basketball Records & History," Illinois High School Association, accessed February 27, 2024, www.ihsa.org/Sports-Activities/Boys-Basketball/Records-History.
35. "Girls Basketball Records & History," Illinois High School Association, accessed February 27, 2024, www.ihsa.org/Sports-Activities/Girls-Basketball/Records-History.
36. "Eckersall a Future Maroon," *Chicago Tribune*, October 26, 1902; "Hyde Park Wins by Large Score," *Chicago Inter Ocean*, December 1, 1901; "Hyde Park Again Ahead," *Chicago Inter Ocean*, February 2, 1902; "Hyde Park Makes a Big Total," *Chicago Inter Ocean*, October 12, 1902; "High School Boys Busy," *Chicago Tribune*, February 8, 1903; "Schoolboys Still at It," *Chicago Tribune*, June 1, 1903.
37. "North Division's Pennant," *Chicago Tribune*, April 27, 1903; "North Division Holds Title," *Chicago Tribune*, April 3, 1904; "North Division Is Best," *Chicago Tribune*, April 19, 1903; "North Division Is Winner," *Chicago Tribune*, March 18, 1905; "Boys Track and Field Records & History," Illinois High School Association, accessed February 27, 2024, www.ihsa.org/Sports-Activities/Boys-Track-Field/Records-History; "Tilden Victor in State Meet; 6 Marks Broken," *Chicago Tribune*, May 20, 1928; "Hyde Park and Tilden Tech Tie for Track Title," *Chicago Tribune*, May 19, 1929; "De Correvont Gets 44 Points as Austin Wins," *Chicago Tribune*, October 23, 1937; Edward Burns, "De Correvont Crosses Goal Three Times," *Chicago Tribune*, November 28, 1937; Charles Bartlett, "C.Y.O. to Honor Prep Stars at Stadium Bouts," *Chicago Tribune*, November 30, 1937; George Strickler, "Letourner and Partner Lead 6 Day Bike Race," *Chicago Tribune*, March 14, 1938; "In the Spotlight: Fenwick Star," *Chicago Tribune*, September 15, 1949; Rich Mayor, "A Chicago Lifer," *Chicago Tribune*, November 7, 2014.
38. "Russell All-State," *Chicago Tribune*, March 5, 1962; Larry Casey, "Aguirre Hits Mark to Pace Playoff Romp," *Chicago Tribune*, February 28, 1978; Michael Arndt, "Bullets End Benjy's Fight to Be the Best," *Chicago Tribune*, November 22, 1984; Bob Sakamoto, "Garnett, Fields Fly Farragut to Champaign," *Chicago Tribune*, March 13, 1995; Bob Sakamoto, "Above the Crowd," *Chicago Tribune*, April 9, 1995; Bob Sakamoto, "Above the Rest—and the Rim," *Chicago Tribune*, April 7, 1996; Bob Sakamoto, "Rose-y Finish," *Chicago Tribune*, March 19, 2006; Bob Sakamoto, "Rose Smells Sweet Repeat," *Chicago Tribune*, March 16, 2007.
39. Marlen Garcia, "Capping an Attitude," *Chicago Tribune*, March 26, 2000; Alan Sutton, "Quite a Career Capper," *Chicago Tribune*, March 25, 2001; "Girls Track and Field Records & History," Illinois High School Association, accessed February 27, 2024, https://www.ihsa.org/Sports-Activities/Girls-Track-Field/Records-History; Marlen Garcia, "Alexandria the Greatest," *Chicago Tribune*, May 19,

2002; Barry Temkin, "Morgan Park's Golden Girl Has Bigger Plans," *Chicago Tribune*, May 23, 2004; Nathan Baird, "Anderson Leaps into History," *Chicago Tribune*, May 22, 2005.

6. THE RECRUIT

1. Henry Beach Needham, "The College Athlete," pt. 1, *McClure's* 25 (June 1905): 117, 126; Needham, "The College Athlete," pt. 2, *McClure's* 25 (July 1905): 267; Edward S. Jordan, "Buying Football Victories," pt. 1, *Collier's* 36 (November 11, 1905): 20; Jordan, "Buying Football Victories," pt. 2, *Collier's* 36 (November 18, 1905): 22; Jordan, "Buying Football Victories," pt. 3, *Collier's* 36 (November 25, 1905): 21; Jordan, "Buying Football Victories," pt. 4, *Collier's* 36 (December 2, 1905): 19.
2. AAS Papers, Box 13, Folders 4, 9.
3. "'Badgers' After New Talent," *Chicago Inter Ocean*, March 31, 1902.
4. Kryk, *Stagg vs. Yost*, 141–43; "Sectional Game of High Schools," *Chicago Tribune*, December 6, 1902; "Officials Praise Hyde Park," *Chicago Tribune*, December 7, 1902.
5. "Eckersall a Future Maroon," *Chicago Tribune*, October 26, 1902.
6. "Michigan Alumni at Smoker," *Chicago Tribune*, November 15, 1902.
7. "School Season Is Ended," *Chicago Tribune*, June 28, 1903.
8. "Another Year for Eckersall," *Chicago Daily News*, July 7, 1903.
9. Kryk, *Stagg vs. Yost*, 143–45.
10. Walter Eckersall, "My Twenty-Five Years of Football," pt. 3, *Liberty* 3 (October 30, 1926): 73.
11. "Eckersall Joins Stagg's Eleven," *Chicago Tribune*, September 15, 1903; Kryk, *Stagg vs. Yost*, 145–46.
12. "Stagg Lands Most Lads," *Chicago Tribune*, September 6, 1903.
13. "Eckersall Joins Stagg's Eleven."

7. COACH STAGG

1. Stagg, *Touchdown!*, 110–12; Lester, *Stagg's University*, 3.
2. Lester, *Stagg's University*, 122, 130.
3. Stagg, *Touchdown!*, 110, 131–32.
4. Stagg, *Touchdown!*, 143–44.
5. Chernow, *Titan*, 37–38, 60, 132, 222–26, 302–8; Stagg, *Touchdown!*, 144–46.
6. Chernow, *Titan*, 307–10; Goodspeed, *History of the University of Chicago*, 29.
7. Rockefeller, *Random Reminiscences*, 178–79.
8. Chernow, *Titan*, 308, 312; Goodspeed, *History of the University of Chicago*, 66–69, 83–88.
9. Chernow, *Titan*, 316–19, 497; Lester, *Stagg's University*, 4–6; Goodspeed, *History of the University of Chicago*, 136–37.
10. Lester, *Stagg's University*, 16; Stagg, *Touchdown!*, 148, 153–54; "Stagg Will Not Come to Chicago," *Chicago Tribune*, November 28, 1891.
11. Lester, *Stagg's University*, 17–19.

12. Goodspeed, *History of the University of Chicago*, 377–79; Stagg, *Touchdown!*, 105.
13. "The Mighty Stagg," *Chicago Inter Ocean*, October 2, 1892.
14. Stagg, *Touchdown!*, 154–55.
15. Lester, *Stagg's University*, 199–200; "Stagg on Athletics," *Chicago Tribune*, October 9, 1892; "Chicago Varsity Defeats Englewood," *Chicago Tribune*, October 11, 1892; "Stagg's Schedule Arranged," *Chicago Tribune*, October 13, 1892; Stagg, *Touchdown!*, 161.
16. Stagg, *Touchdown!*, 191, 199.
17. "Boys Must Not Slug," *Chicago Tribune*, January 12, 1895.
18. "Draw the Line Close," *Chicago Tribune*, February 9, 1896; "Seven in the Contest," *Chicago Tribune*, September 30, 1896.
19. Lester, *Stagg's University*, 200–202.
20. Sumner, *Amos Alonzo Stagg*, 191–96.
21. "Faith in Stagg Cheers Chicago," *Chicago Tribune*, October 30, 1903; Stagg, *Touchdown!*, 137.

8. FRESHMAN PHENOM

1. "Clean Sweep by Chicago Teams," *Chicago Tribune*, February 27, 1903; "High School Boys Fast," *Chicago Tribune*, March 1, 1903; "First Regiment Wins Big Meet," *Chicago Tribune*, March 8, 1903; "Chicagoans First in Athletic Meet," *St. Louis Republic*, March 22, 1903.
2. "Eckersall Is Under the Ban," *Chicago Tribune*, August 27, 1903.
3. "Interstate Season Closes," *Chicago Tribune*, October 5, 1903.
4. "Eckersall Barred from Maroon Team," *Chicago Inter Ocean*, September 16, 1903.
5. "Stagg Defies A.A.U. in Eckersall Case," *Chicago Inter Ocean*, September 17, 1903.
6. "Linginger [*sic*] in Town," *Chicago Inter Ocean*, September 22, 1903.
7. "Hollister Picks Michigan," *Chicago Tribune*, October 3, 1903.
8. "Chicago Kickers Score 40 Points," *Chicago Tribune*, September 18, 1903.
9. Walter Eckersall, "My Twenty-Five Years of Football," pt. 3, *Liberty* 3 (October 30, 1926): 74.
10. "Maroons Beat Lombard 34 to 0," *Chicago Inter Ocean*, September 20, 1903; "Maroons Shut Out North Division," *Chicago Inter Ocean*, September 24, 1903; "Chicago Wins from Lawrence," *Chicago Tribune*, September 27, 1903; "Stagg's Kickers Make 108 Points," *Chicago Tribune*, October 1, 1903.
11. "What a Man Must Not Do on a College Football Team," *Chicago Inter Ocean*, October 4, 1903.
12. "Maroons Win the First Real Game," *Chicago Tribune*, October 4, 1903.
13. "Maroons Defeat Cornell Eleven," *Chicago Tribune*, October 8, 1903; "Maroons Defeat Purdue by 22 to 0," *Chicago Inter Ocean*, October 11, 1903; "Chicago Beats Purdue 22 to 0," *Chicago Tribune*, October 11, 1903; "Medics Easy for Maroon Scrubs," *Chicago Inter Ocean*, October 15, 1903.
14. "0 to 0 Score at Marshall Field," *Chicago Tribune*, October 18, 1903.

15. "Eckersall Faces Many Ugly Rumors," *Chicago Inter Ocean*, October 22, 1903.
16. "A.A.U. to Keep Eckersall Out," *Chicago Tribune*, October 21, 1903.
17. "Swears to Story of Pay," *Chicago Tribune*, October 25, 1903.
18. "Charges Denied by Eckersall," *Chicago Tribune*, October 23, 1903.
19. "Stagg's Statement in Eckersall Case," *Chicago Inter Ocean*, October 30, 1903.
20. "Maroons Beat Illini by 18 to 6," *Chicago Inter Ocean*, October 25, 1903.
21. Lester, *Stagg's University*, 78–79; Revsine, *Opening Kickoff*, 122–23.
22. "Chicago Scores Great Victory," *Chicago Tribune*, November 1, 1903.
23. "Score Twice on Chicago Eleven," *Chicago Tribune*, November 8, 1903.
24. "Penalty Costs Chicago a Game," *Chicago Tribune*, November 15, 1903.
25. Louis A. Dougher, "Short Sport Takes," *Washington Times*, December 5, 1917; Grantland Rice, "Where Are the Old Stars Now?" *Collier's* 74 (October 18, 1924): 46; Harvey Woodruff, "In the Wake of the News: Heston and Eckersall," *Chicago Tribune*, October 30, 1932.
26. "Michigan Victor in Final Contest," *Chicago Tribune*, November 27, 1903.
27. "Experts' Views of the Game," *Chicago Tribune*, November 27, 1903.
28. "Stars Picked for the All-Western," *Chicago Inter Ocean*, November 29, 1903; "Selections for All-Western 11," *Chicago Tribune*, November 29, 1903.
29. Camp, *Spalding's Official Foot Ball Guide* (1905), 3, 17, 33, 35.
30. "Rumor Accuses Eckersall," *Chicago Inter Ocean*, December 4, 1903; "Goodby, Walter, Goodby!" *Chicago Tribune*, December 5, 1903; "Badgers May Get Eckersall," *Chicago Inter Ocean*, December 6, 1903; "Eckersall Is Out for Good," *Chicago Inter Ocean*, December 10, 1903.
31. "Stagg Is Able to Be About," *Chicago Tribune*, December 14, 1903.
32. "Doors Closed to 'Eckie,'" *Chicago Tribune*, December 15, 1903.
33. "Approves Pattengill's Stand," *Chicago Tribune*, December 16, 1903; "Eckersall Is Down and Out," *Chicago Inter Ocean*, January 4, 1904.
34. "Illinois Freshmen Victors," *Chicago Tribune*, February 7, 1904; "Illini Wins from Chicago, 45 to 41," *Chicago Inter Ocean*, February 28, 1904; "Freshmen Down Sophomores," *Chicago Tribune*, March 20, 1904.
35. "Eckersall May Be Professional," *Chicago Inter Ocean*, March 29, 1904.
36. "Eckersall Now Eligible," *Chicago Inter Ocean*, July 3, 1904.

9. ALL-AMERICAN

1. "Eckersall Will Run for Chicago," *St. Louis Globe-Democrat*, June 22, 1904.
2. "Eckersall's Case Up Today," *Chicago Tribune*, June 25, 1904; "Chicago Team Beats Princeton Tigers," *St. Louis Republic*, June 26, 1904.
3. "Notes of the Midway Athletes," *Chicago Tribune*, August 5, 1904.
4. "Young Man Drowned," *St. Joseph (MI) Herald*, August 26, 1904; "Pigskin's Boom Delights Midway," *Chicago Inter Ocean*, September 4, 1904.
5. "Maroons Have an Easy Time with Lombard," *Chicago Inter Ocean*, September 18, 1904; "Englewood Too Light for the Maroon Team," *Chicago Inter Ocean*, Septem-

ber 22, 1904; "Chicago Beats Light Lawrence Team 29 to 0," *Chicago Inter Ocean*, September 25, 1904; "North Siders Hold Maroons to Low Score," *Chicago Inter Ocean*, September 29, 1904.

6. "Chicago Walked Over the Indiana Eleven," *Detroit Free Press*, October 2, 1904.
7. "Chicago, 20; Purdue, 0," *Chicago Tribune*, October 9, 1904.
8. "Maroons Again Seek Honors in Immense Score," *Chicago Inter Ocean*, October 16, 1904.
9. "Big Game in Detail," *Chicago Inter Ocean*, October 23, 1904.
10. "Chicago Eleven Ties with Illini," *Chicago Tribune*, October 30, 1904.
11. "Chaff for Yost and Heston," *Chicago Tribune*, November 6, 1904.
12. "Texas Team Easy for the Maroons," *Chicago Tribune*, November 6, 1904.
13. "Coach Yost Hands a Few to Alonzo Stagg and Others," *Chicago Inter Ocean*, October 28, 1904.
14. Thomas S. Hammond, as told to Harvey Woodruff, "My Greatest Thrill in Football," *Chicago Tribune*, November 6, 1932.
15. "Michigan Colors Wave in Triumph," *Chicago Tribune*, November 13, 1904; Harry W. Ford, "Weight Triumphs over Maroons," *Chicago Inter Ocean*, November 13, 1904.
16. "Eckersall Is Again Winner over Wisconsin," *Chicago Inter Ocean*, November 25, 1904.
17. O'Loughlin, "The Journal's All Western," *Minneapolis Journal*, November 28, 1904; "Pick of Football Stars," *Chicago Tribune*, November 27, 1904; "All Westerners for '04 Season," *Chicago Inter Ocean*, November 27, 1904; Harry W. Ford, "Only Four Men Meet Approval of All Critics," *Chicago Inter Ocean*, November 28, 1904; "Hammond Overlooked as Tackle Selection," *Detroit Free Press*, November 27, 1904; Camp, *Spalding's Official Foot Ball Guide* (1905), 37.
18. Camp, *Spalding's Official Foot Ball Guide* (1905), 5, 29.
19. "First Tryout for Maroons," *Chicago Tribune*, December 11, 1904; "Maroons in Good Tryout," *Chicago Tribune*, January 29, 1905; "Dual Track Meet Won by Illinois," *Chicago Tribune*, February 12, 1905; "Maroons Win Dual Meet," *Chicago Tribune*, March 19, 1905.
20. "Armour Beaten Again," *Chicago Inter Ocean*, March 31, 1905; "First Game to Michigan," *Chicago Tribune*, April 16, 1905; "Maroons Lose by One Run," *Chicago Tribune*, April 23, 1904; "Maroons' Hitting Frightens Illini," *Champaign (IL) Daily News*, April 27, 1905.
21. University of Chicago, *Cap and Gown* 11 (1906): 270–73.
22. "Eckersall Case May Cause Hitch in I.A.C. Plans," *Chicago Tribune*, March 14, 1905; "Confer on Eckersall Case," *Chicago Tribune*, March 18, 1905.
23. "Pave Way for 'Eckie's' Return," *Chicago Tribune*, March 23, 1905.
24. "Not Yet Cleared," *Rock Island (IL) Argus*, March 24, 1905; "Handicaps for Coliseum Meet Are Given Out," *Chicago Inter Ocean*, March 26, 1905.

10. CHAMPIONS OF THE WEST

1. "Simple Life for Eckersall," *Chicago Daily News*, September 2, 1905; Stagg to Harper, September 11, 1905, AAS Papers, Box 9, Folder 11.
2. "Maroon Squad Begins Regular Football Work," *Chicago Inter Ocean*, September 12, 1905; "Transfer Power to Rule," *Chicago Tribune*, June 3, 1905.
3. "Heavy Team for Chicago," *Chicago Tribune*, September 3, 1905; "Begin Work on Gridiron," *Chicago Tribune*, September 12, 1905.
4. "One Maroon Place Open," *Chicago Tribune*, September 10, 1905.
5. "Good Kicking by Eckie," *Chicago Tribune*, September 15, 1905.
6. "Maroons Defeat North Division by 26 to 0 Score," *Chicago Inter Ocean*, September 17, 1905; "Chicago Team Scores 33," *Chicago Tribune*, September 24, 1905.
7. "Maroons Defeat Wabash by Small Score of 15 to 0," *Chicago Tribune*, October 1, 1905.
8. "Now to Build Up Team Work," *Chicago Tribune*, October 2, 1905; "Made to Work After the Game," *Chicago Tribune*, October 5, 1905.
9. "Maroons Roll Up Good Score on Hawkeye Team," *Chicago Inter Ocean*, October 8, 1905.
10. "Maroons Will Meet Sheldon's Hoosiers Today," *Chicago Inter Ocean*, October 14, 1905.
11. Merrill C. "Babe" Meigs, "The Greatest Football Player in the World—Walter Eckersall," *American Weekly*, October 26, 1947.
12. "Maroons Defeat Indiana Team," *Chicago Tribune*, October 15, 1905.
13. "Stagg Predicts Maroon Victory," *Chicago Tribune*, October 20, 1905.
14. "Steffen Is Back in Midway Fold," *Chicago Tribune*, October 11, 1905.
15. "Eckersall Scores Another Victory for the Maroons," *Chicago Inter Ocean*, October 22, 1905.
16. "Gil Dobie Hands Palm to Eckersall," *Lincoln (NE) State Journal*, September 7, 1924; "Greatest Play Gil Dobie Ever Saw," *Lincoln (NE) State Journal*, September 8, 1924.
17. "Drop Kick Wins for the Maroons," *Chicago Tribune*, October 22, 1905.
18. "Greatest Play Gil Dobie Ever Saw."
19. "Tests Purple on Chicago Plays," *Chicago Tribune*, October 24, 1905.
20. "Chicago Runs Up 32 Points on M'Cornack's Men," *Chicago Inter Ocean*, October 29, 1905.
21. "Illini No Match for Wolverines," *Chicago Tribune*, November 5, 1905.
22. Edward S. Jordan, "Buying Football Victories," pt. 1, *Collier's* 36 (November 11, 1905): 19.
23. Jordan, "Buying Football Victories," pt. 1, 20.
24. "General Denial of Charges Against Western Athletes," *Chicago Inter Ocean*, November 8, 1905.
25. "Chicago Winner over Purdue, 19–0," *Chicago Tribune*, November 12, 1905.

26. "Celebration of Maroon Victory Held at Midway," *Chicago Inter Ocean*, December 5, 1905.
27. "Maroons Beat Illinois," *Chicago Tribune*, November 19, 1905.
28. "Opinions of Experts," *Chicago Inter Ocean*, November 19, 1905.
29. "Tag Ends of the Big Game," *Chicago Tribune*, December 1, 1905; "Winners Cash in Big Bets," *Chicago Tribune*, December 1, 1905.
30. AAS Papers, Box 47, Folder 7.
31. Lester, *Stagg's University*, 68–69.
32. "Assert Proof of Professionalism of Capt. Eckersall," *Chicago Inter Ocean*, January 11, 1906.
33. "Umpire Talks of Curtis Case," *Chicago Tribune*, December 1, 1905.
34. Camp, *Spalding's Official Foot Ball Guide* (1906), 13.
35. Walter Eckersall, "Fighting Man of Football Does His Bit," *Chicago Tribune*, February 10, 1918.
36. "Chicago Is Victor; Leads the West," *Chicago Tribune*, December 1, 1905; "Stagg's Warriors Wreck Yost's Scoring Machine," *Chicago Inter Ocean*, December 1, 1905; "Details of Play Which Gave the Maroons the Western Championship," *Chicago Inter Ocean*, December 1, 1905.
37. "Maroons Wild with Joy," *Chicago Tribune*, December 1, 1905.
38. "Stagg and His Players Talk," *Chicago Tribune*, December 1, 1905; Walter H. Eckersall, "Year of College Sport," *Chicago Tribune*, December 31, 1905.
39. "From Michigan, 'The Fallen,'" *Chicago Tribune*, December 1, 1905.
40. "Celebration of Maroon Victory Held at Midway," *Chicago Inter Ocean*, December 5, 1905; "Hereafter It's Capt. Eckersall," *Chicago Tribune*, December 6, 1905.
41. Lardner, "Eckie."
42. "All Western Is Picked for 1905," *Chicago Tribune*, December 1, 1905; Camp, *Spalding's Official Foot Ball Guide* (1906), 31.
43. Camp, *Spalding's Official Foot Ball Guide* (1906), 13.
44. Camp, *Spalding's Official Foot Ball Guide* (1906), 23.
45. James Vautravers, "1905 College Football National Championship," Tip Top 25, accessed September 22, 2022, https://tiptop25.com/champ1905.html.
46. "A.A.U. Reinstates 'Eckie,'" *Chicago Tribune*, November 21, 1905.
47. "Eckersall out of Maroon Track Athletics; In Business," *Chicago Inter Ocean*, January 10, 1906; "Withdrawal of Eckersall Merely a Passing Rumor," *Daily Maroon*, January 10, 1906; "Eckersall and Bezdek Sought," *Chicago Inter Ocean*, December 22, 1905; "Eckersall Socker [*sic*] Convert," *Chicago Tribune*, December 14, 1905; "Assert Proof of Professionalism of Capt. Eckersall," *Chicago Inter Ocean*, January 11, 1906.
48. "Athletes to Study Bible," *Chicago Tribune*, December 22, 1905; "'Eckie' Returns to Midway," *Chicago Tribune*, January 15, 1906; Walter H. Eckersall, "Year of College Sport," *Chicago Tribune*, December 31, 1905.
49. "Football May Be Abolished on the Midway," *Chicago Inter Ocean*, January 17, 1905.

50. "Maroons Tie Two World's Records," *Chicago Inter Ocean*, February 4, 1906; "Western Sprinters Lose at Boston," *Chicago Inter Ocean*, February 11, 1906; "Maroons Beaten by Illini Team," *Chicago Tribune*, February 17, 1906; "Illinois Team Again Wins by the Pole Vault," *Chicago Inter Ocean*, March 4, 1906.
51. "Callahan Joins the 'Scrubs,'" *Chicago Tribune*, April 4, 1906.
52. University of Chicago, *Cap and Gown* 12 (1907): 214–17; "Maroons Beat Northwestern," *Chicago Tribune*, April 26, 1906; "Michigan Beats Chicago in an Eleven Inning Game," *Chicago Tribune*, May 10, 1906; "Maroons Win Good Game," *Chicago Tribune*, May 15, 1906; "Maroons Win in Tenth," *Chicago Inter Ocean*, June 3, 1906.
53. "Paw Paw Lake," *Chicago Tribune*, June 24, 1906.

11. YEAR OF REFORM

1. Miller, *Big Scrum*, 174–204.
2. "Football Year's Death Harvest," *Chicago Tribune*, November 26, 1905.
3. "Ten Yards, Three Downs," *Chicago Tribune*, February 11, 1906.
4. "At Work with Pigskin," *Chicago Tribune*, August 26, 1906.
5. "More Studies for Athletes," *Chicago Tribune*, May 2, 1906.
6. "Puts Football on a Shelf," *Chicago Tribune*, May 1, 1906.
7. "Eckie and Parry at the Midway," *Chicago Tribune*, September 18, 1906; "Maroon Football Candidates Take Light Practice," *Chicago Inter Ocean*, September 18, 1906; "Stagg Stops the Football Work," *Chicago Tribune*, September 25, 1906.
8. "Purdue Is Easy for the Maroons," *Chicago Tribune*, October 21, 1906.
9. "Chicago Winner by a Big Margin," *Chicago Tribune*, October 28, 1906; "Chicago Swamps the Strong Indiana Veterans, 33 to 8," *Chicago Inter Ocean*, October 28, 1906.
10. "Wants Michigan Game Next Year," *Chicago Tribune*, October 31, 1906.
11. "Coach Stagg Has 75 Plays to Use in Minnesota Contest," *Chicago Inter Ocean*, November 6, 1906.
12. "Brighter Story from the Midway," *Chicago Tribune*, November 8, 1906.
13. Walter Eckersall, "Neglected Play Cost N.U. Win Over Michigan," *Chicago Tribune*, November 5, 1919; Walter Eckersall, "Purple Brains and Lewis' Toe Sink Wolverines in Morass," *Chicago Tribune*, November 8, 1925.
14. "That Safety—How It Happened," *Minneapolis Journal*, November 13, 1906.
15. "Minnesota Wins from Chicago, 4–2," *Chicago Tribune*, November 11, 1906; "Gophers' Brawn and Marshall's Toe Victorious," *Chicago Inter Ocean*, November 11, 1906; "How the Minnesotans Showed Chicago," *Minneapolis Journal*, November 11, 1906.
16. "Opinions of the Experts," *Chicago Tribune*, November 11, 1906.
17. "An Incident of the Chicago-Illinois Game of 1906 Which Chicago Won 63–0," dictated May 5, 1932, AAS Papers, Box 16, Folder 10.
18. "Maroons Smother Illinois Men, 63 to 0," *Chicago Inter Ocean*, November 18, 1906; "Maroons Victor over Illini, 63–0," *Chicago Tribune*, November 18, 1906.

19. "Eckersall Stars in His Last Game," *Chicago Inter Ocean*, November 25, 1906; "Maroons Defeat Nebraska, 38–5," *Chicago Tribune*, November 25, 1906; "Cross the Line," *Lincoln (NE) State Journal*, November 25, 1906.
20. "Opinions of the Experts," *Chicago Tribune*, November 25, 1906.
21. "'All Western' as Picked for 1906," *Chicago Tribune*, November 25, 1906.
22. Camp, *Spalding's Official Foot Ball Guide* (1907), 19, 21.

12. MAROON FOOTBALL AFTER ECKERSALL

1. Walter H. Eckersall, "Chicago Defeats Indiana, 27 to 6," *Chicago Tribune*, October 13, 1907; "Stagg's Maroons Romp Away with Indiana, 27 to 6," *Chicago Inter Ocean*, October 13, 1907; "One Western Man on All-American," *Chicago Tribune*, December 24, 1907.
2. I. E. Sanborn, "Maroons Clinch Champion Title," *Chicago Tribune*, November 22, 1908; James Vautravers, "1908 College Football Top 25," Tip Top 25, accessed September 22, 2022, https://tiptop25.com/top25_1908.html.
3. R. W. Lardner, "Kicks by Russell Down Purdue, 6–0, Before Big Crowd," *Chicago Tribune*, October 25, 1913.
4. R. W. Lardner, "Title to Maroons; Crush Wisconsin in Last Game, 19–0," *Chicago Tribune*, November 23, 1913; Walter Camp, "Des Jardien and Craig on Walter Camp's All-American," *Chicago Inter Ocean*, December 14, 1913.
5. Harvey T. Woodruff, "Why Not Call It Stagg Field?" *Chicago Tribune*, October 26, 1913.
6. Walter H. Eckersall, "Maroons Choice in Gridiron Race," *Chicago Tribune*, October 27, 1913.
7. "Alumni Indorse 'Stagg Field' Idea," *Chicago Tribune*, November 18, 1913; Maroon, "'Tribune's' Name of Stagg Field Made Official," *Chicago Tribune*, November 3, 1914.
8. Stagg, *Touchdown!*, 323–24.
9. Stagg, *Touchdown!*, 320.
10. Stagg, *Touchdown!*, 342.
11. Robert M. Lee, "Chicago-Illinois Tie: 21–21," *Chicago Tribune*, November 9, 1924; "Pretty Busy Day for Red Grange, and His Gains Total 300 Yds.," *Chicago Tribune*, November 9, 1924; Stagg, *Touchdown!*, 341–49.
12. Lester, *Stagg's University*, 126.
13. "Stagg to Quit as Director of Athletics," *Chicago Tribune*, October 14, 1932; David Condon, "Clark Shaughnessy, Wizard of T-Formation, Dead at 78," *Chicago Tribune*, May 16, 1970; Lester, *Stagg's University*, 150–63.
14. Lester, *Stagg's University*, 174–86; Charles Bartlett, "University of Chicago Gives Up Football," *Chicago Tribune*, December 22, 1939.

13. THE MYTH OF FRANK MERRIWELL

1. Revsine, *Opening Kickoff*, 71–81; Robert H. Boyle, "Frank Merriwell's Triumph," *Sports Illustrated*, December 4, 1962.

2. Des Jardins, *Walter Camp*, 46.
3. Miller, *Big Scrum*, 85; Des Jardins, *Walter Camp*, 107; Lester, *Stagg's University*, 12, 19–20.
4. Theodore Roosevelt, "What We Can Expect of the American Boy," *St. Nicholas* 27, no. 7 (May 1900): 571, 573, 574.
5. Hall, *Spalding's Official Foot Ball Guide* (1926), 19.
6. Lester, *Stagg's University*, 57–58; "All Is Denied by Stagg," *Chicago Tribune*, October 30, 1903; "Eckersall Is Down and Out," *Chicago Inter Ocean*, January 4, 1904; "Athletes Behind in Studies," *Chicago Tribune*, January 5, 1904.
7. "Indoor Season Is Begun," *Chicago Tribune*, January 3, 1907; "'Big Nine' Keeps Athletic Lid On," *Chicago Tribune*, January 13, 1907.
8. "Maroons Begin Practice," *Chicago Tribune*, January 23, 1907.
9. "Warrant for Eckersall; 'Forgot Something'—$40, Tailor Alleges," *Chicago Inter Ocean*, January 25, 1907; "Eckersall to Face Trial," *Chicago Tribune*, January 26, 1907.
10. "Eckersall Pays for Coat," *Chicago Tribune*, February 3, 1907.
11. Lester, *Stagg's University*, 60–61.
12. "Lyon May Rejoin Maroons," *Chicago Tribune*, February 6, 1907; University of Chicago, *Cap and Gown* 12 (1907): 55.
13. "Eckersall Makes Record in Bowling Tournament," *Daily Maroon*, February 1, 1907; "Eckersall Not Eligible; Bowlers Are Perplexed," *Daily Maroon*, February 6, 1907.
14. "Bezdek Is Selected as Assistant Football Coach," *Chicago Tribune*, June 19, 1907.
15. "General Sporting Field," *Chicago Tribune*, June 20, 1907; "Eckersall to Referee," *St. Louis Post-Dispatch*, June 22, 1907; "Sporting News at Home and Abroad," *Benton Harbor (MI) News-Palladium*, June 26, 1907.
16. Stagg to Professor W. S. Langston, Agricultural College, Logan, Utah, June 19, 1907, AAS Papers, Box 14, Folder 3.
17. Stagg to President W. L. Bryan, University of Indiana, August 20, 1905, AAS Papers, Box 14, Folder 3; Stagg to President Wm. T. [*sic*] Bryan, Indiana University, November 28, 1906, AAS Papers, Box 14, Folder 3; Stagg to President J. C. Hardy, Mississippi Agricultural and Mechanical College, January 8, 1906, AAS Papers, Box 14, Folder 3; Stagg to Samuel Plantz, Lawrence College, March 1, 1909, AAS Papers, Box 14, Folder 3; Stagg to Mr. P. B. Shumway, Northwestern University, January 20, 1914, AAS Papers, Box 14, Folder 5.
18. "Bullet Closes Girl's Gay Night," *Chicago Tribune*, December 20, 1908; "Midnight Revel Ends with Mortal Wound," *Chicago Inter Ocean*, December 20, 1908.
19. "Actress Fatally Shot," *Los Angeles Times*, December 20, 1908; "Walter Eckersall in Shooting Scrape," *Decatur (IL) Herald*, December 21, 1908.
20. ISMI for Walter Herbert Eckersall and Elizabeth Louise Jahn, August 18, 1909; CCBCI for Elizabeth Louise Eckersall, December 20, 1909.
21. "Eckersall Wedded at the Hub, Long Ago," *Lake County (IN) Times*, May 5, 1910; USCR for Elizabeth Bateman and Elizabeth Eckersall, 1930; "Eckersall Married,"

South Bend (IN) Tribune, August 20, 1909; McCarthy, *Making Men*, 266; Sperber, *Shake Down the Thunder*, 313.

22. Walter H. Eckersall, "Stagg Tries Out Forward Passes," *Chicago Tribune*, March 4, 1910.
23. USCR for Walter and Mary Eckersall and family, 1910, and for Elizabeth J. and Elizabeth L. Eckersall, 1910.
24. "Say Valente Killed Jahn," *Chicago Tribune*, February 17, 1898; "August John's [*sic*] Wound Fatal," *Chicago Daily News*, February 15, 1898.
25. "Football Star Is Sued by His Wife," *Salt Lake City Evening Telegram*, December 19, 1911; "Sues Eckersall for Divorce," *Chicago Tribune*, December 16, 1911; "Mrs. Eckersall Wins Divorce," *Chicago Tribune*, February 17, 1912; "Divorce for Mrs. Eckersall," *Chicago Daily News*, February 16, 1912.
26. "Eckersall Faces Contempt," *Chicago Daily News*, January 9, 1915.

14. SEMIPRO

1. "Turkey Day Game Sure," *Chicago Inter Ocean*, November 18, 1906.
2. Angell-to-Judson and Judson-to-Angell telegrams, November 14, 1906, AAS Papers, Box 9, Folder 16; "Alumni Contest Is Off," *Chicago Inter Ocean*, November 25, 1906.
3. "Massillon Beats College 'Pros,'" *Chicago Tribune*, November 30, 1906; "Massillon Beats All-Western in Bruising Contest," *Chicago Inter Ocean*, November 30, 1906.
4. "Eckersall's Promises," *Glen Falls (NY) Morning Star*, January 19, 1907.
5. "Anson After Eckersall," *Chicago Inter Ocean*, February 28, 1907.
6. "Will Play at League Park," *Chicago Tribune*, April 20, 1907; "Normals Lead Park Team in Chicago," *Joliet Herald*, July 28, 1907; "Sporting News and Comment," *Chicago Tribune*, June 15, 1907.
7. "Eckersall a Base Ball Player," *Appleton (WI) Evening Crescent*, May 1, 1907.
8. "Eckersall Becomes Semi-Pro," *Chicago Tribune*, June 16, 1907; "Anson's Men Beat Giants," *Chicago Inter Ocean*, June 16, 1907.
9. "Saves His Life," *Benton Harbor (MI) News-Palladium*, July 11, 1907; "Eckersall Again a Hero," *Chicago Inter Ocean*, July 11, 1907.
10. Walter Eckersall, "My Twenty-Five Years of Football," pt. 5, *Liberty* 3 (November 13, 1926): 79.
11. "Eckersall's Team Is Winner," *Chicago Tribune*, October 7, 1907; "Eckersalls Defeat Aurora Tigers by Score of 34 to 0," *Chicago Tribune*, October 14, 1907; "Eckersalls Again Win," *Chicago Inter Ocean*, October 21, 1907.
12. "Eckersalls, 5; Morris A.C., 0," *Chicago Tribune*, October 29, 1907; "Mohawks Win, 5 to 0, from Englewood A.C. Eleven," *Chicago Tribune*, November 4, 1907; "Eckersalls Register Victory over the Woodstock Eleven," *Chicago Tribune*, November 11, 1907; "Easy Win for Eckersalls over South Chicago Team," *Chicago Tribune*, November 18, 1907.
13. "Eckersalls Have Close Call," *Chicago Inter Ocean*, November 29, 1907.

14. "Eckersalls, 6; Thistles, 0," *Chicago Tribune*, December 2, 1907.
15. "Football Title Swamped in Mud," *Chicago Tribune*, December 9, 1907.
16. "Bars Eckersalls and Mohawks from the Football League," *Chicago Inter Ocean*, December 14, 1907.
17. "Eckersall May Retire," *Chicago Inter Ocean*, December 20, 1907.
18. "Eckersalls' Victory over First Regiment Protested," *Chicago Tribune*, December 23, 1907.
19. "Semi-Pros to Open Season," *Chicago Inter Ocean*, April 5, 1908.
20. "'Cap' Anson Not Like Casey," *Chicago Tribune*, May 31, 1908.
21. "Anson's Men Balk, Draw Releases," *Chicago Tribune*, June 2, 1908.
22. "Feature of 'Semi-Pro' Day Proves Interesting," *Chicago Tribune*, July 22, 1907.
23. "Good Performances Feature Field Day," *Chicago Inter Ocean*, June 29, 1908.
24. "Ansons Take Title from the Normals," *Chicago Inter Ocean*, December 21, 1908.
25. "Eckersall New Coach," *Decatur (IL) Herald*, September 14, 1908.
26. St. Viator College, "The Coach," *The Viatorian* 26, no. 1 (October 1908): 27–28.
27. "Marquette, 63; St. Viateurs, 0," *Chicago Inter Ocean*, October 18, 1908; "Morgan Park Wins Its Game," *Chicago Tribune*, October 25, 1908; "Notre Dame Easily Wins Battle, 46–0," *South Bend (IN) Tribune*, November 19, 1908.
28. "Good Work at St. Viateur's [*sic*]," *Chicago Tribune*, October 30, 1908.
29. Harold Iddings, "Kelly Changes Mind and Maroon Fatted Heifer Is Sliced Up," *Chicago Inter Ocean*, October 29, 1908.
30. "Easy Win for St. Viateur's [*sic*]," *Chicago Tribune*, November 27, 1908.
31. "Eckersalls and Deans in Drawn Gridiron Game, 4–4," *Chicago Tribune*, November 27, 1908; W. F. Allen, "All-Star Teams Battle to 4 to 4 Tie at Nicollet Park," *Minneapolis Tribune*, November 27, 1908.
32. Eckersall, "My Twenty-Five Years of Football," pt. 5, 80.
33. Walter H. Eckersall, "Eckersalls Win by 12 to 4," *Chicago Tribune*, January 2, 1909; "Eckersall Boots Chicago Victory," *St. Louis Globe-Democrat*, January 2, 1909.
34. Eckersall, "My Twenty-Five Years of Football," pt. 5, 80.
35. "Anson's Colts Start on Long Journey," *Chicago Inter Ocean*, March 29, 1909; "Walter Eckersall to Join Semi-Pros at River Forest," *Chicago Inter Ocean*, February 25, 1909.
36. "River Forest Team Organized," *Chicago Inter Ocean*, March 21, 1909.
37. "Gunthers Bumped into Third Place," *Chicago Tribune*, October 4, 1909.
38. "Semi-Pro Gates Open Today," *Chicago Tribune*, March 27, 1910; "Logan Squares Open Season," *Chicago Tribune*, March 28, 1910.

15. WORLD'S GREATEST NEWSPAPER

1. "Sixty Years of the Tribune," *Chicago Tribune*, June 10, 1907.
2. "The Chicago Tribune for the Year 1856," *Bloomington (IL) Pantagraph*, December 26, 1855.
3. Wendt, *Chicago Tribune*, 17–38, 64–65, 74–76, 86, 89–104, 111–28, 139, 171, 189–99.

4. Wendt, *Chicago Tribune*, 452; "Trotting Races," *Chicago Tribune*, June 20, 1858; "Base Ball Match," *Chicago Tribune*, July 8, 1858; "The Great Prize Fight," *Chicago Tribune*, September 18, 1863.
5. "The Last Prize-Fight," *Chicago Tribune*, November 22, 1867.
6. "Sports," *Chicago Tribune*, December 29, 1865.
7. Oriard, *King Football*, 58.
8. "Base Ball as a Confidence Game," *Chicago Tribune*, July 28, 1867.
9. "Opening of the Base Ball Campaign at St. Louis," *Chicago Tribune*, April 30, 1870.
10. "White Above the Red," *Chicago Tribune*, September 8, 1870.
11. Wendt, *Chicago Tribune*, 291.
12. "The Club Races," *Chicago Tribune*, June 29, 1884; "Scenes on the Ground," *Chicago Tribune*, June 29, 1884; "The American Derby," *Chicago Tribune*, June 27, 1886; "Spokane the Victor," *Chicago Tribune*, June 23, 1889; "Fame for Uncle Bob," *Chicago Tribune*, June 22, 1890.
13. "Gambling a Crime," *Chicago Tribune*, September 25, 1894.
14. "For Reliable Sporting News Read THE TRIBUNE," *Chicago Tribune*, September 12, 1897.
15. "Foot-Ball," *Chicago Tribune*, November 21, 1875.
16. "Sundry Sports," *Chicago Tribune*, May 31, 1879.
17. "Sporting Affairs," *Chicago Tribune*, November 22, 1885.
18. "Chicago Athletics First Game," *Chicago Tribune*, October 9, 1892; "Chicagos Won Again," *Chicago Tribune*, October 25, 1892; "Beaten by Harvard," *Chicago Tribune*, October 27, 1892; "Lost by Two Points," *Chicago Tribune*, October 30, 1892; "Strung Out Tigers," *Chicago Tribune*, November 3, 1892; "Played a Weak Draw," *Chicago Tribune*, November 6, 1892.
19. "Football Prices Arranged," *Chicago Tribune*, November 16, 1892; "Boston the Victor," *Chicago Tribune*, November 25, 1892.
20. "Stagg's Men Lose Again," *Chicago Tribune*, November 11, 1900; "Michigan Loses to Iowa, 28 to 5," *Chicago Tribune*, November 11, 1900; "Diagram of Northwestern and Chicago's Hard Struggle," *Chicago Tribune*, November 11, 1900; "Make Gophers Earn Game," *Chicago Tribune*, November 11, 1900; "Badgers Win with Ease," *Chicago Tribune*, November 11, 1900.
21. Wendt, *Chicago Tribune*, 345–48.
22. Wendt, *Chicago Tribune*, 359, 363, 385; Charles Bartlett, "A City and a Sports Department," *Chicago Tribune*, January 24, 1942; "Briggs, Famous Cartoonist of You and Me, Dies," *Chicago Tribune*, January 4, 1930; "Ring Lardner Dead After Long Illness," *Chicago Tribune*, September 26, 1933.

16. THE SCRIBE

1. Lester, *Stagg's University*, 234; Walter H. Eckersall, "Year of College Sport," *Chicago Tribune*, December 31, 1905.
2. Eckersall to Camp, April 19, 1907, WCCP, Box 10, Folder 261.

3. Camp, *Spalding's Official Foot Ball Guide* (1907), 271.
4. Camp, *How to Play Foot Ball*, 54–63.
5. Linn, *James Keeley*, 102.
6. Walter H. Eckersall, "Gridiron Gossip by Eckersall," *Chicago Tribune*, September 15, 1907.
7. Walter H. Eckersall, "Quakers Are Easy for the Indians," *Chicago Tribune*, October 27, 1907.
8. Lardner, "Eckie."
9. "Every Sunday, the Champions and Stars of the Sports World Parade the Pages of the Great Sunday Tribune!" *Chicago Tribune*, March 17, 1929.
10. Walter H. Eckersall, "Little Man Wins Big Auto Classic," *Chicago Tribune*, May 31, 1911.
11. Walter Eckersall, "Harmon Mum but Chicago Gets Hockey," *Chicago Tribune*, March 19, 1926.
12. Walter H. Eckersall, "Again the First Nationals," *Chicago Tribune*, June 19, 1910; Walter H. Eckersall, "Luther League Skating Honors to Bethlehem," *Chicago Tribune*, February 20, 1916; Walter H. Eckersall, "First Prize Won by Himschoot in Cycle Grind," *Chicago Tribune*, January 2, 1915.
13. Walter H. Eckersall, "Racquet Title to Mullins," *Chicago Tribune*, February 5, 1911.
14. Don Maxwell, "Eckie—As We Knew Him," *Chicago Tribune*, March 25, 1930.
15. "Our Town," *Chicago Tribune*, July 22, 1928.
16. Walter H. Eckersall, "Goodwin Star in A.A.U. Water Meet," *Chicago Tribune*, August 6, 1911.
17. Walter Eckersall, "Running Attack of Rockne Crew Trims Army 13–7," *Chicago Tribune*, October 19, 1924.
18. Grantland Rice, "Notre Dame Again Trims West Point," *Boston Globe*, October 19, 1924.
19. Edward Burns, "Eckersall . . . Football Immortal," *Chicago Tribune Grafic*, November 24, 1946.
20. Bob Sink, "Along the Line," *Decatur Herald*, March 27, 1930.
21. Sink, "Along the Line."
22. Linn, *James Keeley*, 102–3.
23. "Champion to Box with H.C. Lytton," *Chicago Tribune*, December 15, 1910.
24. Walter H. Eckersall, "Champion Boxes Two Fast Bouts," *Chicago Tribune*, December 16, 1910.
25. "'Square Shooters' in Sportdom and News Work Succeed, Says Eckersall," *Editor and Publisher*, January 8, 1927.
26. Maxwell, "Eckie."

17. THE OFFICIAL

1. "Heston's Leg Broken," *New York Sun*, November 30, 1906.

2. Walter Eckersall, "My Twenty-Five Years of Football," pt. 5, *Liberty* 3 (November 13, 1926): 81.
3. Walter Eckersall, "Ragged Game by Indiana," *Chicago Tribune*, October 6, 1907; Walter Eckersall, "Quakers Are Easy for the Indians," *Chicago Tribune*, October 27, 1907.
4. "Punts and Passes," *Kansas City Star*, November 22, 1911; "Was Illinois Touchdown Legal? Camera Says 'NO,'" *Lincoln (NE) Star*, October 8, 1924; Leslie A. Young, "Charts Disagree with Referee Eckersall on Down That Ended Notre Dame Game," *Hartford Courant*, November 15, 1928; "Referee Eckersall Passes the Buck in Who-Has-the-Ball Case," *New York Daily News*, November 14, 1928.
5. "Fans, Mad, Mob Referee over Close Ruling," *Chicago Tribune*, November 18, 1923.
6. Bryn Griffiths, "Wisconsin vs. Eckersall," *Madison (WI) Capital Times*, November 19, 1923.
7. Red Mich, "Wolverines Win from Badgers on Fluke Decision, 6–3," *Madison (WI) State Journal*, November 18, 1923.
8. "Eckersall to Officiate at Packard Park," *Detroit Free Press*, October 27, 1915.
9. "The Pan American Bank Nominates an All-American Football Team!" *Los Angeles Evening Express*, November 28, 1928.
10. "Rockne Recalls," *Lincoln (NE) State Journal*, February 8, 1931.
11. "Rockne Recalls."
12. "Eckie Called as Coast Official," *Chicago Tribune*, December 29, 1915.
13. Halas, *Halas by Halas*, 41.
14. "Eckersall Still in Shape," *Buffalo Times*, November 15, 1917.
15. Walter Camp, "Doctor, Big League Umpire, Former Star and Army Man Best Football Officials," *Fort Worth (TX) Star-Telegram*, October 15, 1922.
16. "Grid Officials Seek More Pay," *Lexington (KY) Herald*, January 17, 1929.
17. "In the Wake of the News: Football Officials," *Chicago Tribune*, September 25, 1928.

18. THE SWEET SCIENCE

1. "Knockout for Prize Fighting," *Chicago Tribune*, December 18, 1900.
2. Walter H. Eckersall, "Chicago Mecca for Boxers," *Chicago Tribune*, August 24, 1912.
3. Walter H. Eckersall, "J. Johnson Home on 34th Birthday," *Chicago Tribune*, April 1, 1912; Walter H. Eckersall, "Jack Quits Stage for Fight," *Chicago Tribune*, April 11, 1910; Walter H. Eckersall, "Johnson in City Ready to Train," *Chicago Tribune*, April 29, 1912; Walter H. Eckersall, "Champion Eager to Re-Enter Ring," *Chicago Tribune*, June 1, 1911; Walter H. Eckersall, "Johnson Demands $30,000 for Fight," *Chicago Tribune*, December 24, 1910; Walter H. Eckersall, "Negroes Plan Reception for J. Johnson on Return Today," *Chicago Tribune*, July 6, 1912; Walter H. Eckersall, "Johnson Dead? Yarn a Hoax," *Chicago Tribune*, December 19, 1910.
4. Walter H. Eckersall, "Jack Wires Jeff His Best Wishes," *Chicago Tribune*, April 16, 1910.

5. Walter H. Eckersall, "Kaufman a Comer, Says Jack," *Chicago Tribune*, August 11, 1910; Walter H. Eckersall, "Next Title Fight on Foreign Soil," *Chicago Tribune*, August 9, 1910; Walter H. Eckersall, "J. Johnson Home on 34th Birthday," *Chicago Tribune*, April 1, 1912.
6. Walter H. Eckersall, "Johnson Denies Brooklyn Story," *Chicago Tribune*, August 6, 1910.
7. Walter H. Eckersall, "Fight Edict from New York Stirs Blood of Mr. Johnson," *Chicago Tribune*, January 12, 1912.
8. Walter H. Eckersall, "Kelly Has Shade over Ed M'Goorty," *Chicago Tribune*, May 7, 1910.
9. Walter H. Eckersall, "Referee Eckersall Says Bloom Never Had Chance," *Chicago Tribune*, April 8, 1911.
10. Walter Eckersall, "Mandell Wins Kansas' Title on Points," *Chicago Tribune*, July 4, 1926.
11. Walter H. Eckersall, "Pugilistic Fans in Joyful Mood," *Chicago Tribune*, May 4, 1911.
12. Walter Eckersall, "Shuffle, No. 8 of the Callahans, All Irish Though Half German," *Chicago Tribune*, March 28, 1926; Walter Eckersall, "Ring Fans Hail Mushy Callahan Real Champion," *Chicago Tribune*, February 7, 1927; Walter H. Eckersall, "Fighters Ready for Gong Clang," *Chicago Tribune*, April 7, 1911; Walter H. Eckersall, "Williams to Box Coulon on Coast," *Chicago Tribune*, February 2, 1914; Walter Eckersall, "Sailor Freedman and Dundee Box Ten Round Draw," *Chicago Tribune*, May 28, 1921.
13. Walter H. Eckersall, "Packey Too Fast for Bronson," *Chicago Tribune*, May 30, 1912.
14. "Everlasting Winners," *Los Angeles Times*, April 29, 1991; Steve Marantz, "'100 Greatest Boxers' Surely a Target and a Hit," *Boston Globe*, December 2, 1984; Ray Pearson, "Rainbow Trail in Ring Sport Lures Unwary," *Chicago Tribune*, May 26, 1918; "Packey McFarland, Long Uncrowned Lightweight Champion, Dies at 48," *St. Louis Post-Dispatch*, September 23, 1936.
15. Walter H. Eckersall, "Athletic Clubs Lobby for Bouts," *Chicago Tribune*, May 5, 1911; Walter H. Eckersall, "Says Boxing Bill Has Good Chance," *Chicago Tribune*, March 2, 1915; Walter Eckersall, "Loop Clubs to Stage Boxing as Soon as Lowden Signs Bill," *Chicago Tribune*, June 20, 1919; Walter Eckersall, "Service Men of Illinois to Back New Boxing Bill," *Chicago Tribune*, May 29, 1920; "Senate Defeats Boxing Because of Dexter Riot," *Chicago Tribune*, June 20, 1923.
16. Walter H. Eckersall, "Ketchel Draws with Wolgast at Forest Park," *Chicago Tribune*, August 1, 1915; Walter Eckersall, "Mullen to Promote Indoor Shows; Charity Card First," *Chicago Tribune*, January 8, 1923; Walter Eckersall, "Frankie Genaro, Joe Lynch Win Whirlwind Gos," *Chicago Tribune*, April 5, 1923; Walter Eckersall, "Title Mat Bout Features Storm Benefit Tonight," *Chicago Tribune*, April 6, 1925.
17. Walter Eckersall, "Sammy Mandell Wins Bout When Spencer Fouls," *Chicago Tribune*, April 8, 1922; Walter Eckersall, "Garcia Beats Sammy; Wins Scrap on Boat," *Chicago Tribune*, February 10, 1923.

18. Walter H. Eckersall, "Cutler Draws with Shanks," *Chicago Tribune*, July 3, 1914; Walter Eckersall, "Burman Beats Flannigan and Looks the Champ," *Chicago Tribune*, January 30, 1923.
19. "Boxing Is Within Law," *De Kalb (IL) Daily Chronicle*, July 24, 1922.
20. Walter Eckersall, "Boxing Bill Is Warmly Lauded by Chicagoans," *Chicago Tribune*, July 5, 1925; Walter Eckersall, "Chicago Boxing Depends on Voters Tuesday," *Chicago Tribune*, April 11, 1926; "Boxing Wins in Chicago by 300,000," *Chicago Tribune*, April 14, 1926.
21. Eckersall, "Mandell Wins Kansas' Title on Points."
22. Walter Eckersall, "Promoters Hit Snags Staging Chicago Fights," *Chicago Tribune*, June 27, 1927.
23. Walter Eckersall, "Dempsey Glad; Ready to Fight to Hold Title," *Chicago Tribune*, July 5, 1919; Walter Eckersall, "Dempsey Jabs Beat Me, Bill Miske Says Praising His Rival," *Chicago Tribune*, September 7, 1920.
24. Harvey Woodruff, "Tunney's Left Hand Punches Win Title," *Chicago Tribune*, September 24, 1926; Walter Eckersall, "Title Bout Here May Draw Gate of 2,800,000," *Chicago Tribune*, July 25, 1927.
25. Walter Eckersall, "Rickard Fixes Sept. 22 as Date of Title Bout," *Chicago Tribune*, August 4, 1927.
26. Walter Eckersall, "Dempsey Opens Training Camp to the Public," *Chicago Tribune*, August 28, 1927; Walter Eckersall, "Wiggins Butts Tunney on Eye; Opens Long Gash," *Chicago Tribune*, September 7, 1927; Walter Eckersall, "Estelle Turns Head as Jack Battles Foes," *Chicago Tribune*, August 29, 1927; Walter Eckersall, "Tunney Picks Bronson to Handle His Corner," *Chicago Tribune*, September 13, 1927; Walter Eckersall, "Jack Rests His Fists; Takes on Old Man Par," *Chicago Tribune*, August 30, 1927; Walter Eckersall, "Tunney Rests Harder as Big Battle Nears," *Chicago Tribune*, September 14, 1927.
27. Ed Hughes, "Lytton and Eckersall Favored by Chicagoans for Much Disputed Post," *Brooklyn Daily Eagle*, September 20, 1927.
28. "The Fight by Rounds," *Chicago Tribune*, September 23, 1927. This nonbylined account was later credited as Eckersall's work. See Charles Bartlett, "A City and a Sports Department," *Chicago Tribune*, January 15, 1942.
29. Walter Eckersall, "Tunney's Ring Craft Is Credited for His Victory; Given 8 of 10 Rounds," *Chicago Tribune*, September 23, 1927.

19. FOOTBALL GOES TO WAR

1. Walter H. Eckersall, "Let Our Freshmen Play Football and Save Game," *Salt Lake City Herald-Republican*, July 22, 1917.
2. Walter Eckersall, "Gridiron Teams at War Camps Will Help Game," *Anaconda (MT) Standard*, August 19, 1917.
3. Walter Eckersall, "Stars of Football Join U.S. Ranks, but Game Will Keep On," *Chicago Tribune*, September 9, 1917.

4. Walter Eckersall, "College Players in Service Boost to Camp Football," *Chicago Tribune*, November 16, 1917.
5. Walter Eckersall, "Pat Smith and Erickson Star in Jackies' Victory," *Chicago Tribune*, November 30, 1917.
6. Walter Eckersall, "Sports at Camp Bring Spirit to New Army Men," *Chicago Tribune*, December 23, 1917.
7. Walter Eckersall, "Fighting Man of Football Does His Bit," *Chicago Tribune*, February 10, 1918; Walter Eckersall, "Eckie Recalls Gridiron Feats of Col. Hackett," *Chicago Tribune*, February 3, 1918; Walter Eckersall, "Carlisle Hero Now a Captain for Uncle Sam," *Chicago Tribune*, March 24, 1918; Walter Eckersall, "Jimmy Turner Another Grid Hero in Army," *Chicago Tribune*, April 21, 1918.
8. Walter Eckersall, "Sam Ransom Fearless in War or Sport," *Pittsburgh Post*, July 21, 1918.
9. WWIDR for Walter Eckersall, September 12, 1918.
10. Walter Eckersall, "Bluejackets and Iowa Varsity Usher in Football Season," *Chicago Tribune*, September 28, 1918.
11. Walter Eckersall, "Service Teams Seem to Have College Elevens Outclassed," *Chicago Tribune*, October 14, 1918.
12. Walter Eckersall, "Clash Will Be Day's Feature for Midwest," *Chicago Tribune*, October 19, 1918.
13. Walter Eckersall, "Former College Stars in Grant-Taylor Game Saturday," *Chicago Tribune*, November 6, 1918.
14. Walter Eckersall, "Cleveland Navy Wrests Victory from Soldiers," *Chicago Tribune*, November 24, 1918.
15. Walter Eckersall, "Hawkeyes and Dodge in Scoreless Draw; Snow Banks Field," *Chicago Tribune*, December 1, 1918.
16. "Paddy Driscoll Is Fatal to Rutgers," *New York Tribune*, November 17, 1918; "Weird Tackle as Great Lakes Defeats Annapolis, 7 to 6," *Chicago Tribune*, November 24, 1918.
17. Walter H. Eckersall, "That California Trip, as Told by 'Eckie' Himself," *Great Lakes Recruit*, March 1919.
18. Walter Eckersall, "Great Lakes Grid Players Spend Xmas on Drill Field," *Chicago Tribune*, December 26, 1918; Walter Eckersall, "Great Lakes in Acid Grid Test New Year's Day," *Chicago Tribune*, December 27, 1918.
19. Davis, *Papa Bear*, 45.
20. Walter Eckersall, "Great Lakes Eleven Earns National Service Title, 17–0," *Chicago Tribune*, January 2, 1919; "Six Capstone Football Greats in Rose Bowl Hall of Fame," *Birmingham (AL) News*, April 16, 1944.
21. Walter Eckersall, "Great Lakes Eleven Earns National Service Title, 17–0," *Chicago Tribune*, January 2, 1919; Walter Camp, "Walter Camp Calls Great Lakes Eleven Champion Football Team of Country," *Chicago Herald and Examiner*, January 19, 1919.

20. THE SUNDAY GAME

1. Walter Eckersall, "More Football Than Ever with 'Pro' Elevens in Action," *Chicago Tribune*, September 24, 1919.
2. Eckersall, "More Football Than Ever." Emphasis added.
3. "East Chicago, 20; Mitchell A.C., 0," *Chicago Tribune*, October 30, 1916; "Birk Brothers Gain on Field in Pin Circuit," *Chicago Tribune*, October 30, 1916; "Americans Win Most Contests; Defeat Swedes," *Chicago Tribune*, October 30, 1916; "Cy Young and Normals Blank Grand Crossing," *Chicago Tribune*, October 30, 1916; "At the Billiard Rooms," *Chicago Tribune*, October 30, 1916; Walter H. Eckersall, "Gophers Look Like Best Bet in Conference," *Chicago Tribune*, October 30, 1916; "Massillon Eleven Wins," *Chicago Tribune*, October 30, 1916.
4. "Famed Brickley Heads $20,000 Hammond Team," *Moline (IL) Dispatch*, September 20, 1919.
5. I. E. Sanborn, "Hammond 'Pro' Team Books Cub Park for Season in Football," *Chicago Tribune*, October 18, 1919.
6. "Hammond Plays Scoreless Tie with Cleveland," *Chicago Tribune*, November 3, 1919.
7. "Hammond Grid Skipper Is Jailed: Bad Checks," *Moline (IL) Dispatch*, December 16, 1919; "Parduhn Freed; Players' Checks to Be Made Good," *Chicago Tribune*, December 18, 1919.
8. Walter Eckersall, "Pro Football Looms as Danger to Great College Game," *Chicago Tribune*, November 26, 1919.
9. Walter Eckersall, "'Big Ten' to Take Action Against Grid Pros Today," *Chicago Tribune*, December 6, 1919.
10. "1500 See Local Team Crush Visitors Under Fast Fierce Attack," *Decatur (IL) Herald*, October 4, 1920.
11. Walter Eckersall, "Staleys and Akron Battle to 0–0 Tie for Pro Grid Title," *Chicago Tribune*, December 13, 1920; Walter Eckersall, "Akron Pros Held to a Scoreless Tie by the Decatur Staleys," *Akron Beacon-Journal*, December 13, 1920.
12. Walter Eckersall, "Chicago Schools Make Fair Showing in Illinois Meet," *Chicago Tribune*, May 22, 1921.
13. Walter Eckersall, "Grange Is Illinois 'Punch' That Fells Nebraska, 24 to 7," *Chicago Tribune*, October 3, 1923.
14. James Crusinberry, "Grange Thrills Huge Crowd by Racing to 5 Touchdowns," *Chicago Tribune*, October 19, 1924.
15. Walter Eckersall, "Eckie Discusses Passes and How to Play Them," *Chicago Tribune*, October 17, 1924; Walter Eckersall, "Zuppke Should Have Credit for Grange's Feats," *Chicago Tribune*, October 24, 1924; Walter Eckersall, "Illini, Aided by Wind, Beat Hawks, 36–0," *Chicago Tribune*, November 2, 1924.
16. "Voice of the People: Eckie Gets Panned," *Chicago Tribune*, November 8, 1924.
17. Walter Eckersall, "Eckersall Picks Big 10 Honor Teams," *Chicago Tribune*, December 6, 1925.

18. "Eckersall Thinks 'Red' Grange Will Give Enemies of College Athletics Food for Knocking," *Albuquerque (NM) Morning Journal*, November 24, 1925.
19. Walter Eckersall, "Grange's Injury Logical Result of Overstrain," *Chicago Tribune*, December 11, 1925.
20. "Eckersall May Lead Pro Loop," *Fort Worth (TX) Record-Telegram*, February 17, 1926.
21. James Crusinberry, "Pyle's New Pro Grid League Formed with Seven Clubs In," *Chicago Tribune*, February 18, 1926.
22. "Committees Are Picked to Run C.A.A.U. Athletics," *Chicago Tribune*, November 11, 1924.

21. CHICAGO GOES FOR GOLD

1. "First of the Olympic Games," *Chicago Tribune*, April 8, 1896; "Americans Make Good Showing," *Chicago Tribune*, April 12, 1896; Grace Corneau, "So Easy as to Be a Joke," *Chicago Tribune*, July 29, 1900.
2. "C.A.A. Athletes Unable to Gain," *Chicago Tribune*, September 1, 1904; "Olympic Games Result in Feats," *Chicago Tribune*, September 2, 1904; "Final Olympic Events Today," *Chicago Tribune*, September 3, 1904; "Local Swimmer Wins at St. Louis," *Chicago Tribune*, September 6, 1904; "Swimming Events at St. Louis," *Chicago Tribune*, September 7, 1904.
3. Hugo M. Friend, "Letter of Mr. Friend," *Chicago Tribune*, April 8, 1906; "Hugo Friend Talks of Trip," *Chicago Tribune*, June 26, 1906; A. A. Stagg, "World Athletes Ready for Games," *Chicago Tribune*, July 13, 1908; A. A. Stagg, "More Honors Won by U.S. Athletes," *Chicago Tribune*, July 17, 1908; A. A. Stagg, "Americans Raise Flag of Victory," *Chicago Tribune*, July 21, 1908.
4. Walter H. Eckersall, "Eckersall's Observations on Amateur Sports," *Nashville American*, May 3, 1908; Walter H. Eckersall, "On Form Americans Should Sweep Boards at London," *Buffalo Courier*, July 6, 1908; Walter H. Eckersall, "American Records Made in England," *Buffalo Courier*, August 30, 1908.
5. Walter H. Eckersall, "Olympic Contests of 1912 Promise to Be Greatest in Athletic History," *Chicago Tribune*, December 24, 1911.
6. Walter H. Eckersall, "Chicago May Get 15 Olympic Men," *Chicago Tribune*, March 3, 1912.
7. "The Chicago Athletic Association," *Chicago Tribune*, April 12, 1890; "Club-House Will Be Opened Tonight," *Chicago Tribune*, July 15, 1893.
8. Walter Eckersall, "George Dawson, Former C.A.A. Boxing Teacher, Visits Here," *Chicago Tribune*, July 9, 1925.
9. "Shuts Out Athletic Club," *Chicago Tribune*, February 16, 1900; *New Illinois Athletic Club*, 17, 39.
10. Walter H. Eckersall, "Big Local Clubs to Bury Hatchet," *Chicago Tribune*, December 14, 1911; Walter Eckersall, "New Swimming Row Between Big Clubs Started over Polo," *Chicago Tribune*, April 5, 1918; Walter Eckersall, "Central A.A.U. Board Slaps at E.C. Brown of Title Committee," *Chicago Tribune*, January 21, 1919.

11. Walter Eckersall, "Coast Natator Swims to Fame in Olympic Trial," *Chicago Tribune*, July 12, 1920; Walter Eckersall, "Chicago Stars Grab Honors in Olympic Meet," *Chicago Tribune*, July 18, 1920; Walter Eckersall, "Fourteen C.A.A. Men Picked for Olympic Squad," *Chicago Tribune*, July 19, 1920.
12. Walter Eckersall, "Americans Are Picked to Win," *Los Angeles Times*, June 22, 1924.
13. Walter Eckersall, "Prep Tank Stars of City Against Best of Nation," *Chicago Tribune*, March 2, 1921; Walter Eckersall, "Records Crack as Weiss Takes Howell's Scalp," *Chicago Tribune*, April 2, 1924; Amateur Athletic Union, *Official Swimming Handbook*, 235–38, 252–57.
14. Walter Eckersall, "Prout Named Chief of National A.A.U.," *Chicago Tribune*, November 23, 1921; "Ross Shatters Mark for 500 Meters in Naval Station Tank," *Chicago Tribune*, March 16, 1921; "Chicago Unknown Beats World Champ in 100-Yard Swim," *LaCrosse (WI) Tribune*, August 7, 1921.
15. Walter Eckersall, "Tribune to Host Aquatic Meet at Lincoln Park," *Chicago Tribune*, July 9, 1922.
16. Amateur Athletic Union, *Official Swimming Handbook*, 225–52.
17. Walter Eckersall, "I.A.C. Wins National A.A.U. Meet," *Chicago Tribune*, September 2, 1923; Walter Eckersall, "I.A.C. Leads National Swim Meet," *Chicago Tribune*, April 6, 1927; Walter Eckersall, "N.A.A.U. Swim Meet Opens at C.A.A. Tonight," *Chicago Tribune*, April 2, 1928.
18. Walter H. Eckersall, "M'Dermott Sets New Mark," *Chicago Tribune*, March 14, 1912; Walter H. Eckersall, "Hawaiian Wins 50 Yard Title in C.A.A. Tank," *Chicago Tribune*, April 27, 1916; Walter Eckersall, "Coast Natator Swims to Fame in Olympic Trial," *Chicago Tribune*, July 12, 1920; Walter Eckersall, "M'Gillivray vs. Kahanamoku in Three Events," *Chicago Tribune*, July 9, 1918; Walter Eckersall, "Duke and Pals Exhibit Today in C.A.A. Pool," *Chicago Tribune*, July 12, 1918; Walter Eckersall, "Over 40,000 See Duke Win Feature at Water Carnival," *Chicago Tribune*, July 15, 1918.
19. Walter Eckersall, "Chicago Stars Grab Honors in Olympic Meet," *Chicago Tribune*, July 18, 1920; Walter Eckersall, "Paddock Proves Most Notable of Sprinting Stars," *Chicago Tribune*, April 3, 1921; Walter Eckersall, "Fastest Human Stops Here on Way to Paris," *Chicago Tribune*, April 15, 1923; Walter Eckersall, "Charley Paddock Tells Walter Eckersall His Side of Controversy with the A.A.U.," *Chicago Tribune*, December 27, 1923.
20. Walter Eckersall, "Flying Nurmi Beats Ray and Cracks Record," *Chicago Tribune*, January 27, 1925; Walter Eckersall, "Nurmi Victor in Loyola Feature; Holy Cross Wins," *Chicago Tribune*, April 20, 1925; Walter Eckersall, "Conger Defeats Peltzer by Ten Yards," *Chicago Tribune*, February 11, 1928.
21. Walter Eckersall, "Olympic Games Are Goal of Stars in Big 10 Meet," *Chicago Tribune*, May 17, 1928.
22. Walter Eckersall, "Kockler Leads Bike Riders in Olympic Trial," *Chicago Tribune*, June 7, 1920.

23. Walter Eckersall, "Shoot Titles to Marksmen from Illinois," *Chicago Tribune*, August 19, 1917; Walter Eckersall, "Mark Arie and Troeh May Be Matched for Supremacy at Traps," *Chicago Tribune*, May 9, 1919; Walter Eckersall, "Mark Arie Wins Board of Trade Target Trophy," *Chicago Tribune*, June 9, 1920; Walter Eckersall, "Arie Champion Single Shot in State Tourney," *Chicago Tribune*, June 21, 1920.
24. Walter Eckersall, "Henry Gliders Win City-Wide Skate Tourney," *Chicago Tribune*, February 4, 1923.
25. Walter Eckersall, "Dark Horse, Allen, Wins Silver Skates," *Chicago Tribune*, January 21, 1924.
26. Walter Eckersall, "Silver Skates Races Drawing Record Entry," *Chicago Tribune*, January 11, 1925; Walter Eckersall, "500 Kids Enter Silver Skates Juvenile Derby," *Chicago Tribune*, January 18, 1925; Walter Eckersall, "45,000 See Farrell Win Tribune Skating Derby," *Chicago Tribune*, January 26, 1925; Walter Eckersall, "Silver Skates Derbies Carded for Jan. 21–22," *Chicago Tribune*, December 18, 1927; William Shirer, "O'Neil Farrell Ties for 3d in Olympic Race," *Chicago Tribune*, February 14, 1928.

22. SILVER SKATES AND GOLDEN GLOVES

1. Walter H. Eckersall, "Skating Club to Boost Plan for Carnival," *Chicago Tribune*, December 6, 1915; Walter H. Eckersall, "Mayor To Give Ice Rinks for Young Skaters," *Chicago Tribune*, December 8, 1915; Walter H. Eckersall, "Boys Speed on Roller Skates for 'Trib' Races," *Chicago Tribune*, January 24, 1916; Walter H. Eckersall, "Boy Skaters, 10,000 Strong, in 'Trib' Tests," *Chicago Tribune*, January 9, 1916.
2. Walter H. Eckersall, "Crowd of 5,000 Sees Finals for Trophies," *Chicago Tribune*, February 6, 1916.
3. Grossman et al., *Encyclopedia of Chicago*, 754–55.
4. Walter Eckersall, "Silver Skates Go to Victor in 'Trib' Derby," *Chicago Tribune*, January 7, 1917.
5. Walter Eckersall, "30,000 Cheer as Art Staff Wins Silver Skates," *Chicago Tribune*, January 29, 1917.
6. Don Maxwell, "Eckie—As We Knew Him," *Chicago Tribune*, March 25, 1930.
7. Stephan Benzkofer, "When Speedskating Was King of Winter," *Chicago Tribune*, February 16, 2014.
8. Walter Eckersall, "10,000 Cheer Boys in 'Tribune' Meet," *Chicago Tribune*, June 30, 1918; Walter Eckersall, "Tribune to Sponsor Bicycle Derby," *Chicago Tribune*, August 13, 1922; Walter Eckersall, "Tribune to Hold Aquatic Meet at Lincoln Park," *Chicago Tribune*, July 9, 1922.
9. Hugh Fullerton, "Amateurs to Box in Huge Tournament Here," *Chicago Tribune*, February 22, 1923; Justin L. Faherty, "The DeMille of Sport: Arch Ward Is Originator of Big Tournaments," *St. Louis Globe-Democrat*, January 20, 1946; "Patrolling

the Sport Highway with Al Warden," *Ogden (UT) Standard-Examiner*, February 12, 1948.

10. "Boxing Entry Blank," *Chicago Tribune*, February 28, 1923; Walter Eckersall, "658 Amateurs to Fight for Tribune Golden Gloves," *Chicago Tribune*, February 17, 1929.
11. "Amateur Boxing Vox Pop," *Chicago Tribune*, March 1, 1923.
12. "Our Boxing Tournament," *Chicago Tribune*, March 2, 1923.
13. Walter Eckersall, "Tribune A.A. Picks Boxing Place, Dates," *Chicago Tribune*, February 28, 1923.
14. Walter Eckersall, "Crown City's Glove Champs This Evening," *Chicago Tribune*, March 28, 1923; Walter Eckersall, "Great Crowd Sees Howard Boxers Win," *Chicago Tribune*, March 29, 1923.
15. Walter Eckersall, "Praise Galore for Tribune A.A. Boxing Tourney," *Chicago Tribune*, March 30, 1923; Walter Eckersall, "Great Crowd Sees Howard Boxers Win," *Chicago Tribune*, March 29, 1923.
16. Paul Gallico, "The News Announces Amateur Ring Tourney," *New York Daily News*, February 14, 1927; Paul Gallico, "Golden Gloves Tourney a Fixture," *New York Daily News*, March 30, 1927.
17. Walter Eckersall, "Tribune to Help Uncle Sam Find Olympic Boxers," *Chicago Tribune*, May 8, 1927; Walter Eckersall, "404 Amateurs to Fight for Golden Gloves," *Chicago Tribune*, March 4, 1928.
18. Walter Eckersall, "5,000 Cheer Winners of Golden Gloves," *Chicago Tribune*, March 10, 1928.
19. Walter Eckersall, "Kestian, Too Light for Grid Sport, Makes Good in Ring," *Chicago Tribune*, March 15, 1928; Walter Eckersall, "Fosco Primes K.O. Wallop for New York Welterweight," *Chicago Tribune*, March 19, 1928; Walter Eckersall, "Radka, Tribune Heavyweight, Hardens Muscles in Foundry," *Chicago Tribune*, March 16, 1928; Walter Eckersall, "Maier, Tribune Battler, Never Beaten in Ring," *Chicago Tribune*, March 20, 1928.
20. Walter Eckersall, "Tickets for Inter-City Meet Today," *Chicago Tribune*, March 12, 1928; Paul Gallico, "Golden Glovers to Chicago," *New York Daily News*, March 19, 1928; Walter Eckersall, "Chicago and New York Fight to Draw," *Chicago Tribune*, March 25, 1928; Paul Gallico, "Glovers Split Victories," *New York Daily News*, March 25, 1928.
21. Walter Eckersall, "9,000 See Final Battles for Golden Gloves," *Chicago Tribune*, February 24, 1929.
22. Walter Eckersall, "Golden Gloves Fights Told Blow by Blow," *Chicago Tribune*, March 28, 1929; "Individual Effort: Boxing," *Chicago Tribune*, August 10, 1997.
23. Walter Eckersall, "Chicago Boys Start Battle for Golden Gloves Tonight," *Chicago Tribune*, February 11, 1930; Walter Eckersall, "Out of Town Golden Gloves Army Plans Its Invasion," *Chicago Tribune*, February 17, 1930.
24. Walter Eckersall, "Chicago Golden Gloves Prelims Run Two Days," *Chicago Tribune*, February 6, 1930.

25. Don Maxwell, "Chicago Hails Golden Gloves Champions," *Chicago Tribune*, March 1, 1930; French Lane, "Chicago Boys Beat Country Cousins, 5 to 3," *Chicago Tribune*, March 1, 1930.
26. Walter Eckersall, "Blow by Blow Account of Fights for Golden Glove Intercity Championship," *Chicago Tribune*, March 20, 1930.
27. "Here Are All Eight of Them—Golden Gloves Champions of Chicagoland," *Chicago Tribune*, March 10, 1934; Howard Barry, "22,132 Hail New Golden Gloves Champions," *Chicago Tribune*, March 11, 1939; Wilfrid Smith, "Round by Round Account of Golden Gloves Final Bouts," *Chicago Tribune*, March 7, 1953; Maurice Shevlin, "Hail Glove Kings! Next—Intercity," *Chicago Tribune*, March 12, 1959; Maurice Shevlin, "14 Bouts Bring 8 New Glove Champs," *Chicago Tribune*, March 10, 1960.

23. COLOR LINES

1. Pruter, *Rise of American High School Sports*, 15; Grossman et al., *Encyclopedia of Chicago*, 363–64.
2. Walter Eckersall, "Sam Ransom Fearless in War or Sport," *Pittsburgh Post*, July 21, 1918.
3. "Englewood Beats Hyde Park 5 to 0," *Chicago Inter Ocean*, November 29, 1903.
4. Eckersall, "Sam Ransom Fearless."
5. Walter H. Eckersall, "Johnson Works to Lose Weight," *Chicago Tribune*, November 30, 1910; Walter H. Eckersall, "Jack Johnson to Open Café," *Chicago Tribune*, April 16, 1912; Walter H. Eckersall, "Negroes Plan Reception for J. Johnson on Return Today," *Chicago Tribune*, July 6, 1912; Walter H. Eckersall, "'Black Belt' Coin Goes on Johnson to Defeat Moran," *Chicago Tribune*, June 23, 1914; Walter H. Eckersall, "Negroes Refuse to Bet on Jack," *Chicago Tribune*, February 21, 1915.
6. J. Lincoln Davis, "Chicago and Jack Johnson," *Tampa (FL) Morning Tribune*, October 27, 1912; "Conviction of a Black Brute," *Jones County (MS) News*, May 22, 1913; "The Prize Fight," *Jackson (MS) Daily News*, July 5, 1910; "Jack Johnson an Undesirable," *Charlotte (NC) News*, October 27, 1912; Walter H. Eckersall, "Jack Wires His Best Wishes," *Chicago Tribune*, April 16, 1910; Walter H. Eckersall, "Kaufman a Comer, Says Jack," *Chicago Tribune*, August 11, 1910.
7. Walter H. Eckersall, "Willard Refuses Offer for Match," *Chicago Tribune*, January 6, 1913; Walter H. Eckersall, "Attention, Pugs! Wanted—A 'Hope,'" *Chicago Tribune*, May 16, 1911; Walter H. Eckersall, "New 'White Hope' a Local Product," *Chicago Tribune*, June 18, 1911; Walter H. Eckersall, "Fight Edict from New York Stirs Blood of Mr. Johnson," *Chicago Tribune*, January 12, 1912.
8. Walter H. Eckersall, "Johnson Ordered Away From 'Gym,'" *Chicago Tribune*, January 10, 1913.
9. Walter H. Eckersall, "Athlete of South Draws Color Line," *Chicago Tribune*, August 9, 1911.

10. Walter Eckersall, "Forget Color Lines in Gridiron Games Under Army Regime," *Chicago Tribune*, December 3, 1918.
11. Oriard, *King Football*, 291–92.
12. Oriard, *King Football*, 294.
13. Walter H. Eckersall, "Purple Preps Meet Winners," *Chicago Tribune*, May 28, 1911; Walter H. Eckersall, "Evanston 'Preps' Take Tiger Meet; Lane Tech Second," *Chicago Tribune*, February 11, 1912; Prep, "Lane Victor in Hard Game," *Chicago Tribune*, October 13, 1911.
14. Walter H. Eckersall, "Brown Beaten by Washington in 14–0 Combat," *Chicago Tribune*, January 2, 1916; Walter H. Eckersall, "West Gets Four Places on All-American Team," *Chicago Tribune*, December 10, 1916.
15. Walter H. Eckersall, "Staleys and Akron Battle to 0–0 Tie for Pro Grid Title," *Chicago Tribune*, December 13, 1920.
16. "West High and Clinton Play Tie Contest," *Davenport (IA) Daily Times*, November 27, 1914.
17. Walter Eckersall, "Great Lakes Team Downs Iowa in Football Opening, 10–0," *Chicago Tribune*, September 29, 1918.
18. Walter Eckersall, "Iowa Eleven Will Keep 'Big Ten' Foes Stepping Lively," *Chicago Tribune*, October 3, 1918; Walter Eckersall, "Football Coaches Forget Sterling Plays of Old Game?" *Chicago Tribune*, October 31, 1919; Walter Eckersall, "Iowa to Invade Midway with Great Team in Top Form," *Chicago Tribune*, November 12, 1919.
19. Walter H. Eckersall, "Badgers Win Meet from Maroons by One Point," *Chicago Tribune*, June 6, 1915; Walter H. Eckersall, "Records Fall in A.A.U. Meet; Joie Ray Star," *Chicago Tribune*, July 18, 1915; Walter H. Eckersall, "Illini Swamp Maroon Squad in Dual Meet," *Chicago Tribune*, May 13, 1916.
20. Walter Eckersall, "Chicago Stars Grab Honors in Olympic Meet," *Chicago Tribune*, July 18, 1920; "Yank Athletes Earn Points in Olympic Games," *Chicago Tribune*, August 18, 1920.
21. Walter Eckersall, "World Broad Jump Record Smashed!" *Chicago Tribune*, June 25, 1925.
22. Walter Eckersall, "Ontario Preps Win Marquette Relay Games," *Chicago Tribune*, May 6, 1928.
23. Walter H. Eckersall, "Langford Due Here Today," *Chicago Tribune*, May 24, 1911; Walter H. Eckersall, "Langford Fails to Show Up," *Chicago Tribune*, May 25, 1911; Walter H. Eckersall, "Langford 'On Parade' Today," *Chicago Tribune*, May 26, 1911; Walter H. Eckersall, "Langford Spars at Speedy Pace," *Chicago Tribune*, May 27, 1911; Knockout, "Governor Stops Kenosha Fight," *Chicago Tribune*, May 30, 1911.
24. Walter H. Eckersall, "Johnson Offered $25,000 Go," *Chicago Tribune*, April 9, 1912; Walter Eckersall, "Dempsey Willing If Public Wants Bout with Wills," *Chicago Tribune*, December 22, 1921; Walter Eckersall, "Dempsey Here, Ready to Meet Wills for Title," *Chicago Tribune*, August 31, 1922; Walter Eckersall, "Georges Is Next; Bout With Wills Remote," *Chicago Tribune*, September 1, 1922.

25. Walter Eckersall, "George Dawson, Former C.A.A. Boxing Teacher, Visits Here," *Chicago Tribune*, July 9, 1925.
26. Walter Eckersall, "Bogash, Flowers Mix Tonight at Aurora," *Chicago Tribune*, July 24, 1925.
27. Walter Eckersall, "Walker Wrests Title from Flowers," *Chicago Tribune*, December 4, 1926.
28. "Mr. Eckersall, Tribune Reporter," *Chicago Defender*, February 3, 1912.
29. Walter Eckersall, "Track Meet for Public Aug. 16 in Grant Park," *Chicago Tribune*, July 30, 1919; Walter Eckersall, "Foxy Coaches Prime Teams for Big Event," *San Antonio Evening News*, July 31, 1919; Walter Eckersall, "16-Year-Old Chicago Girl Swim Victor," *Chicago Tribune*, August 3, 1919; Walter Eckersall, "Banner Year in Football With A.E.F. Men Back," *Anaconda (MT) Standard*, August 3, 1919.
30. Walter H. Eckersall, "Orioles Lead in Homan A.A. Meet," *Chicago Tribune*, February 22, 1911.
31. Walter Eckersall, "Gov. Lowden Views Exhibition Boxing of 'Homecoming Day,'" *Chicago Tribune*, June 25, 1919.
32. Camp and Eckersall, "Some Negro Football Stars," 152–53.

24. THE SEEDY SIDE OF SPORTS

1. Walter H. Eckersall, "Negroes Refuse to Bet on Jack," *Chicago Tribune*, February 21, 1915.
2. Walter H. Eckersall, "Johnson Will Beat Willard, Chicago Tip," *Chicago Tribune*, April 4, 1915; Walter Eckersall, "Jack Johnson Now Thrives as a Medicine Man," *Chicago Tribune*, April 19, 1919.
3. Walter H. Eckersall, "Declares Fight Was Honest," *Chicago Tribune*, February 4, 1911; Walter Eckersall, "Barrett Goes Down and Out in 3d Round," *Chicago Tribune*, February 5, 1927.
4. Walter Eckersall, "Coulon Charges Boxing Chief Staged Political Shakedown," *Chicago Tribune*, June 4, 1927; Walter H. Eckersall, "Sheriff Ends Go; Foul Work Cause," *Chicago Tribune*, September 11, 1912; Walter Eckersall, "Canzoneri Pins Faith on K.O. in Title Bout," *Chicago Tribune*, August 1, 1929.
5. Walter H. Eckersall, "Masked Marvel Takes Feature Bout at C.A.A.," *Chicago Tribune*, March 12, 1916; Walter Eckersall, "'Strangler' and Gardini Ready to Go to Mat," *Chicago Tribune*, April 3, 1923; Walter Eckersall, "Lewis Crushes Dempsey to Mat in 'Mixed' Battle," *Chicago Tribune*, April 2, 1922; Walter Eckersall, "Mat Match Square, or Referee Quits," *Chicago Tribune*, February 13, 1919; Walter Eckersall, "Fake Mat Bouts Aired in Quiz; May Bar Sport," *Chicago Tribune*, June 7, 1927.
6. Walter Eckersall, "Texans Learn Foot Race Trick Back in the '70s," *Chicago Tribune*, March 16, 1919; Walter Eckersall, "Here's a Stunt Made 'Suckers' Out of Bookmakers," *Chicago Tribune*, May 4, 1919; Walter Eckersall, "'Doped' Coffee Tricks Bettors on a Foot Race," *Chicago Tribune*, April 13, 1919.

7. Walter H. Eckersall, "M'Farland Takes Final Training," *Chicago Tribune*, February 13, 1912.
8. Walter H. Eckersall, "Slow Up in Work for Big Battle," *Chicago Tribune*, November 22, 1907; Walter H. Eckersall, "Gridiron Rivals Are Confident," *Chicago Tribune*, October 30, 1908; Walter H. Eckersall, "Await Whistle for Clash," *Chicago Tribune*, November 12, 1908; Walter H. Eckersall, "Maroons Happy; Expect Victory," *Chicago Tribune*, November 20, 1908; Walter H. Eckersall, "Two 'M' Elevens Await Whistle," *Chicago Tribune*, November 20, 1909; Walter H. Eckersall, "Western Rivals Await Whistle," *Chicago Tribune*, November 19, 1910.
9. Walter Eckersall, "Great Lakes in Acid Grid Test on New Year's Day," *Chicago Tribune*, December 27, 1918.
10. Walter Eckersall, "California Team Shows Power in Drill for W.J.," *Chicago Tribune*, December 29, 1921.
11. Walter Eckersall, "N. Dame Squad Is Due at Scene of Battle Today," *Chicago Tribune*, December 31, 1924; Walter Eckersall, "City Welcomes Irish, Trojans Today," *Chicago Tribune*, November 25, 1927; Walter Eckersall, "Trojans Rated 2 to 1 Favorite Over Tech Team," *Chicago Tribune*, December 13, 1929.
12. Walter H. Eckersall, "M'Goorty Victor in Bout at Gary," *Chicago Tribune*, June 24, 1911.
13. Walter Eckersall, "Meyers Wins as Foe Plays Safe and Fans Jeer," *Chicago Tribune*, April 4, 1922; Walter Eckersall, "Stormy Scenes as Ed Lewis Headlocks Zyb," *Chicago Tribune*, February 27, 1924.
14. Walter Eckersall, "Walker Gets a Scare, but Wins over Freedman," *Chicago Tribune*, August 25, 1925; Walter Eckersall, "Miller Draws with Herman in Slow Bout," *Chicago Tribune*, September 18, 1925; Walter Eckersall, "Ad Stone Beats Owens as Fans Boo at E. Chicago," *Chicago Tribune*, September 22, 1925.
15. Walter Eckersall, "Toledo Returns to Quiet Life over the Night," *Chicago Tribune*, July 6, 1919.
16. "Complete Schedule for the State High School Tourney Is Announced for the First Time," *Bloomington (IL) Pantagraph*, March 15, 1921; "Gunman Slays Alfred Lingle in I.C. Subway," *Chicago Tribune*, June 10, 1930; John O'Brien, "Tribune Reporter Becomes a Crime Statistic," *Chicago Tribune*, June 12, 1997.
17. Walter Eckersall, "Boxing War On; Rival Promoters Announce Cards," *Chicago Tribune*, April 13, 1923.
18. "'Wop Tommy' Now Sought as Enright Killer," *Chicago Tribune*, February 6, 1920; "Former Wife of Colosimo Eludes Police," *Chicago Tribune*, May 13, 1920; Walter Eckersall, "Dundee to Mix with Henry on Boat Tonight," *Chicago Tribune*, May 19, 1922; Walter Eckersall, "Bob Martin Arrives for Schmader Mill," *Chicago Tribune*, August 30, 1922.
19. Walter Eckersall, "Boxing War Ends—2 Star Shows Monday, Tuesday," *Chicago Tribune*, April 20, 1923.
20. "Who's Who in War of Beer Running Bandits," *Chicago Tribune*, September 18, 1923.

21. Walter Eckersall, "Boxers Tangle in St. Malachy Benefit Tonight," *Chicago Tribune*, May 21, 1923.
22. "Notes of the Boxers," *Chicago Tribune*, September 29, 1923. This article was not bylined but most likely written by Eckersall.
23. Walter Eckersall, "Forty Federal Sleuths after Ticket Scalpers," *Chicago Tribune*, September 30, 1919; Walter Eckersall, "Says Pikers Who Sell to Scalpers Should Pay Tax," *Chicago Tribune*, October 1, 1919; Walter Eckersall, "Local Bettors Take Sudden Liking to Reds," *Chicago Tribune*, October 2, 1919.
24. Westbrook Pegler, "Nobody's Business," *Chicago Tribune*, November 13, 1932.

25. THE AUTHORITY

1. Bob Sink, "Along the Line," *Decatur (IL) Herald*, March 27, 1930.
2. Walter H. Eckersall, "Eckersall Picks the All Western," *Chicago Tribune*, November 28, 1909.
3. Walter H. Eckersall, "Likes New Football Rules," *Chicago Tribune*, October 6, 1907.
4. Walter H. Eckersall, "Look for Battle on Forward Pass," *Chicago Tribune*, February 2, 1912; Walter H. Eckersall, "Better Football Under New Code," *Chicago Tribune*, February 5, 1912.
5. Walter H. Eckersall, "Football Stars of West," *Chicago Tribune*, November 24, 1907; Walter H. Eckersall, "Three Leading Critics' All-American Elevens," *Chicago Tribune*, December 26, 1907.
6. Walter H. Eckersall, "All-American Team Chosen by Eckersall," *Chicago Tribune*, December 6, 1914; Walter H. Eckersall, "'Eckie' Names Four of West for All-Stars," *Chicago Tribune*, December 5, 1915; Walter H. Eckersall, "West Gets Four Places on All-American Team," *Chicago Tribune*, December 10, 1916; Walter Eckersall, "Harley and Meyers on Eckersall's All-American Team," *Chicago Tribune*, December 15, 1919; Walter Eckersall, "Array of Greats on All-American Picked by Eckie," *Chicago Tribune*, December 11, 1921.
7. "Walter H. Eckersall Ill; Football Overwork Cause," *Chicago Tribune*, December 4, 1917; Walter Eckersall, "Jackies Get Star Skater as Ice Coach," *Chicago Tribune*, December 21, 1917.
8. Walter Eckersall, "Eckersall Picks Four from West in All-American," *Chicago Tribune*, December 16, 1917.
9. "Expert Pulls Boner on Star Selection," *Salt Lake Telegram*, December 19, 1917; Guy Butler, "Topics of the Tropics," *Miami Daily News*, October 27, 1950; George Wallace, "Avalanche of Sports," *Lubbock (TX) Morning Avalanche*, November 25, 1958.
10. Harold E. O'Neill, "Sporting Topics," *New Brunswick (NJ) Daily Home News*, December 24, 1917.
11. Eckersall, "Harley and Meyers"; Eckersall, "Array of Greats."
12. Walter Eckersall, "Eckersall Names All-American Team," *Chicago Tribune*, December 12, 1920.

13. Walter H. Eckersall, "Football Queries," *Chicago Tribune*, October 27, 1907.
14. Walter H. Eckersall, "How to Play Football for Beginners," *Chicago Tribune*, September 1, 1912; "Play Football! Eckersall Tells You How," *Chicago Tribune*, September 16, 1928; "Now Ready—'Eckie's' Football Articles in Booklet Form!" *Chicago Tribune*, October 15, 1928.
15. Walter Eckersall, "Willie Heston Heads List of Michigan Stars," *Chicago Tribune*, September 23, 1923; Walter Eckersall, "Aubrey Devine Leads All Iowa Gridiron Heroes," *Chicago Tribune*, September 16, 1923; Walter Eckersall, "Chick [*sic*] Harley's Great Record Earns Him Honor as Leading Buckeye Grid Hero," *Chicago Tribune*, October 7, 1923; Walter Eckersall, "George Gipp Rated Greatest of Notre Dame Grid Stars," *Chicago Tribune*, October 14, 1923.
16. Harvey Woodruff, "Eckersall Greatest Maroon Grid Star, Woodruff Says," *Chicago Tribune*, December 30, 1923; Harvey Woodruff, "In the Wake of the News," *Chicago Tribune*, March 27, 1930.
17. "Wisconsin Star Out," *Indianapolis News*, October 12, 1909; "Claim an Injustice," *Oshkosh (WI) Daily Northwestern*, October 13, 1909; "Student Body Demands Reinstatement of Moll," *Indianapolis News*, October 16, 1909.
18. Walter H. Eckersall, "Moll Reinstated; Wisconsin Happy," *Chicago Tribune*, October 21, 1909. Emphasis added.
19. Walter H. Eckersall, "Season of 1915 Greatest Ever in Gridiron Play," *Chicago Tribune*, December 26, 1915; "Fifteen Boys Killed in Football This Year," *New York Times*, November 28, 1915.
20. Walter H. Eckersall, "Danger Element Is Zest to Sport," *Chicago Tribune*, November 23, 1909; Walter H. Eckersall, "Unfit Player Brings Death to Grid Sport," *Chicago Tribune*, October 20, 1915.
21. Walter H. Eckersall, "Maroons' Defeat Seems Certain," *Chicago Tribune*, October 25, 1910.
22. "Eckersall to Speak Before Grid Committee," *Chicago Tribune*, March 4, 1927; "No Drastic Changes Made by Grid Rules Committee," *Brooklyn (NY) Daily Times*, February 5, 1928; Walter Eckersall, "Football Rules Committee Clarifies Grid Code," *Chicago Tribune*, February 7, 1928.
23. Hugh Fullerton, "Collegiate Post Is Offered Eckersall," *Chicago Tribune*, February 12, 1923; James Crusinberry, "Pyle's New Pro Grid League Formed with Seven Clubs In," *Chicago Tribune*, February 18, 1926; "Athletic Czar on West Coast," *Collyer's Eye*, July 27, 1929; "Eckersall Is Mentioned for Boxing Board," *Belleville (IL) News-Democrat*, August 6, 1929.
24. "Plan 12 Months' Olympiad at Chicago World's Fair in 1933," *Chicago Tribune*, February 14, 1928.
25. "Committees Are Picked to Run C.A.A.U. Athletics," *Chicago Tribune*, November 11, 1924.
26. Walter Eckersall, "Charley Paddock Tells Walter Eckersall His Side of Controversy with the A.A.U.," *Chicago Tribune*, December 27, 1923.

27. Walter Eckersall, "Major Griffith Attacks A.A.U. Olympic Tactics," *Chicago Tribune*, April 16, 1928.
28. Walter Eckersall, "New Defects Pointed Out in A.A.U. Rule Here," *Chicago Tribune*, April 17, 1928; Walter Eckersall, "Athletic Paper Attacks A.A.U. Olympic Control," *Chicago Tribune*, April 18, 1928; Walter Eckersall, "A.A.U. Controls Selections for U.S. Olympic Squad," *Chicago Tribune*, April 19, 1928.
29. "Interpreting Sports for Sunday Readers," *Editor and Publisher*, October 3, 1925; "'Square Shooters' in Sportdom and News Work Succeed, Says Eckersall," *Editor and Publisher*, January 8, 1927.
30. Walter H. Eckersall, "Present Game a Hybrid, Says Gridiron Expert," *Pittsburgh Press*, September 24, 1907.
31. "How to Play Football, by Walter Eckersall," *Chicago Tribune*, September 16, 1928.

26. THE FRIEND

1. HEK, "Some Offside Plays," *Chicago Tribune*, November 20, 1904.
2. "Celebration of Maroon Victory Held at Midway," *Chicago Inter Ocean*, December 5, 1905; "Warrant for Eckersall," *Chicago Inter Ocean*, January 25, 1907; "Eckersall to Face Trial," *Chicago Tribune*, January 26, 1907.
3. Lester, *Stagg's University*, 61–62.
4. Lardner, "Eckie."
5. Ralph Cannon, "The Campus Canopy," *Chicago Daily News*, April 17, 1930.
6. Bert Demby, "W.H. Eckersall, Sport Writer, Dies Suddenly," *Lancaster (PA) Daily Intelligencer Journal*, March 25, 1930.
7. Don Maxwell, "Eckie—As We Knew Him," *Chicago Tribune*, March 25, 1930.
8. Lardner, "Eckie."
9. Merrill C. "Babe" Meigs, "The Greatest Football Player in the World—Walter Eckersall," *American Weekly*, October 26, 1947.
10. Don Maxwell, "Speaking of Sports," *Chicago Tribune*, March 28, 1929.
11. "Chicago Gets Ready to Fete Flying Amelia," *Chicago Tribune*, July 18, 1928; Kathleen McLaughlin, "City Ready to Cheer Amelia; 'Home' Today," *Chicago Tribune*, July 19, 1928; Kathleen McLaughlin, "City Welcomes Miss Earhart Home," *Chicago Tribune*, July 20, 1928.
12. Walter Eckersall, "Eckie Recalls Gridiron Feats of Col. Hackett," *Chicago Tribune*, February 3, 1918; Walter Eckersall, "Maroons' Game with Michigan Recalls Battle," *Chicago Tribune*, November 7, 1920; Walter Eckersall, "Fighting Man of Football Does His Bit," *Chicago Tribune*, February 10, 1918.
13. "Arrangements Completed for Walter Eckersall's Last Rites," *Chicago Tribune*, March 26, 1930.
14. Lardner, "Eckie."
15. Harvey Woodruff, "Eckersall Greatest Maroon Grid Star, Woodruff Says," *Chicago Tribune*, December 30, 1923; Bert Demby, "Walter Eckersall, Greatest

Grid General of Middle West, Dies," *Brooklyn Citizen*, March 25, 1930; Maxwell, "Eckie—As We Knew Him."

16. USCR for Walter and Mary Eckersall and family, 1910; "Walter Eckersall Sr. Dies," *Chicago Tribune*, November 15, 1914.
17. "Building Permits," *Chicago Tribune*, November 10, 1914.
18. "Walter Eckersall Sr. Dies"; "Rites for W. Eckersall Sr.," *Chicago Tribune*, November 16, 1914.
19. CCMI for Stephen R. Anderson and Jessie M. Eckersall, April 27, 1915; USCR for Mary, Etta, and Walter Eckersall, 1920; Sperber, *Shake Down the Thunder*, 312–13.
20. Ted Rakstis, "Eckersall Family Living Near Coloma," *Benton Harbor (MI) News-Palladium*, November 15, 1957.
21. "Aldermen Honor Walter Eckersall; Funeral Today," *Chicago Tribune*, March 27, 1930.
22. "Mrs. Eckersall, Mother of Noted Writer, Is Dead," *Chicago Tribune*, November 10, 1928; "Walter Eckersall, Outstanding Sport Figure, Is Dead," *Decatur (IL) Herald*, March 25, 1930.
23. USCR for Elizabeth Bateman and Elizabeth Eckersall, 1930; Nancy McDonald, "Not a Woman to Take Chances, 'Jappy' Heeds Advice of Friends," *St. Petersburg (FL) Times*, September 18, 1951.
24. "20,410 Students Get Diplomas in Schools of City," *Chicago Tribune*, February 3, 1929; "Walter Eckersall's Daughter Injured in Accident Here," *Decatur (IL) Herald*, May 24, 1929.
25. John P. Gallagher, "Like Father Like Daughter," *Los Angeles Times*, October 19, 1930.
26. Nona Parker, "Like Father, Like Daughter!" *St. Petersburg (FL) Times*, December 8, 1938.
27. USCR for Angus, Elizabeth, and Gay Gordon, and Elizabeth Eckersall, 1940; USSSA for Elizabeth Louise Eckersall, February 22, 1973.
28. "Famous Pitchers Get Their Smoke from Tuxedo," *Nashville (TN) Banner*, October 8, 1912; "John McGraw Drinks Coca-Cola," *Sacramento Bee*, August 16, 1916; "Batting Eyes of Ty Cobb, Super-man Greatest Baseball Player, Tells How Nuxated Iron Gave Him New Life," *Fort Wayne (IN) Daily News*, June 23, 1916; Katie Nodjimbadem, "Babe Ruth Hit a Home Run with Celebrity Product Endorsements," *Smithsonian Magazine*, August 10, 2016.
29. "Walter Eckersall, Famous Football Authority Says: 'Give Sensible Attention to Your Underwear This Winter,'" *Moline (IL) Dispatch*, September 30, 1929; "Walter Eckersall Tells Jim Henry 'I Like That Winning Kick . . . MAN, It's a Great Shaving Cream,'" *Popular Science Monthly*, November 1929; "America's Famous Football Coaches and Officials Line Up for POSTUM," *Liberty*, November 17, 1928; "Take Off Fat," *New York Daily News*, August 19, 1928; "Eckersall's Indoor Football Game," *Chicago Tribune*, November 12, 1922.
30. Sumner, *Amos Alonzo Stagg*, 34.

31. "Amelia M. Earhart, First Woman to Fly the Atlantic by Aeroplane, Says—," *Chicago Tribune*, August 2, 1928; "Al Jolson, Famous Comedian and Star of Song," *Chicago Tribune*, January 24, 1929; "'I Appreciate Lucky Strike' Says George M. Cohan," *Chicago Tribune*, February 28, 1928; "Here Is the Complete Statement as Authorized by James A. Farley," *Chicago Tribune*, October 28, 1930; "Eddie Cantor, Famous Star of Musical Comedy and the Follies," *Chicago Tribune*, April 19, 1927.
32. "I Can't Afford to Get Fat," *New York Daily News*, December 6, 1928.
33. UADR, Box 11, Folders 67, 68; Sperber, *Shake Down the Thunder*, 216.
34. "Students Gather to Cheer for Eckersall," *Daily Maroon*, November 24, 1906.
35. Walter H. Eckersall, "Stagg's Critics Forget Feats of Winning Years," *Chicago Tribune*, November 9, 1916; Walter Eckersall, "Stagg's Defense May Upset Zup's Best Laid Plans," *Chicago Tribune*, November 7, 1924.
36. "Kelly Changes Mind and Maroon Fatted Heifer Is Sliced Up," *Chicago Inter Ocean*, October 29, 1908; Harvey T. Woodruff, "Graduates O.K. 'Stagg Field,'" *Chicago Tribune*, November 20, 1913.
37. Walter H. Eckersall, "Football Season Formally Opened," *Chicago Tribune*, September 24, 1907; Walter H. Eckersall, "Smaller Teams Given a Chance," *Chicago Tribune*, October 7, 1907; Walter H. Eckersall, "Football Gossip by Eckersall," *Chicago Tribune*, October 13, 1907; Walter H. Eckersall, "Football May Hurt Runner," *Chicago Tribune*, September 26, 1911; University of Chicago, *Cap and Gown* 17 (1912): 216; University of Chicago, *Cap and Gown* 18 (1913): 208, 210.
38. Lester, *Stagg's University*, 62.
39. "Walter Eckersall at St. Luke's Hospital," undated memo by Amos Alonzo Stagg, AAS Papers, Box 16, Folder 10.
40. "Arrangements Completed for Walter Eckersall's Last Rites."

27. –30–

1. Harland Rohm, "Hawks Leave for Montreal," *Chicago Tribune*, March 25, 1930; "N.U. Splashers Beat Stanford; Go East Today," *Chicago Tribune*, March 25, 1930; "Swiderski and Retzlaff Win at White City," *Chicago Tribune*, March 25, 1930.
2. Harvey Woodruff, "Heart Attack Takes Walter Eckersall," *Chicago Tribune*, March 25, 1930; Bert Demby, "W. Eckersall, Greatest Grid General, Dies," *Belleville (IL) Daily News Democrat*, March 25, 1930; Bert Demby, "W.H. Eckersall, Sport Writer, Dies Suddenly," *Lancaster (PA) Daily Intelligencer Journal*, March 25, 1930; "Walter Eckersall Claimed by Death," *Boston Globe*, March 25, 1930; John P. Gallagher, "Death Signals for Eckersall," *Los Angeles Times*, March 25, 1930.
3. ICOD for Walter H. Eckersall, filed March 26, 1930.
4. Woodruff, "Heart Attack Takes Walter Eckersall."
5. ICOD for Walter H. Eckersall; Walter Eckersall, "New York's Golden Glovers Leave for Home," *Chicago Tribune*, March 21, 1930.
6. "Walter H. Eckersall Ill; Football Overwork Cause," *Chicago Tribune*, December 4, 1917.

7. Demby, "W. Eckersall, Greatest Grid General, Dies"; Gallagher, "Death Signals for Eckersall."
8. Demby, "W. Eckersall, Greatest Grid General, Dies."
9. "Athletes and Hearts," *Kenosha (WI) Evening News*, March 28, 1930.
10. McHugh et al., "Cardiovascular Health of Retired Field-Based Athletes."
11. "Walter Eckersall Claimed by Death"; Sperber, *Shake Down the Thunder*, 313.
12. Harvey Woodruff, "In the Wake of the News," *Chicago Tribune*, March 29, 1929.
13. Wilhelmsen et al., "Heart Failure in the General Population of Men."
14. "Divorce for Mrs. Eckersall," *Chicago Daily News*, February 16, 1912; Linn, *James Keeley*, 102; "Walter Eckersall at St. Luke's Hospital," undated memo by Amos Alonzo Stagg, AAS Papers, Box 16, Folder 10.
15. "Hospital Liquor Seized; Doctor Is on Warpath," *Chicago Tribune*, August 4, 1926.
16. Sumner, *Amos Alonzo Stagg*, 167; Wikipedia, "Walter Eckersall," accessed April 17, 2022, https://en.wikipedia.org/wiki/Walter_Eckersall; Hall, *Amos Alonzo Stagg*, 25–27.
17. Don Maxwell, "Eckie—As We Knew Him," *Chicago Tribune*, March 25, 1930.
18. Woodruff, "Heart Attack Takes Walter Eckersall"; "Sport Leaders Join in Tribute to Eckersall," *Chicago Tribune*, March 25, 1930; Knute Rockne, "Campus Comment," *Lincoln (NE) Evening Journal*, April 5, 1930.
19. "Arrangements Completed for Walter Eckersall's Last Rites," *Chicago Tribune*, March 26, 1930.
20. "Aldermen Honor Walter Eckersall; Funeral Today," *Chicago Tribune*, March 27, 1930; Chicago City Council, *Journal of the Proceedings of the City Council*, 2547.
21. "Eckersall Laid to Rest Near the Old Grid Field," *Chicago Tribune*, March 28, 1930.

28. LEGACY

1. Walter Camp, "W.H. Eckersall on All-Time Eleven," *Chicago Tribune*, January 25, 1910; Grantland Rice, "The Sport-Light," *New York Tribune*, November 16, 1917; "Hurry-Up" Yost, "Eckersall, Coy, Heston and Thorpe His Selections in All-Star Backfield," *Buffalo Courier*, December 22, 1925; Charles P. Ward, "Mr. Football, Alias Jim Thorpe, Lines Up All-Time Team on Memory's Gridiron," *Detroit Free Press*, November 18, 1942; "Red Grange Selects All-Time Backfield," *Miami Herald*, February 21, 1934; Arch Ward, "Remember Him? Walter Eckersall of the Maroons, Called Greatest Quarter Back—Three Times an All American," *Chicago Tribune*, January 1, 1937; Grantland Rice, "Jim Thorpe Voted Greatest Grid Player of All Time by Jury of Leading Coaches; Yost, Edwards, Warner, Heisman Pick 'Em," *Rock Island (IL) Argus*, November 3, 1920; "Coaches Pick Best Backs of All Time," *Franklin (PA) News-Herald*, December 30, 1924; C. William Duncan, "Who Is Football's Greatest Player?" *Cincinnati Enquirer*, November 22, 1931; Charles Dunkley, "Eckersall Joins Greats in Grid Poll," *Decatur (IL) Review*, April 7, 1951.

2. George A. Barton, "Sportographs," *Minneapolis Tribune and Star Journal*, March 29, 1942.
3. Merrill C. "Babe" Meigs, "The Greatest Football Player in the World—Walter Eckersall," *American Weekly*, October 26, 1947.
4. "First Group Picked for Football's Hall of Fame," *Tampa Tribune*, November 4, 1951.
5. Red Blaik, "All-Time Eleven Tough to Beat," *Camden (NJ) Courier-Post*, September 30, 1969.
6. "Relay Kings Arrive Early," *Des Moines (IA) Register*, April 24, 1930; Wilfrid Smith, "Team Entries Pour in for Silver Skates," *Chicago Tribune*, January 16, 1931; Wilfrid Smith, "Dentist Wins Silver Skates Title," *Chicago Tribune*, January 24, 1955.
7. "Schools Snub E. Side Chamber," *Daily Calumet*, November 11, 1948; "Open Field Today; Fete for Eckersall," *Chicago Tribune*, September 17, 1949; "Select Names for 7 New or Planned Parks," *Chicago Tribune*, November 26, 1955.
8. "Gift From Venezuela," *Chicago Tribune*, September 1, 1959.
9. "Suggests Bust of Eckersall in University Hall," *Chicago Tribune*, March 29, 1930.
10. "First-Round Picks," *University of Chicago Magazine*, October 2003, accessed March 11, 2024, magazine.uchicago.edu/0310/features/hof-class.shtml.
11. Stephan Benzkofer, "When Speedskating Was King of Winter," *Chicago Tribune*, February 16, 2014.
12. Ron Grossman, "Meet Arch Ward, the Sports Editor Who Created MLB's All-Star Game," *Chicago Tribune*, July 15, 2022; Rick Kogan, "Molding Boxers, Shaping Lives," *Chicago Tribune*, March 12, 2023; Chicago Golden Gloves, "History," accessed July 25, 2024, mail.chicagogoldengloves.com/history.html; Golden Gloves of America, "Hall of Fame," accessed February 27, 2024, http://www.goldenglovesusa.org/hall-of-fame.
13. Ron Grossman, "Meet Arch Ward," *Chicago Tribune*, July 17, 2022; Don Pierson, "NFL and the Media: How the Times Have Changed," *Chicago Tribune*, December 14, 2014; Arch Ward, "All-America Football Conference Formed," *Chicago Tribune*, September 3, 1944; Arch Ward, "In the Wake of the News," *Chicago Tribune*, September 5, 1944.
14. Wendt, *Chicago Tribune*, 726–27, 782–83; "The Chicago Tribune's Wilfrid Smith Takes Off for His Fourth Olympics," *Chicago Tribune*, October 10, 1964; "For the Most Complete Sports Coverage . . . ," *Chicago Tribune*, March 14, 1976.
15. Michael Moran, "Hinckley & Schmitt Football Books by James Peterson," Francis D. "Hap" Moran website, accessed February 27, 2024, www.hapmoran.org.
16. Peterson, *Eckersall of Chicago*.
17. "Stagg, 94, Talks to Old Midway Stars at Lunch," *Chicago Tribune*, August 8, 1957.
18. Andrew Bagnato, "Who's Who—and Who's Not," *Chicago Tribune*, July 31, 1995; "Goodness, Greatness," *Chicago Tribune*, August 22, 1999.
19. Sperber, *Shake Down the Thunder*, 89–90, 259–61.

20. Savage, *American College Athletics*, 184.
21. Lester, *Stagg's University*, 55–63.
22. Sperber, *Shake Down the Thunder*, 90, 259.
23. Sperber, *Shake Down the Thunder*, 261.
24. Lou Smith, "Sport Snarks," *Cincinnati Enquirer*, November 12, 1934.
25. Willis, *Red Grange*, 331, 345–47, 354–58, 363–67.
26. *Sports Illustrated* Staff, "Who Would Have Won the Heisman from 1900–1934," *Sports Illustrated*, December 12, 2008, www.si.com/college/2008/12/12/early-heisman.
27. ESPN Staff, "The All-Time All-America Team for College Football's 150th Anniversary," ESPN, December 26, 2019, www.espn.com/college-football/story/_/id/28356861/the-all-america-team-college-football-150th-anniversary; Dennis Dodd and CBS Sports Staff, "College Football Turns 150," CBS Sports, August 14, 2019, www.cbssports.com/college-football/news/college-football-turns-150-all-time-all-america-team-features-the-games-greatest-ever.
28. Al Carbone, "Celebrating College Football 150—Walter Camp's All-Time All-America Team," Walter Camp Football Foundation, January 15, 2020, www.waltercamp.org/celebrating-college-football-150-walter-camps-all-time-all-america-team.
29. Matt Brown, "150 Years of College Football: The Athletic's All-Time Team," *The Athletic*, November 6, 2019, www.theathletic.com/1353588/2019/11/06/college-football-all-time-all-america-teams-150th-anniversary.
30. Matt Brown, "Best of the 1900s: Michigan Scores a Point a Minute, Chicago Answers and the East Monopoly Is Challenged," *The Athletic*, March 11, 2019, www.theathletic.com/858710/2019/03/11/college-football-best-1900s-players-teams-coaches-games-michigan.

BIBLIOGRAPHY

ARCHIVES AND MANUSCRIPT MATERIALS

AAS Papers. Amos Alonzo Stagg Papers, Hanna Holborn Gray Special Collections Research Center (SCRC), University of Chicago Library.

CCBCI. Cook County Birth Certificates Index, 1871–1922. Accessed via Ancestry.com.

CCMI. Cook County Marriages Index, 1871–1920. Accessed via Ancestry.com.

ICOD. Illinois Standard Certificate of Death. Obtained from Cook County Clerk Vital Records Office, February 28, 2022.

ISMI. Indiana Select Marriages Index. Accessed via Ancestry.com.

UADR. University Athletic Director's Records, University of Notre Dame Archives.

USCR. United States Census Record. Accessed via Ancestry.com.

USSSA. United States Social Security Application and Claim Index. Accessed via Ancestry.com.

WCCP. Walter Chauncey Camp Papers, Manuscripts and Archives, Yale University Library. Accessed via microfilm through Hesburgh Libraries, University of Notre Dame.

WWIDR. World War I Draft Registration Cards. Accessed via Ancestry.com.

PUBLISHED WORKS

Amateur Athletic Union of the United States. *Official Swimming Handbook, 1957–1958*. N.p., 1957.

Brown, Timothy P. *How Football Became Football: 150 Years of the Game's Evolution*. West Bloomfield MI: Brown House, 2020.

Camp, Walter, ed. *How to Play Foot Ball*. New York: American Sports, 1917.

———. *Spalding's Official Foot Ball Guide*. New York: American Sports, 1905, 1906, and 1907.

Camp, Walter, and Walter Eckersall. "Some Negro Football Stars." In *The Ann Arbor Negro Year-Book, 1918–1919*. Ann Arbor MI: George H. Wright, 1918.

Chernow, Ron. *Titan: The Life of John D. Rockefeller Sr*. New York: Random House, 1998.

Chicago City Council. *Journal of the Proceedings of the City Council of the City of Chicago, Illinois*. Regular Meeting, March 26, 1930.

Davis, Jeff. *Papa Bear: The Life and Legacy of George Halas*. New York: McGraw Hill, 2005.

Des Jardins, Julie. *Walter Camp: Football and the Modern Man*. New York: Oxford University Press, 2015.

Goodspeed, Thomas Wakefield. *A History of the University of Chicago, Founded by John D. Rockefeller. The First Quarter-Century*. Chicago: University of Chicago Press, 1916.

Grossman, James R., Ann Durkin Keating, and Janice L. Reiff, eds. *The Encyclopedia of Chicago*. Chicago: University of Chicago Press, 2004.

Halas, George, with Gwen Morgan and Arthur Veysey. *Halas by Halas: The Autobiography of George Halas*. New York: McGraw Hill, 1979.

Hall, E. K., ed. *Spalding's Official Foot Ball Guide*. New York: American Sports, 1926.

Hall, Jennifer Taylor. *Amos Alonzo Stagg: College Football's Man in Motion*. Charleston SC: History Press, 2019.

Kitagawa, Evelyn M., and Karl E. Taueber, eds. *Local Community Fact Book, Chicago Metropolitan Area 1960*. Chicago: Chicago Community Inventory, University of Chicago, 1963.

Kryk, John. *Stagg vs. Yost: The Birth of Cutthroat Football*. Lanham MD: Rowman and Littlefield, 2015.

Lardner, Ring. "Eckie." In *The Best American Sports Writing of the Century*, edited by David Halberstam, 191–98. Boston: Houghton Mifflin, 1999. Originally published in *Saturday Evening Post*, October 22, 1932.

Lester, Robin. *Stagg's University: The Rise, Decline, and Fall of Big-Time Football at Chicago*. Urbana: University of Illinois Press, 1995.

Linn, James Weber. *James Keeley: Newspaperman*. Indianapolis: Bobbs-Merrill, 1937.

McCarthy, Erin. "Making Men: The Life and Career of Amos Alonzo Stagg, 1862–1933." PhD dissertation, Loyola University of Chicago, 1994.

McHugh, Cliodha, Karen Hind, Daniel Davey, and Fiona Wilson. "Cardiovascular Health of Retired Field-Based Athletes: A Systematic Review and Meta-analysis." *Orthopaedic Journal of Sports Medicine* 7, no. 8 (August 19, 2019).

Miller, John J. *The Big Scrum: How Teddy Roosevelt Saved Football*. New York: HarperCollins, 2011.

New Illinois Athletic Club: Articles of Incorporation, By-Laws, List of Officers and Roll of Members. Chicago: Darrow Printing, 1906.

Oriard, Michael. *King Football: Sport and Spectacle in the Golden Age of Radio and Newsreels, Movies and Magazines, the Weekly and the Daily Press*. Chapel Hill: University of North Carolina Press, 2001.

Peterson, James. *Eckersall of Chicago*. Chicago: Hinckley and Schmitt, 1957.

Pruter, Robert. *The Rise of American High School Sports and the Search for Control, 1880–1930*. Syracuse NY: Syracuse University Press, 2013.

Revsine, Dave. *The Opening Kickoff: The Tumultuous Birth of a Football Nation*. Guilford CT: Lyons Press, 2014.

Rockefeller, John D. *Random Reminiscences of Men and Events*. New York: Doubleday, Page, 1909.

Savage, Howard J. *American College Athletics*. New York: Carnegie Foundation for the Advancement of Teaching, 1929.

Sperber, Murray. *Shake Down the Thunder: The Creation of Notre Dame Football*. Bloomington: Indiana University Press, 1993.

Stagg, Amos Alonzo, as told to Wesley Winans Stout. *Touchdown!* New York: Longmans, Green, 1927.

Sumner, David E. *Amos Alonzo Stagg: College Football's Greatest Pioneer*. Jefferson NC: McFarland, 2021.

United States Patent Office. *Official Gazette, Volume XXXIV, January 5 to March 30, Inclusive, 1886*. Washington: Government Printing Office, 1886.

Wendt, Lloyd. *Chicago Tribune: The Rise of a Great American Newspaper*. New York: Rand McNally, 1979.

Wilhelmsen, L., et al. "Heart Failure in the General Population of Men: Morbidity, Risk Factors, and Prognosis." *Journal of Internal Medicine* 249, no. 3 (March 2001).

Willis, Chris. *Red Grange: The Life and Legacy of the NFL's First Superstar*. Lanham MD: Rowman and Littlefield, 2019.

INDEX

Page numbers in italics refer to illustrations.